National Geographic Picture Atlas of

OurWorld

National Geographic Picture Atlas of

Our World

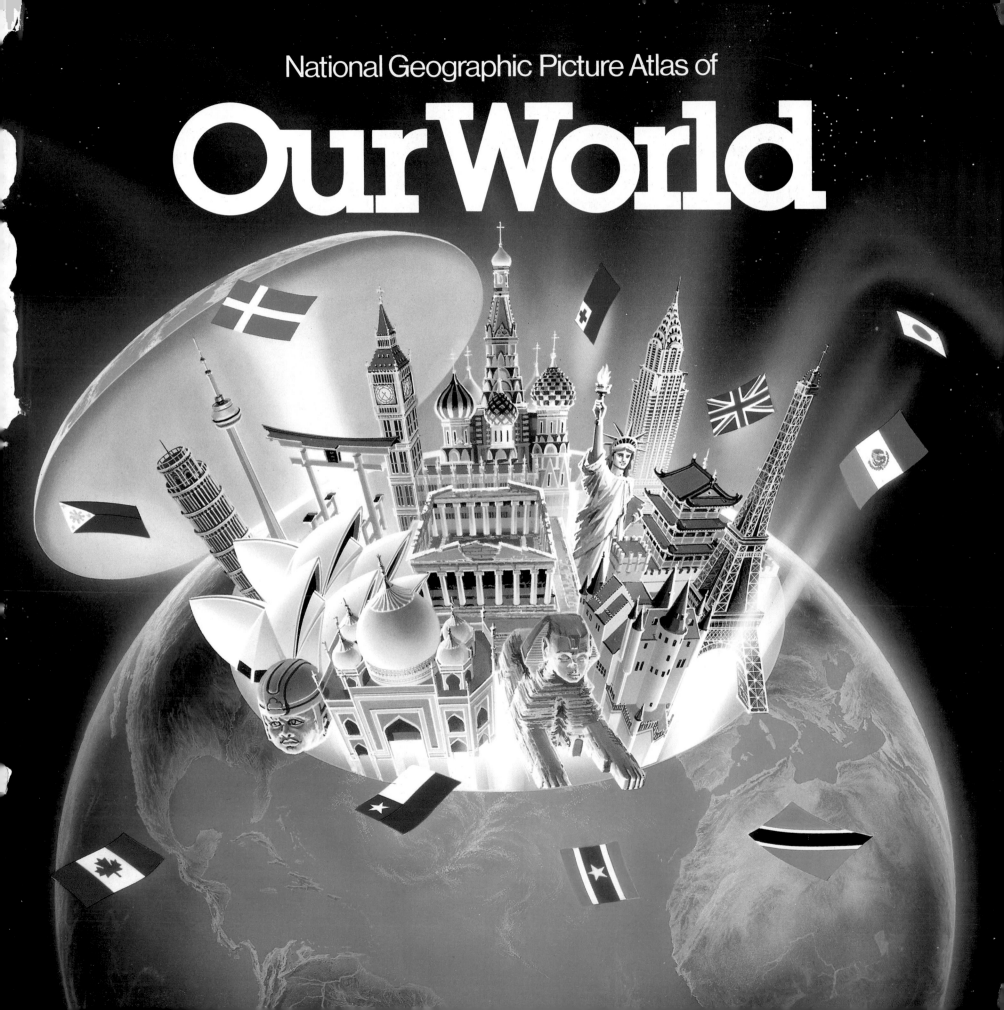

National Geographic Picture Atlas of

Our World

Published by
The National Geographic
Society

Gilbert M. Grosvenor
*President and
Chairman of the Board*

Michela A. English
Senior Vice President

Prepared by
The Book Division

William R. Gray
*Vice President and
Director*

Margery G. Dunn
Charles Kogod
Assistant Directors

Charles O. Hyman
*National Geographic
Book Service*

Staff for this book

Mary B. Dickinson
Editor

Carolinda E. Hill
Jean Kaplan Teichroew
Assistant Editors

Greta Arnold
Linda B. Meyerriecks
Illustrations Editors

David M. Seager
Art Director

Charlotte Golin
Designer

Jennifer Gorham Ackerman
Catherine Herbert Howell
Edward Lanouette
David F. Robinson
Writer-Editors

Joseph Alper
Elisabeth B. Booz
Margo Browning
Carol Dana
Elizabeth L. Newhouse
Catherine O'Neill
Melanie Patt-Corner
Suzanne K. Poole
Margaret Sedeen
John Thompson
Anne E. Withers
Contributing Writers

Ratri Banerjee
Cathryn P. Buchanan
Paulette L. Claus
Marguerite Suarez Dunn
Susan C. Eckert
James B. Enzinna
Joyce B. Marshall
Lise Swinson Sajewski
Penelope A. Timbers
Anne E. Wain
Editorial Researchers

James B. Enzinna
Art Coordinator

Karen Dufort Sligh
Laurie A. Smith
Jean C. Stringer
Illustrations Assistants

Richard S. Wain
Production Project Manager

Andrea Crosman
Emily F. Gwynn
Production

George V. White
Director
John T. Dunn
Associate Director
and R. Gary Colbert
*Manufacturing and
Quality Management*

Karen F. Edwards
Elizabeth G. Jevons
Sandra F. Lotterman
Teresita Cóquia Sison
Marilyn J. Williams
Staff Assistants

George I. Burneston, III
Indexer

Maps by Publications Art
John D. Garst, Jr.
Virginia L. Baza
Peter J. Balch
Timothy E. Burdick
Sven M. Dolling
Gary M. Johnson
Andrew J. Karl
Darrah Long
Isaac Ortiz

Maps for 1993 Edition
Carl Mehler
Map Manager

Megan M. Ullman
Researcher

New and Revised Maps
Mapping Specialists, Limited
Madison, Wisconsin

Kevin P. Allen
Nancy L. Clapsaddle
Neal J. Edwards
Charles W. Gotthardt, Jr.
Daniel J. Ortiz
Juan J. Valdés
Susan Young
Alfred L. Zebarth
Cartographic Division
John F. Shupe
Chief Cartographer

Globe Maps by
Tibor G. Toth

Artwork by
Shusei Nagaoka

Contributions by
Aileen Buckley
Alice J. Dunn
Alexander M. Tait
Jonathan B. Tourtellot

Sue Appleby Purcell
Educational Consultant

John P. Augelli,
  The University of Kansas,
  Latin America
Stephen S. Birdsall,
  The University of North
  Carolina at Chapel Hill,
  North America
Michael E. Bonine,
  The University of Arizona,
  *North Africa and the
  Middle East*
John D. Eyre,
  The University of North
  Carolina at Chapel Hill,
  Oceania
Jack D. Ives,
  University of California
  at Davis, *The Poles*
C. Gregory Knight,
Marieta P. Staneva
  The Pennsylvania State
  University,
  Sub-Saharan Africa
Thomas R. Leinbach,
  University of Kentucky,
  Southeast Asia
Clifton W. Pannell,
  The University of Georgia,
  Far East
Joseph E. Schwartzberg,
  University of Minnesota,
  Twin Cities, *South Asia*
Roger L. Thiede,
  University of Wisconsin
  at Eau Claire, *Former
  Soviet Union Republics*
Craig ZumBrunnen,
  University of Washington,
  Europe
Regional Consultants

Cover Photography: Michel
Tcherevkoff

Revised 1993
276 pages, 290 illustrations,
130 maps, 27 paintings.

Contents

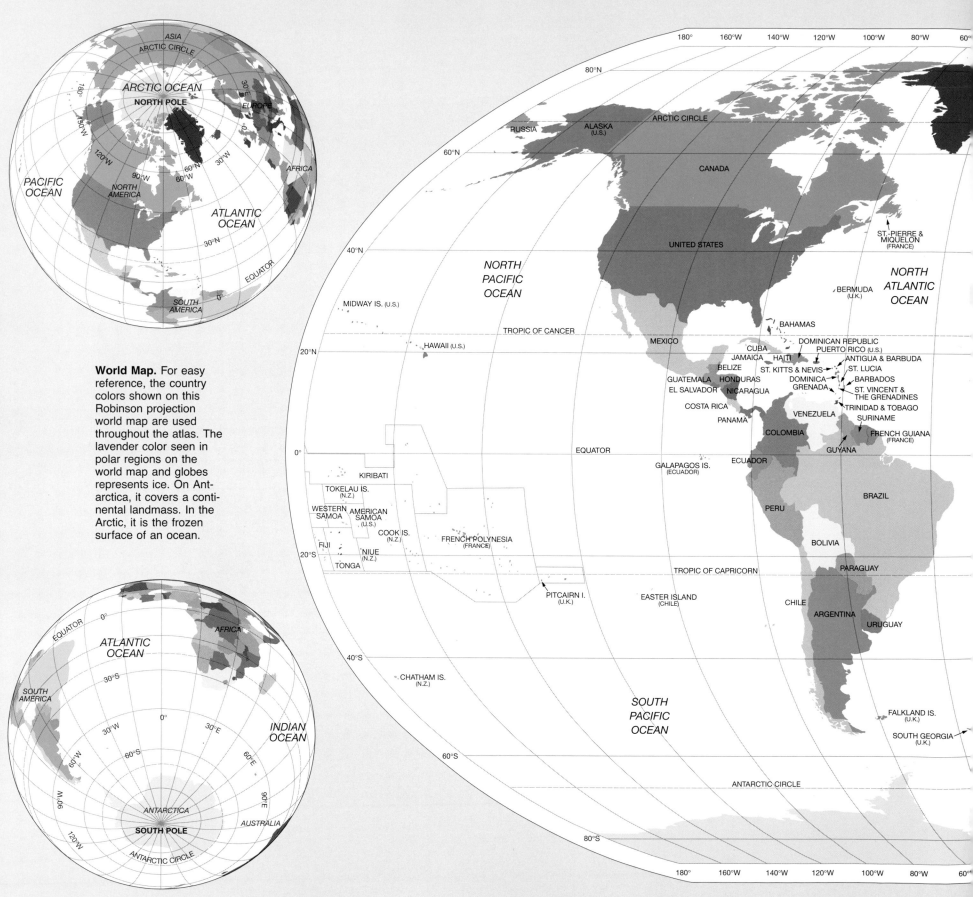

World Map. For easy reference, the country colors shown on this Robinson projection world map are used throughout the atlas. The lavender color seen in polar regions on the world map and globes represents ice. On Antarctica, it covers a continental landmass. In the Arctic, it is the frozen surface of an ocean.

ASIA
ARCTIC CIRCLE
ARCTIC OCEAN
NORTH POLE
EUROPE
PACIFIC OCEAN
NORTH AMERICA
AFRICA
ATLANTIC OCEAN
SOUTH AMERICA

EQUATOR
ATLANTIC OCEAN
AFRICA
SOUTH AMERICA
INDIAN OCEAN
ANTARCTICA
SOUTH POLE
AUSTRALIA
ANTARCTIC CIRCLE

180° 160°W 140°W 120°W 100°W 80°W 60°

80°N

RUSSIA ALASKA (U.S.) ARCTIC CIRCLE

60°N CANADA

UNITED STATES ST.-PIERRE & MIQUELON (FRANCE)

40°N
NORTH PACIFIC OCEAN BERMUDA (U.K.) NORTH ATLANTIC OCEAN

MIDWAY IS. (U.S.)

TROPIC OF CANCER MEXICO BAHAMAS

20°N CUBA DOMINICAN REPUBLIC PUERTO RICO (U.S.)
HAWAII (U.S.) JAMAICA HAITI ANTIGUA & BARBUDA
BELIZE ST. KITTS & NEVIS ST. LUCIA
GUATEMALA HONDURAS DOMINICA BARBADOS
EL SALVADOR NICARAGUA GRENADA ST. VINCENT & THE GRENADINES
COSTA RICA TRINIDAD & TOBAGO
PANAMA VENEZUELA SURINAME
COLOMBIA FRENCH GUIANA (FRANCE)
GUYANA
EQUATOR ECUADOR
GALAPAGOS IS. (ECUADOR)

KIRIBATI BRAZIL
TOKELAU IS. (N.Z.) PERU
WESTERN SAMOA AMERICAN SAMOA (U.S.)
COOK IS. (N.Z.) BOLIVIA
FIJI FRENCH POLYNESIA (FRANCE)
20°S NIUE (N.Z.)
TONGA TROPIC OF CAPRICORN PARAGUAY

PITCAIRN I. (U.K.) EASTER ISLAND (CHILE) CHILE
ARGENTINA URUGUAY

40°S
CHATHAM IS. (N.Z.)

SOUTH PACIFIC OCEAN FALKLAND IS. (U.K.)
SOUTH GEORGIA (U.K.)

60°S

ANTARCTIC CIRCLE

80°S

180° 160°W 140°W 120°W 100°W 80°W 60°

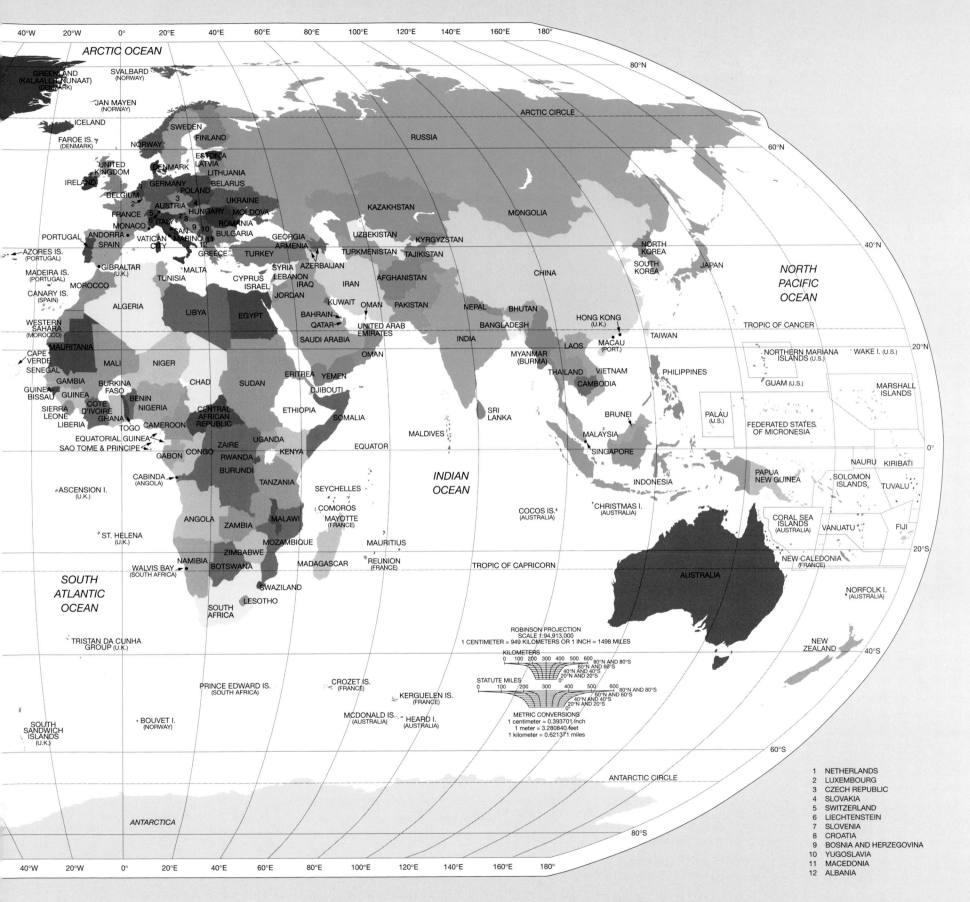

ARCTIC OCEAN

GREENLAND
(KALAALLIT NUNAAT)
(DENMARK)

SVALBARD
(NORWAY)

80°N

JAN MAYEN
(NORWAY)

ARCTIC CIRCLE

ICELAND

60°N

FAROE IS.
(DENMARK)

SWEDEN
FINLAND

NORWAY

RUSSIA

UNITED
KINGDOM

ESTONIA
LATVIA
DENMARK
LITHUANIA

IRELAND

GERMANY
BELGIUM

POLAND
BELARUS

3

UKRAINE

AUSTRIA
FRANCE   5   HUNGARY   MOLDOVA

KAZAKHSTAN

MONACO   6   ITALY   8
SAN   9   10   ROMANIA
MARINO   11

2

4

NORTH
KOREA

JAPAN

NORTH
PACIFIC
OCEAN

PORTUGAL   ANDORRA   •   12
SPAIN   VATICAN   BULGARIA
CITY

GEORGIA
ARMENIA

UZBEKISTAN

KYRGYZSTAN

40°N

AZORES IS.
(PORTUGAL)

GREECE   TURKEY
MALTA

TURKMENISTAN

TAJIKISTAN

MADEIRA IS.
(PORTUGAL)

GIBRALTAR
(U.K.)

SYRIA
CYPRUS   LEBANON
ISRAEL

AZERBAIJAN

AFGHANISTAN

CHINA

SOUTH
KOREA

MONGOLIA

TUNISIA

IRAQ   IRAN

MOROCCO

JORDAN

CANARY IS.
(SPAIN)

KUWAIT

PAKISTAN

NEPAL

BHUTAN

HONG KONG
(U.K.)

TAIWAN

TROPIC OF CANCER

WESTERN
SAHARA
(MOROCCO)

ALGERIA

LIBYA

EGYPT

BAHRAIN
QATAR

OMAN

UNITED ARAB
EMIRATES

BANGLADESH

MACAU
(PORT.)

20°N

MAURITANIA

SAUDI ARABIA

INDIA

MYANMAR
(BURMA)

LAOS

NORTHERN MARIANA
ISLANDS (U.S.)

WAKE I. (U.S.)

CAPE
VERDE

MALI

NIGER

OMAN

GUAM (U.S.)

MARSHALL
ISLANDS

SENEGAL

CHAD

SUDAN

ERITREA

YEMEN

THAILAND

VIETNAM

PHILIPPINES

GAMBIA

BURKINA
FASO

DJIBOUTI

CAMBODIA

GUINEA
BISSAU

GUINEA

BENIN

NIGERIA

CENTRAL
AFRICAN
REPUBLIC

ETHIOPIA

SRI
LANKA

BRUNEI

PALAU
(U.S.)

FEDERATED STATES
OF MICRONESIA

SIERRA
LEONE

COTE
D'IVOIRE   GHANA

SOMALIA

MALDIVES

MALAYSIA

LIBERIA

TOGO   CAMEROON

EQUATORIAL GUINEA

UGANDA

EQUATOR

SINGAPORE

0°

SAO TOME & PRINCIPE

GABON   CONGO

ZAIRE

RWANDA
BURUNDI

KENYA

NAURU   KIRIBATI

CABINDA
(ANGOLA)

TANZANIA

SEYCHELLES   ·

INDIAN
OCEAN

INDONESIA

PAPUA
NEW GUINEA

SOLOMON
ISLANDS   TUVALU

ASCENSION I.
(U.K.)

COMOROS

COCOS IS.
(AUSTRALIA)

CHRISTMAS I.
(AUSTRALIA)

CORAL SEA
ISLANDS
(AUSTRALIA)

VANUATU

FIJI

ANGOLA   ZAMBIA   MALAWI

MAYOTTE
(FRANCE)

ST. HELENA
(U.K.)

ZIMBABWE

MOZAMBIQUE

MADAGASCAR

MAURITIUS

NEW CALEDONIA
(FRANCE)

20°S

NAMIBIA

WALVIS BAY
(SOUTH AFRICA)

BOTSWANA

REUNION
(FRANCE)

TROPIC OF CAPRICORN

AUSTRALIA

NORFOLK I.
(AUSTRALIA)

SOUTH
ATLANTIC
OCEAN

SWAZILAND

LESOTHO

SOUTH
AFRICA

TRISTAN DA CUNHA
GROUP (U.K.)

NEW
ZEALAND

40°S

ROBINSON PROJECTION
SCALE 1:94,913,000
1 CENTIMETER = 949 KILOMETERS OR 1 INCH = 1498 MILES

PRINCE EDWARD IS.
(SOUTH AFRICA)

CROZET IS.
(FRANCE)

KILOMETERS
0   100 200 300 400 500 600   80°N AND 80°S
60°N AND 60°S
40°N AND 40°S
20°N AND 20°S

KERGUELEN IS.
(FRANCE)

STATUTE MILES
0   100   200   300   400   500   600   80°N AND 80°S
60°N AND 60°S
40°N AND 40°S
20°N AND 20°S

BOUVET I.
(NORWAY)

MCDONALD IS.
(AUSTRALIA)

HEARD I.
(AUSTRALIA)

METRIC CONVERSIONS
1 centimeter = 0.393701 inch
1 meter = 3.280840 feet
1 kilometer = 0.621371 miles

SOUTH
SANDWICH
ISLANDS
(U.K.)

60°S

ANTARCTIC CIRCLE

ANTARCTICA

80°S

1   NETHERLANDS
2   LUXEMBOURG
3   CZECH REPUBLIC
4   SLOVAKIA
5   SWITZERLAND
6   LIECHTENSTEIN
7   SLOVENIA
8   CROATIA
9   BOSNIA AND HERZEGOVINA
10   YUGOSLAVIA
11   MACEDONIA
12   ALBANIA

Mapping Our World

More than two decades ago, on my first field assignment for the National Geographic Society, I explored the pastoral, lake-studded highlands of Slovenia while gathering material for a book on the Alps. Slovenia then was a small, quiet republic in a much larger federation, Yugoslavia. The Slovenes—warm, open, industrious—were strongly involved with their nation. But it was clear that they considered themselves to be Slovenes first and Yugoslavs second.

When political change began sweeping the world in the early months of this decade, the Slovenes were one of the first peoples to desire, to fight for, and to gain their independence. Their new country of Slovenia, with its historical ties to Western Europe renewed and strengthened, is struggling forward with pride and dignity, despite severe economic challenges and civil strife in neighboring parts of the former Yugoslavia.

This is but one example, though, of the unprecedented cascade of changes that in recent years have transformed not only the map of the world but also the very course of history. To understand a rapidly changing world and to put into context the manifold and complex character of those changes, we all need to know and understand more about our global neighbors—and thus about ourselves.

In 1990, when the Society published the previous edition of the *Picture Atlas of Our World*, the Berlin Wall had just been breached. That event came to symbolize change and actually seemed to stimulate it. In just three years, the world has turned dramatically: Two Germanies have become one; Yugoslavia has broken up into five countries; the Soviet Union has fragmented into fifteen countries; Czechoslovakia has divided into two countries; and, in mid-1993, Eritrea proclaimed its independence from Ethiopia.

Because of these changes and the international attention focused on them, we have come to perceive the Slovenes and the Slovaks, the Tajiks and the Turkmens differently—as individual peoples with rich cultures and traditions and not simply as parts of larger, monolithic states. Likewise, we have come to see long-familiar nationalities with different eyes than in the past: the Russians . . . the Germans . . . the Poles . . . and many more.

The early 1990s have produced so many news headlines about international events that we would be lost without a knowledge of geography. Timely maps of the Middle East in 1991 helped Americans follow the Iraqi invasion of Kuwait that escalated into the Gulf War. When Mount Pinatubo erupted with cataclysmic force that same year in the Philippines, satellite images provided maps of the atmosphere that helped us understand the possible effect on global weather patterns. And the map of Africa has become familiar to most of us, as we witnessed the repeal of the *apartheid* policy in South Africa, the UN-sponsored effort to stabilize Somalia and relieve starvation there, and the bitter civil wars in several other African countries.

I hope that this atlas—fully updated with new cartography, new photography, and current information—will contribute to a better understanding of the intricate fabric of life in all corners of the globe. I also hope that it will help put into perspective the changes that have overtaken us in recent years. In striving to meet the National Geographic Society's educational mission, the staff of this book has worked long and diligently to gather and present accurate information about the world, parts of which are still remote or in turmoil.

In the *Picture Atlas of Our World*, we encounter a world that has irrevocably changed. Tiny Slovenia, long dominated by the Carolingian, Holy Roman, and Austro-Hungarian Empires and more recently a component of Yugoslavia, now stands truly independent—for the first time in more than 1,400 years. The crescendo of change seems to have slackened; now the Slovenes and the citizens of the other new nations in Europe, Asia, and Africa strive to adapt to today's global environment—while the rest of the world learns to understand and respect the unique heritage of each new country.

William R. Gray
*Vice President and
Director, The Book Division*

Where in the World?

A world globe helps us to find our way around the earth. Using a globe is like using a street map. Suppose you want to meet a friend on the corner of Third Avenue and Main Street. To find the intersection on a map, you might follow Third Avenue until it meets Main Street. On a globe, there are no streets or avenues. Instead, you can use the grid formed by lines of latitude and longitude. If you have the latitude and longitude coordinates, you can find any place on earth.

Lines of latitude run east and west around the globe and are evenly spaced from the Equator to the North and South Poles. They are also called parallels, because they are parallel to each other. Parallels become shorter toward the Poles.

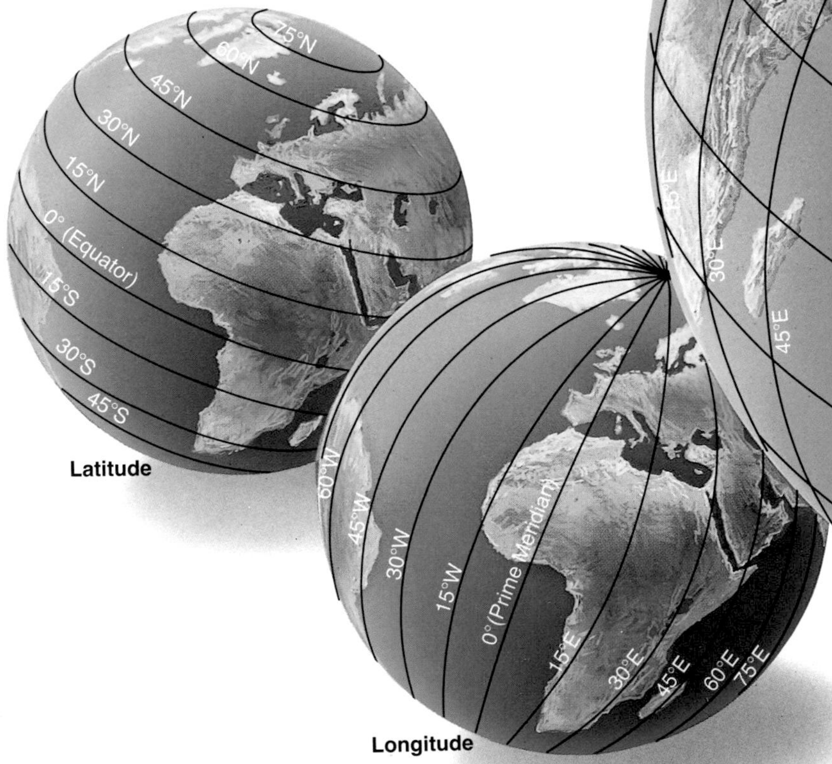

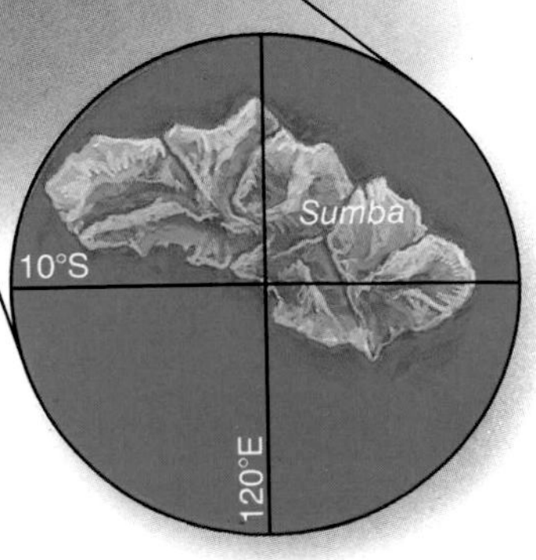

Latitude

Longitude

Finding Sumba. *Globes do not show every line of latitude or longitude, but just a few at regular intervals. The two small globes above show lines of* latitude *(left) and* longitude *(right) spaced 15 degrees apart. The Equator is at 0° latitude, and the Prime Meridian is at 0° longitude. Combining the two sets of lines forms a grid, shown on the large globe. You can use this grid to find any spot on earth. For example, Sumba, one of the Lesser Sunda Islands of Indonesia, is located at about latitude 10° S, longitude 120° E. To find it, follow the Equator east to 120° E, then go south. Just before 15° S, you will find Sumba.*

Lines of longitude run north and south. They are also called meridians. All meridians are the same length, and they come together at the North and South Poles. By international agreement, the meridian that runs through Greenwich, England, is called the Prime Meridian.

Together, meridians and parallels form an imaginary grid that defines positions on earth in terms of their distance from the Equator and Prime Meridian. Latitude measures distance north or south of the Equator, and longitude is the distance east or west of the Prime Meridian. Both latitude and longitude are measured in degrees (°). Latitude goes from 0° to 90° north and south of the Equator, and longitude from 0° to 180° east and west of the Prime Meridian. Each degree is further divided into 60 minutes ('), and each minute is divided into 60 seconds ("). Geographers use all these measurements to pinpoint the locations of places in the world.

Parallels never meet, so the distance between two lines of latitude does not change. One degree of latitude is about 69 miles (111 km), one minute of latitude is about 1.15 miles (1.85 km), and one second of latitude is approximately 101 feet (31 m). Because meridians do meet, one degree of longitude is shorter at the Poles than at the Equator. However, no matter where, 15 degrees of longitude equals the amount of the earth that passes the sun in one hour.

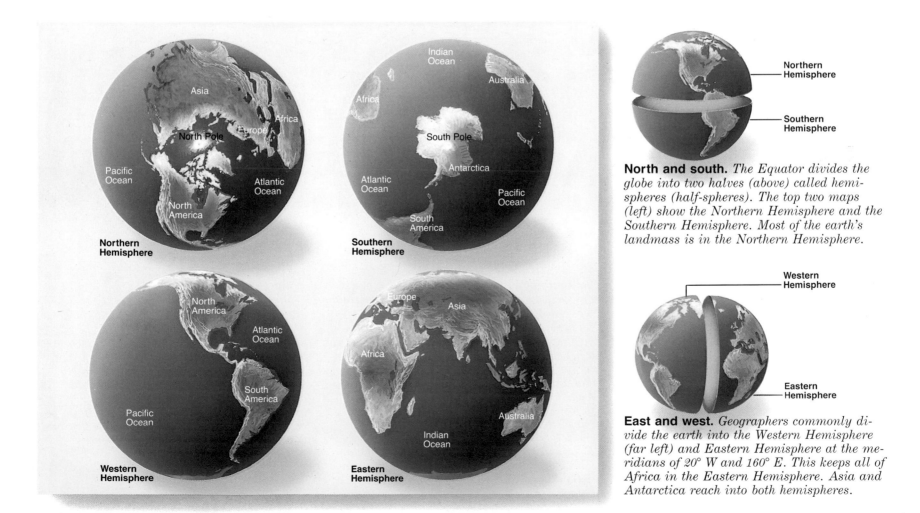

North and south. *The Equator divides the globe into two halves (above) called hemispheres (half-spheres). The top two maps (left) show the Northern Hemisphere and the Southern Hemisphere. Most of the earth's landmass is in the Northern Hemisphere.*

East and west. *Geographers commonly divide the earth into the Western Hemisphere (far left) and Eastern Hemisphere at the meridians of 20° W and 160° E. This keeps all of Africa in the Eastern Hemisphere. Asia and Antarctica reach into both hemispheres.*

The Round Earth on Flat Paper

Maps teach us about the world by showing the sizes and shapes of countries, displaying earth's mountains, rivers, lakes, and other features, and showing the distance between places. Maps can also show us the worldwide distribution of such things as deserts, cities, people, or resources like oil fields. Maps, though, are not the best way to show the round earth. A globe is.

A globe is a scale model of the earth showing its shape, lands, distances, and directions in their true proportions. But a globe is too bulky and awkward to carry around, and pictures of a globe do not make good maps in an atlas. For one thing, they show only half of the world at a time. So mapmakers make flat maps instead.

Changing the globe into a map is not simple, however. Imagine cutting a globe in half and trying to flatten the two hemispheres. They would wrinkle, and their shapes would distort. In fact, every map has some distortion. A map can show either the correct *size* of countries or the correct *shapes* of small areas, but not both.

There are many ways to project a round globe onto flat paper. Each produces a certain type of map. Imagine a glass globe with lines etched on it. Lines running parallel to the Equator are called parallels of latitude; those connecting the Poles are called meridians of longitude. Shining a light through the globe onto paper projects shadows of the lines and landmasses onto the paper (see below). These can be copied on paper to make a map, but the method is limited. Computers are needed to make most map projections.

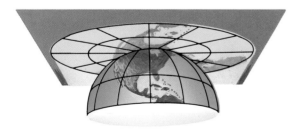

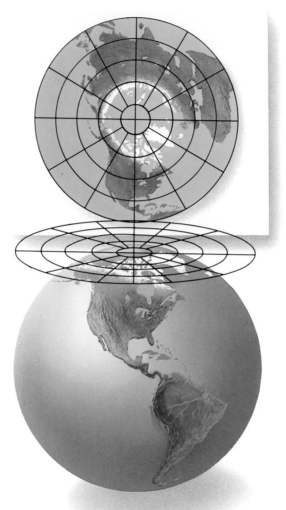

Plane projection. *Each type of map is suited for displaying a particular view of the world. The map above is useful for displaying an entire hemisphere. It also represents areas in their proper proportions: If you put a dime over two different places on the map, the areas represented under each coin will be the same size. This map is called a Lambert Azimuthal Equal-Area map, and it is made by projecting half of the earth onto a plane that touches the globe at one point. That point becomes the central projection point of the map. Directions from the map's center to another point on the map are correct, but all other directions are distorted. This projection also distorts the* shapes *of countries.*

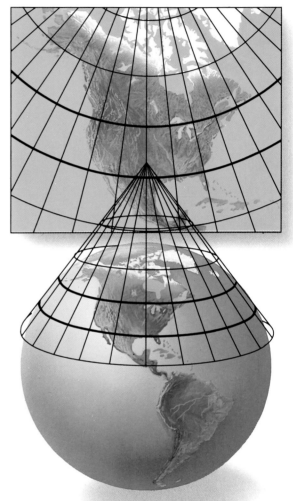

Conic projection. *A Lambert Conformal Conic map is made by projecting the globe onto a cone. The latitude lines where the cone and globe touch, shown darker than the others, are called the standard parallels. The word "conformal" means that this map represents the* shape *of limited areas accurately. Conic maps are used to show parts of the globe that run primarily east and west in the middle latitudes. The United States would be one example. Unlike the map at left, this one distorts* size *from one area to another.*

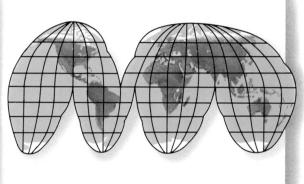

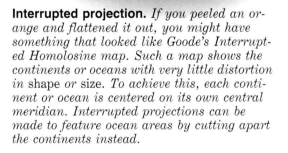

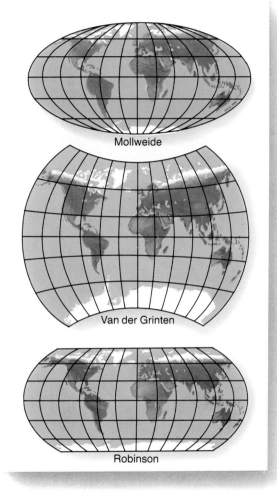

Cylindrical projection. *The Mercator projection map is very commonly used. It is suitable for navigating at sea because a line connecting any two points gives the best compass direction between them. For areas close to the Equator, this type of map accurately represents the shape, but it badly distorts the relative sizes of landmasses the nearer they are to the North and South Poles. Alaska, for example, looks about half the size of South America on such a map, when South America is, in fact, more than 11 times bigger.*

Interrupted projection. *If you peeled an orange and flattened it out, you might have something that looked like Goode's Interrupted Homolosine map. Such a map shows the continents or oceans with very little distortion in shape or size. To achieve this, each continent or ocean is centered on its own central meridian. Interrupted projections can be made to feature ocean areas by cutting apart the continents instead.*

Map evolution. *Cartographers are always looking for a more accurate way to project the round earth onto flat paper. The Mollweide projection (top), developed in 1805, is good for accurately representing the relative size of the world's landmasses, but it distorts their shapes. The Van der Grinten projection (middle) became the National Geographic Society's standard map in 1922. It does a better job of representing shapes, but it distorts the relative sizes of many countries, particularly Canada, Greenland, and Russia. In 1988 the Society adopted a map based on the Robinson projection as its official standard, believing that it provides the best compromise in representing both* shape *and* size.

Spinning Through Day and Night

While people on North America's Pacific coast stir in early morning slumber at 4 a.m., those on the east coast are eating breakfast, and the residents of central Africa have finished their midday meal. Because it is 8 to 10 p.m. in Australia, people there are probably thinking about bed. The reason for these time differences is that the earth rotates from west to east, spinning through 15 degrees of longitude every hour.

In the days when communication among different areas was slow, each town set its clocks by observing the sun's position—it was noon local time when the sun was directly overhead. Thus in the United States, at noon in Washington, D. C., it was 12:12 p.m. farther east in New York City. But as transportation and communication technology advanced, it became important to have a standard system of time.

In 1883, U. S. railroad officials created four time zones, each 15 degrees wide, to span the country. These zones were centered on the meridians at 75°, 90°, 105°, and 120° west of the Prime Meridian running through Greenwich, England. Soon other countries began adopting this system, creating a series of standard time zones centered on meridians spaced 15 degrees apart. Today, all but a few countries set their local time according to these time zones. As a result, we can determine accurately what time it is anywhere in the world.

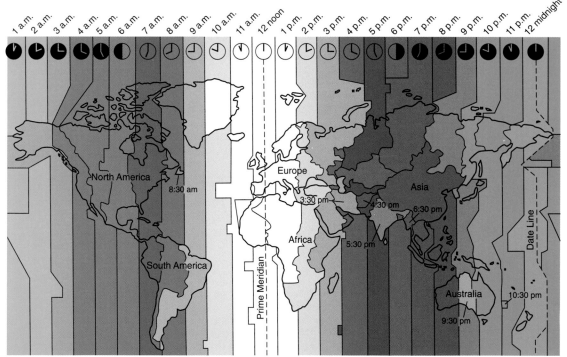

Variations in color indicate irregular time zones.

World time zones. *The map above shows the 24 standard time zones. The colors correspond to the meridians on which they are centered, which encircle the globe at right. Notice that the borders of each time zone are not straight lines. That is so that entire countries or neighboring communities can have the same time zone. For example, the date line, at 180° longitude, zigs and zags to avoid splitting up island groups in the Pacific Ocean. China, by decree of its government, has only one time zone even though it spans some 60 degrees of longitude. It shows up as a single zone under the Asia label.*

Earth's rotation. *A day—approximately the time it takes the earth to complete one rotation on its axis—is made up of 24 hours. Because the planet is divided into 360 degrees, it travels 15 degrees each hour. The globe below shows the meridians, spaced at intervals of 15 degrees longitude. Each hour a different meridian is opposite the sun. The white line is the Prime Meridian at 0° longitude, and the time zone centered on it is called Universal Time (UT), formerly Greenwich Mean Time (GMT). The zigzagging green line on the opposite side of the earth is the date line, the boundary where each calendar day begins.*

Revolving with the Seasons

Every 365¼ days, the earth completes its orbit of the sun. During that trip, the weather over much of the world changes in a regular pattern known as seasons. Year after year, spring, summer, fall, and winter follow one another. Spring always begins around March 21 in the Northern Hemisphere, while fall starts on that same date in the Southern Hemisphere.

The earth has seasons because its axis is tilted. You can see by looking at a mounted globe that the North and South Poles are tipped at an angle of about 23½ degrees. The earth always leans in the same direction as it revolves around the sun, so the amount of sunlight hitting the Northern and Southern Hemispheres changes seasonally as the planet pursues its orbit.

On about June 22, when the Northern Hemisphere is tilted toward the sun, countries such as the United States enjoy the first day of summer. This is the longest day of the year, and the sun's rays are never more direct. Meanwhile, it is the shortest day in the Southern Hemisphere, as the South Pole points away from the sun.

Six months later, the Southern Hemisphere leans toward the sun. Winter grips northern latitudes, while Australia heads into summer. Between the extremes of summer and winter come spring and fall. During these seasons, earth's axis is perpendicular to the sun's rays, and neither hemisphere has much sunlight advantage.

In the Northern Hemisphere. *As the earth orbits the sun, most areas pass through four seasonal phases (below). On about June 22, the Tropic of Cancer receives the sun's most direct rays. In the Northern Hemisphere, this is the summer solstice, when summer begins. As the earth moves on around the sun, the rays strike the globe most directly farther south, crossing the Equator about September 23, the fall equinox. By about December 22, the winter solstice, the Tropic of Capricorn is exposed to the sun's most direct rays. They move north across the Equator again on the spring equinox, about March 21. On the two equinoxes, most places on earth have nearly equal hours of daylight and dark.*

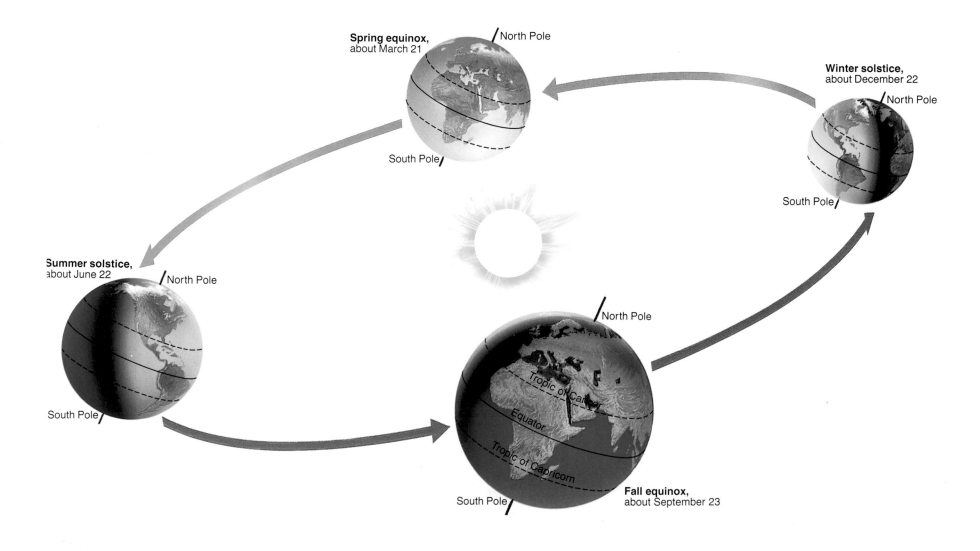

Spring equinox, about March 21
North Pole
South Pole

Winter solstice, about December 22
North Pole
South Pole

Summer solstice, about June 22
North Pole
South Pole

North Pole
Tropic of Cancer
Equator
Tropic of Capricorn
South Pole
Fall equinox, about September 23

Arctic zone

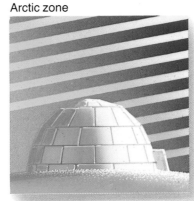

Temperate zone

Tropical zone

Heat and light. *Temperatures may change with the seasons, but it is always warmer at the Equator than it is near the North and South Poles. The reason for this is that the earth is round. In the world's tropical areas, symbolized by the tropical house, the sun's rays hit the earth nearly vertically, and the ground and air above it become warm. But because the earth is curved, the angle of the sun's rays becomes lower as you move away from the Equator. A house in the United States (middle, above) receives less direct sunlight. In the Arctic, still less reaches the igloo, because the sun's rays are nearly parallel to the ground. The sun's energy is dissipated and the Arctic stays generally colder.*

Nature's Power Shapes the Land

Earth's changing surface is formed of thick slabs of rock called plates. They divide the planet's rigid crust into a patchwork of seven vast pieces and several small ones. The huge plates carry the continents and form the ocean floor.

Propelled by forces from within the planet, the plates move slowly around the globe. Most of the time, plate movement is so gradual that it can't be felt. The slabs of rock usually advance only a few inches each year. As they move, the plates interact. They may plow into each other, pull apart, or slide past each other. Geologists call this activity plate tectonics.

Plate tectonics is the force that creates many of earth's physical features. In fact, "tectonic" comes from a Greek word that means "builder."

Where plates collide, great mountain chains rise, such as the Himalaya in Asia. Where the edge of one plate slides beneath another, creating deep valleys called trenches, the interaction triggers volcanic activity. Around three sides of the Pacific plate, hundreds of active volcanoes form the zone known as the Ring of Fire.

As plates sliding alongside each other catch,

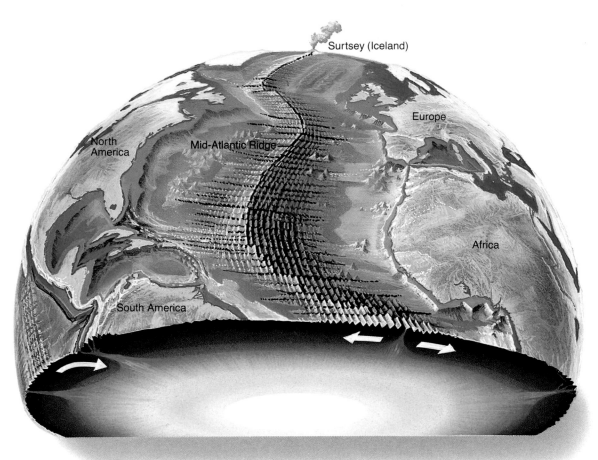

Surtsey (Iceland)

Europe

North America

Mid-Atlantic Ridge

Africa

South America

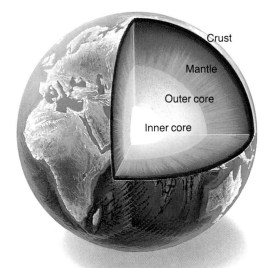

Crust

Mantle

Outer core

Inner core

Layered Planet. *A superhot, solid inner core lies at the center of the planet. It is surrounded by the liquid outer core. The mantle, a thick layer of hot, dense rock, lies above the iron core. The crust, the earth's rocky shell, forms the surface. As little as 5 miles (8 km) thick in places, it is the earth's thinnest layer.*

Mid-Atlantic Ridge. *The diagram above shows the Atlantic section of the Mid-Ocean Ridge. A rift, or deep crack, splits the ridge, allowing molten rock called magma to well up between the plates. The magma hardens, creating new ocean floor and volcanic landforms such as the distant island of Surtsey.*

Patchwork of plates. *Seven large plates and several small ones form the earth's crust. Red lines on the map below represent plate boundaries. Yellow dots stand for the many active volcanoes found along them. Volcanic zones develop where molten material from inside the earth erupts through the crust.*

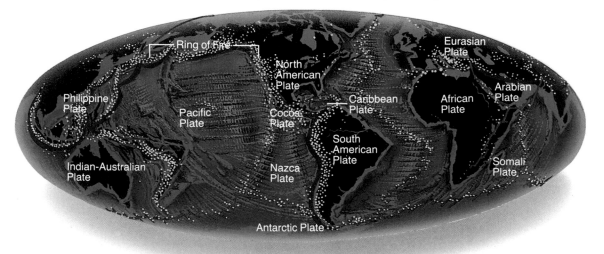

Ring of Fire

Eurasian Plate

North American Plate

Caribbean Plate

African Plate

Arabian Plate

Philippine Plate

Pacific Plate

Cocos Plate

Indian-Australian Plate

South American Plate

Nazca Plate

Somali Plate

Antarctic Plate

Along a fault. *Earthquakes occur along faults, or cracks, in the earth's rigid crust. The dark vertical line on the diagram below shows the location of a fault. As two plates grind past each other along a fault, strain builds up in the rocks. Eventually the strain becomes so great that the rocks snap and* move. *This movement releases pent-up energy along the fault, causing an earthquake. The ground trembles as shock waves move through it away from the place where the rocks snapped apart. Earthquakes can topple houses and power lines and tear apart sections of roads and railroad tracks.*

Fault

Crust

Mantle

Fault

Crust

Mantle

Crater

Funnel

Caldera

Magma chamber

they build up tension. When the tension releases, it causes earthquakes such as those that have repeatedly shaken California. Where plates pull apart, usually on the floor of the oceans, molten rock from within the earth wells up. This material creates new seafloor and builds an undersea mountain chain that rings the earth, the Mid-Ocean Ridge.

Earth scientists have not pinpointed exactly what fuels plate tectonics. But they think that heat rising from the earth's core may create slowly moving currents within the mantle, the thick, hot layer of rock below the crust. Over millions of years, these slowly churning currents may have shifted the plates around.

Scientists estimate that plate tectonics has been shaping the earth's surface for 2.5 to 4 billion years. The activity continues today. The peaks of the Himalaya are getting higher as the Indian landmass pushes against them; Hawaii is inching toward Japan; Europe and North America are drifting apart. Millions of years from now, plate tectonics will have sculptured a whole new face for our dynamic planet.

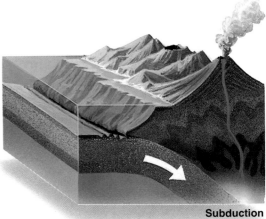

Subduction

Volcanic eruption. *A cloud of ash and gas spews from a volcano as red-hot magma rises to the surface (left). Volcanoes usually form along boundaries where one plate plunges beneath another (above). The rocky slab melts as it dives down into the hot mantle, and the molten material rises to forge volcanoes.*

The Language of Maps

archipelago—a group or chain of islands.

bay—a body of water partially surrounded by land; bays are usually smaller and less deeply indented than **gulfs.**

canyon—a deep, narrow valley with steep sides; it is usually wider and longer than a gorge.

cape—a piece of land that extends into a river, a lake, or an ocean.

delta—a lowland composed of silt, sand, and gravel deposited by a river at its mouth.

divide—the high boundary between areas drained by different river systems; water flows in a different direction on either side.

dormant volcano—a temporarily inactive volcano; a totally inactive one is called extinct.

escarpment—a cliff separating two nearly flat land surfaces that lie at different levels.

glacier—a large, slowly moving mass of ice.

harbor—a body of water sheltered by natural or artificial barriers and deep enough to moor ships.

iceberg—a large, floating chunk of ice broken away from a glacier or an ice shelf.

isthmus—a strip of land connecting two larger land areas and separating two bodies of water.

lagoon—a shallow body of water that opens on the sea but is protected by a sandbar or coral reef.

mesa—a broad, flat-topped landform with steep sides found in arid or semiarid regions.

oasis—a green area in a desert, with a spring or water hole often fed by an underground aquifer.

peninsula—a long piece of land almost surrounded by water but connected to a larger landmass.

plateau—a large, flat area that rises higher than the land around it; it is larger than a mesa.

reef—an offshore ridge of rocks, coral, or sand.

sound—a long, broad ocean inlet usually parallel to the coast, or a long stretch of water separating an island from the mainland.

strait—a narrow passage of water that connects two larger bodies of water.

tributary—a stream that flows into a larger river.

How to Read Our Maps

Each map in this book is full of information. To find the locations of towns, rivers, and other features, study the place-name labels. If you understand the symbols, you can discover even more. Refer to the key, or map legend, below. On the map at right, you'll see that Argentina's capital is Buenos Aires. The label size also tells you that, like Montevideo, it has a population of more than a million. The towns of Viedma and Rawson have the smallest size dot and label, meaning they have fewer than 50,000 people.

The other symbols represent man-made and physical features. Look at the painting of a geographic landscape on the opposite page. Keep that picture in mind when you see a canal, waterfall, glacier, or reef symbol on a map.

In this picture atlas each country appears on a map like the one at right and on a locator map that places it on its continent. Each has a story and a fact box, and flags are shown for all independent countries. Foreign words and place-names in the stories often have accent marks called diacriticals that help in pronunciation. Diacriticals appear on the wall map that comes with this book but not on the book's own maps.

⊛ *Country Capital*

⊙ *Dependency Capital*

● **Montevideo** *1 million people and over*

● **Cordoba** *100,000 to under 1 million people*

• Copiapo *50,000 to under 100,000 people*

· Viedma *under 50,000 people*

Lake, Reservoir		*Swamp*	
Intermittent Lake		*Internal Boundary*	
Dry Salt Lake		*Disputed Area*	
River		*Road*	
Intermittent River		*Railroad*	
Disappearing River	)(	*Pass, Tunnel*	
Canal	//	*Waterfall*	
Reef	I	*Dam*	
Mountains	+	*Mountain Peak*	
Glaciers	▫	*Site*	

How to find a place:
Look up Comodoro Rivadavia, Argentina, in the Index. It will say **74** P5. Turn to page 74. Find the letter P on the side of the map and the number 5 at the bottom. Follow imaginary arrows, represented by real ones on this page, to where they meet. There you'll find Comodoro Rivadavia.

North America

The first humans set foot on North America in what is now Alaska about 30,000 years ago. These early migrants crossed from Asia on a strip of land long since submerged under the Bering Strait. Their descendants survive today as the Indians of the Americas. As they spread southward, they peopled a continent that ranks third out of seven in size, after Asia and Africa.

North America measures some 4,000 miles (6,437 km) between the coasts of Alaska and Newfoundland, but it pinches to 31 miles (50 km) at its southernmost reach in Central America. There, North America is about 500 miles (805 km) from the Equator. Its northernmost point, a tip of the world's largest island, Greenland, comes about that close to the North Pole.

North America's great geographical diversity has led to great diversity in the way people live. Along the continent's Atlantic coast and the Gulf of Mexico runs a low coastal plain. Much of this land abounds in fertile soil that has grown cotton, corn, tobacco, and other important crops since the days when European colonists settled there. Rich oil deposits lie in the southern part of the plain and in the Gulf of Mexico. Their development often threatens the region's ecology.

The forested ridges of the Appalachian Mountains stretch from Newfoundland to the southern United States. The Appalachians are among earth's oldest mountains; 300 million years ago they stood perhaps as high as today's Rocky Mountains. As erosion wore down the mountains, layers of mud, silt, and sand buried dead plants. Millions of years of heat and pressure underground turned them into coal. This resource has brought wealth to Kentucky, West Virginia, and other states, but at a cost: Mines scar Appalachian hillsides. Miners risk accidents and lung disease, and shutdowns have brought poverty.

Rapids and waterfalls mark places where rivers rush from the Appalachian foothills to meet the coastal plain. In the early days of the United States, ships could sail no farther upriver, and cities grew where there was waterpower for industry. They now form a string of densely populated metropolitan areas along the East Coast.

In Canada, the lowlands of the St. Lawrence River lie west of the Appalachians. This river highway to the Great Lakes and its fertile valley helped cities to thrive. Once the development of

steam power freed industry from its dependence on rushing water, cities grew up near raw materials such as iron and coal. Just as eastern cities drew immigrants, first from Europe, later from Asia and Latin America, these inland cities became home to many different cultural groups.

In the center of the continent, plains and lowlands sweep west from the Appalachians to the foot of the Rocky Mountains. Some 14,000 years ago, glaciers covered parts of the northern plains. These ice sheets sculptured a rolling landscape with thousands of lakes, the biggest of which are the five Great Lakes. Great river systems formed from the runoff of melting glaciers. Among others, the Missouri, Mississippi, and Ohio became highways traveled by Indians and pioneers and by today's barges and ships.

The western plains lie in the rain shadow of the Rocky Mountains. Too dry for forests, the plains were grasslands until settlers' plows broke the sod. Now farmers grow wheat and ranchers graze cattle. In Canada's southern prairies, agriculture and mineral resources have brought wealth, and cities have flourished.

In Canada's north, the prairies give way to the conifer forests of the taiga and, farther north, to tundra. People in isolated lumber camps, mining towns, and fishing villages face a frigid climate and harsh terrain. To the east, shaped like an enormous broken doughnut, the Canadian Shield arcs around Hudson Bay and dips into parts of the United States. The Shield is named for the rock that lies under its thin soil, rock that formed about three billion years ago, when the first forms of life appeared on earth.

To the west, the plains slope upward to the Rocky Mountains, a jagged range of lofty peaks stretching from northern Alaska through western Canada almost to Mexico. These are young mountains. At the southern end, volcanic eruptions that ended ten million years ago created peaks and basins; the rich mineral deposits that were found there drew prospectors and miners. The spine of the Rockies forms part of the Continental Divide. East of the divide, rivers flow to the Gulf of Mexico and the Atlantic or to the Arctic Ocean. West of it they flow to the Pacific.

Between the Rockies and the Pacific coast ranges of the United States lies a series of plateaus and basins, the latter flooded thousands of

A Missouri tallgrass prairie

The Continental Divide in Montana

A Lake Superior shoreline in Wisconsin

years ago with huge lakes. Now the dry lake beds are hard and flat as pavement. On one of them, shuttles land after their sojourns in space. Across one plateau the Colorado River slices the mile-deep Grand Canyon, the biggest gorge on earth. Irrigation allows some farming, but much of this region is rangeland and desert.

Along the Pacific coast grew the greatest conifer forest on earth before loggers came to it. Today's remnants are a reminder of what western North America was like before Europeans appeared. Redwoods here are the world's tallest trees, giant sequoias are the largest, and bristlecone pines are more than 4,000 years old, among the oldest living things on earth.

To the south, a high, rugged plateau forms the heart of Mexico, rimmed on east and west by mountains that converge in volcanic peaks. In sight of these peaks stands one of the world's fastest growing urban areas, Mexico City. Seeking work, impoverished peasants flood into the city. Over the years millions of Mexicans, as well as other Latin Americans, have found their way into the United States.

The smaller nations of North America range through Central America and arc across the Caribbean Sea. Many of the Caribbean islands are the peaks of submerged volcanoes. Coastal plains and sandy beaches edge the islands. Some are among the world's most densely populated places. Much of the good land is on plantations owned by wealthy people, and businesses are often owned by outsiders. A major source of income in Mexico and the islands is remittances, money sent home by those who leave to work in Canada or the United States. Still, the Caribbean nations have made great strides in building up their tourist industry, which became their prime foreign-currency earner in the mid-1980s.

Most of North America's poorer people aspire to the affluence of the American life-style. With some of earth's greatest resources at their disposal, the United States and Canada have developed standards of living largely unmatched in the rest of the world. In recent years, though, a greater understanding has grown of the vulnerability of those natural assets and of the need to protect the environment, to check consumption, to lessen air pollution—to preserve the quality of life for future generations.

Mexico City, like many cities, faces overcrowding and pollution.

Facts About North America

Area: 9,357,293 sq mi (24,235,280 sq km)
Population: 435,800,000
Highest Point: Mt. McKinley, Alaska, 20,320 ft (6,194 m) above sea level
Lowest Point: Death Valley, California, 282 ft (86 m) below sea level
Largest Country: *(by area)* Canada 3,849,670 sq mi (9,970,610 sq km)
Largest Country: *(by population)* United States 255,570,000
Largest Island: *Greenland 840,004 sq mi (2,175,600 sq km)
Largest Metropolitan Areas: *(by population)*

New York, U. S.	18,087,300
Mexico City, Mexico	15,000,000
Los Angeles, U. S.	14,531,500

Longest Rivers: *(mi and km)*

Mississippi-Missouri	3,710	5,971
Mackenzie-Peace	2,635	4,241

Largest Lakes: *(sq mi and sq km)*

Superior, U. S.-Canada	31,699	82,100
Huron, U. S.-Canada	23,012	59,600
Michigan, U. S.	22,300	57,800

*World record

Glossary

campesino—a resident of a Latin American rural area.

contras—an organized group of rebels who fought the Sandinista government in Nicaragua.

Creole—a mixture of several languages, which serves as an indigenous form of speech.

ejido—in Mexico, redistribution of farmland by the government to individuals or collectives after the 1910 Mexican Revolution.

guerrilla—a person who carries on warfare behind enemy lines through ambushes, raids, and sabotage of transport and communications.

hacienda—a large estate or plantation in Latin America, or its main house.

Maya—an Indian civilization of Mexico and Central America that built cities and temple-pyramids and devised a calendar and a writing system.

patois—a regional dialect.

plantation—a large estate that grows a cash crop; usually worked by unskilled or semiskilled labor.

taiga—subarctic coniferous forest largely consisting of firs and spruces.

tundra—a treeless plain found mostly in Arctic regions; it has permanently frozen subsoil and low-growing plants.

Of the 50 United States, 48 are contiguous, which means they touch each other. That leaves two: Alaska, which borders on Canada, and Hawaii in the Pacific Ocean. To fit Alaska (right) and the contiguous states on the same page at the scale indicated above, the maps here show them far out of their true geographic relationship to each other. A map of Hawaii, using a larger scale, appears on the facing page. The deep blue areas on the small map of North America show the correct locations of all the states.

0 KILOMETERS 500
0 STATUTE MILES 250
For map legend see page 21.

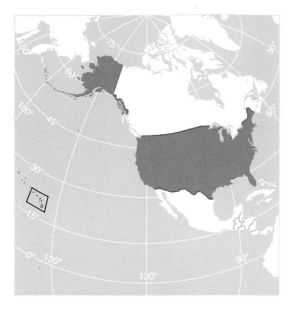

United States

Ocean waves slap the rocks of Oregon and wash the sands of Florida. Deserts cover the Southwest and forests the Pacific Northwest. In California's Death Valley it seldom rains; at the top of Hawaii's Mount Waialeale the rain seldom stops. Few other nations match the United States' variety of landscapes and climates.

The fourth largest country in area and third in population was born on the East Coast while Spanish colonists settled the Southwest. It grew westward, from 13 colonies on the Atlantic coast to 50 states stretching as far as Alaska and Hawaii. In longitude it reaches a third of the way around the globe. In latitude it spans more than 50 degrees, from southernmost Hawaii where the ground never freezes to northernmost Alaska where the ground never thaws.

Three-fourths of the United States lies west of the Mississippi River. But more than half of the 30 largest metropolitan areas lie east of it. As you travel east to west, you see reasons why.

On the East Coast, colonists built towns and cleared farmland. Abundant resources such as lumber, fish, and iron, and crops such as tobacco and cotton funneled through seaports en route to other colonies and Europe. Cities with skyscrapers now stand where ports grew around harbors on the coast and up the rivers.

In the hilly Northeast, swift rivers gave power for factories run by waterwheels. So along with farming and lumbering, a host of industries such as textiles and firearms arose. With the coming of railroads, industrial hubs such as Detroit and Pittsburgh prospered, close to both transportation and sources of raw materials.

In the Southeast, land and climate were ideal for planting cotton and tobacco. Some of the millions of Africans brought over as slaves worked these fields. Descendants of slaves now make up about a tenth of the U. S. population.

Inland, you reach the low Appalachian Mountain ridges. Their mines help make the United States a world leader in coal production. But for many years these forested ridges slowed westward travel. To the east the colonies threw off British rule and forged a nation of 13 states, while lands to the west and south remained largely Indian territory. But settlers soon crowded out the Native Americans whose land this had been for thousands of years.

The land smoothes out in the central farmlands and dairy pastures and the Great Plains beyond. Here farmers grow half the world's corn and more wheat for export than any other country. Here, too, lie sheep and cattle ranges.

Cities sprinkle the nation's midsection and the rugged Rocky Mountain area. Many started as mining towns, others as rail hubs where cattle and crops were shipped, still others as port cities along rivers like the Mississippi that served as vital highways of commerce and expansion.

Farther west you cross deserts in the rain shadow of the Sierra Nevada. Over that mountain range lie California croplands and the Coast Range, then the Pacific Ocean.

Head northwest past the dense forests of the Pacific Northwest and you find Alaska, where some fishing towns are linked by air and sea without a road across the rugged land. Far out to sea you come to the Hawaiian Islands, the summits of undersea volcanoes, where pineapples and sugarcane grow and tourists frolic.

The United States is the world's leading industrial power. Machines now do much of the work of farms and factories, driving millions of people to desert the fields and mills of small-town America and turn to service jobs in the cities: banking, finance, government, entertainment, and medical care. Fewer than two Americans in a hundred still work on farms. But as cities have swelled, so have their problems, and those of smaller towns, too: economic worries, overcrowding, pollution, crime, drugs.

Americans trace their roots to immigrants. Some were refugees from hard times or political upheavals in Europe. Some were brought against their will from Africa. Many now pour in from Southeast Asia and Latin America. The American people are as varied as their land, a mix more diverse than in any other nation.

Official name: *United States of America*
Area: *3,618,770 sq mi (9,372,614 sq km)*
Population: *255,570,000*
Capital: *Washington, D. C. (pop. 589,000)*
Ethnic groups: *white, African American, Hispanic, Asian, Native American*
Language: *English*
Religious groups: *Christian, Jewish, other*
Economy: *Agr: grains, cotton, tobacco, oilseeds, livestock, sugar, vegetables, fruit. Ind: machinery, metals, food processing, chemicals, motor vehicles, aerospace, telecommunications, oil, electronics, consumer goods, fishing, lumber, paper, mining*
Currency: *U. S. dollar*

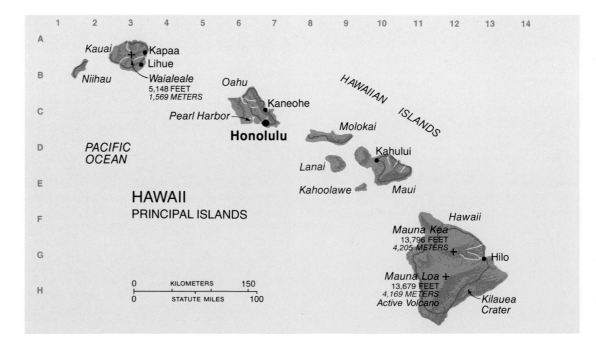

HAWAII
PRINCIPAL ISLANDS

United States

1 *Autumn paints the hills of Burke Hollow in Vermont, a New England state famed for fall colors and winter skiing.*

2 *Space shuttle* Columbia *roars off the pad at Cape Canaveral, Florida, home base for U. S. space vehicles since the 1950s.*

3 *New York City lights up the night. Lights and cars help make the United States the world's biggest consumer of energy.*

4 *A high school band joins a presidential inaugural parade in Washington, D. C., the nation's capital since 1800.*

5 *Fishermen explore a Louisiana bayou. Such slow-moving streams crisscross the Mississippi Delta, where the river fans out near its mouth.*

1 *Vermont, U. S.*

2 *Florida, U. S.*

3 *New York, U. S.*

4 *Washington, D. C., U. S.*

5 *Louisiana, U. S.*

1 *Washington, U.S.*

United States

1 *A self-leveling combine harvests wheat on a slope in Washington. This state ranked fourth in U.S. wheat production in 1990.*

2 *Freeways tie a knot in Los Angeles. Such high-speed roads link the city's downtown core to its sprawling suburbs.*

3 *Mount McKinley, North America's highest peak, soars over campers in Alaska. Indians call the mountain Denali, "high one."*

4 *Logs for export, cut from vast forests of the Pacific Northwest, crowd both the ships and the water at Longview, Washington.*

5 *Apache cowboys rope a calf on a ranch, one of several cooperatives that raise cattle on the grasslands of the Fort Apache Indian Reservation in Arizona.*

2 *California, U.S.*

3 *Alaska, U.S.*

4 *Washington, U. S.*

5 *Arizona, U. S.*

A B C D E F G H J K L M N O P Q R S T U

ARCTIC OCEAN

GREENLAND SEA

Alert

Ellesmere Island

GREENLAND
(KALAALLIT NUNAAT)
(DENMARK)

Qaanaaq (Thule)

+ North Magnetic Pole

Parry Islands

Baffin Bay

Tasiilaq

BEAUFORT SEA

Resolute

ARCTIC CIRCLE

Banks Island

Illulissat

Aasiaat

Davis Strait

ALASKA
(UNITED STATES)

Tuktoyaktuk

Inuvik

Victoria Island

Baffin Island

Sisimiut

Maniitsoq

YUKON TERRITORY

Cambridge Bay

Nuuk (Godthab)

Paamiut

Cape Farewell

Qaqortoq

Mount Logan
19,524 FEET
+ 5,951 METERS

Great Bear Lake

Mackenzie River

Iqaluit

LABRADOR SEA

Yukon River

Whitehorse

NORTHWEST TERRITORIES

Hudson Strait

Yellowknife

Ivujivik

Ungava Peninsula

ATLANTIC OCEAN

Great Slave Lake
Hay River

CANADA

Rankin Inlet

Kuujjuaq

NEWFOUNDLAND

Fort Smith

BRITISH COLUMBIA

Lake Athabasca

HUDSON BAY

LABRADOR

Prince Rupert

Dawson Creek

ALBERTA

Churchill River

Churchill

Nelson River

Fort Severn

Churchill Falls

St. John's

Prince George

ROCKY MOUNTAINS

Edmonton

SASKATCHEWAN

MANITOBA

QUEBEC

Island of Newfoundland

PACIFIC OCEAN

Fraser River

Chisasibi

TRANS-CANADA HIGHWAY

Prince Albert

Lake Winnipeg

Fort Albany

James Bay

Sept-Iles

Gulf of St. Lawrence

ST.-PIERRE AND MIQUELON (FRANCE)

Vancouver Island

Vancouver

Calgary

Saskatoon

NEW BRUNSWICK

PRINCE EDWARD ISLAND

Victoria

Lethbridge

Regina

Winnipeg

ONTARIO

St. Lawrence River

Fredericton

Charlottetown

TRANS-CANADA HIGHWAY

Thunder Bay

TRANS-CANADA HIGHWAY

Quebec

Halifax

Lake Superior

Sudbury

Montreal

NOVA SCOTIA

UNITED STATES

Lake Huron

Ottawa

Bay of Fundy

Oshawa

Toronto

Lake Ontario

Hamilton

London

Lake Erie

Lake Michigan

Windsor

Most of Greenland, the world's largest island, lies above the Arctic Circle. Most of Canada sprawls below it. In these two lands, people live farther north than anywhere else in the Western Hemisphere. Far more Canadians live in the south, though, near the border with the contiguous United States, the world's longest open border. More than 100 million people cross it every year.

0 KILOMETERS 600
0 STATUTE MILES 400

For map legend see page 21.

1 2 3 4 5 6 7 8 9 10 11 12 13 14 15 16 17 18 19

Canada

Look at a Canadian ten-dollar bill and you'll see the words "Ten Dollars Dix." *Dix* is the French word for ten. It's there because Canada's history has given the country two official languages.

In 1497 John Cabot sailed to Newfoundland and staked a claim for England. Nearly 40 years later, Jacques Cartier sailed to the mouth of the St. Lawrence River and laid claim for France. While English settlements sprouted along the seaboard and Hudson Bay, the French headed inland. Their settlements in the present-day province of Quebec became part of New France, the French colonial empire in North America that lasted for more than a century until the British seized control in 1763.

Canada is now a democracy, modeled in part after British law and government. The country recognizes the British Queen as its sovereign, a largely ceremonial echo of British rule. But in Quebec, French is the main language, and the legal system is much like that of France. Montreal, Quebec's largest city, is the largest French-speaking city in the world except Paris.

Canada and the United States share an unfortified border more than 5,000 miles (8,045 km) long. Eight out of ten Canadians live within 100 miles (160 km) of it. That leaves almost 80 percent of this huge land nearly uninhabited. Yet this wilderness is Canada's treasure chest. Thirty percent of the world's newsprint, the paper in your newspaper, comes from forests that cover half the country. Hundreds of mines make Canada a leading exporter of minerals.

Canada is the largest country in area after Russia. Five regions make up this immense landmass. At the northern end of the Appalachian Mountains is a region of hills and rolling plains stretching from New Brunswick to Newfoundland. A neighboring region of fertile flatlands rims the Great Lakes and the St. Lawrence River. Half of Canada's people live in these two regions. Half of its vegetables and nearly all of its corn come from farms there.

In the last 50 years steel mills, refineries, car factories, and other plants have been built along the shores of the Great Lakes in Ontario. Ontario's abundant hydroelectricity and, lately, nuclear power have contributed greatly to industrial development. The St. Lawrence River waterway links industrial centers such as Toronto and Montreal with seaports of the world.

Most of eastern Canada rests on an ancient sheet of bedrock called the Canadian Shield that extends into the United States. Thick evergreen forests cover its southern reaches. Farther north, taiga forests overlap the permafrost region. In the latter, the subsoil is permanently frozen, and most plants are tundra species such as low shrubs and lichens. Few plants survive in the ice and snow of the Shield's Arctic extremes.

West of the Shield lies a belt of plains, wooded in the north, rippling with wheat in the south. Besides bumper crops that rank Canada second only to the United States as a wheat-exporting country, the region yields lumber and minerals.

West of these forests and wheat fields rise the majestic Canadian Rockies, the beginning of a mountainous region that stretches to the Pacific coast. Rough terrain and a cold climate help keep this region sparsely settled, though Vancouver and other coastal centers thrive on fishing, shipping, and other activities.

A land of striking contrasts, Canada embraces the extremes of wilderness and urban development, of agriculture and industry, of European and indigenous cultures. Its vast natural resources and far-flung population supply an urbanized, industrial heartland with the raw materials that keep the economy going.

Official name: *Canada*
Area: *3,849,670 sq mi (9,970,610 sq km)*
Population: *27,300,000*
Capital: *Ottawa (pop. 572,200)*
Ethnic groups: *British, French, and other European origin, indigenous Indian and Inuit*
Language: *English, French*
Religious groups: *Roman Catholic, Protestant*
Economy: *Agr: wheat, livestock, feed crops, oilseeds, tobacco, fruit, vegetables. Ind: transportation equipment, food processing, petroleum products, wood and paper products, chemicals, metals, minerals, fishing*
Currency: *Canadian dollar*

Greenland

Greenland is like an elongated bowl filled with ice. A huge ice sheet, two miles thick in places, covers nearly all the island. Its heavy weight helps push the land down below sea level, leaving a surrounding rim of mountains.

Greenland is the world's biggest island. Here, in the tenth century, Viking explorer Erik the Red found patches of green in fjords and coastal meadows. To lure settlers from Iceland, he named the island Greenland. Other people already lived there. Inuit hunters had crossed the ice from Ellesmere Island generations before.

From their day to ours, most people have found Greenland's ice-choked northern coasts unfit to live on and have settled on the southwestern coastal fringe. There, commercial fishermen can put out to sea and herders can grow hay and tend sheep or reindeer. Many residents of Greenland fish for salmon, halibut, and cod, or work in plants that process the catch. Few roads link towns along the rugged coast; boats, snowmobiles, and aircraft take people to visit, attend school, or find a job.

Nearly all Greenlanders are of Inuit or Inuit-European descent. They govern themselves, but their island, known officially by its Greenlandic name, Kalaallit Nunaat, remains part of Denmark, home of Vikings centuries ago. A nationalist minority calls for full independence.

Official name: *Greenland (Kalaallit Nunaat)*
Area: *840,004 sq mi (2,175,600 sq km)*
Population: *57,000*
Capital: *Nuuk (Godthåb) (pop. 12,217)*
Ethnic groups: *Greenlander, Danish*
Language: *Danish, Greenlandic*
Religious groups: *Lutheran*
Economy: *Agr: hay, sheep, vegetables. Ind: fishing, lead and zinc mining, sealing, handicrafts*
Currency: *Danish krone*

St.-Pierre and Miquelon

Of its once-great Canadian lands, France holds only these eight rocky islets. With little soil for gardens, the islanders—French citizens, but self-governing—raise vegetables and livestock for home use and work in a fishing fleet and a fish processing plant. Tourism helps the economy.

Official name: *Territorial Collectivity of St.-Pierre and Miquelon*
Area: *93 sq mi (242 sq km)*
Population: *6,000*
Capital: *St.-Pierre (pop. 5,683)*

1 *British Columbia, Canada*

Canada

1 *Lions Gate Bridge leads toward Vancouver, Canada's most important Pacific port, where tall forests grow down to the sea.*

2 *Grain elevators store wheat in Saskatchewan, one of the Prairie Provinces and a leading grower of wheat.*

3 *Canadian Rockies peaks frame a camper in Banff National Park in Alberta, a province famed for high-country scenery.*

2 *Saskatchewan, Canada*

4 *Quebec, Canada*

5 *Newfoundland, Canada*

3 *Alberta, Canada*

6 *Greenland*

Canada

4 *Château Frontenac hotel towers over Quebec, Canada's oldest city and capital of the French-speaking province of Quebec.*

5 *Atlantic codfish are netted inshore in Newfoundland. Inshore and offshore fishing have yielded a rich catch for centuries.*

Greenland

6 *Inuit hunters make sealskin leather. Inuit, or Eskimos, range North America's Arctic and subarctic regions.*

A

Tijuana ● **Mexicali**

Ensenada

UNITED STATES

B
Nogales ● **Ciudad Juarez**

Colorado River

C

D
Rio Bravo del Norte (Rio Grande)

Hermosillo

E
Chihuahua ●

Conchos River

Yaqui River

Guaymas ●
Delicias

F
Santa Rosalia ● **Ciudad Obregon**
● Hidalgo del Parral
● **Nuevo Laredo**

Gulf of California

G
Monclova
Reynosa

Los Mochis ●
Gomez Palacio
Monterrey
Matamoros

H
Torreon
Saltillo **Guadalupe**

*PACIFIC
OCEAN*

*GULF
OF
MEXICO*

Culiacan

J
● La Paz
Durango
Ciudad Victoria

K
Mazatlan ●
MEXICO

Zacatecas ●
Ciudad Mante ●

L
Ciudad Madero
Tampico

San Luis Potosi
*Panuco
River*

M
Aguascalientes

Tepic
Leon

Zapopan **Guadalajara**
Guanajuato ●
Poza Rica

N
Puerto Vallarta ●
Salamanca
El Tajin

Tlaquepaque **Irapuato**
Queretaro
Celaya

O
Lake Chapala
Zamora ●
Teotihuacan ■
Pachuca
Xalapa
Veracruz

Morelia
Mexico

Manzanillo ●
Colima ●
Uruapan
Toluca
Cordoba

P
Cuernavaca
Puebla
Orizaba

Popocatepetl
17,930 FEET
5,465 METERS
*Pico de
Orizaba*
18,855 FEET
5,747 METERS
Highest point
in Mexico

Balsas River

Q
Chilpancingo ●

SIERRA MADRE DEL SUR
Oaxaca

R
Acapulco ●
Salina Cruz ●

S
*Gulf of
Tehuantepec*

SIERRA MADRE OCCIDENTAL
SIERRA MADRE ORIENTAL
CENTRAL PLATEAU
Lerma River

BAJA CALIFORNIA

Mexico's northern bor-
der, patrolled by the
United States against il-
legal crossings, marks
the northern boundary of
Latin America.
  The name refers chief-
ly to countries of North
America, South America,
and the Caribbean Sea
where Spanish or Portu-
guese is spoken, but it
may include French-
speaking areas. Some-
times its meaning
broadens to embrace all
the countries south of
Mexico's border with the
United States.

0   KILOMETERS   250
0   STATUTE MILES   150

For map legend see page 21.

T

1 2 3 4 5 6 7 8 9 10 11 12 13 14 15 16 17 18 19 20

TROPIC OF CANCER

Progreso

Cancun

Merida

Cancun I.

Chichen Itza

Cozumel Island

Uxmal

Bay of Campeche

Campeche

YUCATAN

PENINSULA

Chetumal

Usumacinta River

BELIZE

Villahermosa

Palenque

Tuxtla Gutierrez

Salinas River

Grijalva River

GUATEMALA

Tapachula

Mexico

Like a great stone wall, a range of mountains winds north from western Central America and deep into Mexico. There it splits into two ranges, the Sierra Madre Oriental (East) and Occidental (West). Between them spreads a cool, high plateau, 500 miles (805 km) wide and 1,500 miles (2,415 km) long that is home to half of Mexico's people. Where the ranges divide stands Mexico City with one of the largest urban populations in the world. Latest estimates run to more than 15 million residents in the metropolitan area.

Frequent earthquakes jolt the city. Pollution fouls its air, partly because the surrounding mountains often keep winds from blowing away factory smoke and the exhaust of cars, buses, and trucks. Yet thousands more people arrive in Mexico City each week, looking for jobs and a place to live. Many end up jobless in the shanty-towns at the city's fringes.

For thousands of years this central plateau has been a magnet for settlers. Indians found a pleasant climate, fertile soil, and enough rainfall for their staple crops of corn, beans, and squash. Six centuries ago the Aztec built their capital here, on an island in a lake. Now the lake is gone, drained and filled in by Spanish conquerors for a capital that developed into modern Mexico City. But Indians remain. About a third of Mexico's people descend from the native peoples who farmed and traded in Mexico before the Spaniards came. The rest are mostly mestizos of mixed Indian and Spanish blood.

The Spaniards divided the plateau, and much of the rest of Mexico, into haciendas, sprawling estates where landowners prospered on cattle ranching and farming. Later, a government program called *ejido* redistributed nearly half of the farmland to individuals or to community groups. Despite this effort, reminders of the old hacienda system linger today in large landholdings worked by campesinos, farm workers who often have no farmland of their own.

Little more than a tenth of Mexico's land is good for farming. Only a small fraction of that is permanently cultivated, often by using irrigation. In the deserts of the north and west there is not enough rain for crops; in the mountains the terrain is too steep and the climate too cold; the southeast lacks dependable water sources. Yet farming is still the mainstay of Mexico's economy. Large farms yield coffee, cotton, fruit, and vegetables and export much of the crop.

In rural areas, campesinos tend plots to feed their families or work for pay on the commercial farms. When crop prices fall, landholders cannot make a profit on crops they grow to sell, and thus cannot pay the campesinos. Out of jobs, the workers move to urban centers. Mexico's population boom forces still more people into the already crowded cities.

Some find jobs in Mexico's well-developed industries. Workers help produce chemicals, textiles, and steel, and assemble everything from audiocassettes to automobiles. An increasing number of factories are near the U. S. border. Here more than a thousand factories receive parts from American firms and ship back assembled goods to the United States. In December 1992, leaders of the U. S., Canada, and Mexico signed a free trade agreement that is expected to have a huge impact on Mexico's economy.

Mexico is a world leader in silver production. Miners also extract gold, sulfur, lead and zinc ores, and about 40 other minerals. In the 1970s a big oil discovery in the hot, humid lowlands along the Gulf of Mexico gave the nation's economy a much-needed boost. Then oil prices fell, leaving Mexico with massive foreign debt.

Tourists, most of them from the United States, help ease the nation's money problems. They come to seaside resorts such as Puerto Vallarta and Acapulco on the Pacific shore, and island getaways such as Cancún and Cozumel in the Caribbean Sea. Many travelers visit the impressive Maya ruins that dot the lowlands of the Yucatán Peninsula.

Mexicans come to the United States too, but most aren't on vacation. Millions live legally in the United States. No one knows how many more have crossed the border illegally. These people are refugees from Mexico's population boom and lack of jobs.

Officially, Latin America ends at the U. S. border. But Mexico once stretched much farther north, and the border states still have strong Spanish ties. Today Mexico has the highest population of any Spanish-speaking country in the world. Its roots are in Spain, and in the former grandeur of civilizations such as those of the Aztec and the Maya.

Official name: *United Mexican States*
Area: *756,066 sq mi (1,958,201 sq km)*
Population: *87,715,000*
Capital: *Mexico (City) (pop. 8,237,000, met. pop. 15,000,000)*
Ethnic groups: *mestizo, Indian, white*
Language: *Spanish, Indian languages*
Religious groups: *Roman Catholic*
Economy: *Agr: corn, wheat, coffee, cotton, sugarcane, fruit, vegetables, sorghum, oilseeds, livestock, tobacco. Ind: oil, food processing, chemicals, steel, minerals, textiles, motor vehicles, tourism, fishing*
Currency: *peso*

1 *Mexico*

Mexico

1 *Popocatépetl, sacred volcano of the Aztec, towers over a church built by Spanish conquerors atop an Aztec temple-pyramid.*

2 *Near pyramids built between A.D. 300 and 1100 at El Tajín, Totonac Indians tend corn much as their ancestors did.*

3 *Imitating the gaudy quetzal, a bird prized by the Aztec and Maya, dancers honor old beliefs at a fair near Mexico City.*

4 *Mexicans wade the Rio Grande at Ciudad Juárez. Some make money carrying others across this boundary into the U. S.*

5 *Sparks fly as factory workers make car exhaust pipes in Querétaro. The U. S.-owned factory helps boost Mexico's economy.*

6 *Once a fishing village, Cancún was chosen in 1970 to be a big tourist center. Now hotels fill this islet in the Caribbean Sea.*

7 *Cacao pods ripen in southeastern Mexico. The beans inside are used to make cocoa.*

2 *Mexico*

3 *Mexico*

4 *Mexico*

5 *Mexico*

6 *Mexico*

7 *Mexico*

A B C D E F G H J K L M N O P Q R S T U

MEXICO

Hondo River

Belize City

Turneffe Islands

PETEN ▫Tikal

Belize River

Usumacinta River

Lake Peten Itza •Flores

⊗Belmopan

Pasion River

BELIZE

CARIBBEAN SEA

Bahia Islands

Gulf of Honduras

Puerto Barrios

Puerto Cortes
•Tela

La Ceiba

GUATEMALA *Lake Izabal*

Rio Negro •Coban

San Pedro Sula
•El Progreso

Aguan River

La Esperanza Mountains

Patuca River

Caratasca Lagoon

Motagua River

Ulua River

Tajumulco Volcano +
13,845 FEET
4,220 METERS

•Quetzaltenango •Zacapa

□Copan

Lake Yojoa

•Juticalpa

Coco River

Mosquito Coast

Highest point in Central America

Antigua Guatemala

•Santa Rosa de Copan

HONDURAS

•Siguatepeque

Cordillera Isabella

⊗**Guatemala**

•Mazatenango

•Tiquisate

•Escuintla

Lempa River

•Comayagua

⊗**Tegucigalpa**

•San Jose

Santa Ana

•Comayaguela

•Danli

Rio Grande de Matagalpa

EL SALVADOR

•Sonsonate

•Sensuntepeque

NICARAGUA

•Acajutla

⊗**San Salvador**

•Esteli

•Jinotega

•La Libertad

•San Miguel

•Matagalpa

Nueva San Salvador

•Usulutan

•La Union

•Choluteca

PACIFIC OCEAN

Gulf of Fonseca

•Chinandega

CARIBBEAN SEA

Leon

Lake Managua

Escondido River

Managua⊗

•Tipitapa

•Masaya

•Bluefields

•Diriamba

•Granada

Lake Nicaragua

•Rivas

San Juan River

San Carlos River

•Liberia

Arenal → +
5,358 FEET
1,633 METERS

COSTA RICA

•Alajuela

•Puntarenas

•Heredia ⊗**San Jose**

•Puerto Limon

Mosquito Gulf

•Cartago

Gulf of Nicoya

+*Mount Chirripo*
12,530 FEET
3,819 METERS

Osa Peninsula

•David

Puerto Armuelles

Gulf of Chiriqui

Coiba Island

Seven small nations crowd onto the tapering isthmus that links Mexico to South America. Together they are known as **Central America.** Six of them share a Spanish colonial and Indian heritage. Belize, a former British colony, has greater cultural ties to the English-speaking Caribbean islands.

0 KILOMETERS 150
0 STATUTE MILES 100

For map legend see page 21.

1 2 3 4 5 6 7 8 9 10 11 12 13 14 15 16 17 18 19 20

sparsely settled northern third of the country, the Petén, stand Maya ruins such as Tikal, a maze of stone palaces and temple-pyramids.

About half of Guatemala's people are Indians. Nowhere on the North American continent is there an Indian culture so little changed by the coming of Europeans. Most of the native peoples speak Mayan languages and tend plots of corn, beans, and squash as their forebears did.

Official name: *Republic of Guatemala*
Area: *42,042 sq mi (108,889 sq km)*
Population: *9,710,000*
Capital: *Guatemala (City) (pop. 1,675,589)*
Ethnic groups: *Indian, ladino*
Language: *Spanish, Mayan languages*
Religious groups: *Roman Catholic, Protestant*
Economy: *Agr: coffee, cotton, sugarcane, bananas, corn, beans, livestock, rubber, cardamom. Ind: food processing, textiles, chemicals, oil, tourism*
Currency: *quetzal*

El Salvador

El Salvador lies along a double row of volcanoes, and some of them are very much alive. Yet Salvadoran peasants farm even the steep sides of the cones. Land is precious in the smallest and most densely populated country in Central America, and much of the farmland is owned by an elite few.

On the slopes the farmers tend small plots of corn and other staples, tilling with hoes and planting with pointed sticks. Many live in squarish thatched-roof houses with dirt floors. After the fall harvest, thousands trek to commercial plantations in the highlands to pick the coffee beans that sustain El Salvador's economy.

Although 40 percent of Salvadoran workers are employed in agriculture, the country is highly industrialized. Factories are located around the larger cities and towns. The economy is in trouble, though, slowed by drought and a devastating 1986 earthquake, and sabotaged by a civil war that dragged on for 12 years. Tens of thousands of civilians died in the war's cross fire, and perhaps a million fled their homeland. Many headed to the United States. The tourist industry has suffered too; fewer visitors come to enjoy the lakes and mountains of the cool interior or the beaches along the Pacific Ocean fringe.

Official name: *Republic of El Salvador*
Area: *8,124 sq mi (21,041 sq km)*
Population: *5,574,000*
Capital: *San Salvador (pop. 481,400)*
Ethnic groups: *mestizo, Indian*
Language: *Spanish*
Religious groups: *Roman Catholic*
Economy: *Agr: coffee, cotton, corn, sugarcane, beans, rice, sorghum, wheat. Ind: food processing, textiles, clothing, chemicals, oil, cement, fishing*
Currency: *Salvadoran colón*

Guatemala

Cool tropical highlands hold most of Guatemala's people and much of its industry. There stands the biggest city in Central America—Guatemala City, the nation's capital. The metropolitan area's population has grown fourfold in three decades. Farmers come in from the countryside to seek jobs because they own little or no land to farm. Half the farmland is owned by less than 5 percent of the population, who prosper on coffee, bananas, cotton, and other export crops.

Other people flee to the city from rural homelands wracked by decades of war between government troops and rebel guerrillas. In 1976, thousands flocked in when their villages crumbled in a mighty earthquake.

Among the highlands volcanoes rise—a few still active, but most of them dormant like Tajumulco, Central America's highest peak. In the

Belize

Legend says English sailors shipwrecked in 1638 founded the first British settlement in what is now Belize. Established as a crown colony named British Honduras in 1862, Belize won independence in 1981. English is the official language, and most Belizeans also speak an English Creole somewhat like those of the Caribbean islands. The British influence gives Belize a distinctive flavor in Central America.

From coastal swamps and forests the terrain slopes upward to low mountains. Two natural treasures bring in much needed tourist income: a spectacular coral reef second in size to Australia's Great Barrier Reef, and a rain forest full of tropical birds and animals. Sugarcane, fruit, and fish are the other mainstays of an economy with very little manufacturing.

Belize has the smallest population in Central America. Half its people trace roots to black Africa. Most Belizeans live in Belize City and other coastal communities, where steady sea breezes relieve the hot, humid climate.

Official name: *Belize*
Area: *8,867 sq mi (22,965 sq km)*
Population: *229,000*
Capital: *Belmopan (pop. 5,300)*
Ethnic groups: *black, mestizo, Indian*
Language: *English, English Creole, Spanish*
Religious groups: *Roman Catholic, Protestant*
Economy: *Agr: sugarcane, citrus fruit, bananas, corn, rice, beans, livestock. Ind: food processing, clothing, fertilizer, lumber, rum, fishing, tourism*
Currency: *Belize dollar*

Honduras

In the late 16th century, Spanish prospectors found silver in the mountainous interior of Honduras. Mule paths that linked scattered dwellings later became the winding streets of Tegucigalpa, once a mining town, today the capital. Some say its name comes from an ancient Indian language: *taguzgalpa*, meaning "silver hill."

Honduran miners still dig for silver and other minerals, mainly in the western mountains. And the manufacturing of textiles, cement, and wood products has been developed, especially in San

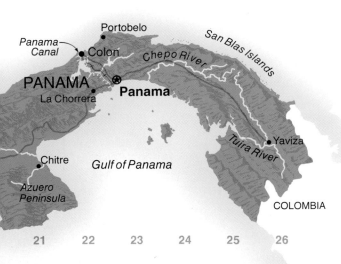

Pedro Sula. Shrimp, lobsters, coffee, and meat bring in export income, but bananas rule the economy. They grow mostly in lowlands along the Caribbean Sea, where American firms own large plantations.

Honduras is the least developed and poorest country in Central America. Sparsely populated, it is a magnet for refugees from strife-torn neighboring nations. Only a few years ago nearly half the people could not read or write. To fight illiteracy, greater emphasis was placed on education, and today 73 percent of the population age 15 and over can read and write.

Official name: *Republic of Honduras*
Area: *43,277 sq mi (112,088 sq km)*
Population: *5,462,000*
Capital: *Tegucigalpa (pop. 608,100)*
Ethnic groups: *mestizo, Indian, black*
Language: *Spanish, Black Carib*
Religious groups: *Roman Catholic*
Economy: *Agr: bananas, coffee, sugarcane, corn, beans, rice, tobacco, livestock. Ind: food processing, textiles, clothing, wood products, mining, fishing*
Currency: *lempira*

Nicaragua

Two big lakes called Lake Managua and Lake Nicaragua nestle between the mountain ranges of western Nicaragua. Most Nicaraguans make their home in the plains along the Pacific coast and the highlands around the lakes. There campesinos herd cattle and grow cotton, coffee, and bananas in the fertile volcanic soil. There too stand most of Nicaragua's urban areas, including the biggest, the capital city of Managua.

Earthquakes wrecked Managua in 1931 and again in 1972. Ghostly ruins dot the old downtown area, while businessmen and government workers come and go in the rebuilt city. Textile and food-processing plants cluster nearby.

Sandinista rebels seized power in 1979 after overthrowing the 42-year dictatorship of the Somoza family. Then the Sandinistas fought for a decade against guerrillas known as contras. In 1990 opposition leader Violeta Barrios de Chamorro was elected president. She soon faced a major challenge: trying to determine the ownership of property confiscated by the Sandinistas.

The country looks like a big triangle set askew. From the mountainous western region, the hills slope down eastward to broad, swampy plains, thick with tropical forests but only thinly populated. Indians such as the Miskito dwell

along the Caribbean shore, known as the Mosquito Coast. Thousands of Miskitos jammed refugee camps in Honduras when the Sandinistas leveled their villages and tried to resettle them in new ones out of the path of war.

Official name: *Republic of Nicaragua*
Area: *50,193 sq mi (130,000 sq km)*
Population: *4,096,000*
Capital: *Managua (pop. 682,100)*
Ethnic groups: *mestizo, white, black, Indian*
Language: *Spanish*
Religious groups: *Roman Catholic*
Economy: *Agr: coffee, cotton, sugarcane, rice, corn, beans, sorghum, cattle, bananas. Ind: food processing, chemicals, metal products, textiles, oil refining*
Currency: *new córdoba*

Costa Rica

Costa Rica lies across the Central American isthmus like a saddle, its sides dropping to seacoasts, its middle rising to mountains. The capital city, San José, sits squarely in the seat on a central highland in the ridge that runs the country's length.

Politically, Costa Rica is like the calm eye of one of the hurricanes that on rare occasions roar in from the Caribbean Sea. In 1949 the Costa Ricans, who call themselves Ticos, abolished their armed forces. Since then their country has become known as a haven of peace in a region of strife. In 1987 then President Oscar Arias Sánchez received a Nobel Peace Prize for his plan to restore peace to Central America.

Ticos take pride in the highest literacy rate in Central America. Nine out of ten adults can read and write, and nearly all children of school age attend school. To guard a natural heritage of rain forests, volcanoes, and sandy beaches, a park system protects a tenth of the nation's lands, a model for other countries worldwide. The economy balances agriculture—mainly coffee, bananas, and beef—with food processing, chemical, and textile industries.

Official name: *Republic of Costa Rica*
Area: *19,730 sq mi (51,100 sq km)*
Population: *3,187,000*
Capital: *San José (pop. 294,200)*
Ethnic groups: *white, mestizo, black*
Language: *Spanish*
Religious groups: *Roman Catholic*
Economy: *Agr: coffee, bananas, sugarcane, rice, corn, cattle. Ind: food processing, textiles, chemicals*
Currency: *Costa Rican colón*

Panama

Panama is like two bridges: a land link between continents and a sea link between oceans. Panama's mountainous S-curve connects the North and South American continents by land. Since 1914 the Panama Canal has sliced across Central America to link the Pacific Ocean with the Atlantic via the Caribbean Sea. Built by the United States, the canal is jointly administered by the U. S. and Panama.

Panama City, the capital, located on the canal's Pacific end, and Colón, about 50 miles (80 km) away on the Caribbean end, have prospered from trade that funnels through the strategic Big Ditch. Panama normally receives millions of dollars a month for use of the canal and an oil pipeline that crosses the isthmus.

By treaty, Panama will take over the canal in the year 2000. With the announced aim of protecting American lives and the canal treaties, the U. S. sent troops in 1989 to remove dictator Manuel Antonio Noriega. Power was restored to the government elected earlier in the year, which Noriega had blocked from taking office. As the new government attempts to bring political stability to the country, it also faces the challenge of improving the struggling economy.

Panama has about 100 banks that serve customers worldwide. Merchant ships of many nations sail under Panamanian registry, making it a world leader in the licensing of cargo ships. Perhaps a quarter of Panama's workers are farmers who tend family plots or grow cash crops. But the country's economy relies on the canal and service industries associated with it.

Official name: *Republic of Panama*
Area: *29,762 sq mi (77,082 sq km)*
Population: *2,431,000*
Capital: *Panama (City) (met. pop. 439,300)*
Ethnic groups: *mestizo, black, white, Indian*
Language: *Spanish, English*
Religious groups: *Roman Catholic*
Economy: *Agr: bananas, sugarcane, coffee, rice, corn, beans. Ind: finance, transport, food processing*
Currency: *balboa*

Costa Rica

1 *Arenal Volcano fumes and rumbles in the northern mountains of Costa Rica. Volcanoes that sprinkle the ridges of the Central American isthmus mark the seams where great shifting slabs of earth's crust, called tectonic plates, slowly collide and grind against each other.*

1 *Costa Rica*

Panama

1 *Skyscrapers sprout in Panama's capital, Panama City, the Pacific Ocean gateway to the canal that cuts across the isthmus.*

El Salvador

2 *A Salvadoran harvests red, ripe coffee berries, each containing two coffee beans, from shrubs in the highlands.*

Nicaragua

3 *Oxen plow a field on a small farm in the Nicaraguan countryside.*

Guatemala

4 *Steep temple-pyramids jut from the Guatemalan rain forest at ancient Tikal, a sprawling Maya ruin.*

Honduras

5 *Streets and sidewalks pulse with life in Comayagüela. Workers tote the wares of stores and open-air market stalls.*

Belize

6 *Rainbows of fish in coral gardens lure divers to Lighthouse Reef and other undersea wonders just off the shore of Belize.*

1 *Panama*

2 *El Salvador*

3 *Nicaragua*

4 *Guatemala*

5 *Honduras*

6 *Belize*

A B C D E F G H J K L M N O P Q R S T U

UNITED STATES

Grand Bahama Island
Freeport
Abaco Island

Eleuthera Island

Straits of Florida

Nassau
⊛
New Providence Island

Andros Island

Cat Island

San Salvador

TROPIC OF CANCER

BAHAMAS

Great Exuma

Long Island

Havana ⊛ **Guanabacoa**
• Cardenas
Matanzas
Pinar del Rio
Cienfuegos
Santa Clara

Acklins Island

Mayaguana Island

CUBA
Bay of Pigs

Isle of Youth

Sancti Spiritus
Ciego de Avila

Camaguey

Great Inagua Island

Turks and Caicos Islands
(UNITED KINGDOM)
⊛ Grand Turk

Las Tunas • **Holguin**

Manzanillo • **Bayamo**

Santiago de Cuba • **Guantanamo**

Cap-
Haitien
Port-de-Paix •

DOMINICAN REPUBLIC

ATLANTIC OCEAN

Puerto Plata •

Santiago •
San Francisco de Macoris •

Gonaives •
Pico Duarte
10,417 FEET
3,175 METERS +

Cayman Islands
(UNITED KINGDOM)
George Town ⊛

HAITI

JAMAICA
Montego Bay •
May
Pen •
Mandeville •
Kingston
⊛
Spanish
Town

Port-au-Prince ⊛
• San Juan

San Juan
Bayamon

Santo Domingo
⊛ • La Romana

HISPANIOLA
Bani •

San Pedro
de Macoris

PUERTO RICO
(UNITED STATES) **Ponce**

Les Cayes •

G R E A T E R

CARIBBEAN SEA

A N T I L L E S

When Columbus sighted these islands in 1492, he thought he had reached islands near India in Asia, and so he named them the Indies. Now they are known as the **West Indies,** because of their location in the Western Hemisphere. The two main island groups in the West Indies are the Greater Antilles and Lesser Antilles. The Antilles separate the Caribbean Sea from the Atlantic Ocean. A third group, the Bahamas, lies in the Atlantic.

0 KILOMETERS 250
0 STATUTE MILES 150
For map legend see page 21.

ARUBA
(NETHERLANDS)
Oranjestad

NETHERLANDS ANTILLES
(NETHERLANDS)
Curacao
Bonaire

Willemstad

L E S S E R

COLOMBIA

VENEZUELA

1 2 3 4 5 6 7 8 9 10 11 12 13 14 15 16 17 18 19 20

BERMUDA
(UNITED KINGDOM)

St. George's Island

Somerset Island

Hamilton

St. David's Island

Bermuda Island

0 KILOMETERS 15
0 STATUTE MILES 10

U.S. Virgin Islands
British Virgin Islands
Anguilla (UNITED KINGDOM)
St. Martin (St. Maarten) (FRANCE & NETHERLANDS)
Charlotte
Amalie
St. Barthelemy (FRANCE)
Saba (NETH.)
Barbuda
St. Croix   St. Eustatius   Basseterre
(U.S.)   (NETH.)   St. John's   ANTIGUA AND
ST. KITTS   Antigua   BARBUDA
AND NEVIS
Redonda   Montserrat (UNITED KINGDOM)
Guadeloupe (FRANCE)
Basse-Terre   Pointe-a-Pitre

DOMINICA
Roseau

St.-Pierre
Fort-de-France   Martinique
(FRANCE)

Castries   ST. LUCIA

St. Vincent   BARBADOS
Kingstown   Bridgetown
ST. VINCENT AND
THE GRENADINES

GRENADA
St. George's

A N T I L L E S

Tobago
TRINIDAD AND TOBAGO
Port of Spain   Arima
Trinidad
San Fernando

21   22   23   24   25   26

Bermuda

The British colony of Bermuda is made up of hundreds of coral islands lying 650 miles (1,046 km) east of North Carolina. Only 20 are inhabited. Many are too small to show up on our map.

Nowhere else in the world do you find coral islands this far north. Bermuda's famed beaches owe their pink tint to grains of coral. The warm Gulf Stream ensures balmy breezes, flowers—and tourists, the core of Bermuda's prosperity. Exports of flowers and bananas, plus a little manufacturing, round out a healthy economy.

Spanish explorer Juan de Bermudez spotted the hilly islands in 1503. The first occupants were British seafarers shipwrecked in 1609. Later, African slaves were brought in; today three-fifths of Bermudians descend from them.

Official name: *Bermuda*
Area: *20 sq mi (53 sq km)*
Population: *61,000*
Capital: *Hamilton (pop. 2,000)*
Ethnic groups: *black, white*
Language: *English*
Religious groups: *Protestant, Roman Catholic*
Economy: *Agr: bananas, vegetables, Easter lilies, citrus fruit. Ind: tourism, finance, manufacturing*
Currency: *Bermuda dollar*

Bahamas

On one of the 700 Bahama Islands, Columbus first landed in the New World five centuries ago. Later a British colony, the Bahamas won independence in 1973. Millions of visitors arrive each year, making tourism the leading industry. Finance is second, with more than 300 banks serving customers around the world. Shipping adds to an economy that includes little agriculture. Much income may also derive from drug trafficking.

Nowhere in the world can you find clearer seas than here, because these low, sandy islands have no rivers to cloud the water with silt. Though 30 islands are inhabited, six out of ten Bahamians live on only one: New Providence, site of the major port and capital city, Nassau.

Official name: *The Commonwealth of The Bahamas*
Area: *5,382 sq mi (13,939 sq km)*
Population: *264,000*
Capital: *Nassau (met. pop. 153,000)*
Ethnic groups: *black, white*
Language: *English, English Creole*
Religious groups: *Protestant, Roman Catholic*
Economy: *Agr: vegetables, fruit, livestock. Ind: tourism, banking, shipping, cement, rum, fishing*
Currency: *Bahamian dollar*

British Dependencies

Once the British West Indies embraced many islands, but now only a sprinkling remain under British rule. These include the **British Virgin Islands**, a double arc of some 15 inhabited islands and about 20 islets. More than three-fourths of the people of this volcanic archipelago live on Tortola. Most are black; about 10 percent are of white or other origin. Poor soils and hilly terrain make large-scale farming or herding difficult, and there are few industries. Many people seek work in the U. S. Virgin Islands. The economy relies on tourists, some of whom sail to coves where pirates like Blackbeard and Captain Kidd once lurked between raids on passing ships.

Abundant rain gives mountainous **Montserrat** a wealth of streams, waterfalls, and forests. Its economy also depends on tourism, along with fruit, vegetable, and livestock farming. One 1989 visitor, Hurricane Hugo, left almost all of the 12,000 residents homeless. Rebuilding has been expensive but quicker than expected.

In recent years the low-lying **Cayman Islands** have become an important financial center and tax haven. A turtle farm founded on the Caymans in 1968 breeds the endangered green sea turtle. Some are released into the wild and some eaten locally. The low, dry **Turks and Caicos Islands** are another financial center. On rocky **Anguilla** people make salt by evaporating seawater. Islanders also fish for clawless lobsters and for conch, the large marine snails eaten here.

Cuba

The world's top exporter of sugar, Cuba sold most of its output to the United States until a revolt led by Fidel Castro turned the island nation to communism in 1959. For 30 years the Soviet Union supported Cuba's economy, providing cheap oil and cut-rate loans while buying sugar at up to triple the going price. Then the Soviet empire broke apart. Trade between its former republics and Cuba declined dramatically, and Cuba's economy deteriorated. In 1992 the largest of the ex-Soviet republics, Russia, reached an agreement with Cuba on developing a new trade policy.

Sugarcane covers more than half of Cuba's farmland, most of which lies in the fertile central plains. Before Castro, much of the cropland was owned by foreigners, but now the state owns most of the land.

The state owns the factories too. Cigars, the

best-known product, have been a Cuban export since Columbus's sailors saw Indians puffing on rolls of leaves they called *tobacos*. The Indians died out long ago. Today's Cubans are mostly blacks, whites, and mulattos, descendants of Spaniards and their black plantation slaves.

Cuba's fine climate, beaches, and mountain scenery attract a growing tourist trade. Visitors once flocked to Havana, largest city in the Caribbean, for its old Spanish buildings, showy nightclubs, and nonstop fun. Though the glamour has faded, Cuba's capital remains a major port and commercial hub.

Official name: *Republic of Cuba*
Area: *42,804 sq mi (110,861 sq km)*
Population: *10,846,000*
Capital: *Havana (pop. 2,077,900)*
Ethnic groups: *mulatto, white, black*
Language: *Spanish*
Religious groups: *Roman Catholic*
Economy: *Agr: sugarcane, tobacco, rice, root crops, citrus fruit, coffee, livestock. Ind: oil refining, food processing, nickel, textiles, chemicals, fishing*
Currency: *Cuban peso*

Jamaica

"*Irie*," say some Jamaicans of their island. In their dialect it means "wonderful." Tourists agree as they raft down a river or admire the scenery of this mountainous tropical island, third largest in the Caribbean. Many enjoy beach resorts, where they sip local rum and dance to reggae. Most tourists do not see Jamaica's other, grimmer face: the slums of urban areas like Kingston, the capital.

Three-fourths of Jamaicans descend from African slaves who worked plantations under British colonial rule. Many now tend small farms all over the island, raising corn, yams, coffee, or other crops—even marijuana. Some work modern sugarcane and banana plantations, or make clothing, tires, cement, and other manufactured goods in urban centers. Few countries surpass Jamaica's output of bauxite—the ore from which aluminum is made—a major export.

Official name: *Jamaica*
Area: *4,244 sq mi (10,991 sq km)*
Population: *2,507,000*
Capital: *Kingston (met. pop. 641,500)*
Ethnic groups: *black, mulatto*
Language: *English, English Creole*
Religious groups: *Protestant*
Economy: *Agr: sugarcane, citrus fruit, bananas, pimiento, coconuts, coffee, cacao, tobacco. Ind: bauxite, tourism, textiles, food processing, rum, cement*
Currency: *Jamaican dollar*

Haiti

In the 1700s Haiti was a rich French colony of sugarcane and coffee plantations. Today this western third of the island of Hispaniola is one of the world's poorest countries. Forests that covered its mountainous terrain are all but gone. As erosion strips away the exposed soil, Haitians continue to cut trees to make charcoal for fuel. Coffee is still an important export, but most farmers tend only small family plots of corn, rice, and beans. Factories assemble toys, electronic equipment, and sporting goods, including baseballs.

Most Haitians descend from African slaves who revolted and formed the first black republic in 1804. Many practice voodoo, a blend of African and Christian beliefs. After decades of dictatorship, Haiti elected a new president in 1990, but military leaders soon forced him out. The United Nations called for his reinstatement.

Official name: *Republic of Haiti*
Area: *10,714 sq mi (27,750 sq km)*
Population: *6,432,000*
Capital: *Port-au-Prince (pop. 514,400)*
Ethnic groups: *black, mulatto*
Language: *French, Haitian Creole*
Religious groups: *Roman Catholic, voodoo*
Economy: *Agr: coffee, sugarcane, corn, rice, beans, cacao. Ind: food processing, textiles, manufacturing*
Currency: *gourde*

Dominican Republic

In 1492 some of Columbus's sailors settled on the island that he named Hispaniola. There, four years later, Spanish colonists founded Santo Domingo, the first permanent European settlement in the New World. Today it's the capital of the Dominican Republic, a nation that occupies the eastern two-thirds of the island.

The highest point in the Caribbean is in the middle of this mountainous country: 10,417-foot (3,175 m) Pico Duarte in the Cordillera Central, one of four ranges that corrugate the landscape. To its north lies the Cibao Valley, a major farming area. Another is the wide plain in the southeast where sugarcane plantations and sugar refineries produce the nation's leading export. Small farms yield much of the coffee crop, another important export. Farming employs almost half the country's workers.

Miners dig silver, nickel, and other minerals. The nation has the biggest active gold mine in the Caribbean. Yet most Dominicans are poor, their economy crippled by inflation and a growing foreign debt. New resorts help, as tourists discover Dominican beaches, sportfishing grounds, and old Spanish-style architecture.

Official name: *Dominican Republic*
Area: *18,816 sq mi (48,734 sq km)*
Population: *7,471,000*
Capital: *Santo Domingo (met. pop. 1,600,000)*
Ethnic groups: *mulatto, white, black*
Language: *Spanish*
Religious groups: *Roman Catholic*
Economy: *Agr: sugarcane, coffee, rice, cacao, tobacco. Ind: food processing, mining, textiles, cement*
Currency: *Dominican Republic peso*

Puerto Rico

Commonwealth, state, or independent nation? For years Puerto Ricans have argued over what their island should be. Since 1952 it has been a "commonwealth associated with the United States." It sends a resident commissioner to the U. S. Congress, but Puerto Ricans can't vote for president and don't pay federal income tax.

During four centuries of Spanish control, the fortunes of this mountainous island depended on sugarcane, coffee, and tobacco. By the 1950s, the markets for these crops had declined, fields had become unproductive, and there was not enough food or work for the booming population. Being U. S. citizens, Puerto Ricans could emigrate freely to the mainland. More than half a million people left the island in search of jobs. Most crowded into neighborhoods called barrios in cities like New York and Chicago.

Federal aid and investment by U. S. companies helped the Puerto Rican government create jobs in industries such as clothing, electrical equipment, and food processing. Thousands who had left came home. Many settled around San Juan, the capital. Now manufacturing and tourism help to make Puerto Rico one of the wealthiest Caribbean islands, though still poorer than the poorest state in the U. S.

Official name: *Commonwealth of Puerto Rico*
Area: *3,435 sq mi (8,897 sq km)*
Population: *3,721,000*
Capital: *San Juan (pop. 437,745)*
Ethnic groups: *Hispanic*
Language: *Spanish, English*
Religious groups: *Roman Catholic*
Economy: *Agr: livestock, sugarcane, coffee, bananas, yams, pineapples. Ind: medicines, petrochemicals, food processing, electronics, textiles*
Currency: *U. S. dollar*

United States Virgin Islands

There is not much level land in the 3 hilly islands and about 50 islets of the U. S. Virgin Islands. Rainfall is erratic; when it comes, most of it runs off the hard clay soil, sometimes in floods. Yet for 250 years, Dutch, British, French, then Danish planters raised sugarcane and other crops on plantations sprawling up the hillsides.

After slaves were set free in the mid-1800s, the plantations fell idle. Today visitors roam ruins of sugar mills and homes on islands that now belong to the U. S., bought from Denmark in 1917. More than a million tourists come here each year. Many arrive on big cruise ships that dock, sometimes a dozen a day, at Charlotte Amalie, the capital and seaport on **St. Thomas.** There they find resorts and duty-free shops.

Some take a ferry to **St. John,** where a national park covers half the island and more than 5,000 acres (2,025 ha) of coral gardens offshore. The largest island is **St. Croix,** site of rum distilleries and of one of the world's largest oil refineries.

These islands depend on tourists. But there aren't enough islanders to staff the hotels and cafés, drive the cabs, and sell the souvenirs. Thousands of people from poorer islands have come here for jobs.

Official name: *Virgin Islands of the United States*
Area: *136 sq mi (352 sq km)*
Population: *99,000*
Capital: *Charlotte Amalie (pop. 12,331)*
Ethnic groups: *black, white*
Language: *English, Spanish, French*
Religious groups: *Protestant, Roman Catholic*
Economy: *Agr: vegetables, fruit, sorghum, cattle. Ind: tourism, oil refining, watches, rum, textiles*
Currency: *U. S. dollar*

St. Kitts and Nevis

St. Kitts and Nevis are one country, but they are almost like two. On St. Kitts, the larger island, workers raise sugarcane on government plantations that cover the lower slopes of its volcanic peaks. Factories turn out electronic goods, textiles, and shoes. Resorts cater to upscale tourists, who pour into shops and casinos in the fast-paced capital, Basseterre.

Two miles (3 km) away on Nevis, cotton and vegetables ripen on the slopes of a single peak, its summit hidden in clouds nearly every day. Gone are the sugarcane plantations of British colonial times; renovated sugar mills and houses now welcome tourists as quaint, quiet inns.

In 1623 St. Kitts became the first British settlement in the Caribbean. Together St. Kitts and Nevis won independence in 1983, but Nevisians kept the right to secede from the union.

Official name: *Federation of St. Kitts and Nevis*
Area: *101 sq mi (261 sq km)*
Population: *40,000*
Capital: *Basseterre (pop. 18,500)*
Ethnic groups: *black*
Language: *English*
Religious groups: *Protestant*
Economy: *Agr: sugarcane, cotton, coconuts. Ind: sugar, tourism, clothing, beverages, electronics*
Currency: *East Caribbean dollar*

Antigua and Barbuda

Antiguans say that if you visit a beach a day, it will take you a year to see all the beaches on their hilly island of many coves and bays. In a bay called English Harbour, a British fleet set up a base in the 1700s to protect its Caribbean colonies. For 185 years a family named Codrington leased nearby Barbuda from Britain's monarchs for "one fat pig" a year, and used the island for fishing and raising livestock to feed slaves on Antigua's sugarcane plantations.

In 1981 a nation was formed of Antigua, low, forested Barbuda, and uninhabited Redonda. The country is striving to ease its dependence on tourism with fishing, farming, and the manufacture of appliances, clothing, and rum.

Official name: *Antigua and Barbuda*
Area: *170 sq mi (440 sq km)*
Population: *64,000*
Capital: *St. John's (pop. 36,000)*
Ethnic groups: *black*
Language: *English, local dialects*
Religious groups: *Protestant*
Economy: *Agr: cotton, livestock, fruit, vegetables. Ind: tourism, clothing, appliances, rum, fishing*
Currency: *East Caribbean dollar*

French Overseas Departments

Now and then, disaster hits mountainous **Martinique**—a hurricane, an earthquake, a volcanic eruption. One of the worst struck in 1902, when Mount Pelée erupted and wiped out the old capital, St.-Pierre. In minutes, more than 30,000 people died. Today St.-Pierre is a quiet village rich in history, and a new capital flourishes at sophisticated, French-flavored Fort-de-France.

The eruption crippled the sugar industry, the main source of export income during 350 years of French rule. Much cropland is still owned by *békés*, descendants of white settlers, but now most sugar goes to the island's rum distilleries. Bananas and pineapples add to an economy that includes oil refining, cement making, tourism, and subsidies from the French government.

Guadeloupe, some 70 miles (113 km) north, is a group of islands and islets. The main landmass is not one island but two. A saltwater channel named Rivière Salée separates the volcanic western island from the low, rolling eastern island. Sugar is important here too, and so is coffee, but bananas bring in half the export income.

Administered as part of Guadeloupe are France's other Caribbean possessions: small, quiet St. Barthélemy, whose name is often shortened to St. Barts, and St. Martin, the northern two-thirds of an island whose southern third is Dutch. Migration from the overseas departments to France is widespread.

Dominica

Forests cover much of this rugged, rainy island nation, a British possession until 1978. Bananas, coconuts, and limes ripen in its rich soil, and factories process foodstuffs and make soap and cigars.

Dominica has few white sand beaches and no casinos or nightlife to lure tourists as other Caribbean islands do. Instead, nature lovers hike to gauzy waterfalls, lush rain forests, hot springs, and a steaming lake in a volcanic basin.

With high peaks to wring out clouds, parts of Dominica get up to 20 feet (6 m) of rain a year, so much that it exports water to other islands. It has the only reservation for Caribs, once-fierce Indians who gave the Caribbean Sea its name. Some Dominicans speak both English and a French patois, an echo of British-French wrangling over the island in the 1700s. On the reservation you can hear the ancient Carib language.

Official name: *Commonwealth of Dominica*
Area: *290 sq mi (751 sq km)*
Population: *87,000*
Capital: *Roseau (pop. 8,300)*
Ethnic groups: *black, Carib Indian*
Language: *English, French patois*
Religious groups: *Roman Catholic, Protestant*
Economy: *bananas, citrus fruit, coconuts, soap*
Currency: *East Caribbean dollar*

St. Lucia

Before becoming a British colony in 1814, St. Lucia changed hands 14 times as France and Britain vied for control. The British profited for the next 165 years from sugarcane plantations in the island's broad valleys. Most St. Lucians descend from the African plantation slaves. English is the official language, but many people speak instead a French patois left over from the years of conflict. The nation gained independence in 1979.

Bananas and coconuts in sprawling groves ripen in the rich volcanic soil, but hurricanes often ruin the crops. The economy has been broadened to include manufacturing and food processing. Tourists come in growing numbers, drawn by beaches, mountain scenery, and bubbling sulfur springs left from the island's volcanic origin. Oil tankers come too, for near the capital of Castries stands a modern tanker port.

Official name: *St. Lucia*
Area: *238 sq mi (617 sq km)*
Population: *156,000*
Capital: *Castries (pop. 56,100)*
Ethnic groups: *black, mixed, East Indian*
Language: *English, French patois*
Religious groups: *Roman Catholic*
Economy: *Agr: bananas, coconuts, cacao. Ind: clothing, beverages, cardboard boxes, tourism*
Currency: *East Caribbean dollar*

St. Vincent and the Grenadines

This small nation of islands was a British colony until 1979. It is a leading grower of arrowroot, a source of starch used in medicines and flour. The plant is also now used in paper that makes copies without carbons and in computer paper, giving growers and the economy a boost. Bananas, rum, and flour are the mainstays. Still, the main island of St. Vincent remains one of the eastern Caribbean's poorest.

Vincentians are a little better off on the Grenadines, a kite-tail of six main islands and nearly a hundred islets strung out to the south. Many tourists visiting this country go to the swanky resorts in the Grenadines or explore their bays and beaches by private yacht. The southernmost Grenadines belong to Grenada.

Mountainous St. Vincent faces constant peril. Soufrière, one of the region's two most active volcanoes (the other is Pelée on Martinique),

erupted in 1979 and could again any day. Hurricanes can also ravage the islands.

Official name: *St. Vincent and the Grenadines*
Area: *150 sq mi (388 sq km)*
Population: *115,000*
Capital: *Kingstown (met. pop. 29,300)*
Ethnic groups: *black, mulatto, white*
Language: *English, French patois*
Religious groups: *Protestant, Roman Catholic*
Economy: *Agr: bananas, arrowroot, coconuts. Ind: food processing, cement, furniture, rum*
Currency: *East Caribbean dollar*

Barbados

"Not British but English," says one Barbadian of this nation's heritage. Settlers arrived from England in 1627, and Barbados never changed hands until independence in 1966. Generations of Englishmen ran sugarcane plantations and molasses and rum operations on the coastal lowlands and slopes of the central ridge. These families still own much of the land, but descendants of slaves make up most of the population, one of the world's densest at more than 1,500 people per square mile. Barbadians call their island Bimshire and themselves Bajans.

Tourism and small factories now surpass sugar on this easternmost Caribbean island. Unlike its volcanic neighbors, it is a low coral outcrop.

Official name: *Barbados*
Area: *166 sq mi (430 sq km)*
Population: *258,000*
Capital: *Bridgetown (pop. 7,500)*
Ethnic groups: *black, mulatto, white*
Language: *English, Bajan dialect*
Religious groups: *Protestant*
Economy: *Agr: sugarcane. Ind: tourism, food processing, electronic components assembly, clothing*
Currency: *Barbados dollar*

Grenada

The oval on the left of Grenada's flag is a nutmeg. Grind the seed inside, and you have the spice that flavors cookies and eggnog. Grind the lacy husk around the seed, and you have mace, another spice. For 200 years the nutmeg has ripened on the fertile slopes of this volcanic outcrop, often called the Isle of Spice. Sugar ruled before that. Now descendants of the sugarcane plantation slaves grow nutmeg, fruit, and vegetables on

small plots sprinkled over the wooded island.

Once a British colony, Grenada became a nation in 1974. When radicals staged a coup and began executing rivals, the United States and several Caribbean countries invaded in 1983 to restore democracy. Though it includes Carriacou and islets to the north, Grenada is one of the Western Hemisphere's tiniest nations.

Official name: *Grenada*
Area: *133 sq mi (344 sq km)*
Population: *84,000*
Capital: *St. George's (pop. 7,500)*
Ethnic groups: *black, mulatto*
Language: *English, French patois*
Religious groups: *Roman Catholic, Protestant*
Economy: *nutmeg, mace, cacao, bananas, tourism*
Currency: *East Caribbean dollar*

Trinidad and Tobago

Imagine a lake of black, oozy tar. On the island of Trinidad there really is one: Pitch Lake, the world's leading source of natural asphalt. Petroleum has oozed up through porous rock to create this 100-acre (40 ha) wonder. One of the first nations in the world to drill for oil, Trinidad now produces its own and refines oil from the Middle East.

Lying off the east coast of Venezuela, Trinidad and Tobago together were a British colony before they became a nation in 1962. But while Tobago is a quiet, mountainous tourist haven, Trinidad has steel mills, chemical plants, factories, and livestock farms. Big estates, mostly on the western side, grow sugarcane. Small farms produce cacao and other crops.

Trinidad has resorts too. They fill up during Carnival, two days of merrymaking before the 40 fasting days of Lent. Costumed bands hammer on steel drums made from oil barrels, adding witty lyrics to a catchy beat in music called calypso. Nearly half of the people descend from African slaves, most of the rest from Asian workers brought in when slavery ended.

Official name: *Republic of Trinidad and Tobago*
Area: *1,981 sq mi (5,130 sq km)*
Population: *1,263,000*
Capital: *Port of Spain (pop. 58,300)*
Ethnic groups: *black, East Indian, mixed*
Language: *English, English Creole, other*
Religious groups: *Christian, Hindu*
Economy: *Agr: sugarcane, cacao, coffee, rice, citrus fruit. Ind: oil, chemicals, tourism, food processing*
Currency: *Trinidad and Tobago dollar*

Netherlands Dependencies

Remembering three of these six islands is as easy as ABC: Aruba, Bonaire, and Curaçao. The ABCs lie close to Venezuela. The others are some 500 miles (805 km) northeast: St. Eustatius, Saba, and St. Maarten, part of an island that also holds French St. Martin. The Netherlands has ruled these islands known as the **Netherlands Antilles** for most of their history. In 1986 **Aruba** took the first step toward full independence and split off from the others to become a separate dependency with its own capital, Oranjestad.

The hallmark of these islands is diversity. The ABCs are mainly coral, the others mostly volcanic. Schools teach in Dutch on the ABCs and in English on the other islands. In the ABCs people also speak Papiamento, a mix of Spanish, Portuguese, Dutch, English, and African dialects that mirrors the history of the Caribbean.

Tourism is a major industry on all the islands. Four have fine beaches, but rugged Saba and St. Eustatius jut from the sea without the wide, sandy beaches that many tourists seek. They offer serenity and scenery instead. Saba has lush vegetation, but arid Aruba is nearly barren.

Dutch merchants have made Willemstad, the Netherlands Antilles capital on Curaçao, a commercial and financial center. It is also a visual delight with its colorful, ornamented wooden shops and houses. Curaçao has one of the Western Hemisphere's biggest ship-repair dry docks. Workers on nearby Bonaire and on St. Maarten, hundreds of miles to the north, produce salt. Bonaire is also a major grower of aloes—plants used in medicines and ointments—and a magnet for scuba divers lured to its fish-filled coral reefs. Oil from Venezuela once fed refineries on the ABCs, but the oil industry has declined, causing serious economic hardship.

French Overseas Departments

1 *Mount Pelée looms over St.-Pierre on volcanic Martinique. An eruption in 1902 wiped out the capital city that stood here.*

Trinidad and Tobago

2 *Swirls of scarlet frame a masquerader at Trinidad's Carnival, a pre-Lenten funfest held also in Tobago.*

Grenada

3 *Just picked on Grenada, nutmegs show red husks that yield a spice called mace. Seeds inside yield another spice, nutmeg.*

1 *Martinique, French Overseas Departments*

2 *Trinidad, Trinidad and Tobago*

3 *Grenada*

1 *Haiti*

2 *New Providence Island, Bahamas*

3 *United States Virgin Islands*

4 *Barbados*

5 *Cuba*

6 *Dominican Republic*

Haiti

1 *Haitians at a sacred waterfall join a voodoo festival that commemorates a vision of the Virgin of Miracles, Vyèj Mirak.*

Bahamas

2 *Nassau schoolchildren decorated this Bahamian street with colors and images of island life: fishing, marketing, churchgoing.*

United States Virgin Islands

3 *A diver swims among fragile corals in the Buck Island Reef National Monument.*

Barbados

4 *Sugarcane burdens a Barbadian field hand. Leaves are used for tying bundles; sap in the stalk yields sugar.*

Cuba

5 *Havana cigar makers sample their world-famous product. They can puff all the cigars they want by day and take one home.*

Dominican Republic

6 *Villagers take a break in the western hill country near the border with Haiti.*

South America

Among the seven continents of the world, South America is middle size—fourth after Asia, Africa, and North America. But unlike some other continents, South America is largely wilderness—a land of high mountains, sweeping forests, and sprawling plains. The continent extends about 4,700 miles (7,560 km) between the sunny beaches of the Caribbean Sea and the cold, storm-lashed islands of Tierra del Fuego near Antarctica. Most people find much of the land inhospitable—too hot or too cold or too dry or too wet.

South America is a continent of extravagances. The Andes form the longest mountain range on any continent. They are second in elevation only to Asia's Himalaya. More than 45 Andean peaks rise above 20,000 feet (6,100 m), most of them higher than any summit in North America. Angel Falls in Venezuela is the world's tallest waterfall, and the falls of Iguazú, shared by Argentina and Brazil, are among the most spectacular.

Want to find one of the world's stormiest places? Then try the coast of Chile, around 40 or 50 degrees south latitude—the roaring forties and furious fifties that have made Cape Horn a notorious graveyard of ships and sailors.

Between the Andes and the Pacific Ocean lies a narrow strip of coastal plain. Here you find the Atacama Desert, the world's driest place. Before 1971 some parts of the Atacama hadn't felt a drop of rain in centuries. Ocean currents flowing from Antarctica cool the air along the coast, preventing the buildup of rain clouds.

Many Andean mountains are volcanoes formed by molten rock rising through the earth's crust as the floor of the Pacific Ocean slowly grinds beneath the continent. Ecuador alone has some 50 volcanoes, about 30 of them active. From time to time earthquakes rumble through the mountains, or volcanoes spew ash and lava onto surrounding slopes. Over the last half century or so, about 100,000 Andean people have been killed in landslides and avalanches touched off by earthquakes.

Though destructive, volcanic eruptions add minerals to the soil, creating fertile fields in which farmers can grow their crops.

In the northern half of the Andes, broad, high plateaus called altiplanos lie between parallel mountain ranges. Many of the people who live on these altiplanos are Indians, descendants of the Inca and other groups who flourished here before the arrival of Spanish explorers in the 16th century. They live in small communities isolated from one another and the outside world by rugged terrain and lack of good roads. Most villagers are farmers who grow barely enough food to feed themselves, and herd sheep or llamas and alpacas. In recent years, many farmers have taken to growing coca as a cash crop. It's easy to see why: An acre of coca, the raw ingredient of cocaine, brings in $5,000 to $10,000; an acre of corn, $150 or so.

Because of elevation, life in the highlands can be uncomfortably cold, even in the summer. People who have lived there for generations have enlarged hearts and lungs that enable them to live and work in the rarefied air. Visitors unaccustomed to such heights find it difficult to get about without gasping for breath.

South America has other highlands, too, but much lower ones than the Andes. In the north, the Guiana Highlands border the Amazon Basin and are covered with tropical forests. South of the Amazon rise the Brazilian Highlands, mostly rolling hills and plateaus.

Farther south, the Brazilian Highlands give way to the grassy plains, or Pampas, of Uruguay and Argentina—a region known for cattle ranches and farms that grow huge crops of wheat, rice, oats, and corn. Beyond the Pampas, where the continent narrows, stretch the rolling tablelands of Patagonia, a cold, windy, almost treeless place where sheep are raised.

Between the Guiana and Brazilian Highlands lies the Amazon Basin, a hot, humid region nearly as big as the contiguous United States. Through the lowlands flows the 4,000-mile-long (6,437 km) Amazon River and more than a thousand of its tributary streams. Seven tributaries are more than 1,000 miles (1,600 km) long. One of them, the Madeira River, winds 2,013 miles (3,240 km) through the forest. All in all, the mighty Amazon carries more water than the combined flow of the world's next six largest rivers—and it carries the water through the world's largest rain forest.

The mouth of the Amazon measures 200 miles (320 km) across, wide enough to hold Marajó, an

Salt lakes amid volcanic peaks in the high Andes

Angel Falls in Venezuela

NORTH AMERICA

CARIBBEAN SEA

CENTRAL AMERICA

Llanos

Orinoco River

Angel Falls

GUIANA HIGHLANDS

Marajo Island

Galapagos Islands

Amazon

Amazon River

River

Basin

SOUTH AMERICA

Madeira

BRAZILIAN

Mato Grosso Plateau

HIGHLANDS

Sao Francisco River

Lake Titicaca

Altiplano

Atacama Desert

A N D E S

Paraguay River

Gran Chaco

Iguazu Falls

PACIFIC OCEAN

Parana River

Uruguay River

Pampas

Rio de la Plata

Easter Island

Mt. Aconcagua
22,834 FEET
6,960 METERS
Highest point in
South America

Patagonia

Valdes Peninsula
−131 FEET
−40 METERS
Lowest point in
South America

Falkland Islands

Tierra del Fuego

South Georgia

Strait of Magellan

Cape Horn

South Sandwich Islands

ANTARCTICA

AFRICA

TROPIC OF CANCER

EQUATOR

TROPIC OF CAPRICORN

ATLANTIC OCEAN

ANTARCTIC CIRCLE

island nearly the size of Denmark. Large ocean-going vessels travel 1,000 miles (1,600 km) upstream to the city of Manaus. Smaller ships can navigate all the way to Iquitos in Peru, 2,300 miles (3,700 km) from the Atlantic Ocean.

Tropical rain forest covers much of the Amazon Basin. More than 100 tree species can be found in a single acre, among them hardwoods such as mahogany and cedar; edible palms; rubber trees; the Brazil nut tree; and the cumaru, from which come perfumes and medicines. By contrast, temperate forests usually have fewer than five tree species per acre.

Much of the forest is deeply shadowed and parklike, covered by a dense, leafy canopy that blocks out sunlight. Near clearings or along riverbanks where light reaches the ground, the forest becomes a jungle, a tangle of vegetation impenetrable to anyone on foot without a machete to hack through the undergrowth.

But now the rain forest is in trouble. To encourage settlement and develop the interior, Brazilians have been bulldozing roads through the wilderness and cutting or burning vast tracts of forest to open up new lands for crops and cattle.

About 90 percent of all South Americans live within 200 miles (320 km) of the coast in large, modern cities such as São Paulo, Rio de Janeiro, Buenos Aires, Santiago, and Lima. About half of them speak Spanish. The other half—in Brazil—speak Portuguese because Portugal colonized Brazil some 500 years ago.

Today, the more temperate parts of South America, a broad band running from southern Brazil through Uruguay and Argentina to central Chile, are among the world's most rapidly industrializing areas. Only about a quarter of all South Americans still work on farms and ranches. Since 1950, people have moved to cities in droves, hoping to escape rural poverty and the turmoil caused by roving terrorist bands. This migration of millions of people has placed Buenos Aires, Rio de Janeiro, and São Paulo among the world's ten largest and fastest growing metropolitan areas. But on the outskirts of these gleaming, skyscrapered cities huddle vast slums—sprawling shantytowns largely filled with country folk seeking jobs and a better life for themselves and their children.

Development imperils the Amazon rain forest in Brazil.

Facts About South America

Area: 6,880,637 sq mi (17,820,770 sq km)
Population: 299,900,000
Highest Point: Mount Aconcagua, Argentina, 22,834 ft (6,960 m) above sea level
Lowest Point: On Valdés Peninsula, Argentina, 131 ft (40 m) below sea level
Largest Country: *(by area)* Brazil 3,286,488 sq mi (8,511,965 sq km)
Largest Country: *(by population)* Brazil 150,794,000
Largest Metropolitan Areas: *(by population)*

São Paulo, Brazil	15,000,000
Buenos Aires, Argentina	11,125,600
Rio de Janeiro, Brazil	9,600,500
Lima, Peru	6,404,500

Longest Rivers: *(mi and km)*

Amazon	4,000	6,437
Paraná	2,485	3,999
Purus	2,100	3,380

Largest Lakes: *(sq mi and sq km)*

Maracaibo, Venezuela	5,217	13,512
Titicaca, Peru-Bolivia	3,200	8,288

Tallest Waterfall:
* Angel Falls, Venezuela, 3,212 ft (979 m)

*World record

Glossary

alpaca—a domesticated mammal with long, woolly hair; related to the llama.
altiplano—a high plateau that lies between higher mountains.
coca—a shrub whose leaves are made into a drug called cocaine.
conquistador—a soldier in the Spanish conquest of the Americas.
coup, coup d'état—the forcible overthrow of a government by a small group, usually from within.
guanaco—a mammal with a soft, thick coat; probably the original ancestor of both the alpaca and the llama.
Inca—an empire in the Andes that ruled an area from Colombia to Chile before the Spanish conquest.
landlocked country—a country surrounded by land, without access to the sea.
llama—a mammal used as a pack animal and a source of wool; related to the camel.
llano—an open, grassy plain.
mestizo—a Latin American of mixed European and American Indian ancestry.
pampa—an extensive grassland.
rain forest—dense forest composed mainly of broad-leaved evergreens found in wet tropical regions.

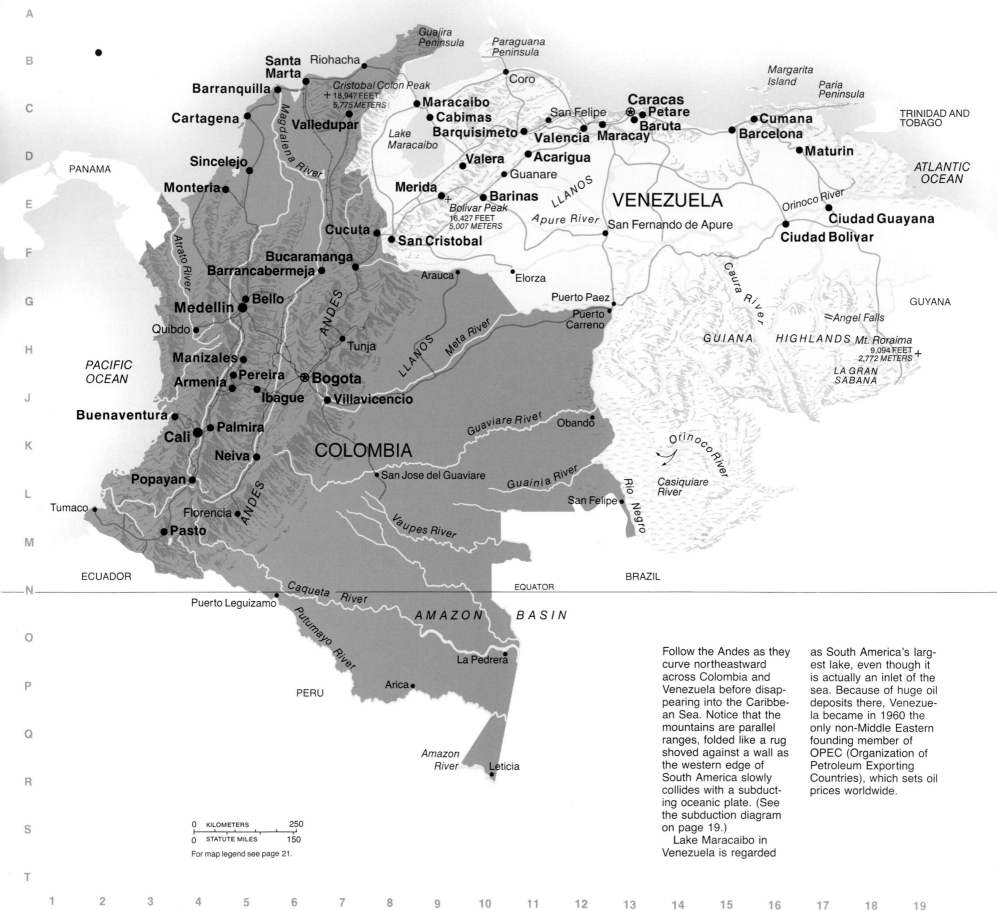

CARIBBEAN SEA

PANAMA

Guajira
Peninsula

Paraguana
Peninsula

Margarita
Island

Paria
Peninsula

TRINIDAD AND
TOBAGO

Riohacha

**Santa
Marta**

Barranquilla

Cristobal Colon Peak
+ 18,947 FEET
5,775 METERS

Coro

Cartagena

Magdalena River

Valledupar

Maracaibo
Cabimas

Lake
Maracaibo

San Felipe

Caracas
⊛ **Petare**
Baruta

Cumana
Barcelona

ATLANTIC
OCEAN

Sincelejo

Barquisimeto

Valencia
Maracay

Maturin

Monteria

Valera
Acarigua

Merida

Guanare

LLANOS

VENEZUELA

Orinoco River

Cucuta

Atrato River

Bolivar Peak
16,427 FEET
5,007 METERS

Barinas

Apure River

San Fernando de Apure

Ciudad Guayana

San Cristobal

Ciudad Bolivar

Bucaramanga

Barrancabermeja

Arauca

Elorza

GUYANA

ANDES

Puerto Paez

Caura River

Angel Falls

Medellin
Bello

Quibdo

Puerto
Carreno

GUIANA   HIGHLANDS Mt. Roraima
9,094 FEET
2,772 METERS +

PACIFIC
OCEAN

Tunja

LLANOS

Meta River

LA GRAN
SABANA

Manizales

Armenia
Pereira
Ibague

⊛ **Bogota**

Villavicencio

Buenaventura

Guaviare River

Obando

Orinoco River

Cali
Palmira

COLOMBIA

Casiquiare
River

Neiva

San Jose del Guaviare

Guainia River

San Felipe

Rio Negro

Popayan

Florencia

ANDES

Vaupes River

Tumaco

Pasto

ECUADOR

Caqueta River

EQUATOR

BRAZIL

N

Puerto Leguizamo

AMAZON   BASIN

Putumayo River

PERU

La Pedrera

Arica

Amazon
River

Leticia

0   KILOMETERS   250

0   STATUTE MILES   150

For map legend see page 21.

Follow the Andes as they curve northeastward across Colombia and Venezuela before disappearing into the Caribbean Sea. Notice that the mountains are parallel ranges, folded like a rug shoved against a wall as the western edge of South America slowly collides with a subducting oceanic plate. (See the subduction diagram on page 19.)

Lake Maracaibo in Venezuela is regarded as South America's largest lake, even though it is actually an inlet of the sea. Because of huge oil deposits there, Venezuela became in 1960 the only non-Middle Eastern founding member of OPEC (Organization of Petroleum Exporting Countries), which sets oil prices worldwide.

Colombia

Colombia is the only South American country that has coastlines washed by both the Caribbean Sea and the Pacific Ocean. Its land is rugged and varied. It includes snowcapped mountains nearly 19,000 feet (5,800 m) high, rolling hills and upland plateaus, coastal deserts, and low-lying tropical rain forests.

Most of Colombia's people live in the mountainous western third of the country. There, in broad, high valleys, rich volcanic soil provides fertile farmland, and the weather is usually cool and comfortable. East of the mountains, cattle graze the grasslands. To the south spreads the Amazon Basin, a hot, humid region cut by streams that flow into the Amazon River.

Gold brought Spanish settlers to Colombia in the early 1500s. Soon after, they began to hear stories of a golden man—El Dorado, they called him. He was an Indian chief, it was said, whose subjects dusted him with gold on ceremonial occasions. Spanish treasure hunters soon took up the search for El Dorado. They never found him or his treasure, but they did find gold and forced the local people to mine it for them.

To this day Colombia is one of South America's leading gold producers. It is rich in emeralds, too, mining about 95 percent of the world's supply of the lustrous green gems. Colombia has many other minerals as well, chiefly salt, coal, and metal ores such as copper and iron.

The nation's capital, Bogotá, is also its largest city. Situated on a plateau about 8,600 feet (2,620 m) high, it is home to four million people.

Cartagena, a port on the Caribbean Sea, ranks as one of Colombia's oldest cities. Founded in 1533, its massive fortress guarded against pirate attacks on treasure fleets that gathered there to sail back to Spain. In both cities modern, high-rise buildings stand amid carefully preserved tile-and-stucco homes and churches of those bygone colonial days.

Medellín, the second largest city, is an industrial center noted for its textile mills and steel plants. Surrounded by mountains, it lies in a rich coffee-growing region. Most Colombian coffee is grown on small family farms. Prized for its flavor, it is an important source of export income.

Over the years Medellín and Cali, to the south, have become major centers for illegal drugs such as marijuana and cocaine. Colombia recently rewrote its constitution and began social and economic reforms, but drug trafficking and guerrilla efforts to destabilize the government remain serious problems.

Colombia's position at the meeting place of two continents, and its variety of terrain and climate, give it many different kinds of plants and animals, including about 1,500 bird species—a world record. The birds range from moth-size hummingbirds to the large harpy eagle that can swoop off with a monkey or a sloth. Pumas, jaguars, and ocelots roam the wilds, and Colombia counts more species of bats, including the bloodthirsty vampire, than any other country.

Official name: *Republic of Colombia*
Area: *439,737 sq mi (1,138,914 sq km)*
Population: *34,252,000*
Capital: *Bogotá (met. pop. 4,176,800)*
Ethnic groups: *mestizo, white, mulatto, black*
Language: *Spanish*
Religious groups: *Roman Catholic*
Economy: *Agr: coffee, grains, potatoes, sugarcane, bananas, cotton, livestock, flowers. Ind: textiles, food processing, oil, chemicals, metals, cement, mining*
Currency: *Colombian peso*

Venezuela

Venezuela jumped into the modern world in the 1920s when it began to produce oil, a lot of it. The oil was found in vast deposits beneath the waters of Lake Maracaibo on the Caribbean coast. Soon Venezuela was the richest country in South America. By 1926 oil had replaced coffee as the nation's most important export. Cities boomed, burgeoning with glass-and-steel buildings. Highways called *autopistas* linked major urban centers.

But then trouble struck. Over the years Venezuela had borrowed heavily from international banks to expand and modernize its farms and develop its industries. When the price of oil suddenly dropped in 1986, the deeply indebted nation could not pay off its loans. Venezuela's standard of living declined. The 1990s brought another large drop in oil prices, a recession, and attempted coups against the government.

Venezuela has 2,000 miles (3,220 km) of coast along the northern reaches of the continent. Two-thirds of its people—and most of its major cities, including the capital, Caracas—are found in the highlands that stretch along the Caribbean Sea. The highlands are spurs of the Andes. Their elevation gives them a mild climate, and some of the higher mountains in the west are snow covered year-round.

In the northwest corner of the country, oil-rich lowlands extend from the coast to Lake Maracaibo. The large, shallow lake is dotted with thousands of oil-drilling derricks.

Sixteenth-century explorers sailing along the coast found Indians living on the lake in houses built on stilts. Houses and canoes reminded the explorers of Venice, Italy, so they named the place Venezuela, Spanish for Little Venice.

Maracaibo, a large modern city near the lake, is a commercial and industrial center, and home to more than a million Venezuelans.

In the interior, beyond the mountains and north of the Orinoco River, stretch the Llanos, or plains. This is cattle ranching country, populated by cowboys called *llaneros* and great herds of humpbacked zebu cattle. The government has begun to develop industries in the Llanos because of their rich iron and aluminum ore deposits and immense oil reserves.

South of the river lie the Guiana Highlands, a barely explored forest from which rise high, flat-topped mountains known as *tepuis*. From one of them, Auyan-tepui, Devil Mountain, spills the world's tallest waterfall, 3,212-foot (979 m) Angel Falls. It was discovered in 1935 by an American aviator, Jimmy Angel, while he was searching for gold and diamonds—deposits modern prospectors still hope to find.

Official name: *Republic of Venezuela*
Area: *352,144 sq mi (912,050 sq km)*
Population: *18,883,000*
Capital: *Caracas (pop. 1,290,000)*
Ethnic groups: *mestizo, white, black, Indian*
Language: *Spanish*
Religious groups: *Roman Catholic*
Economy: *Agr: corn, fruit, sugarcane, coffee, rice. Ind: oil, iron ore, building materials, food processing, textiles, steel, aluminum, motor vehicles*
Currency: *bolívar*

1 *Colombia*

2 *Colombia*

3 *Colombia*

4 *Venezuela*

5 *Venezuela*

Colombia

1 *Stone walls of a 17th-century fortification surround the heart of Cartagena. The walls, 60 feet (18 m) thick in places, were built to protect the city from pirates.*

2 *Emeralds from a mine near Bogotá are prized worldwide for their color and brilliance. Found only in small clusters, the stones must be dug out with hand tools.*

3 *A Colombian farmer harvests coca leaves, used to make cocaine. Demand for the illegal drug makes coca an irresistible cash crop for poor farmers of the Andes.*

Venezuela

4 *Oil-drilling rigs rise from the waters of Lake Maracaibo. These wells tap petroleum deposits lying beneath the lake bed.*

5 *Flat-topped Mount Roraima rises 9,094 feet (2,772 m) through the mist. Rare birds and plants live in isolation on this mesa called a* tepui, *Indian for "mountain."*

6 *A Makiritare girl from the rain forest of the Orinoco region rests in a hammock with her pet toucan.*

6 *Venezuela*

Ecuador got its name be-
cause the Equator—*el
ecuador* in Spanish—
runs right through it.

For many years before
Mount Everest's height
was measured in the
1850s, Ecuador's tallest
volcano, Chimborazo,
was believed to be
earth's highest mountain
above sea level. Surveys
revealed that other
peaks besides Everest
topped it, including the
two named here in Peru.

The Galápagos
Islands, part of Ecuador
since 1832, get their
name from the giant tor-
toises—*galápagos* in
Spanish—that live there.

0 KILOMETERS 250
0 STATUTE MILES 150

For map legend see page 21.

Esmeraldas

Ibarra

EQUATOR

Quito ⊗

Latacunga   + *Cotopaxi*
                19,347 FEET
                5,897 METERS

Manta

Portoviejo   Quevedo   **Ambato**

Chimborazo +
20,702 FEET   **Riobamba**
6,310 METERS

Guayaquil   **ECUADOR**

*Gulf of
Guayaquil*   **Cuenca**

Tumbes   **Machala**

Loja

Talara

Sullana

Piura

*SECHURA
DESERT*

Moyobamba   Yurimaguas

Chachapoyas

Chiclayo

Cajamarca

PACIFIC OCEAN

Trujillo

Chimbote   Yungay   + *Mount Huascaran*
                            22,205 FEET
                            6,768 METERS

Huaraz

Huanuco

Cerro de Pasco

La Oroya

Callao   ⊗ **Lima**   **Huancayo**

Huancavelica

Pisco   Ayacucho   Abancay

Ica

Nazca

Mount Coropuna
21,079 FEET
6,425 METERS +

Mollendo

COLOMBIA

Napo River

Putumayo River

Iquitos

Amazon River

Maranon River

AMAZON BASIN

Ucayali River

PERU

BRAZIL

Pucallpa

Urubamba River

Apurimac River

Puerto Maldonado

Machu Picchu

Cuzco

ANDES

BOLIVIA

*Lake
Titicaca*

Puno

Arequipa

Moquegua

ALTIPLANO

Tacna

CHILE

GALAPAGOS ISLANDS
(ECUADOR)

0 KILOMETERS 100
0 STATUTE MILES 75

*PACIFIC
OCEAN*

Pinta Island

Marchena Island

EQUATOR

San Salvador Island

*Fernandina
Island*

Santa Cruz Island

*Isabela
Island*   Puerto
Baquerizo Moreno

*San Cristobal
Island*

Santa Maria Island

Espanola Island

Ecuador

There are two kinds of eruptions you can almost always count on in Ecuador, volcanic and political. This Equator-straddling country has about 30 active volcanoes. From time to time they rumble and belch ashes onto surrounding villages.

Almost as restless as the volcanoes are the politicians. Until recently, few presidents managed to serve out a full, four-year term. Coups and countercoups were a way of life as government after government was overthrown. At one stage in its modern history, Ecuador had 22 presidents or heads of state within 23 years.

Geography and the state of the economy play a big part in Ecuador's political instability. About half of its people live in the fertile, coastal lowlands, where bananas, coffee, cacao, and other export crops flourish. The major city here is Guayaquil, a busy modern port that has grown rapidly since the late 1960s when oil was discovered in the eastern provinces. Most lowlanders are of European or mixed Indian-European extraction. Living near the coast encourages them to be outward-looking in matters of trade and commerce, and exposes them to new ideas.

The other half of Ecuador's people—many of them Indians—live in isolated highland towns and villages nestled in the Andes. Most highlanders lead traditional, slow-paced lives as farmers who raise dairy cattle or wheat, corn, barley, and potatoes. Their isolation makes them less receptive to change.

Quito, the capital, lies in the highlands at an elevation of 9,300 feet (2,830 m). Its churches, plazas, and public buildings preserve some of South America's finest examples of Spanish colonial architecture. Change comes slowly to Quito—and to most highlanders. Getting them to agree with lowlanders on politics can be tricky.

East of the mountains stretches Ecuador's oil region, a sparsely populated area covered by dense tropical forests. Oil discovered here in 1967 helped to fuel Ecuadorian prosperity until oil prices fell in the mid-1980s. Today Ecuador, like other South American oil producers, faces slow economic growth and heavy debt from borrowing when oil prices were high.

Ecuador's offshore waters swarm with tuna, other fish, and shrimp. Farther offshore, some 600 miles (965 km) to the west, lie the Galápagos Islands. This cluster of volcanic islands belonging to Ecuador is home to giant tortoises, marine lizards, and other animals found nowhere else. They have fascinated scientists ever since naturalist Charles Darwin visited the islands in 1835. In 1959, Ecuador declared most of the archipelago a national park.

Official name: *Republic of Ecuador*
Area: *109,484 sq mi (283,561 sq km)*
Population: *9,996,000*
Capital: *Quito (pop. 1,094,300)*
Ethnic groups: *mestizo, Indian, white, black*
Language: *Spanish, Quechua*
Religious groups: *Roman Catholic*
Economy: *Agr: bananas, coffee, cacao, sugarcane, corn, potatoes, rice, livestock. Ind: food processing, textiles, chemicals, fishing, lumber, oil, shrimp*
Currency: *sucre*

Peru

Peru, stronghold of the once proud Inca Empire, is a land high, wild, beautiful—and cruel. Many of South America's highest mountains rise here, snowcapped peaks thrusting 20,000 feet (6,100 m) or more above the sea. Although these Andean mountains are beautiful, they are also deadly. In 1962 Peru's highest mountain, 22,205-foot (6,768 m) Huascarán, let loose a cascade of mud and ice that killed 4,000 people. And in 1970 an earthquake touched off a series of avalanches that killed 60,000 people.

Streams and rivers have carved awesome canyons in the highlands and plateaus where half of Peru's people live. Some of these gorges plunge two miles (3 km)—twice as deep as the Grand Canyon. After the conquest of Peru by Spain in 1532, Inca survivors may have hidden out in the mountains north of the old Inca capital of Cuzco. Here, on a ridge between two mountain peaks rising from the forest, stands Machu Picchu, now thought to be a royal estate built by Pachacuti, founder of the Inca Empire.

Most of the people who live in the central highlands and valleys are Indians, Quechua-speaking descendants of the Inca whose fabulously rich empire reached from Chile to Colombia. Many of them farm small plots of corn, potatoes, and coca (much of which is shipped to Colombia to be made into cocaine). Their children herd sheep and llamas, valued for meat and wool. Other workers mine copper, lead, and silver.

The high plateau, or Altiplano, of southern Peru is also the site of Lake Titicaca, shared by Peru and Bolivia. Indians here live in reed huts and sail the lake in boats made of reed bundles.

Living for generations at elevations of 12,000 to 14,000 feet (3,660 to 4,270 m), highland Indians have developed extra-large lungs and hearts. Most of them are desperately poor. They have few roads, schools, or hospitals. One out of ten babies dies before its first birthday. These problems have led to social unrest and the formation of armed rebel bands who try to overthrow the government with terrorist tactics. In the 1990s, several powerful earthquakes and a deadly cholera epidemic added to Peru's social, economic, and political woes.

Narrow coastal lowlands fringe the western flanks of the mountains. They are mainly desert, created by a cold ocean current, the Peru Current, which cools the air flowing across it so that rain clouds don't form. The current also supports shoals of anchovies that are caught and ground into pig and chicken feed for export.

Peru's capital, Lima, founded on this coastal strip by conquistadores in 1535, is a center of commerce, art, and industry, along with its port city, Callao. Most lowlanders descend from Spanish or Spanish and Indian ancestors.

East of the mountains lies the great basin through which flow the headwaters of the Amazon River. The thick, largely unexplored forests of this region cover about 60 percent of Peru, but are home to only 5 percent of its people.

Official name: *Republic of Peru*
Area: *496,225 sq mi (1,285,220 sq km)*
Population: *22,454,000*
Capital: *Lima (met. pop. 6,404,500)*
Ethnic groups: *Indian, mestizo, white*
Language: *Spanish, Quechua, Aymara*
Religious groups: *Roman Catholic*
Economy: *Agr: sugarcane, potatoes, rice, corn, coffee, cotton, livestock. Ind: minerals, oil, fishing, textiles, food processing, cement, motor vehicles, steel*
Currency: *inti*

1 *Peru*

2 *Peru*

3 *Peru*

Peru

1 *Spinning wool into yarn, an Indian woman near Cuzco uses a spindle to twist the fibers together. Mother and napping child wear traditional dyed-wool clothing.*

2 *Farmers in the Andean highlands harvest potatoes, a crop that can grow successfully at elevations of up to 14,000 feet (4,270 m).*

3 *Machu Picchu, built by the Inca in the 15th century, crowns a ridge in the Andes. Scientists now believe the ruins were once part of a royal estate.*

Ecuador

4 *Shoppers stroll amid an open-air market in Quito. South America's oldest capital, Quito was established in 1534 and preserves much of its colonial heritage.*

5 *A giant tortoise in the Galápagos Islands displays its armor. These endangered animals can weigh up to 600 pounds (270 kg) and may live 150 years.*

4 *Ecuador*

5 *Ecuador*

A B C D E F G H I J K L M N O P Q R S T U

VENEZUELA

Georgetown
Linden
Nieuw
Nickerie
Paramaribo
Devil's Island
GUYANA
Lake Van
Blommestein
Kourou
Cayenne
SURINAME **FRENCH GUIANA**
(FRANCE)

COLOMBIA

GUIANA HIGHLANDS

ATLANTIC OCEAN

Neblina Peak
9,888 FEET
+ 3,014 METERS

EQUATOR

Rio Negro

Amazon River

Marajo
Island

Belem

Amazon River

Manaus

TRANS-AMAZON
HIGHWAY

Sao Luis

AMAZON BASIN

Madeira River

Tapajos River

Tocantins River

Fortaleza

Teresina
Crateus

Purus River

Natal

BRAZIL

Porto Velho

Xingu River

Parnaiba River

Joao Pessoa

Recife

Rio Branco

PERU

Juazeiro

Maceio

Sao Francisco River

Aracaju

Feira de Santana

BOLIVIA

MATO GROSSO

BRAZILIAN HIGHLANDS

Salvador

PLATEAU

⊗**Brasilia**

Goiania

Brazil, the giant of South
America, covers nearly
half the continent. It extends some 2,700 miles
(4,345 km) from north to
south and east to west. It
holds more than half the
continent's population,
too. The Portuguese col-
onized coastal areas in
the 1500s, and because
of the rugged interior,
most cities remain near
the coast.

Guyana, Suriname,
and French Guiana to
Brazil's north are the
only countries in South
America without a Portu-
guese or Spanish heri-
tage. The first was a
British colony, the sec-
ond a Dutch one, and
the third still is French.

**Campo
Grande**

**Sao Jose do
Rio Preto**

**Belo
Horizonte**

Vitoria

Ribeirao Preto

Juiz de Fora

Parana River

Campinas

Campos

PARAGUAY

Sorocaba

Rio de Janeiro

Sao Paulo

**Sao Jose
dos Campos**

TROPIC OF CAPRICORN

Santos

*Iguazu
Falls*

Curitiba

ARGENTINA

Uruguay River

Porto Alegre

*Patos
Lagoon*

0   KILOMETERS   500

0   STATUTE MILES   300

URUGUAY

For map legend see page 21.

1 2 3 4 5 6 7 8 9 10 11 12 13 14 15 16 17 18

Guyana

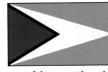

In Guyana they speak English. It's the country's official language, which makes Guyana the only English-speaking nation in South America. That's because, for 150 years—until it won independence in 1966—Guyana was a colony ruled by the United Kingdom. It was known as British Guiana.

Guiana is an Indian word. It means "land of waters" and refers to the coastal swamps, marshes, and lagoons formed by four major rivers as they flow into the Atlantic Ocean from the interior highlands. Spanish explorers sailing along the coast here in 1498 took one look at all the mud, silt, jungles, and alligators—and sailed on to Venezuela. It was the Dutch, in the early 1600s, who realized that so much mud and water was worth a king's ransom in rich farmland, but only if the water could be drained.

Dutch settlers dredged and built, and brought in slaves from Africa to work on their sugarcane plantations. The British eventually took over, and brought in thousands of indentured workers from India, Portugal, and China. Today, Guyanese call their country "the land of six peoples."

Most of Guyana's people live in the humid coastal lowlands. They grow rice and sugarcane. A few thousand American Indians, descendants of the Caribs and Arawaks, live inland. Georgetown, the capital, is a city of wooden buildings, many of them raised on stilts to escape flooding.

Gold and diamonds have been found in Guyana's interior, but the nation's real mineral wealth lies in its immense deposits of bauxite.

During World War II Guyana supplied the United States with nearly all the bauxite needed for aluminum to build fighter planes and bombers.

Official name: *Co-operative Republic of Guyana*
Area: *83,000 sq mi (214,969 sq km)*
Population: *805,000*
Capital: *Georgetown (pop. 150,400)*
Ethnic groups: *East Indian, black, mixed, Indian*
Language: *English*
Religious groups: *Christian, Hindu, Muslim*
Economy: *Agr: sugarcane, rice, fruit, vegetables. Ind: bauxite, lumber, fishing, textiles, gold, rum*
Currency: *Guyana dollar*

Suriname

The British and the Dutch arranged a land swap in 1667. In exchange for a colony named New Amsterdam in North America, the Dutch got part of a British colony in South America. New Amsterdam would become New York City and Dutch Guiana became Suriname, which won its independence in 1975.

Suriname rises gradually from a low, swampy coastal belt to heavily forested interior highlands. About 90 percent of the land is covered by thousands of different kinds of trees. One of them, the rot-resistant greenheart, has wood so dense and hard that it will not float.

Suriname's biggest export is the bauxite dug from its mines and processed into aluminum. Power to run the factories comes from a hydroelectric plant that taps one of the world's largest man-made lakes, 600-square-mile (1,555 sq km) Lake Van Blommestein.

Most of Suriname's people live along the coast on farms and plantations that export rice and bananas. Here, too, stands the capital, Paramaribo, a city of about 246,000 people. Suriname's citizens, like those in neighboring Guyana, came originally from many lands. Most Surinamers speak a polyglot tongue commonly called Taki-Taki, which is made up of English, Dutch, French, African, and Asian words.

Official name: *Republic of Suriname*
Area: *63,037 sq mi (163,265 sq km)*
Population: *437,000*
Capital: *Paramaribo (met. pop. 246,000)*
Ethnic groups: *East Indian, Creole, Javanese, black, Indian*
Language: *Dutch, Sranan Tongo (Taki-Taki)*
Religious groups: *Christian, Hindu, Muslim*
Economy: *Agr: rice, bananas, sugarcane. Ind: bauxite, wood products, food processing, shrimp*
Currency: *Suriname guilder*

French Guiana

French Guiana is noted mainly for two things: the spicy red pepper named after its capital, Cayenne, and Devil's Island, the dreaded prison colony surrounded by sharks and swirling currents. Between 1852 and 1946, some 70,000 prisoners languished in several prisons here, now shut. Most never lived to see France again.

Long a colony, French Guiana became an overseas *département* in 1946, with an elected representative in Paris. Its people, chiefly of African descent, are French citizens. Most live in and around Cayenne. The heavily forested countryside has few roads and, away from the coast, rises to low hills. Shrimp processing and rum distilling are among French Guiana's industries, along with a commercial rocket-launching station at Kourou, which takes advantage of earth's greater rotational speed near the Equator to loft satellites into orbit.

Official name: *Department of French Guiana*
Area: *34,749 sq mi (90,000 sq km)*
Population: *105,000*
Capital: *Cayenne (pop. 41,200)*
Ethnic groups: *black, mulatto, white, East Indian, Chinese, Indian*
Language: *French, French Creole*
Religious groups: *Roman Catholic*
Economy: *Agr: rice, cassava, bananas, vegetables, sugarcane. Ind: construction, shrimp, lumber, rum*
Currency: *French franc*

Brazil

Almost everything about Brazil is big: big land, big forests, big rivers, big cities—big debt. Brazil is far and away the largest nation in South America. It covers nearly half the continent and shares a common border with all other South American countries except Chile and Ecuador. Brazil is also the only Portuguese-speaking nation in South America, thanks to its discovery by Portuguese mariners in 1500.

The country's Atlantic coast extends more than 4,600 miles (7,400 km). About 90 percent of the Brazilian people—a mixture of Europeans, Africans, Indians, and Asians—live along a coastal strip between the ocean and a wall-like escarpment that averages 2,600 feet (790 m) high. Behind the escarpment spread large plateaus and the Amazon Basin.

Parts of the plateaus and basin are covered with grass and shrubs—excellent for cattle ranching. But most of the basin is covered by a rain forest so immense it could blanket much of the United States. Many giants live in this shadowy world—trees more than 200 feet (60 m) high, lily pads big enough for small children to float on, toads and spiders as big as dinner plates, snakes big enough to swallow a deer.

Here, too, flows the 4,000-mile-long (6,437 km) Amazon River, second in length only to Egypt's 4,145-mile (6,671 km) Nile. Millions of plant and animal species live in the surrounding rain forest. One tree, *pau-brasil*—brazilwood—gave the country its name and provided 16th-century Europe with a valuable red dye.

But now the forest is in danger. Over the years great swaths have been cut down, burned, or flooded so that farmers, ranchers, and miners could move into the interior. In one recent year a forest area bigger than Belgium went up in smoke. In the 1950s, to encourage settlement, a new national capital, Brasília, was built 600 miles (965 km) inland from the old coastal capital, Rio de Janeiro. Roads were built to link the new capital with the *sertão*, the backcountry.

Scientists and conservationists warn that if such destruction continues, global weather might be seriously affected, and thousands of useful plants and animals might disappear.

Brazil's forests yield lumber, nuts, wax, and latex from rubber trees. Its farms grow much of the world's coffee and oranges. Mills and factories in large, modern industrial cities such as São Paulo and Rio turn out cars, textiles, and television sets. Brazil's mines have some of the world's richest deposits of iron ore, bauxite, gold, manganese, and gemstones.

Brazil also has the biggest debts of any developing nation. Over the years it borrowed heavily to develop farms and factories; to build roads, dams, and cities. In 1990, Brazil's first directly elected president in 30 years took office amid hopes that he would improve the economy. But charges of corruption overshadowed his economic reform efforts, and he resigned three years later. Today the foreign debt is so staggering that many Brazilians say: "This is a land of the future—and always will be!"

Official name: *Federative Republic of Brazil*
Area: *3,286,488 sq mi (8,511,965 sq km)*
Population: *150,794,000*
Capital: *Brasília (pop. 1,596,300)*
Ethnic groups: *white, mulatto, black, Indian*
Language: *Portuguese*
Religious groups: *Roman Catholic*
Economy: *Agr: coffee, rice, corn, sugarcane, cacao, soybeans, cotton, cassava, oranges, livestock, wheat. Ind: textiles, chemicals, cement, lumber, iron ore, steel, motor vehicles, metals, manufacturing, fishing*
Currency: *cruzeiro*

1 *Brazil*

2 *Brazil*

3 *Brazil*

4 *French Guiana*

Brazil

1 *Hacked from the heart of the Amazon forest, the Carajás iron mine in the northern Brazilian Highlands holds the world's largest deposit of high-quality iron ore.*

2 *A woolly spider monkey uses its tail as an extra "hand." Fewer than 400 of these monkeys survive as development destroys their coastal forest habitat.*

3 *Steep-sided mountains called* morros *give Rio de Janeiro its distinctive cityscape.*

French Guiana

4 *Wayana Indian children examine a new toy—a Rubik's Cube. Despite the remoteness of the Wayanas' rain-forest home, the modern world is reaching into their lives.*

A B C D E F G H J K L M N O P Q R S T U

1 2 3 4 5 6 7 8 9 10 11 12 13 14 15 16 17 18

Madeira
River

Cobija

Madre de Dios River

Lake
Rogaguado

Mamore River

Guapore River

PERU

Beni River

Lake
Rogagua

Lake San
Luis

Blanco River

San Martin River

Trinidad

BOLIVIA

San Miguel River

ANDES

Mount Illampu
21,201 FEET
6,362 METERS

Lake
Titicaca

La Paz

Mount Illimani
21,302 FEET
6,462 METERS

Chapare River

BRAZIL

ALTIPLANO

ANDES

Cochabamba

Santa Cruz

Tucavaca River

Oruro

Mount Sajama
21,463 FEET
6,542 METERS

Uncia

Grande River

Lake
Poopo

Sucre

CHILE

Potosi

Salar de
Uyuni

G R A N   C H A C O

Leon Peak
3,280 FEET
1,000 METERS

PARAGUAY

Paraguay River

Pilcomayo River

Tarija

Filadelfia

Pedro Juan Caballero

AMAMBAY MOUNTAINS

Verde River

Concepcion

TROPIC OF CAPRICORN

Monte Lindo River

ARGENTINA

Pilcomayo River

Villa Hayes

Acaray River

Asuncion

Lugue
Caacupe

Ciudad del Este

San Lorenzo

Coronel Oviedo

Paraguari

Villarrica

Tebicuary River

Parana River

Pilar

Encarnacion

0   KILOMETERS   250
0   STATUTE MILES   150
For map legend see page 21.

Bolivia and Paraguay are South America's only landlocked countries, a situation that can put them at an economic disadvantage when they wish to ship their products overseas. It means they must depend on the goodwill of neighbors for access to ocean ports. In 1883, Bolivia lost its coastal lands as a result of the War of the Pacific with Chile.

Paraguay's attempts to keep open the Paraná River, its lifeline to the outside world, in 1865 led to a five-year war with neighboring countries that killed more than half its people.

Bolivia

La Paz, one of Bolivia's two capital cities, lies at such a high elevation—12,000 feet (3,660 m) above sea level— that visitors from the low-lands find themselves huffing and puffing if they try to walk fast. At that height it takes six minutes to boil a three-minute egg, airplanes need extra-long runways to take off, and the people who live there have enlarged lungs that help them breathe the rarefied air more efficiently.

The world's highest capital, La Paz is located on the Altiplano, the windswept plateau that lies between parallel ranges of the Andes. Here, amid snow-covered mountain peaks, condors with 10-foot (3 m) wingspans ride the updrafts, and llamas and alpacas graze the grasses. A few miles away from La Paz sparkles Lake Titicaca, the world's highest navigable lake.

With about a million inhabitants, La Paz is Bolivia's largest city and a center of business. The presidential palace, the national congress, and most of the country's government offices are located there. The other capital city, Sucre, is the judicial capital. It houses the nation's judges and courts of law.

About half of Bolivia's citizens live on the Altiplano. Most are Aymara and Quechua Indians or mestizos, people of mixed Spanish and Indian ancestry. The Indian women are noted for their brightly colored clothes—shawls and skirts worn over a dozen or so petticoats. Men wear *chullos*, colorful knitted caps with earflaps.

Most of the Indians are extremely poor. They earn about $500 a year as laborers, miners, herders, and small farmers. Many cannot read or write, and some speak no Spanish.

In the foothills east of the Andes lie the *yungas*—deep, fertile valleys from which come major crops such as coca, coffee, grains, and fruit. By some estimates, three-quarters of Bolivia's cultivated land is used to grow coca, despite all government attempts to stamp out the practice. The Indians themselves chew dried coca leaves to dull the pain of hunger and cold.

The nation has long been known as a store-house of mineral wealth. Its silver, tin, and copper mines have been among the world's richest. From 1544 to about 1600, Bolivian mines produced half the world's silver. Even today its minerals are an important source of foreign earnings. And the development of oil and gas deposits in the Gran Chaco and near Santa Cruz may someday bring prosperity to its people.

But for now, prosperity eludes Bolivia. Since it won independence from Spain in 1825, Bolivia has lost about two-thirds of its territory in wars with more powerful neighbors. This has left it a landlocked nation, without ports to ship its goods overseas. Political squabbling has done even more damage. In its 168-year history, the republic has suffered 195 coups d'état. From 1978 to 1980, it underwent three general elections, four revolutions, five temporary governments, and more than a thousand strikes by unhappy workers. Such instability has helped keep Bolivia in a chronic state of poverty.

Official name: *Republic of Bolivia*
Area: *424,164 sq mi (1,098,581 sq km)*
Population: *7,802,000*
Capital: *La Paz, administrative (pop. 976,800)*
Sucre, legal and judicial (pop. 105,800)
Ethnic groups: *Indian, mestizo, white*
Language: *Spanish, Quechua, Aymara*
Religious groups: *Roman Catholic*
Economy: *Agr: sugarcane, potatoes, grains, fruit, coffee, cotton. Ind: minerals, oil, lumber, textiles*
Currency: *boliviano*

Paraguay

A landlocked nation in the middle of South America, Paraguay has long been off the beaten track of commerce and industry. For much of its history, the Paraguay River, which divides the country in half, provided the only access, via the Paraná River, to the outside world. Sometimes the nation's isolation was deliberate, decreed by dictators who first took control of Paraguay shortly after it won independence from Spain in 1811.

The first dictator, a despot known as El Supremo, The Supreme One, held office for 30 years. He cut off all foreign trade and contact. In 1865, another ruler involved Paraguay in a war that cost the nation a third of its land and the lives of half its people. The Chaco War in the 1930s claimed several thousand more victims.

In 1954, Gen. Alfredo Stroessner began his 34-year rule as dictator. He built roads, bridges, schools, and dams, and brought a measure of peace and stability to a land that had long been torn by wars, uprisings, and grinding poverty. But he ruled with an iron fist, and political enemies were beaten or jailed or thrown out of Paraguay . . . or killed. The general was ousted in February 1989 by his right-hand man, Gen. Andrés Rodríguez, who then assumed power.

A few months later, General Rodríguez was elected to the presidency on promises of economic reform and democracy. He voiced support for free elections, and Paraguay held its first one in 1993. Voters chose a businessman, Juan Carlos Wasmosy, for president.

Most Paraguayans are part Guaraní Indian and part Spanish. Many people speak both languages. About 95 percent of them live in the country's eastern half, a wooded, rolling plateau with fertile soil. Here they cultivate soybeans, coffee, and rice, as well as tropical fruit. Paraguay has few minerals and not much industry besides selling lumber, making cement, and smuggling everything from cars to cocaine.

The western part of the country, the Gran Chaco, is a grassland area parched in the dry season and swampy when it rains. Here cattle roam on large ranches, and Mennonite farmers near Filadelfia produce fruit, vegetables, and dairy products for sale in the capital, Asunción. The Mennonites, a religious group, migrated to the Chaco from Canada and Europe in the 1920s.

Today, as Paraguay shakes off decades of dictatorship, more than half of its earnings come from the sale of electricity to Brazil. The power is generated by hydroelectric projects on the Paraná River. Initiated by General Stroessner, they were part of his modernization program.

Official name: *Republic of Paraguay*
Area: *157,048 sq mi (406,752 sq km)*
Population: *4,519,000*
Capital: *Asunción (pop. 607,700)*
Ethnic groups: *mestizo, Indian*
Language: *Spanish, Guaraní*
Religious groups: *Roman Catholic*
Economy: *Agr: oilseeds, soybeans, cotton, cassava, sweet potatoes, tobacco, corn, rice, sugarcane, coffee. Ind: meat packing, brewing, textiles, cement, lumber*
Currency: *guaraní*

1 *Paraguay*

2 *Paraguay*

3 *Bolivia*

Paraguay

1 *Soccer players become airborne during a match in Asunción. Futbol is Paraguay's most popular sport.*

2 *Vaqueros, Paraguayan cowboys, round up cattle, crossbreeds of zebus and Brahmans, before driving them to fresh pastures.*

4 *Bolivia*

5 *Bolivia*

6 *Bolivia*

Bolivia

3 *Lake Titicaca's clear waters lie 12,500 feet (3,810 m) above sea level. Indians fish the lake in boats made of bundled totora reeds.*

4 *Sharing a one-room village schoolhouse, two teachers instruct Indian children in two languages, Spanish and Aymara. Separate classes sit back-to-back.*

5 *Tin miners extract ore deep inside a mountain at Potosí. Working in harsh conditions of extreme heat and thin air, they earn about a dollar a day.*

6 *An Aymara Indian plays a sampoña, a reed panpipe, on the streets of Potosí. The music has a breathy, haunting quality.*

PERU

A

Arica

B Iquique
BOLIVIA

Aucanquilcha
20,262 FEET
6,176 METERS
C

Calama
D Antofagasta

San Salvador
de Jujuy

TROPIC OF CAPRICORN

PARAGUAY

Salta
Pilcomayo

GRAN

Copiapo
E

PACIFIC
OCEAN

Paraguay
River

Iguazu Falls

Formosa

Mount Ojos
del Salado
22,572 FEET
6,880 METERS

San Miguel
de Tucuman

Resistencia

Posadas

F
Catamarca

CHACO

Santiago
del Estero

Corrientes

BRAZIL

La Rioja

Parana River

G La Serena
Coquimbo

Santa Fe

Artigas

Rivera

Mount Aconcagua
22,834 FEET
6,960 METERS
Highest point in
South America

Cordoba

Salto

Tacuarembo

H

San Juan

Rio
Cuarto

Parana

Paysandu

Melo

Vina del Mar
Mendoza

Rosario

Mercedes

Uruguay River

J Valparaiso

San Luis

URUGUAY

Santiago
Rancagua

Las Piedras

Buenos Aires

Maldonado

CHILE

La Plata

Rio de la Plata

Montevideo

K Talca

Santa Rosa

L Concepcion

Chillan

Los Angeles

Mar del Plata

PAMPAS

Bahia Blanca

M Temuco

Neuquen

Rio Negro

ATLANTIC
OCEAN

Valdivia

ARGENTINA

Viedma

N Osorno
Puerto Montt

Lake Nahuel Huapi

San Carlos de Bariloche

Valdes
Peninsula

Chiloe
Island

-131 FEET
-40 METERS
Lowest point in
South America

Rawson

O

ANDES

P Coihaique

Comodoro
Rivadavia

Q

R

PATAGONIA

FALKLAND ISLANDS
(UNITED KINGDOM)

S

Strait of
Magellan

Rio Gallegos

West
Falkland

Stanley

Falkland Sound

East
Falkland

T Punta Arenas

TIERRA

Ushuaia

U

DEL
Puerto Williams
FUEGO
Cape Horn

1   2   3   4   5   6   7   8   9   10   11

0 KILOMETERS 400
0 STATUTE MILES 300
For map legend see page 21.

This is a region of extremes. South America's highest and lowest points are both in Argentina. Cape Horn, at the continent's southern tip, lies only about 600 miles (965 km) from Antarctica. Until the opening of the Panama Canal in 1914, sailors voyaging from New York to San Francisco had to face the cape's ferocious storms, as well as an extra journey of 9,000 miles (14,485 km).

A piece of Chile lies 2,300 miles (3,700 km) to its west: Easter Island (see pages 247 and 251).

Chile

Chilli, "where the land ends." That's what the Indians called the world's longest and skinniest country, the Republic of Chile. Pinched between the Pacific Ocean and the high ridges of the southern Andes, Chile extends some 2,650 miles (4,260 km), about the distance between New York and San Francisco. Nowhere is it more than 250 miles (400 km) wide.

Chile is a country of great beauty and stark contrasts. In some places, snowcapped peaks rise straight out of the water. The northern third of the country includes the Atacama Desert, a region so dry that parts of it have gone centuries without rain. The desert is also a mother lode of mineral wealth—copper, silver, gold, and immense deposits of sodium nitrate.

By contrast, Chile's southern part, a wooded maze of fjords and islands, is one of the world's wettest and stormiest places. Some 200 inches (500 cm) of rain a year drench thick forests. Near the continent's tip, winds of up to 200 miles (320 km) an hour lash ice fields and granite peaks. Around the Strait of Magellan, sheep outnumber people fifty to one, and hardy sheepherders mingle with oil and gas drillers. Here, too, live most of Chile's Indians, Mapuche descendants of the warlike Araucanians who successfully resisted armed conquest by Inca and Spaniard.

Most Chileans live in the central section of their country, a region of mild climate and fertile soil. Here farms and ranches produce abundant fruit, vegetables, grains, meat, and dairy products. Here, too, stands Chile's capital, Santiago, and most of its other major cities. The lake district south of Concepción is widely regarded as one of the world's most beautiful resort areas, a land of shimmering lakes and waterfalls set amid sometimes active volcanoes.

Chile's dependence on world copper prices and recent political turmoil cloud its future. In 1970 a communist president was elected to office. Unable to stabilize the nation's economy, he died during a coup three years later and was succeeded by a dictator. In 1990 the country began to get its economy rolling again under a new, democratically elected president.

Official name: *Republic of Chile*
Area: *292,135 sq mi (756,626 sq km)*
Population: *13,600,000*
Capital: *Santiago (met. pop. 4,385,500)*
Ethnic groups: *mestizo, white, Indian*
Language: *Spanish*
Religious groups: *Roman Catholic*
Economy: *Agr: grains, vegetables, sugar beets, fruit, cattle. Ind: copper, minerals, fishing, wood products*
Currency: *Chilean peso*

Argentina

In Argentina they have a saying: "Mexicans descended from the Aztecs. Peruvians descended from the Incas. But we descended from boats." They say this because the ancestors of about 95 percent of the nation's 33 million people came by boat from Europe. Unlike most Latin American countries, Argentina has a very small population of mixed Spanish and Indian blood, and there are few blacks. Most Argentine ancestors came from Italy and Spain. Many also came from France, Germany, Austria, Russia, Great Britain, Switzerland, and Poland.

Perhaps this explains why the capital, Buenos Aires, looks and feels more like a busy European metropolis than most other Latin American cities. Offices and public buildings stand amid chic shops and restaurants along tree-lined boulevards. The area is also home to about a third of Argentina's people. Its factories turn out everything from cars and chemicals to television sets and washing machines.

Argentina is a land of many lands. In the west, along the border with Chile, soar the peaks of the Andes. One of them, 22,834-foot (6,960 m) Mount Aconcagua, is the highest mountain in all the Americas. Amid the mountains farther south lies San Carlos de Bariloche, resembling a town in Switzerland. Settled by Swiss, Germans, and northern Italians, the town has become a resort noted for its chalet-style houses, chocolate shops, and challenging ski runs.

Sweeping eastward across the continent from the foot of the mountains are Argentina's plains—the dry scrublands of the Gran Chaco in the north, the fertile grasslands called Pampas in the middle, and the windswept Patagonian plateau in the south.

Large parts of the Pampas are cattle country, home of the hard-riding gaucho, or cowboy. Here, too, live the wild guanaco, related to the llama, and the ostrich-like rhea. Beef cattle and wheat grown on large *estancias*, ranches, have long provided major Argentine exports. And in Patagonia's desolate reaches roam large flocks of sheep, many of them on ranches established by Scottish and Welsh settlers in the 1800s.

At the tip of the continent lies Tierra del Fuego, Land of Fire, named for the Indian campfires seen by explorer Ferdinand Magellan in 1520 as he sailed through the strait that bears his name. And in the northeast, near Brazil and Paraguay, spread subtropical forests and a tongue of land that reaches to spectacular Iguazú Falls, shared by Brazil and Argentina.

But for all its beauty and productive land, Argentina is a country that went from riches to rags. In the early 1900s, to be "rich like an Argentine" was to be superwealthy. But years of misrule left the nation's economy in shambles. Enormous foreign debts and skyrocketing inflation rates only recently began to come down as a result of government-imposed austerity measures and economic reforms.

Official name: *Argentine Republic*
Area: *1,068,302 sq mi (2,766,889 sq km)*
Population: *33,100,000*
Capital: *Buenos Aires (met. pop. 11,125,600)*
Ethnic groups: *white, mestizo, Indian*
Language: *Spanish*
Religious groups: *Roman Catholic*
Economy: *Agr: grains, sugarcane, oilseeds, livestock. Ind: food processing, motor vehicles, textiles, hides, chemicals, petrochemicals, metals, fishing*
Currency: *austral*

Uruguay

For much of the 20th century Uruguay has seemed blessed. Its gently rolling hills and pasturelands support millions of sheep and cattle. Meat, hides, and wool sold abroad have brought widespread prosperity unknown to most of the other Latin American countries. The government has been generous, providing free schools, hospitals, and other social services.

Nearly half of all Uruguayans live in or around the capital, Montevideo, a modern city at the mouth of the Río de la Plata. Beautiful beaches line the coast. Uruguay's climate is mild, and enough rain falls to grow bountiful crops of sugar, rice, and wheat. In the spring, wildflowers called verbena color the hills, giving Uruguay its nickname, "the purple land."

But in the 1970s, with agricultural production slumping, oil prices and the cost of social services soared. Inflation grew, making the peso worth less and less. Terrorist bands and economic hard times nearly destroyed the nation. The military took control in 1973 and waged a ruthless campaign against the guerrilla bands and leftist political opposition. Today, under a civilian president, Uruguay struggles to repay its debts to foreign lenders, rebuild its shattered economy, and regain its place as one of South America's leading democracies.

Official name: *Oriental Republic of Uruguay*
Area: *68,037 sq mi (176,215 sq km)*
Population: *3,131,000*
Capital: *Montevideo (pop. 1,251,600)*
Ethnic groups: *white, mestizo, black*
Language: *Spanish*
Religious groups: *Roman Catholic*
Economy: *Agr: livestock, wheat, rice, corn. Ind: food processing, leather, textiles, rubber, cement, fishing*
Currency: *Uruguayan new peso*

Falkland Islands

Islands at the end of the world, the Falklands made headlines in 1982 during a brief but bloody war between Argentina and the United Kingdom, which has ruled the Falklands as a colony since 1833. Though defeated, Argentina still claims this Connecticut-size archipelago of some 200 islands that it calls Islas Malvinas. About 2,000 people, mostly sheep ranchers of British extraction, live on these windswept islands. Seals, seabirds, and penguins inhabit their crags and coves; offshore waters teem with squid. Sales of fishing licenses to foreign fleets and of island wool are major sources of income.

Official name: *Colony of the Falkland Islands*
Area: *4,700 sq mi (12,173 sq km)*
Population: *2,000*
Capital: *Stanley (pop. 1,232)*
Ethnic groups: *British*
Language: *English*
Religious groups: *Protestant*
Economy: *Agr: sheep. Ind: wool, fish processing*
Currency: *Falkland pound*

1 *Argentina*

2 *Argentina*

3 *Falkland Islands*

4 *Chile*

Argentina

1 *Gauchos lead a cattle drive in Argentina, where rich grasslands called Pampas nourish beef raised for export.*

2 *Crowds jam the movie district in Buenos Aires, the capital of Argentina. Its metropolitan area has the second largest population in South America.*

Falkland Islands

3 *Black-browed albatrosses perch on cliffs overlooking the South Atlantic Ocean. Their island home lies 300 miles (480 km) off Argentina's coast.*

Chile

4 *Near the southern reaches of the Andes, the glaciated peaks of Torres del Paine National Park harbor rare animal species.*

5 *Nearly four miles (6 km) high, miners break up chunks of sulfur on the slopes of Aucanquilcha, a volcano that rises 20,262 feet (6,176 m) in northern Chile.*

5 *Chile*

Europe

Europe is more a reflection of human culture than of the earth's geography. Physically, it could be described as a large, irregular peninsula hanging off the enormous Eurasian landmass that stretches from the Atlantic to the Pacific Ocean. It is less than one-fourth the size of Asia and only slightly larger than the United States. Of all the continents, only Australia is smaller. Still, Europe's role in world history has been large. At one time or another, Europeans have controlled the vast majority of land on earth. As a result, some traces of European culture—languages, customs, or systems of government—are visible nearly everywhere in the world.

Europe's most important geographic distinction is that no point is very far from an arm of the ocean. This has been a key to its development, for it has given Europeans access to the world. The Arctic Ocean borders it in the north, the Atlantic in the west, and the Mediterranean Sea in the south. Its coastline is more fragmented than that of any other continent, being indented with thousands of fjords and other types of inlets. Not surprisingly, Europeans have been known for centuries as good sailors.

Of the more than 40 European countries, only 13 are landlocked. Even along the continent's eastern border, formed by the Ural Mountains that cross Russia, the Kara Sea and the Black Sea are reachable. The Urals divide Russia into European and Asian portions. Because its larger landmass lies in Asia, Russia appears in the Asian section of this atlas.

The Atlantic Ocean has a great effect on Europe's weather. Its warm currents keep winters mild and summers moderate on much of the continent. Westerly winds from the ocean provide ample rainfall. Because the climate in the western regions is similar to that of the eastern United States, Americans might think that England is straight across the Atlantic Ocean from New York. It's actually opposite icy Labrador.

Four land features dominate the European continent. Rugged highlands cover parts of the British Isles, Brittany, Scandinavia, and the Iberian Peninsula. Here, glaciers scraped away most of the earth, leaving behind thin soil and barren rock. As a result, many people became herders and fishermen. These bleak regions are some of the most sparsely settled in Europe.

The alpine mountain system and related ranges lie across much of southern Europe. Major chains besides the Alps are the Pyrenees, Apennines, Balkans, Dinaric Alps, and Carpathians. Many peaks rise more than 10,000 feet (3,050 m) above sea level, and some reach higher. On Europe's southeastern border, the towering Caucasus Mountains boast the continental record with 18,510-foot (5,642 m) Mount Elbrus.

Mountain passes through alpine ranges are few, but those that do exist provide important routes through which settlers, traders, and armies have passed between southern and northern Europe. The alpine system is still geologically active, so earthquakes and volcanic eruptions periodically shake southern Europe.

North of the Alps lies an upland zone of hilly plateaus that crosses central Europe. Here great rivers, such as the Danube and the Rhine, have long served as important routes for commerce. Europe is blessed with a large number of navigable rivers, scoured out of the landscape when the glaciers retreated at the end of the Ice Age. Most of Europe's major cities, as well as its factories, are on rivers, some of which are fed by the remnants of these glaciers.

The central uplands usually have cool temperatures and abundant rainfall—weather in which grasses and fodder crops thrive. Dairy and livestock farming are important enterprises. Because of rich mineral resources, this area is also a center of mining and industry.

The Northern European Plain stretches across the continent from the Pyrenees to the Ural Mountains. Many of the world's great cities and industrial areas have flourished here amid the gently rolling lowlands. Moderate temperatures and year-round light rains, together with rich soils, have allowed farmers in this part of Europe to be among the most productive in the world. They need to be, in order to help support one of the most densely populated regions on earth. Though Europe covers only 7 percent of the world's land, it is home to 30 million more people than Africa, which covers 20 percent.

Dozens of ethnic groups speaking some 40 languages live within Europe's borders, though not always in harmony. European civilization started with the ancient Greek and Roman cultures. Much of its history is the story of migrations,

The headwaters of the Rhône River

Aurora borealis over Arctic Norway

conquests, and retreats, as different cultures rose to power and then fell before the advance of a stronger group. As the Roman Empire waned, the spread of Christianity provided a common thread for the continent.

Over the centuries, strong military leaders have waged war in attempts to unify Europe under one banner, but without lasting success. Today, Europeans are taking a different route toward unity, letting politicians instead of generals lead the way.

Twelve countries are current members of the European Community (EC), a free-trade zone in Western Europe: Belgium, Denmark, France, Germany, Greece, Ireland, Italy, Luxembourg, the Netherlands, Portugal, Spain, and the United Kingdom. In December 1991, their leaders met in the Dutch city of Maastricht and drew up a treaty adopting a common currency and foreign policy by 1999. The free-trade agreement went into effect in January 1993, but the Maastricht Treaty requires further consideration.

Austria, Finland, Iceland, Norway, Sweden, Liechtenstein, and Switzerland are members of another group, the European Free Trade Association (EFTA), which is negotiating trade agreements with the EC. Some of these and other European countries have applied for EC membership. Some Eastern European countries also have signed agreements with the EC. Most of Europe is moving toward a closer union.

In addition to forging new economic ties, Europeans are seeking ways to improve the continent's rapidly deteriorating environment. Because winds and rivers carry pollutants across national boundaries, it is difficult to enforce environmental protection laws. Toxic chemicals contaminate drinking water. Automobiles and factories produce deadly smog. Scientists blame acid rain—produced by burning large amounts of coal in the factories of central and eastern Europe—for the widespread destruction of trees, including the fabled Black and Bohemian Forests in Germany and the Czech Republic. Following the 1987 nuclear disaster at Chornobyl (Chernobyl), Ukraine, radiation fallout affected people from farmers in Belarus to reindeer herders in Lapland. The EC and other organizations are striving to work out continental solutions to such environmental problems.

Austrian factories belch chemical-laden smoke.

Black Forest trees may be victims of acid rain.

Facts About Europe

Area: 4,065,945 sq mi (10,530,750 sq km)
Population: 684,400,000
Highest Point: Mount Elbrus, Russia, 18,510 ft (5,642 m) above sea level
Lowest Point: Caspian Sea, Europe-Asia, 92 ft (28 m) below sea level
Largest Countries: *(by area)*
  European Russia 1,747,112 sq mi (4,525,000 sq km). Ukraine 233,206 sq mi (604,000 sq km)
Largest Countries: *(by population)*

European Russia	107,219,000
Germany	80,556,000

Smallest Country: *(by area and population)*
* Vatican City 0.2 sq mi (0.4 sq km); pop. 1,000
Largest Metropolitan Areas: *(by population)*

Paris, France	9,060,000
Moscow, Russia	9,000,000
London, U.K.	6,756,400

Longest Rivers: *(mi and km)*

Volga	2,194	3,531
Danube	1,776	2,858

Largest Lake: *(sq mi and sq km)*

Ladoga, Russia	6,835	17,703

*World record

Glossary

autonomy—the right of self-government or freedom from external control.
city-state—an independent country made up of a city and sometimes the surrounding area.
dialect—a regional variety of a language.
duchy—the territory ruled by a duke or duchess.
European Community (EC)—an organization that promotes a common market in Europe.
fjord—a narrow, steep-sided ocean inlet that reaches far into a coastline.
geothermal power—energy provided by heat from inside the earth.
hydroelectric power—electricity produced by capturing the energy of moving water.
maritime—bordering the sea; concerning navigation or commerce on the sea.
medieval—referring to a period of European history known as the Middle Ages, roughly from A.D. 500 to 1500.
monarchy—a government having undivided rule by a single person, such as a king or queen.
parliament—a group of representatives who meet to discuss national affairs and make laws.
privatization—transferal of a business or property from public to private control or ownership.

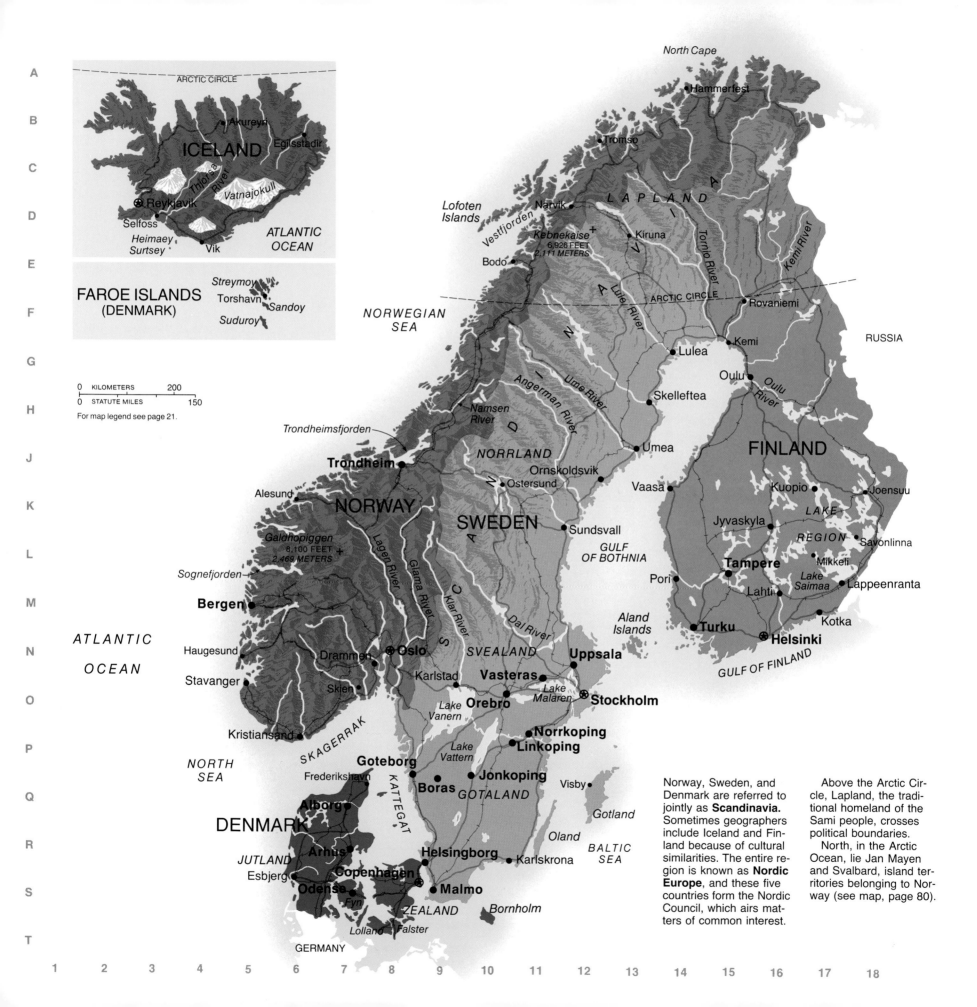

A B C D E F G H J K L M N O P Q R S T

1 2 3 4 5 6 7 8 9 10 11 12 13 14 15 16 17 18

North Cape

Hammerfest

ARCTIC CIRCLE

ICELAND

Akureyn

Egilsstadir

Thjorsa River

Vatnajokull

Reykjavik

Selfoss

Heimaey
Surtsey

Vik

ATLANTIC
OCEAN

FAROE ISLANDS
(DENMARK)

Streymoy

Torshavn *Sandoy*

Suduroy

0 KILOMETERS 200

0 STATUTE MILES 150

For map legend see page 21.

Tromso

LAPLAND

Lofoten
Islands

Narvik

Vestfjorden

Kebnekaise
6,926 FEET
2,111 METERS

Kiruna

Tornio River

Kemi River

RUSSIA

Bodo

NORWEGIAN
SEA

ARCTIC CIRCLE

Rovaniemi

Lulea

Kemi

Oulu

Oulu
River

Angerman River

Ume River

Lule River

Skelleftea

Namsen
River

Trondheimsfjorden

Umea

FINLAND

Trondheim

NORRLAND

Ornskoldsvik

Ostersund

Vaasa

Kuopio

Joensuu

Alesund

NORWAY

SWEDEN

LAKE

Jyvaskyla

REGION

Savonlinna

Galdhopiggen
8,100 FEET
2,469 METERS

Sundsvall

GULF
OF BOTHNIA

Tampere

Mikkeli

Sognefjorden

Lagen River

Glama River

Klar River

Dal River

Pori

Lake
Saimaa

Lappeenranta

Bergen

Lahti

Kotka

Haugesund

ATLANTIC

Drammen

Oslo

Aland
Islands

SVEALAND

Uppsala

Turku

Helsinki

OCEAN

Karlstad

Vasteras

GULF OF FINLAND

Stavanger

Skien

Orebro

Lake
Malaren

Stockholm

Lake
Vanern

Kristiansand

SKAGERRAK

Norrkoping

Linkoping

NORTH
SEA

Goteborg

Frederikshavn

KATTEGAT

Boras

Lake
Vattern

Jonkoping

GOTALAND

Visby

Gotland

Alborg

DENMARK

Arhus

JUTLAND

Esbjerg

Copenhagen

Odense

Fyn

Lolland Falster

ZEALAND

Helsingborg

Malmo

Oland

Karlskrona

BALTIC
SEA

Bornholm

GERMANY

Norway, Sweden, and
Denmark are referred to
jointly as **Scandinavia.**
Sometimes geographers
include Iceland and Fin-
land because of cultural
similarities. The entire region is known as **Nordic
Europe,** and these five
countries form the Nordic
Council, which airs mat-
ters of common interest.

Above the Arctic Cir-
cle, Lapland, the tradi-
tional homeland of the
Sami people, crosses
political boundaries.

North, in the Arctic
Ocean, lie Jan Mayen
and Svalbard, island ter-
ritories belonging to Norway (see map, page 80).

Iceland

Even in winter's chill, Icelanders swim outdoors—in natural hot springs. The springs are heated by volcanoes of an undersea mountain chain called the Mid-Atlantic Ridge. Iceland, part of this chain, rises above the sea and is at the mercy of earth's continual volcanic activity. Every five years, at least one of the country's 200 volcanoes erupts.

Icelanders make the most of life in an unstable environment. They tap geothermal energy to heat most of their homes, buildings, and swimming pools. Greenhouses give them vegetables, tropical fruit, and flowers year-round. Swift rivers supply cheap hydroelectricity for energy-intensive industries such as aluminum refining.

More than half the people live in or near Reykjavik, the capital city. The rest graze sheep and cattle on farms in scattered coastal valleys or live in fishing villages. Because less than 2 percent of the island can be farmed, Icelanders have always turned to the sea to make a living. Iceland's economy depends on fishing, which earns about 75 percent of its export income.

Official name: *Republic of Iceland*
Area: *39,769 sq mi (103,000 sq km)*
Population: *260,000*
Capital: *Reykjavik (met. pop. 149,500)*
Ethnic groups: *Icelander*
Language: *Icelandic*
Religious groups: *Lutheran*
Economy: *Agr: livestock, hay, potatoes, turnips. Ind: fishing, aluminum, ferrosilicon, wool*
Currency: *Icelandic krona*

Norway

Fifteen thousand years ago, Ice Age glaciers slowly ground across what is today Norway. On the seacoast they carved narrow, steep-sided valleys. When the ice eventually melted, the sea level rose and water flooded the valleys, creating fjords and a long, jagged coastline.

Most of Norway is mountainous, and about a quarter of it is covered by forest. Only 3 percent of the land is suitable for farming, much of it in the southeast. Farmers there raise livestock or grow potatoes and barley.

A warm ocean current makes coastal climates temperate. About 80 percent of the population lives in the south within ten miles of the coast, chiefly in urban areas. The state provides free education and insurance covering health care, unemployment, and pensions. Norway's capital, Oslo, is the largest city and the leading industrial, financial, and transportation center.

About a third of Norway lies above the Arctic Circle. Here, in the Land of the Midnight Sun, the sun never sets in the midsummer months. In midwinter it never rises. The long, gloomy winters and rugged landscape may have sparked the imagination of storytellers long ago. Norse mythology from the ninth century tells of gods battling hostile giants to protect humans. Rich folklore was succeeded by a literary tradition that produced writers such as the 19th-century playwright Henrik Ibsen.

The sea has always brought wealth to Norway. Its large merchant marine fleet carries cargoes around the world. The warm ocean current keeps most harbors ice-free all year. Bergen has been a major port and fish market since it was founded almost a thousand years ago.

The ocean's latest gifts are oil and natural gas deposits under the North Sea. Since the mid-1970s they have accounted for up to half of Norway's export income. The United States and the European Community countries are Norway's chief customers. But Norwegians remain divided over a closer association with the EC.

Official name: *Kingdom of Norway*
Area: *125,182 sq mi (324,220 sq km)*
Population: *4,276,000*
Capital: *Oslo (pop. 461,100)*
Ethnic groups: *Norwegian, Sami (Lapp)*
Language: *Norwegian*
Religious groups: *Lutheran*
Economy: *Agr: livestock, feed crops, potatoes, fruit, vegetables. Ind: oil, natural gas, food processing, paper products, machinery, metals, chemicals, fishing*
Currency: *Norwegian krone*

Denmark

Denmark is made up of the Jutland Peninsula and almost 500 islands, connected by a number of ferries and bridges. Throughout history, the country's location has made it a crossroads for people and goods, its islands acting like stepping-stones between Scandinavia and the rest of Europe. Now a further link is planned—a bridge and tunnel to Sweden.

Low, rolling grasslands and a moist, mild climate allow the Danes to farm more than 70 percent of their country. Farmland is considered an important national asset. Before young farmers can purchase land, they must earn a farming license. Danish farmers have long specialized in exports, especially butter and other dairy products. They feed their pigs skim milk, a butter-making leftover—another export is ham.

Despite their agricultural tradition, nearly a quarter of all Danes are employed in industry. A highly skilled work force manufactures a wide range of goods, but most raw materials must be imported. In recent years, products such as ships and diesel engines, furniture and silverware, porcelain figures, hearing aids, and Lego building blocks have accounted for more than 60 percent of the country's export income.

Most factories are near the capital, Copenhagen. More than one-fourth of the population lives in or around this eastern port. Here cargo is collected from vessels too large to enter the shallow Baltic Sea and transferred to smaller freighters. Overlooking Copenhagen's harbor is a statue of the Little Mermaid, a character from a story by the 19th-century Danish author Hans Christian Andersen. "The Ugly Duckling" and his many other tales are told the world over.

Denmark ruled Nordic Europe 600 years ago. Today it only has two self-governing possessions in the North Atlantic—Greenland and the **Faroe Islands,** where fishing provides most of the export income. Only about 2 percent of the rocky archipelago is cultivated, chiefly for potatoes. Grass is another major crop, and a vital one since sheep greatly outnumber people.

Official name: *Kingdom of Denmark*
Area: *16,638 sq mi (43,092 sq km)*
Population: *5,168,000*
Capital: *Copenhagen (met. pop. 1,343,900)*
Ethnic groups: *Danish*
Language: *Danish*
Religious groups: *Lutheran*
Economy: *Agr: livestock, dairy products, grains, root crops. Ind: food processing, machinery, textiles, furs, chemicals, electronics, furniture, fishing*
Currency: *Danish krone*

Sweden

Alfred Nobel, who invented dynamite in 1866, established the Nobel Peace Prize to benefit humanity with the profits from his creation. His explosives, used in mining, helped Sweden develop as an industrial nation. But before 1900, when industry finally brought prosperity, one million Swedes had emigrated to the United States.

Since then Sweden has exploited its natural resources of iron ore, timber, and waterpower. Today the country is a leader in industry, helped by its powerful northern rivers that generate inexpensive hydroelectricity. The heart of Swedish economy is steel production. Huge iron ore deposits around the Arctic town of Kiruna supply factories that manufacture automobiles, machinery, and ships. Timber from the country's extensive forests provides lumber for furniture and wood pulp for newsprint. Forest products account for over a sixth of Sweden's exports.

Much of the northern work force is composed of Sami, or Lapps, an ethnic group that lives north of the Arctic Circle. Traditionally the Sami moved across Lapland herding their reindeer. Now many work in mining and forestry.

Although less than 8 percent of Sweden is suitable for agriculture, its farms furnish nearly all its food. Much of the fertile land is in the south where the climate is mildest. Here farmers raise livestock for dairy products and meat, and grow sugar beets, potatoes, wheat, and barley.

Most major cities and industrial centers are in the south, too. Stockholm, the capital and largest city, is built on a group of islands and is a leading port on the Baltic Sea. Here 90 percent of the residents live in apartments. Even though there is ample land for single homes, large buildings that house many people are more economical to heat during the frigid winters.

Sweden is known for its cradle-to-grave welfare system. But inflation and absenteeism have contributed to a sagging economy. The government is pushing spending reforms and in 1992 applied for European Community membership.

Official name: *Kingdom of Sweden*
Area: *173,732 sq mi (449,964 sq km)*
Population: *8,669,000*
Capital: *Stockholm (pop. 674,500)*
Ethnic groups: *Swedish, Finnish, Sami (Lapp)*
Language: *Swedish, Finnish*
Religious groups: *Lutheran*
Economy: *Agr: livestock, grains, sugar beets, potatoes. Ind: iron, steel, machinery, electronics, wood products, paper, food processing, chemicals, fishing*
Currency: *Swedish krona*

Finland

Finland's location between Sweden and Russia has greatly affected its history. Dominated by Sweden for almost 700 years, Finland became part of tsarist Russia in 1809, then declared independence in 1917. Many Swedish customs remain and, along with Finnish, Swedish is an official language.

Unlike most other European peoples, the Finns came from what is now west-central Siberia in Russia. Probably around 2,000 years ago they settled the town of Turku. Today, most Finns still live in this region on the southwestern coastal plain, primarily in cities. Helsinki, the capital, is Finland's busiest port.

The southwest is also where Finland's best farmland lies. Farmers raise livestock for dairy products and meat, providing all the country's needs. They also grow potatoes and the hardy grains of rye, barley, and oats for domestic use. Finland has a short growing season, so most fruit and vegetables must be imported.

Forests of spruce, pine, and birch that cover about two-thirds of Finland are its greatest resource. Paper, wood, and pulp earn more than a third of its export income. Peat bogs provide fuel, and rivers, flowing from Finland's many lakes, furnish hydroelectric power.

Heavy industry, however, has driven Finland's economy since World War II. The country relied largely on the former Soviet Union for its energy needs, exchanging gas and oil for manufactured goods. But trade relations may take some time to establish with independent Russia. Meantime, Finland is attempting to expand its Western markets, including exploring joint ventures with Estonia to the south—the two peoples speak a similar language and come from the same ethnic stock. In 1992, Finland applied for membership in the European Community.

With snow on the ground for almost six months, cross-country skiing is a national sport. Finns often relax after such activity in a sauna, a wooden room heated by water sizzling on hot stones. There is one sauna for every five Finns.

Official name: *Republic of Finland*
Area: *130,558 sq mi (338,145 sq km)*
Population: *5,028,000*
Capital: *Helsinki (pop. 492,400)*
Ethnic groups: *Finnish, Swedish, Sami (Lapp)*
Language: *Finnish, Swedish*
Religious groups: *Lutheran*
Economy: *Agr: livestock, grains, sugar beets, potatoes. Ind: wood and paper products, machinery, metals, food processing, electronics, textiles, chemicals*
Currency: *markka*

1 *Iceland*

2 *Iceland*

Iceland

1 *Bathers take advantage of naturally heated waters at a geothermal electric plant near Reykjavik, the country's capital.*

2 *A couple shares the task of turning Icelandic wool into distinctively patterned sweaters. This profitable cottage industry helps pass the time during long winter evenings.*

1 *Denmark*

Denmark

1 *Amid the warm glow of Christmas candles, an artist paints a dish with a Royal Copenhagen pattern dating back to 1775.*

Norway

2 *A 12th-century stave church stands on the coast of the Sognefjorden in western Norway. Staves, or wooden posts, form the interior framework of the building.*

Finland

3 *Helsinki's Western Harbor is one of five that make up Finland's biggest seaport. Its shipyards specialize in building icebreakers that keep sea-lanes open in winter.*

Sweden

4 *Actors perform in the public square of Stockholm's Old Town, Gamla Stan, site of buildings from the 16th and 17th centuries.*

5 *A Sami reindeer race draws a crowd in northern Sweden. Reindeer herding was the traditional livelihood of the Sami, but few of them still follow this occupation.*

2 *Norway*

3 *Finland*

4 *Sweden*

5 *Sweden*

Gulf of Finland

ESTONIA

Narva

Kunda
Sillamae
Rakvere
Kohtla-Jarve
Narva R
Paldiski
Tallinn
Keila
Tapa
Vasknarva

Vormsi
Kardla
Haapsalu
Rapla
Turi
Paide
Mustvee
Lake Peipus

Hiiumaa
Emmaste
Muhu
Viljandi

BALTIC SEA

Orissaare
Virtsu
Saaremaa
Kuressaare

Parnu
Viljandi
Tartu
RUSSIA

Moisakula
Torva
Voru

Gulf of Riga

Ainazi
Salacgriva
Valka
Valga

Pskovskoye Lake

Mazirbe
Roja
Valmiera
Smittene
Aluksne

Ventspils
Talsi
Gauja River
Cesis
Gulbene

LATVIA

Venta River
Kuldiga
Jurmala
Madona
Karsava
Pavilosta
Tukums
Riga
Plavinas
Aizpute
Saldus
Daugava River
Rezekne
Zilupe
Liepaja
Jelgava
Jekabpils
Priekule
Auce
Bauska
Livani
Mazeikiai
Daugava River
Skuodas
Naujoji
Akmene
Joniskis
Birzai
Kursenai
Rokiskis
Palanga
Siauliai
Telsiai
Kretinga
Plunge
Radviliskis
Daugavpils
Klaipeda
Rietavas
Panevezys
Zarasai
Nida
Silute
Utena
Ignalina

Courland Lagoon
Taurage
Kedainiai
Ukmerge

LITHUANIA

Pagegiai
Nemunas River
Neris River
RUSSIA
Kaunas
Kaisiadorys
Kybartai
Marijampole
Prienai
Vilnius
Alytus
BELARUS
Salcininkai

POLAND
Varena
Nemunas River
Druskininkai

0 KILOMETERS 50
0 STATUTE MILES 30

For map legend see page 21.

Declarations of independence in 1990 by three small republics on the eastern shores of the Baltic Sea spearheaded the breakup of the Soviet Union. Historically, the **Baltic States** of Estonia, Latvia, and Lithuania have looked to the West for trade and ideas and enjoyed greater prosperity than other peoples under Soviet rule. The three shared a period of independence between the World Wars, and all fiercely resisted Russification of language and culture during eras of tsarist Russian and Soviet control. Many people suffered persecution, execution, or deportation from their homelands. In September 1991, Baltic independence was recognized by a crumbling Soviet Union.

Estonia

Smallest of the Baltic countries, Estonia is mostly flat and watery. Glaciers plowed the area thousands of years ago, leaving it low, with gentle ridges of glacial debris. The country contains more than 1,000 lakes, numerous rivers, and some 800 islands that dot the Baltic Sea. Much of the land is boggy and poor for agriculture, and about one-third of it is forested.

In language, Estonia differs from the other two Baltic republics. Unlike theirs, its language is related to Finnish and Hungarian. The country possesses a rich heritage of folklore and music. Every four years, people flock to Tallinn, the capital, for a huge music and dance festival.

Estonia bears a long history of domination by foreign powers. Beginning in the Middle Ages, Germany, Denmark, and Sweden controlled it at different times. German influence is still seen in the Lutheran faith upheld by 80 percent of ethnic Estonians. Tsarist Russia annexed Estonia in 1721, but the people resisted efforts to force Russian language and culture upon them.

Following a period of independence between the World Wars, Estonia was taken over by the Soviets. They exploited natural resources such as energy-generating oil shale and phosphorite, used to make fertilizer. Many Russians came to work in the new industrial towns of northeastern Estonia and elsewhere. Though its economy has prospered, Estonia suffers severe pollution.

Estonia today still asserts its unique culture, but the denial of citizens' rights worries non-Estonians, about one-third of the population. In 1992, Estonia launched a new currency, the kroon, tied in value to the German mark.

Official name: *Republic of Estonia*
Area: *17,413 sq mi (45,100 sq km)*
Population: *1,581,000*
Capital: *Tallinn (pop. 484,000)*
Ethnic groups: *Estonian, Russian, Ukrainian*
Language: *Estonian, Russian*
Religious groups: *Lutheran, Russian Orthodox*
Economy: *Agr: livestock, dairy products, fodder, vegetables. Ind: machinery, petrochemicals, oil shale processing, textiles, furniture, fishing*
Currency: *kroon*

Latvia

Environmentalists protesting the rampant pollution caused by Soviet industrialization led the way in Latvia's campaign for independence. They were joined by people active in preserving Latvian language and culture. The language is closely related to Lithuanian.

Glacial action produced Latvia's rolling plains and low hills; forests cover one-third of the land. Its natural resources include sand, limestone, and peat—a product of its boggy soils. Recently discovered oil in the far northwest may make Latvia less dependent on imported fuels.

Dairy and livestock farming form the basis of Latvian agriculture, along with a few crops. Industry has focused heavily on machine building, engineering, and chemical manufacturing—a major source of pollution. About one-third of the people live in Rīga, the capital, which has served for centuries as an important Baltic port.

Like its Baltic neighbors, Latvia endured a parade of invaders who suppressed the native Latvian people, also known as Letts.

Now independent, Latvia struggles to return farms to private ownership and to clean up its degraded environment. The future of the country's Russian minority, more than one-third of the population, remains a controversial issue.

Official name: *Republic of Latvia*
Area: *24,942 sq mi (64,600 sq km)*
Population: *2,702,000*
Capital: *Rīga (pop. 915,000)*
Ethnic groups: *Latvian, Russian, Belarusan*
Language: *Latvian, Russian*
Religious groups: *Lutheran, Roman Catholic, Russian Orthodox*
Economy: *Agr: dairy products, livestock, grains, sugar beets. Ind: machinery, engineering, chemicals, shipbuilding, electronics, paper, fishing*
Proposed currency: *lats*

Lithuania

In March 1990, Lithuania declared its independence, leading the way for its Baltic neighbors and, eventually, for the other Soviet republics. Religion unified the Lithuanian people in their quest for freedom. Alone among the peoples of the former Soviet Union, Lithuanians are predominantly Roman Catholic. Their faith is a legacy of an alliance with neighboring Poland from 1385 to 1795; beautiful old churches grace the city of Vilnius, the capital.

Lithuania is mostly low and boggy, crossed with rivers, studded with lakes, and lightly forested. Modest uplands formed of glacial debris rise in the south and east. Most of the world's valuable amber, the fossilized resin of pine trees, is mined on Baltic shores. Lithuanian artisans are famous for creating amber jewelry.

Lithuania's ties to Poland kept it free of the German influence exerted over the other Baltic countries, but could not stop annexation by tsarist Russia in the late 1700s. Today, 80 percent of the people are ethnic Lithuanians, speaking a language related to Latvian and celebrating their heritage with song, dance, and folklore.

Despite widespread industrialization, Lithuania remains the most rural Baltic state. Farmers chiefly raise dairy cows and pigs. Half of all crops grown are used for fodder.

Independent Lithuania is striving to establish a market economy and trade relations with other nations. Inability to purchase expensive fuel (which was heavily subsidized under the Soviets) hinders transportation and keeps homes, offices, and hospitals frigid in winter.

The continuing presence of Russian troops angers many people. Army maneuvers have despoiled thousands of acres of forest, and the dumping of millions of gallons of spent fuels near army bases has polluted soil and water.

Disillusioned by worsening conditions, Lithuanians voted their liberators out of office in November 1992 and elected some officials from the Soviet era, hoping that their more cautious approach to reform would provide greater stability.

Official name: *Republic of Lithuania*
Area: *25,174 sq mi (65,200 sq km)*
Population: *3,736,000*
Capital: *Vilnius (pop. 597,700)*
Ethnic groups: *Lithuanian, Russian, Polish*
Language: *Lithuanian, Russian, Polish*
Religious groups: *Roman Catholic*
Economy: *Agr: livestock, dairy products, grains, flax, sugar beets, vegetables. Ind: machinery, metals, food processing, wood products, fishing*
Proposed currency: *litas*

Latvia

1 *Rīga, Latvia's capital, lines both banks of the Daugava River. An important trading and cultural center in medieval times, it earned the nickname "Paris of the Baltic."*

Estonia

2 *In an international celebration of friendship, an ethnic Estonian from Canada (right) embraces an Estonian national at a song and dance festival in Tallinn.*

Lithuania

3 *Fallen hero: A paint-stained statue of the former Soviet Union leader, Joseph Stalin, gets a dusting at a monument factory in Lithuania's capital, Vilnius.*

4 *A couple tosses hay in the northern countryside. Fodder is an important crop in Lithuania, where livestock farming leads other agricultural activities.*

5 *In Palanga, a craftsman fashions jewelry from amber—fossilized pieces of resin that oozed from pine trees along the shores of the Baltic Sea 30 to 40 million years ago.*

1 *Latvia*

2 *Estonia*

3 *Lithuania*

5 *Lithuania*

4 *Lithuania*

A B C D E F G H J K L M N O P Q R S T U

1 2 3 4 5 6 7 8 9 10 11 12 13 14 15 16 17 18 19

SHETLAND ISLANDS

Unst

Yell

Mainland
Lerwick

ORKNEY ISLANDS

Fair Isle

CHANNEL ISLANDS

Alderney

Guernsey

St. Peter Port   *Sark*

Jersey
St. Helier

FRANCE

0   KILOMETERS   100
0   STATUTE MILES   75

For map legend see page 21.

Kirkwall   *ORKNEY ISLANDS*

Thurso   □ John o'Groats

OUTER HEBRIDES

Stornoway
Isle of Lewis

Ullapool

Moray Firth

Island of Skye

Inverness
Kyle of Lochalsh   *Loch Ness*

Aberdeen

Mallaig

Ben Nevis   *HIGHLANDS*
4,406 FEET   **SCOTLAND**   Balmoral
1,343 METERS   □ *R. Dee*   Castle

Island of Mull

Dundee

Tay R.   Perth   • St. Andrews

Loch Lomond   *Firth of Forth*

INNER HEBRIDES

Greenock   **Edinburgh**

Glasgow   *River Clyde*

Prestwick   *UPLANDS*   *Tweed R.*

Islay   *SOUTHERN*   Hawick

Dumfries   *Hadrian's Wall*   *Tyne R.*   **Newcastle**

NORTHERN IRELAND

Londonderry   *River Bann*

UNITED KINGDOM

Omagh   *Lake Neagh*

Donegal Bay   Armagh   *ISLE OF MAN*   *LAKE DISTRICT*   *NORTH YORK MOORS*   *NORTH SEA*

Sligo   **Belfast**   Douglas   *THE PENNINES*   **GREAT BRITAIN**

Lake Conn   Cavan   Dundalk   *Tees R.*

York

IRISH SEA   **Leeds**   **Kingston upon Hull**

IRELAND   Drogheda   **Bradford**   *THE WOLDS*

CONNEMARA   Galway   *Anglesey*   **Liverpool**   **Manchester**   *R. Trent*

Inishmore Island   *River Shannon*   **Dublin** ◉   Holyhead   **Sheffield**   *The Wash*

Aran Islands   *Barrow River*   *WICKLOW MTS.*   Conwy   **Derby**   **Nottingham**   **Norwich**

ATLANTIC OCEAN   Snowdon +   **Stoke on Trent**   *THE MIDLANDS*   *EAST ANGLIA*

Cliffs of Moher   3,560 FEET   **Leicester**
1,085 METERS

Shannon   Limerick   *CARDIGAN BAY*   **Birmingham**   **Coventry**   **Cambridge**

Tipperary   Kilkenny   Aberystwyth   *CAMBRIAN*   Stratford   **Ipswich**
upon Avon

Blackwater R.   Waterford   *MTS.*   **ENGLAND**

Tralee   Wexford   *St. David's Head*   **Oxford**   *Avon R.*

Carrantuohill +   Rosslare   *CAMBRIAN MTS.*   *WALES*   Hereford   *COTSWOLD HILLS*   **London** ◉   *River Thames*
3,414 FEET   Harbour
1,041 METERS

Killarney   **Cork**   Pembroke   *ST. GEORGE'S CHANNEL*   *Severn River*   **Greenwich**   Canterbury

Blarney   **Newport**   **Oxford**   *NORTH DOWNS*   Dover
Castle

Swansea   **Bristol**   *Strait of Dover*

Cardiff   Cheddar   □ Stonehenge   *NORTH DOWNS*   FRANCE

CELTIC SEA   Barnstaple   *EXMOOR*   *SOUTH DOWNS*   CHANNEL TUNNEL

Tintagel Castle   **Southampton**   **Brighton**

Exeter   *Exe R.*   *DARTMOOR*   **Bournemouth**   **Portsmouth**
Isle of Wight

Truro   **Torbay**   *ENGLISH CHANNEL*

Land's End   Penzance   **Plymouth**

Isles of Scilly

These islands, rich in history, are known by many names. The island of **Great Britain** contains England, Scotland, and Wales. Together with Northern Ireland, they make up the United Kingdom of Great Britain and Northern Ireland.

Ireland is the name of the island that holds Northern Ireland and the Republic of Ireland and is also a short name used for the republic.

The **British Isles** include all the islands shown on these maps. The Channel Islands off the coast of France and the Isle of Man are self-governing crown dependencies of the U.K.

Ireland

Resembling a saucer with a wide rim of hills, the Emerald Isle looks lush and inviting from the air. The green landscape is watered by constant rain and mist.

The Republic of Ireland won independence from the United Kingdom in 1922. Predominantly Roman Catholic, it occupies five-sixths of the island that also holds Northern Ireland. The government advocates peaceful unification with Northern Ireland, presently part of the U.K.

Ireland's eastern half contains the majority of the country's people, cities, and industry. More than 800 foreign companies have invested in factories there. Dublin, the capital, is the manufacturing, publishing, and communications center, and home to a quarter of the population. Waterford in the south is famous for its fine crystal.

In western Ireland, sheep farms and peat bogs give way to a mountainous landscape that in places drops down sheer cliffs to the sea. One-seventh of Ireland is covered with peat, a partially decayed moss that is used as a fuel.

The midlands hold cattle farms. Dry periods are too short here for grain to ripen, although it grows in the drier east. Damp weather was partly responsible for the Great Potato Famine of the 1840s. Infected by a fungus, potatoes rotted in the ground. Starving Irish left by the thousand, most of them emigrating to the United States. Today unemployment has prompted a new exodus, chiefly to the U.K. and Europe.

The Irish are blessed with a gift for language. Their large share of world-renowned writers includes James Joyce and George Bernard Shaw. Efforts have long been under way to preserve the Irish language, which is spoken today only in parts of the far west and south of Ireland.

Official name: *Republic of Ireland*
Area: *27,137 sq mi (70,284 sq km)*
Population: *3,532,000*
Capital: *Dublin (pop. 502,700; met. pop. 921,000)*
Ethnic groups: *Irish, English*
Language: *English, Irish*
Religious groups: *Roman Catholic*
Economy: *Agr: livestock, barley, potatoes, sugar beets, wheat. Ind: food processing, electronics, chemicals, textiles, machinery, tourism, glass, fishing*
Currency: *Irish pound*

United Kingdom

Famed for much of its history as an island fortress, Great Britain hasn't always been an island. In prehistoric times it was connected to continental Europe. Stone Age hunters could walk there. Eventually the sea rose and successive groups of Celts, Romans, Anglo-Saxons, Vikings, and Normans sailed across the English Channel or the North Sea to Great Britain and Ireland. Regional cultures evolved into the countries of England, Scotland, Wales, and Ireland, which merged as the United Kingdom in 1801. The Republic of Ireland won its independence in 1922.

London, near the mouth of the Thames, has been the country's economic center since Roman times and remains one of the largest financial and commercial centers in the world. It is the seat of a parliamentary democracy. While a king or queen reigns in the United Kingdom, the country is governed by a parliament of elected members (the House of Commons) and hereditary or lifetime peers (the House of Lords). Ceremony is a trademark of this great capital.

The Thames, Great Britain's longest river, wanders through lowlands that cover the southeast—a pleasant land of rolling hills and patchwork fields bordered by hedges and stone fences. Resort towns line the south coast from the white cliffs of Dover to the wild countryside of Land's End. The country's best farmland lies in the southeast. Only about 2 percent of the work force is employed in agriculture, so the United Kingdom must import much of its food.

The most crowded region of this densely populated country besides Greater London and the southeast is the Midlands. Here the industrial revolution began in the 1700s. Iron and steel, textile, shipbuilding, and coal industries thrived in northern England, Scotland, and Wales, aided by raw materials from the former British Empire. About a quarter of the work force remains in industry, but foreign competition has led to decline, creating serious unemployment.

North of the Pennines, England's mountain backbone, beyond the Scottish Southern Uplands, lie Scotland's lowlands and its two largest cities, Edinburgh and Glasgow. This region holds most of Scotland's people, farmland, and industry. Still farther north stretch the wind-swept Scottish Highlands, with their heather-covered moors, deep lakes (or lochs), and few trees. Inhabitants raise sheep or fish the seas. The North Sea oil industry based in Aberdeen has brought prosperity, but also the threat of pollution to fishing grounds and coastal wildlife.

In mountainous Wales, the few people who live in the north tend sheep or quarry for limestone and slate. Most of the Welsh live along the coast or in the green valleys of the south, center of a large but now struggling coal industry. Wales is renowned for its poets and singers, who kept the mythology of the Celts alive for centuries before a written language existed.

Across the Irish Sea is Northern Ireland, with a countryside of gentle mountains, valleys, and fertile lowlands. Its livestock and dairy products are exported to Great Britain and Europe, while Irish tweed and linen produced in Londonderry are famous worldwide. Belfast is its major city and port. Northern Ireland's Protestant majority chose in 1922 to stay under British rule when the Republic of Ireland split away, but the Catholic minority feels strongly that all of Ireland should be united. The two groups have clashed repeatedly, with tragic loss of life.

The English Channel, nature's moat protecting the island fortress, has long given the British a sense of security and national identity. But since joining the European Community in 1973, the British have looked increasingly to Europe for trade. A man-made rail link, the Channel Tunnel, scheduled to open in late 1993, will once more join Great Britain to the rest of Europe.

Official name: *United Kingdom of Great Britain and Northern Ireland*
Area: *94,248 sq mi (244,100 sq km)*
Population: *57,763,000*
Capital: *London (pop. 6,756,400)*
Ethnic groups: *English, Scottish, Irish, Welsh*
Language: *English, Welsh, Gaelic*
Religious groups: *Protestant, Roman Catholic*
Economy: *Agr: wheat, barley, potatoes, sugar beets, livestock. Ind: machinery, transportation equipment, oil, coal, food processing, banking, chemicals, electronics, metals, tourism, textiles, fishing.*
Currency: *pound sterling*

1 *England, U.K.*

United Kingdom

1 *Senior judges in ceremonial dress gather at the Palace of Westminster in London for the State Opening of Parliament.*

2 *A familiar London landmark, the Tower Bridge has spanned the River Thames since completion in 1894.*

3 *Coal dust blackens the face of a miner in Rhondda Valley, heart of the Welsh mining industry, which lies outside Cardiff.*

4 *Surrounded by piles of tartans—materials bearing plaid designs usually associated with Scottish clans—a worker stacks cloth in a factory at Hawick, a textile center.*

Ireland

5 *A glass cutter touches up a sample of the fine glassware for which Waterford has been famous since the 18th century.*

6 *Stone walls on Inishmore Island protect man-made soil of sand and seaweed, which transforms barren rock to fertile fields.*

2 *England, U.K.*

3 *Wales, U.K.*

4 *Scotland, U.K.*

5 *Ireland*

6 *Ireland*

A
B

DENMARK

Sylt

North
Frisian
Islands

Kiel Bay *Fehmarn* BALTIC
SEA

Rugen

C *Helgoland* *Kiel Canal* ● **Kiel** Stralsund *Usedom*

● **Rostock**

D NORTH
SEA *East Frisian Islands* ● **Lubeck** ● Wismar MECKLENBURG P O M E R A N I A

E *West Frisian Islands* ● **Wilhelmshaven** ● **Bremerhaven** ● **Schwerin** ● Neubrandenburg

● **Hamburg** *Lake Muritz*

F *IJsselmeer* ● **Groningen** F R I E S L A N D ● **Oldenburg** ● **Bremen** E U R O P E A N *Elbe River* *Oder River* POLAND

G HOLLAND ● Edam Flevoland
Polder ● Enschede N O R T H E R N *Mittelland* *Weser River* ● **Wolfsburg** Brandenburg P L A I N ⊛ **Berlin** Frankfurt
an der Oder

NETHERLANDS ● **Haarlem** ● **Amsterdam** *Canal* ● **Hannover** ● **Potsdam**

H ● **Leiden** ● Delft ● **Utrecht** ● **Arnhem** ● **Osnabruck** ● **Braunschweig** ● **Magdeburg** B R A N D E N B U R G

● **The Hague** ● **Rotterdam** ● **Nijmegen** WESTPHALIA ● **Bielefeld** ● **Dessau** ● **Cottbus**

J *Barrier dam* ● **Dordrecht** *Rhine* *Maas River* ● **Hamm** HARZ MOUNTAINS *Elbe River* *Neisse R.*

Oosterschelde ● **Eindhoven** ● **Essen** ● **Dortmund** ● **Gottingen** ● Stolberg ● **Halle** *Spree R.* *Saale R.*

FLANDERS ● **Duisburg** *Ruhr River* ● **Leipzig** Gorlitz

Ostend ● **Brugge** ● **Antwerp** ● **Dusseldorf** ● **Wuppertal** ● **Kassel** S ● **Dresden**

K ● **Gent** *Scheldt River* **GERMANY** *Fulda* A O R E MOUNTAINS

BELGIUM ● **Maastricht** ● **Koln** ● **Erfurt** *Saale R.* ● **Gera** ● **Chemnitz**

L ⊛ **Brussels** ● **Aachen** ● **Bonn** Gotha ● **Jena** ● **Zwickau** O R E

● Waterloo ● **Liege** *Werra River* *River* ● **Erfurt**

● **Charleroi** ● **Namur** EIFEL ● Plauen

M ARDENNES ● **Koblenz** *River*

● **Wiesbaden** ● **Frankfurt am Main** *Main River* ● Bamberg BOHEMIAN CZECH REPUBLIC

N **LUXEMBOURG** ● **Mainz** ● **Darmstadt**

Mosel River ● **Wurzburg** FOREST

O ⊛ Luxembourg ● **Mannheim** ● **Nurnberg**

Esch ● **Heidelberg**

FRANCE ● **Saarbrucken** BAVARIA

P ● **Heilbronn** ● **Regensburg**

● **Karlsruhe** *Danube River*

Rhine River BLACK FOREST ● **Stuttgart** JURA

Q *Neckar River* SWABIAN ● **Ulm** *Inn River*

● **Augsburg** ● Dachau

R ● **Freiburg** ● **Munich**

S Neuschwanstein
Castle BAVARIAN ALPS

*Lake
Constance* ● Garmisch-
Partenkirchen

SWITZERLAND *Zugspitze*
9,721 FEET
2,963 METERS AUSTRIA

T

Belgium, the Nether-
lands, and Luxembourg
spearheaded the move
toward European unity
by co-founding Benelux.
An economic and social
alliance between the
three countries formed
after World War II, it

was a forerunner of the
European Community.
Germany plays a
major role in the EC.
Despite a deepening re-
cession since unification
of East and West in
1990, Germany remains
an economic giant.

0   KILOMETERS   100

0   STATUTE MILES   75

For map legend see page 21.

U

1 2 3 4 5 6 7 8 9 10 11 12 13 14 15 16 17 18

productive that the Dutch can export cheese, vegetables, and flowers. Their most beloved export, though, may be the tradition of a December visit from St. Nicholas—Sinterklaas. In the U. S., this saint's nickname is Santa Claus.

Official name: *Kingdom of the Netherlands*
Area: *16,023 sq mi (41,500 sq km)*
Population: *15,193,000*
Capital: *Amsterdam (pop. 694,900)*
The Hague, seat of government (pop. 444,242)
Ethnic groups: *Dutch*
Language: *Dutch*
Religious groups: *Roman Catholic, Protestant*
Economy: *Agr: livestock, flowers, grains, potatoes, sugar beets. Ind: food processing, chemicals, oil, metals, natural gas, machinery, electronics, fishing*
Currency: *Netherlands guilder*

Belgium

Belgium's lowlands have been a battleground over the centuries. Most recently, British and American troops fought the Germans there in World War II. From a wide coastal plain the land rolls gently upward to the hilly Ardennes region.

Ruled at times by Spain, Austria, France, or the Netherlands, Belgium won independence from the Dutch in 1830. The country remains divided: In the south live French-speaking Walloons, and in the north dwell Dutch-speaking Flemings. Rivalry is so intense that each group insists on having its own regional government in addition to national rule. By law Brussels, the capital, is bilingual. Its street signs and official documents are printed in both languages.

Brussels is headquarters for both the European Community and the North Atlantic Treaty Organization (NATO)—a defense organization to which the U. S. and Canada belong. Now that the threat of communist attack has subsided and EC nations are discussing their own security measures, NATO's role is being reassessed.

Located near the industrial regions of France, Germany, and the Netherlands, Belgium has long been a trade center. One of the first European countries to industrialize in the 1800s, Belgium has since had a strong manufacturing economy, fed by large coal deposits. As aging factories and mines close in the south and the northern Flemish birthrate exceeds that of the southern Walloons, Belgium's economic power is shifting north, increasing regional tensions.

Most Belgians live in crowded urban areas. The old cities, such as Gent, Brugge, Liège,

and the port of Antwerp (an important diamond-cutting center), charm tourists with the architecture of their medieval buildings.

Official name: *Kingdom of Belgium*
Area: *11,783 sq mi (30,518 sq km)*
Population: *10,041,000*
Capital: *Brussels (pop. 136,700; met. pop. 1,331,000)*
Ethnic groups: *Fleming, Walloon, mixed*
Language: *Dutch, French, German*
Religious groups: *Roman Catholic*
Economy: *Agr: livestock, grains, sugar beets, potatoes. Ind: metals, chemicals, food processing, diamonds, motor vehicles, textiles, glass, oil, coal*
Currency: *Belgian franc*

Luxembourg

The Grand Duchy of Luxembourg began as a castle built in 963 on a rocky cliff, once the site of a Roman fort. Walled towns grew up around the castle, turning the area into a strong fortress whose rulers won great power in the Middle Ages. Today Luxembourg survives as one of Europe's smallest countries. Bordered by Belgium, Germany, and France, the duchy is only 51 miles (82 km) long and 35 miles (56 km) wide.

Scenic forests and deep river valleys in the north give way to the Bon Pays, or "good land," a farming region where wheat, oats, potatoes, and livestock flourish. Along the Mosel River, wine grapes grow in terraced vineyards. Iron ore deposits in the south, which once supported Luxembourg's iron and steel industry, are nearly gone; today most raw materials must be imported from France. The capital city, also called Luxembourg, is an international financial center where about 180 banks have branches.

Luxembourg has three official languages: French and German (used in schools, government, and the press), and Lëtzebuergesch, a Germanic dialect used in conversation. In crowded cities that mix modern and medieval buildings, Luxembourgers enjoy a high standard of living. No wonder their national anthem proclaims, "We want to remain what we are."

Official name: *Grand Duchy of Luxembourg*
Area: *998 sq mi (2,586 sq km)*
Population: *388,000*
Capital: *Luxembourg (pop. 75,600)*
Ethnic groups: *Luxembourger, Portuguese, Italian*
Language: *Lëtzebuergesch, French, German*
Religious groups: *Roman Catholic*
Economy: *Agr: grains, livestock, potatoes, grapes. Ind: banking, iron, steel, food processing, chemicals*
Currency: *Luxembourg franc*

Netherlands

Netherlands means "the lowlands," and true to its name nearly half of this small, flat country lies below sea level. Over the centuries the Dutch have learned how to protect their land and how to reclaim more from the sea.

They stabilized the natural sand dunes along the coasts and built dikes to keep the sea out. Then they cut ditches and canals for drainage and pumped the wetlands dry. Once run by windmills, pumps are now driven by steam or electricity. These drained lands, or polders, have rich farming soil, but the Dutch also build factories, airports, and even towns on them.

Without sea defenses, high tides would flood almost half the country twice a day. The latest engineering feat, the Delta Project completed in 1986, built four huge barriers to keep the North Sea from overflowing the estuary of the Rhine, Maas, and Schelde Rivers during storms.

In the 17th century the Netherlands was a leading sea power, and world trade brought riches. Historic cities such as Amsterdam, Leiden, Delft, and The Hague preserve the art and architecture of this golden age. Still active in trading, the Netherlands has one of the world's busiest ports at Rotterdam. In 1991, Maastricht made modern history as the city where a major European Community treaty was drafted.

Living in a very densely populated country, the Dutch use space cleverly. Houses one room wide rise four stories; apartments span highways. High technology makes small farms so

Germany

The tremendous political changes that swept Eastern Europe in 1989 and 1990 reunited East and West Germany after a separation of 40 years. Berlin became the national capital again, and government offices will gradually move there from Bonn, former capital of West Germany.

Germany was previously united as a country for only 74 years. A group of diverse states joined together in 1871 to form the German nation. It grew into a strong industrial and military power but was defeated in two world wars. After World War II, the four Allied countries divided Germany into four sectors.

In 1949 the areas controlled by the United States, France, and the United Kingdom became the Federal Republic of Germany, or West Germany. A communist state called the German Democratic Republic, or East Germany, was created out of the lands occupied by Soviet forces. The capital, Berlin, was divided, too. East Germany made East Berlin its capital. West Germany, while maintaining ties with West Berlin, set up a separate capital at Bonn. In 1961 East Germans built the Berlin Wall.

Then in 1989, in dramatic response to demonstrations for political freedom, the East German government opened the Berlin Wall and East and West Germans mingled freely once more. Within weeks the Communist Party leaders resigned, free elections were held, and on October 3, 1990, East and West Germany were united. The nation now boasts the largest population in Europe west of the European portion of Russia.

On Germany's northern plain, lakes and marshes punctuate a landscape scattered with large moraines. In places the soil is suitable for pasture, and dairy farming is important. Urban centers of this region include Hamburg, Germany's second largest city and an important port on the Elbe River. Germany's rivers and canals help supply transportation routes for raw materials and manufactured goods. The Rhine, flowing through western Germany's industrial belt, is Europe's major commercial waterway.

On the southern edge of the northern plain, windblown dust and silt, called loess, create fertile soil for farms. Small, efficient farms predominate in the west; in the east, the less productive collectives from communist days are being converted to smaller, privately owned units. Partly because of this fertile land, the northern plain has always been Germany's most urbanized region. Berlin, the largest city as well as capital, is the focal point of the northeast.

Germany's chief coal deposits also lie under the plain, in the heavily industrialized Ruhr River Valley. Here German factory workers, supplemented by "guest workers," mostly from Turkey, Italy, and Yugoslavia, produce steel, chemicals, automobiles, and other goods. In eastern Germany, swift streams in the central uplands provide hydroelectric power for one of Europe's most important textile industries, based in Chemnitz. But other industries nearby use coal-fueled power. Germany's industrial regions and those of its Eastern European neighbors are among Europe's most polluted areas.

Scientists claim that pollution from automobiles and industry is causing the death of Germany's woodlands. Stumps and skeletons of dead pine trees stretch for miles where thick forests once stood. The Bohemian Forest, on Germany's border with the Czech Republic, has been devastated, and many trees have died in the fabled Black Forest in the southwest. Sulfur dioxide emissions, produced by burning lignite, or brown coal, are chiefly blamed.

The Danube River flows east from the Black Forest toward Bavaria. The state's capital and industrial center, Munich, is famed for its beer gardens and Oktoberfest, a 16-day annual spree of feasting and beer-drinking. To the south, the Bavarian Alps rise above dairy farms, bogs, and sparkling glacial lakes. Northwest of Munich stands Dachau, site of Nazi Germany's first concentration camp, established in 1933. A museum there memorializes the former inmates.

Unification of the peoples of the diverse regions of east and west has proved more costly than expected, both socially and economically. Industrial productivity increased in the west but decreased in the east, where unemployment remains high. Disillusionment with increasing taxes and decreasing benefits has sparked tension between east and west, along with persecution of foreign refugees and guest workers by fringe groups. But Germany—an economic giant with one of the world's strongest currencies, pillar of the European Community—continues to strive despite all odds to produce a high standard of living for its united citizenry.

Official name: *Federal Republic of Germany*
Area: *137,857 sq mi (357,046 sq km)*
Population: *80,556,000*
Capital: *Berlin (pop. 3,376,800)*
Ethnic groups: *German*
Language: *German*
Religious groups: *Protestant, Roman Catholic*
Economy: *Agr: grains, potatoes, sugar beets, fruit, livestock. Ind: iron, steel, motor vehicles, machinery, chemicals, electronics, cement, shipbuilding, coal, machine tools, food processing, textiles, beer, wine*
Currency: *Deutsche mark*

1 *Netherlands*

2 *Belgium*

4 *Germany*

3 *Germany*

Netherlands

1 *Street-straddling apartments solve Rotterdam's limited space problem. The city has been largely rebuilt since World War II.*

Belgium

2 *A Godiva worker applies drops of chocolate to fondant-covered cherries. The Brussels-based company is known worldwide.*

Germany

3 *Built in the Bavarian Alps for "Mad" King Ludwig II, 19th-century Neuschwanstein Castle embodied his fantasy of the ideal castle. It inspired the one at Disneyland.*

4 *Jubilant, flag-waving crowds at Berlin's Brandenburg Gate celebrate the unification of Germany at midnight, October 2-3, 1990.*

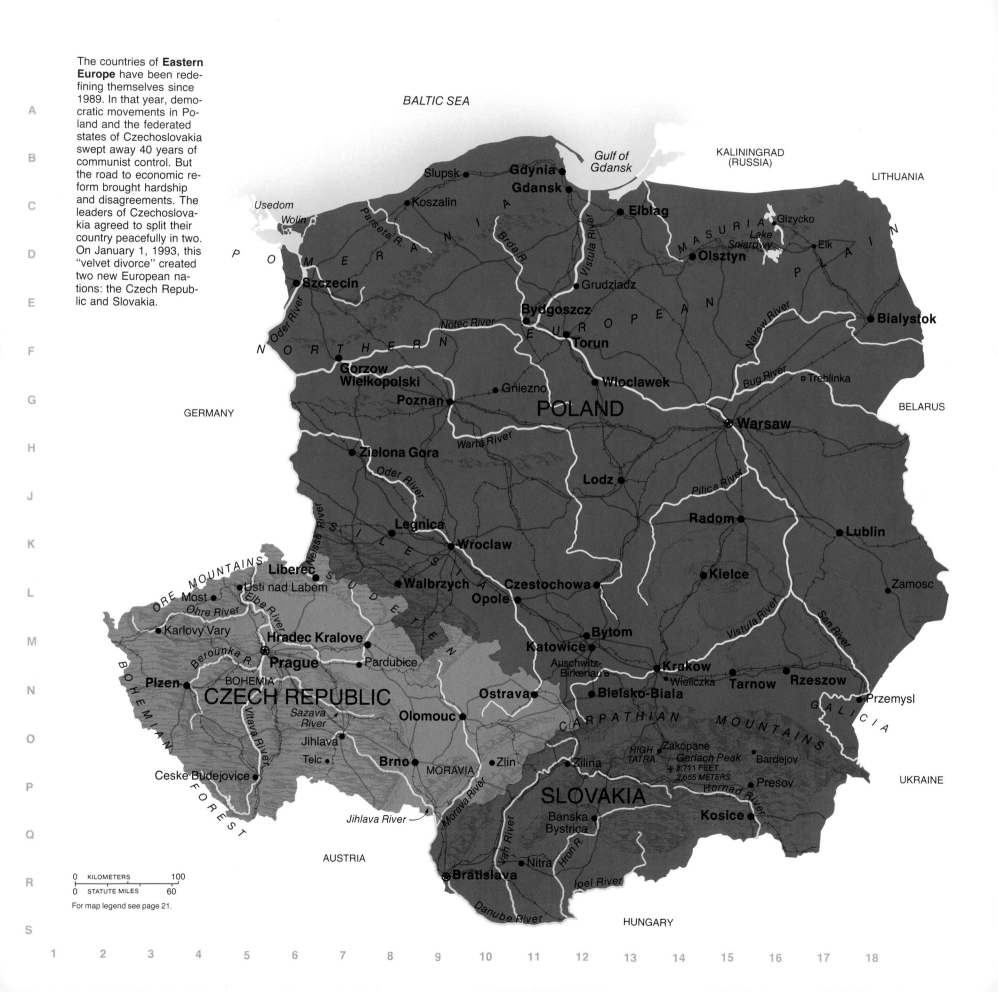

The countries of **Eastern Europe** have been redefining themselves since 1989. In that year, democratic movements in Poland and the federated states of Czechoslovakia swept away 40 years of communist control. But the road to economic reform brought hardship and disagreements. The leaders of Czechoslovakia agreed to split their country peacefully in two. On January 1, 1993, this "velvet divorce" created two new European nations: the Czech Republic and Slovakia.

BALTIC SEA

KALININGRAD
(RUSSIA)

LITHUANIA

Slupsk • **Gdynia**
Gdansk
Gulf of
Gdansk

Koszalin • **Elblag**

Usedom
Wolin

MASURIA
Gizycko
Lake
Sniardwy
Elk

PLAIN

Olsztyn

Parseta R.

Brda R.

POMERANIA

Vistula River

Grudziadz

Szczecin

Bydgoszcz

Bialystok

Oder River

Notec River

Torun

EUROPEAN

Narew River

Gorzow Wielkopolski

NORTHERN

Warta River

Wloclawek

Gniezno

Bug River

Treblinka

Poznan

POLAND

GERMANY

Warsaw

BELARUS

Zielona Gora

Oder River

Lodz

Pilica River

SILESIA

Legnica

Radom

Lublin

Weisse River

Wroclaw

Kielce

Zamosc

ORE MOUNTAINS

Liberec

Walbrzych
SUDETEN

Czestochowa

Opole

Vistula River

San River

Most

Usti nad Labem

Karlovy Vary

Hradec Kralove

Elbe River

Ohre River

Bytom
Katowice

Krakow

Przemysl

Prague

Pardubice

Auschwitz-Birkenau

Wieliczka

Tarnow

Rzeszow

GALICIA

Berounka R.

Ostrava

Bielsko-Biala

CARPATHIAN

MOUNTAINS

Plzen

BOHEMIA

CZECH REPUBLIC

Sazava River

Olomouc

Vltava River

Jihlava

Telc

Brno

MORAVIA

Zlin

Zilina

HIGH TATRA

Zakopane

Gerlach Peak
+ 8,711 FEET
2,655 METERS

Bardejov

UKRAINE

BOHEMIAN

Ceske Budejovice

FOREST

Jihlava River

Morava River

SLOVAKIA

Presov

Kosice

AUSTRIA

Nitra

Van River

Hron R.

Banska Bystrica

Bratislava

Danube River

Ipel River

HUNGARY

0 KILOMETERS 100
0 STATUTE MILES 60

For map legend see page 21.

In 1980, workers led by Lech Walesa formed Solidarity, the first free postwar trade union in Eastern Europe. Bowing to pressure for democratic reform, the government allowed free elections in 1989. The new coalition government moved toward a market economy, including privatization of industry. But "shock therapy," applied to the runaway inflation that followed, led to a recession, and the 29-party parliament was slow in agreeing on solutions. By 1993, signs had appeared of economic growth and stability.

Official name: *Republic of Poland*
Area: *120,725 sq mi (312,677 sq km)*
Population: *38,377,000*
Capital: *Warsaw (pop. 1,655,100)*
Ethnic groups: *Polish*
Language: *Polish*
Religious groups: *Roman Catholic*
Economy: *Agr: grains, potatoes, sugar beets, oilseeds, livestock. Ind: machinery, iron, steel, mining, chemicals, shipbuilding, food processing, textiles*
Currency: *zloty*

Poland

Situated on the huge Northern European Plain, Poland is protected by the Baltic Sea in the north and the Carpathian Mountains in the south. To east and west it lies open, an easy target for invading armies since its founding in the tenth century.

In 1939, Adolf Hitler's German troops overran western Poland in an invasion that started World War II. The people suffered greatly during the war. At least six million Poles died, many in notorious concentration camps such as Treblinka and Auschwitz-Birkenau. Warsaw, the capital, was reduced to ashes and rubble.

After peace came in 1945, the Poles rebuilt their historic capital, and modern Warsaw sprang up around it. The former Soviet Union annexed provinces in eastern Poland and exchanged them for western lands belonging to defeated Germany, sliding Poland westward.

In 1947 a communist government came to power. But the Poles' love of freedom and strong ties to the Roman Catholic Church kept communism from profoundly changing their society. Peasant resistance to Soviet-style collective farms left most of their land in private hands. Crops of potatoes, wheat, rye, and sugar beets are still raised on peasant farms.

The most valuable lands acquired in 1945 contain the Silesian coalfields. These and other rich mineral deposits in the south and southwest fueled an enormous growth in heavy industry. But with industrialization came some of the worst water and air pollution in Europe.

Czech Republic

Three years after crowds gathered in Prague's Wenceslas Square to celebrate the end of communist control in Czechoslovakia, the country divided. The decision was made by Czech and Slovak leaders, not by popular vote.

The new Czech Republic includes the regions of Bohemia and Moravia and holds two-thirds of the former population of Czechoslovakia. Between low mountain ranges, productive farmland yields crops of grain, sugar beets, and hops—used in the famed Czech beer breweries. Coal deposits fuel much of the industry, which is centered around Prague, Brno, and Ostrava.

From the 10th to the 16th century, Bohemia and Moravia formed a powerful empire ruled from Prague, the modern Czech capital. A city of palaces, churches, and one of Europe's oldest universities, Prague remains the cultural, political, and commercial heart of the Czech nation.

Later centuries of Austrian control ended in 1918 with the creation of Czechoslovakia. Communists governed the country after World War II until 1989, when a democratic movement peacefully voted them out of office.

The Czech Republic seems better poised for economic success than does Slovakia. Historically, the Czechs have stronger ties to the West, and they have moved faster in adapting to a market economy. But Czech prosperity is also affected by Slovakia's—the two countries, for now, are tied through trade and currency.

Official name: *Czech Republic*
Area: *30,450 sq mi (78,864 sq km)*
Population: *10,299,000*
Capital: *Prague (pop. 1,213,800)*
Ethnic groups: *Czech, Moravian*
Language: *Czech, Polish*
Religious groups: *Roman Catholic*
Economy: *Agr: grains, sugar beets, hops, livestock. Ind: machinery, machine tools, electrical and transportation equipment, chemicals, wool, leather*
Currency: *koruna*

Slovakia

As Slovakia went its own way after the division of Czechoslovakia on January 1, 1993, it faced far greater challenges than the Czech Republic. Slovakia has only half as many people, a high unemployment rate, and a less developed political and economic structure.

The country is largely mountainous. The Carpathian Mountains provide iron ore, copper, and low-grade coal, as well as recreational opportunities for visitors. Traditionally agricultural, Slovakia industrialized rapidly during the years of communist control following World War II. But vineyards still cover many lower slopes, and potatoes, oats, and flax grow in mountain valleys. Grains, sugar beets, vegetables, and livestock are raised in the fertile valleys of the Danube and other rivers of the south.

One economic hope lies in attracting foreign investment in industry. So far, successes include deals for car assembly, food processing, and the manufacture of household appliances.

Slovakia endured a thousand years of domination by Hungary that ended with World War I. Bratislava, Slovakia's capital, served for a while as capital of the Austro-Hungarian Empire. Today, Hungarians make up 11 percent of the population, but the Slovak government is wary of this strong minority.

Official name: *Slovak Republic*
Area: *18,921 sq mi (49,006 sq km)*
Population: *5,269,000*
Capital: *Bratislava (pop. 441,500)*
Ethnic groups: *Slovak, Hungarian*
Language: *Slovak, Hungarian*
Religious groups: *Roman Catholic*
Economy: *Agr: grains, sugar beets, potatoes, livestock. Ind: armaments, steel*
Currency: *koruna*

1 *Poland*

Poland

1 *A master craftsman tunes the back of a violin that he is making. Poles produce some of the world's finest stringed instruments.*

2 *The High Tatra Mountains form a backdrop to farmers pitching hay onto a wagon. A fifth of the Polish people live on farms, where horses still outnumber tractors.*

Czech Republic

3 *In the historic capital of Prague, floodlit St. Vitus Cathedral rises behind the facade of Prague Castle, high above 14th-century Charles Bridge on the Vltava River.*

Slovakia

4 *A factory worker stitches a shoe. Geared toward heavy industry, Slovakia must now struggle to produce its own consumer items, easily obtained before division.*

2 *Poland*

3 *Czech Republic*

4 *Slovakia*

A
B LATVIA

Druya
Polatsk

C LITHUANIA Vitsyebsk BELARUS

D Hrodna Barysaw Orsha
                    Mahilyow
                    Minsk

E   Byalezina River   Dnipro R.

Baranavichy
F Pisich River Babruysk

G Brest Pinsk Prypyats R. Homyel RUSSIA
POLAND   Pinsk Marshes   Desna R.
H Bug R. Kovel Chornobyl (Chernobyl) Chernihiv
Lutsk Styr River   Sumy
J
Rivne Kyyiv (Kiev)
K Lviv Zhytomyr   Kharkiv RUSSIA
                    UKRAINE Dnipro River
L Ternopil Khmelnytskyy Cherkasy Poltava DONETS RIDGE
SLOVAKIA CARPATHIAN Ivano-Frankivsk Vinnytsya Donets River Slovyansk
M Uzhhorod   PODILSKA UPLAND Uman   Luhansk
HUNGARY MOUNTAINS Dnister River Kirovohrad Dnipropetrovsk
N Tysa R. Chernivtsi Soroca Zaporizhzhya Donetsk
O Prut River Balti Ribnita Kryvyy Rih
MOLDOVA   Melitopol Mariupol
P ROMANIA Chisinau Tiraspol Mykolayiv Berdyansk
Q Bender Comrat Kherson Henichesk SEA OF AZOV
Leova Odesa
R Cahul Bilhorod-Dnistrovskyy CRIMEA Kerch
S BLACK SEA Simferopol
T Sevastopol Yalta
U

1 2 3 4 5 6 7 8 9 10 11 12 13 14 15 16 17 18 19 20

0 KILOMETERS 100
0 STATUE MILES 100
For map legend see page 21.

These three countries, along with the Baltics, long served as a bridge between Europe and Russia, and were coveted by rulers in both. The **Ottoman Empire,** based in Turkey, also had designs on Ukraine and Moldova. Now all three republics hope to capitalize on their location by developing market ties with both East and West.

Alone among the former Soviet republics, Belarus and Ukraine did not need to apply for United Nations membership after independence. They have belonged since 1945—the result of a Soviet move to secure more UN voting power.

Ukraine

The second most populous of the former Soviet republics, Ukraine consists largely of low-lying, temperate grasslands known as the steppe. Mountains rise along the southwestern border and in southern Crimea. The country is well watered. Nearly all of Ukraine's 23,000 rivers drain into the Black Sea or the Sea of Azov.

Historically, Ukraine was part of an alliance of Slavic tribes known as Rus, formed in the ninth century and Christianized in 988 by Vladimir I. Its center was the city of Kiev; known to Ukrainians as Kyyiv, it remains their capital. Kievan Rus lasted some 300 years. Centuries of domination followed, first by the Mongol Empire, then by Lithuania and Poland.

Under the later rule of tsarist Russia and the Soviet Union, Ukrainians suffered centuries of oppression, and their culture declined. Soviet leader Joseph Stalin's forced collectivization of farms caused a famine in the 1930s in which millions of people starved. Millions more perished during the Nazi occupation of World War II.

The 1986 explosion at the Chornobyl (Chernobyl) nuclear power plant brought disaster upon northern Ukraine and Belarus and affected much of the rest of Europe. Ukrainians were angered by incomplete information from Moscow about the accident. After Chornobyl, opposition movements grew, leading to strikes and protests, until independence was gained in 1991.

Ethnic Ukrainians make up nearly three-fourths of the population. They speak Ukrainian, a Slavic language. Most practice the Eastern Orthodox faith. A smaller group of Ukrainian Catholics follow rites of the Eastern church but bear allegiance to the Pope in Rome. There is a Russian population of about 20 percent. Some 200,000 Tatars, a people banished from the Crimea to Central Asia in the 1940s by Stalin, have returned to take up claims in their homeland.

In densely populated Ukraine, villages of more than a thousand inhabitants are common. About two-thirds of the people live in cities. Industry specializes in heavy vehicles such as locomotives, ships, cars, and airliners. Major industrial areas are found in the east, particularly around the coalfields of the Donets basin. But industry suffers from a shortage of oil, materials, and customers ready to pay in currency.

Independent Ukraine faces many other problems, chiefly a chaotic economy with runaway inflation. Ukraine must also work out a division of assets and liabilities with Russia: the naval fleet on the Black Sea, army troops, and a huge debt. And Russia wants to regain control of Crimea, which it ceded to Ukraine in 1954.

But Ukraine's natural resources, such as coal and iron, make the long-term outlook promising. And the fertile soil produces a bountiful yield of grains, fruit, vegetables, meat, and dairy products. A recent study found Ukraine's agricultural, mineral, and industrial potential the highest of all the former Soviet republics.

Official name: *Ukraine*
Area: *233,206 sq mi (604,000 sq km)*
Population: *52,103,000*
Capital: *Kyyiv (Kiev) (pop. 2,587,000)*
Ethnic groups: *Ukrainian, Russian*
Language: *Ukrainian, Russian*
Religious groups: *Ukrainian Orthodox or Catholic*
Economy: *Agr: grains, livestock, vegetables, sugar beets, fruit. Ind: coal, steel, chemicals, machinery, transport equipment, textiles, electronics*
Proposed currency: *hryvnya*

Belarus

When 11 of the former Soviet republics voted in 1991 to create a Commonwealth of Independent States, they chose as their headquarters the city of Minsk, capital of Belarus.

Belarus, or White Russia, was settled around the seventh century by eastern Slavs. It came under the influence of Kiev and was controlled by neighboring powers until independence.

The country is mostly a low plain, watered by rivers, lakes, swamps, and marshes and almost one-third forested. Its natural resources include peat, used for fuel, potash, and small deposits of petroleum. Industry, all but wiped out during World War II, has made a comeback.

Because of Belarus's frontline location, the war also devastated its population, reducing it by nearly one-fourth. Today, about 80 percent of the people are ethnic Belarusans who speak a Slavic language. Independence has brought the problems of operating businesses profitably and finding new markets for goods, while coping with high inflation and skyrocketing fuel prices.

Official name: *Republic of Belarus*
Area: *80,154 sq mi (207,600 sq km)*
Population: *10,263,000*
Capital: *Minsk (pop. 1,589,000)*
Ethnic groups: *Belarusan, Russian*
Language: *Byelorusian, Russian*
Religious groups: *Belarusan Orthodox*
Economy: *Agr: grains, potatoes, flax, livestock. Ind: motor vehicles, machinery, chemicals, textiles*
Proposed currency: *taler*

Moldova

Small and arc-shaped, the Republic of Moldova hugs the border of neighboring Romania. Culturally and historically, Moldova has more in common with Romania than with its Slavic neighbors. Almost two-thirds of its people are ethnic Romanians who speak Romanian, a Romance language. At times independent, at times controlled by foreign powers, Moldova became part of Romania after World War I, only to be seized by the Soviets in 1940.

Moldova's land is fertile, a hilly plain sliced by many rivers into valleys and rocky ravines. Grapes and other fruit and vegetables grow so well in the mild climate that they were exported throughout the former Soviet Union. Wine making and bottling are major Moldovan industries.

Ethnic divisions tax independent Moldova. Russian-speaking Slavs in the industrial area east of the Dnister River have demanded independence. A Turkish Christian minority is also pressing for autonomy. And many Romanian Moldovans desire reunification with Romania.

Official name: *Republic of Moldova*
Area: *13,000 sq mi (33,700 sq km)*
Population: *4,372,000*
Capital: *Chisinau (Kishinev) (pop. 676,000)*
Ethnic groups: *Moldovan, Ukrainian, Russian*
Language: *Romanian, Ukrainian, Russian*
Religious groups: *Romanian Orthodox*
Economy: *Agr: fruit, vegetables, sugar beets, tobacco, grains. Ind: food processing, wine, textiles*
Proposed currency: *Moldovan leu*

Belarus

1 *Houses reflected in still waters at Minsk form part of a reconstructed city. Almost totally destroyed in World War II, the city was rebuilt on its ruins. Belarus's capital, Minsk is a cultural and industrial center.*

Moldova

2 *Pensioners help sort corn at harvesttime. Moldova's rich soil and mild climate produced a quarter of the fruit and vegetables grown in 1990 in the former Soviet Union.*

Ukraine

3 *In Odesa, Ukraine's chief port, passengers land from ferries and sightseeing hydrofoils. Oceangoing freighters at rear can sail world shipping lanes via the Black Sea.*

4 *Ukrainian folk dancers rehearse at a studio in Kyyiv (Kiev). Dressed in traditional costumes, singers, dancers, and musicians of the Veryovka Ukrainian Folk Choir have performed worldwide.*

5 *First graders of Odesa carry flowers for their teachers on the opening day of school.*

1 *Belarus*

2 *Moldova*

3 *Ukraine*

4 *Ukraine*

5 *Ukraine*

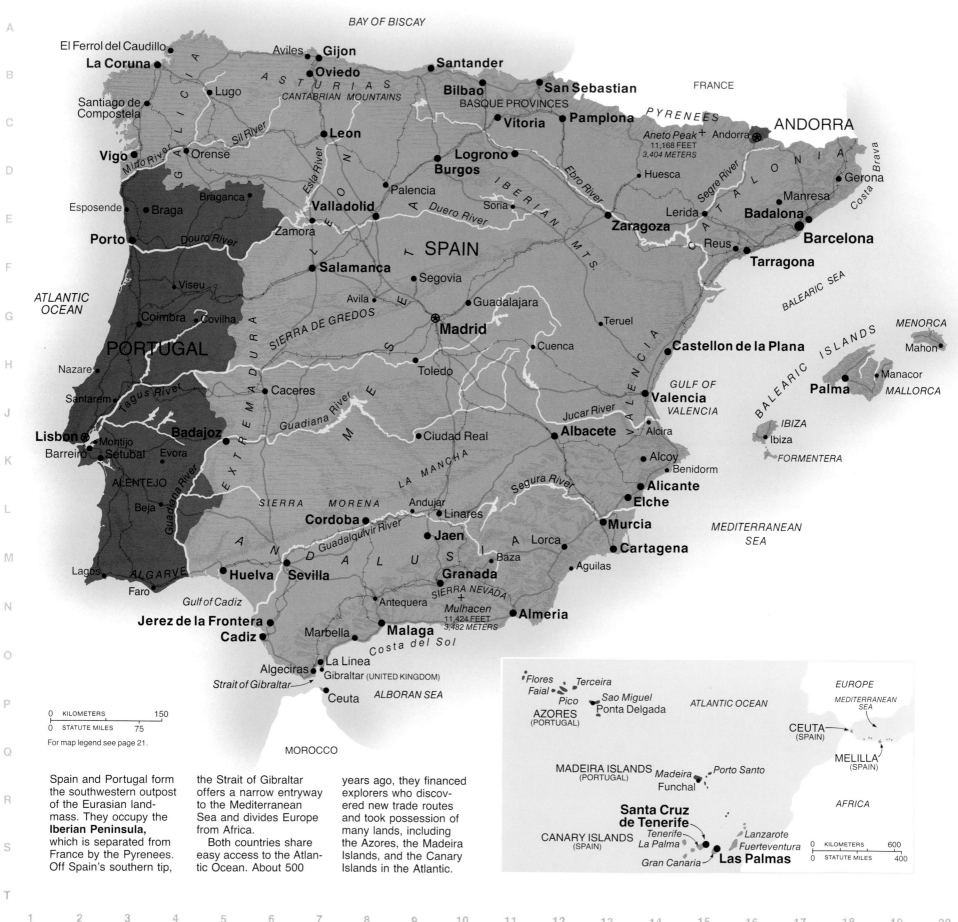

BAY OF BISCAY

A
B
C
D
E
F
G
H
J
K
L
M
N
O
P
Q
R
S
T

El Ferrol del Caudillo
La Coruna
Aviles Gijon
Oviedo
Santander
Bilbao San Sebastian
FRANCE

Lugo
ASTURIAS
CANTABRIAN MOUNTAINS
BASQUE PROVINCES
PYRENEES
ANDORRA

Santiago de
Compostela
GALICIA
Sil River
Vitoria Pamplona
Aneto Peak +
11,168 FEET
3,404 METERS
Andorra

Vigo
Orense
Leon
Burgos
Logrono
Huesca
Segre River
Costa Brava
Gerona

Mino River
Esla River
Palencia
Soria
IBERIAN MTS.
Manresa
Badalona

Esposende Braga
Braganca
Valladolid
Duero River
Ebro River
Zaragoza
Lerida
CATALONIA
Barcelona

Porto
Douro River
Zamora
SPAIN
Reus
Tarragona

Salamanca
Segovia
ATLANTIC
OCEAN
Viseu
SIERRA DE GREDOS
Avila
Madrid
Guadalajara
Teruel
Castellon de la Plana
BALEARIC SEA
MENORCA
Mahon

Coimbra Covilha
Cuenca
GULF OF
VALENCIA
BALEARIC ISLANDS
Palma
Manacor
MALLORCA

PORTUGAL
EXTREMADURA
Caceres
Toledo
Valencia
VALENCIA

Nazare
Tagus River
Guadiana River
Ciudad Real
Jucar River
Alcira
IBIZA
Ibiza

Santarem
Badajoz
Alcoy Benidorm
FORMENTERA

Lisbon
Montijo
Setubal
Evora
Guadiana River
LA MANCHA
Albacete
Segura River
Alicante
Elche

Barreiro
ALENTEJO
Beja
SIERRA MORENA
Andujar
Linares
Murcia
Cartagena
MEDITERRANEAN
SEA

Lagos
ALGARVE
Cordoba
Guadalquivir River
Jaen
Lorca
Baza
Aguilas

Faro
Huelva
Sevilla
ANDALUSIA
Granada
SIERRA NEVADA +
Mulhacen
11,424 FEET
3,482 METERS
Almeria

Gulf of Cadiz
Jerez de la Frontera
Cadiz
Antequera
Marbella
Malaga
Costa del Sol

Algeciras
La Linea
Gibraltar (UNITED KINGDOM)
Strait of Gibraltar
Ceuta
ALBORAN SEA

MOROCCO

0 KILOMETERS 150
0 STATUTE MILES 75
For map legend see page 21.

Spain and Portugal form
the southwestern outpost
of the Eurasian land-
mass. They occupy the
Iberian Peninsula,
which is separated from
France by the Pyrenees.
Off Spain's southern tip,

the Strait of Gibraltar
offers a narrow entryway
to the Mediterranean
Sea and divides Europe
from Africa.
Both countries share
easy access to the Atlan-
tic Ocean. About 500

years ago, they financed
explorers who discov-
ered new trade routes
and took possession of
many lands, including
the Azores, the Madeira
Islands, and the Canary
Islands in the Atlantic.

Flores Terceira
Faial
Pico Sao Miguel
AZORES Ponta Delgada
(PORTUGAL)
ATLANTIC OCEAN
EUROPE
MEDITERRANEAN
SEA

CEUTA
(SPAIN)

MADEIRA ISLANDS
(PORTUGAL) Madeira Porto Santo
Funchal
MELILLA
(SPAIN)

AFRICA

Santa Cruz
de Tenerife
CANARY ISLANDS
(SPAIN)
Tenerife
La Palma
Lanzarote
Fuerteventura
Gran Canaria
Las Palmas

0 KILOMETERS 600
0 STATUTE MILES 400

1 2 3 4 5 6 7 8 9 10 11 12 13 14 15 16 17 18 19 20

The **Azores** and **Madeira**, two strategic archipelagoes hundreds of miles away from Portugal in the Atlantic Ocean, are autonomous regions of the Portuguese Republic. The Azores, covered with lush vegetation, are home to about 253,000 people. Their main products are pineapples, tea, and canned fish. On Madeira, mineral-rich soil, abundant sunshine, and moist sea breezes result in a profusion of flowers. The 275,000 inhabitants support an economy based on sugar, wine, bananas, and hand embroidery, boosted by a growing tourist trade. Visitors arriving by sea or by air are greeted with vistas of plunging cliffs and terraced fields and gardens.

Official name: *Portuguese Republic*
Area: *35,672 sq mi (92,389 sq km)*
Population: *10,481,000*
Capital: *Lisbon (pop. 829,600)*
Ethnic groups: *Portuguese*
Language: *Portuguese*
Religious groups: *Roman Catholic*
Economy: *Agr: grains, potatoes, grapes, olives. Ind: textiles, shoes, wood and cork products, paper, chemicals, appliances, wine, ceramics, fishing, tourism*
Currency: *Portuguese escudo*

Portugal

The Portuguese are proud of their seagoing history. Builders of Europe's first great maritime empire, Portuguese explorers established colonies around the world in the 15th and 16th centuries. Their language is still spoken by 200 million people in Portugal's former possessions in Africa, Asia, and South America.

A member since 1986 of the European Community, Portugal has managed to expand its economy. To supplement traditional pursuits of fishing and farming, the country manufactures such products as textiles, chemicals, and electrical appliances. Lisbon and Porto are the main industrial centers, but most Portuguese live in rural areas along the coast or in river valleys.

The Tagus River flows across the middle of Portugal, dividing it roughly in two. To the north, farmers plant mostly grain crops and potatoes in cool, wet highlands. In vineyards of the Douro River Valley grow the grapes for port wine, one of Portugal's most important exports. The gently rolling plains south of the Tagus River produce fruit, olives, and the cork oak trees that provide another important export, cork. Eighty percent of the world's supply comes from Portugal, chiefly from the Alentejo region.

The Portuguese pour heart and soul into cultural traditions such as the fado—a bittersweet folk song accompanied by two guitars—and popular sports such as soccer and bullfighting. In Portugal, skillful *cavaleiros* fight the bull on horseback, and the bull is not killed at the end.

Spain

In Europe, only Switzerland and Austria are more mountainous than Spain. The Cantabrian Mountains rise on Spain's northern coast, while the Sierra Nevada stretch across the south. The Meseta, a tableland slashed by deep river valleys, covers much of the interior, and the Pyrenees cut off Spain from France. Other ranges ripple across the land, dividing it into regions that are further set apart by speech. Nearly 75 percent of all Spaniards speak Castilian Spanish, the dialect of Castile, a historic region in northern and central Spain. It is the country's official language. Regional languages include Catalan, Galician, and Basque.

Provinces in the western Pyrenees have been home to the Basques for 5,000 years. Bilbao, one of Spain's biggest ports and a center of shipbuilding and steel manufacturing, is located there. Struggling to achieve independence, Basque separatists have clashed often, sometimes violently, with state authorities.

Spain encompasses three climates and agricultural zones. Farmers grow corn, apples, pears, beans, and potatoes in the cool, wet northwest. They also raise beef and dairy cattle there, on the country's best pastureland. On the Meseta, the hot summers, cold winters, and sparse rainfall are better suited for grazing sheep and goats and for growing wheat and barley. The southern coast, with its dry summers and mild winters, abounds in citrus fruit, wine grapes, and olives—major export crops. Spain trades its fruit, vegetable, and grain crops with other countries in the European Community. Two-thirds of all its exports go to the EC.

Madrid, Spain's capital and largest city, is located on the Meseta. It is a busy, rapidly growing financial center. Yet it follows a traditional Spanish rhythm of leisurely two-hour lunches and late-night suppers. Diners rarely sit down before nine o'clock.

Outside Madrid, most Spaniards live in cities on the Mediterranean coast. Spain's second largest city, Barcelona, is a major industrial port. In the 1950s Spain began to modernize its economy, stressing industry rather than agriculture. Automobile production grew rapidly; it now ranks third in Europe. Tourism, another important source of income, attracts more than 50 million visitors a year to sunny beaches, national festivals, and historic sites.

In 711, North Africans later known as Moors conquered Spain. One of their castles, the Alhambra, overlooks the city of Granada. Carved with elaborate Islamic designs, its rooms open onto tiled courtyards with splashing fountains. Spain drove out the last of the Moors in 1492, the year it sponsored Christopher Columbus's voyage to North America. By the mid-1500s, Spain controlled a rich empire in the Americas and was the most powerful country in Europe.

Over the next centuries, Spain suffered a series of wars and rebellions, and eventually lost its empire. In 1936 civil war broke out. Gen. Francisco Franco's forces won in 1939, and he ruled as dictator until his death in 1975. Today the king is chief of state and presides over a parliamentary monarchy. Spain's territories include two ocean communities: the hilly Balearic Islands in the Mediterranean Sea and the Canary Islands, a group of small volcanic islands in the Atlantic Ocean. Awaiting autonomy are the cities of **Ceuta** and **Melilla** on the North African coast, the last of Spain's overseas empire.

Official name: *Kingdom of Spain*
Area: *194,897 sq mi (504,782 sq km)*
Population: *38,554,000*
Capital: *Madrid (met. pop. 2,984,000)*
Ethnic groups: *Spanish, Catalan, Galician, Basque*
Language: *Spanish, Catalan, Galician, Basque*
Religious groups: *Roman Catholic*
Economy: *Agr: grains, fruit, vegetables, olives, livestock. Ind: motor vehicles, iron and steel, chemicals, food processing, textiles, machinery, shoes, electronics, shipbuilding, wine, fishing, tourism*
Currency: *peseta*

Andorra

Tucked into six glacier-carved valleys high in the Pyrenees, Andorra covers an area only one-fifth the size of Rhode Island. The country is landlocked between France and Spain. Up to now the President of France and a Spanish bishop have governed Andorra jointly, according to an agreement made in 1278.

The country had no constitution or legislative powers of its own. Citizenship was restricted to long-established families, leaving a large vote-less population of immigrant workers.

In March 1993, Andorra voted an end to feudalism. Under a constitution negotiated with its "co-princes," it hopes to become a constitutional monarchy with legislative autonomy.

Until the 1950s, Andorra was a poor country of sheepherders, tobacco growers, and smugglers. Since then tourism has made it prosperous. Tax-free shopping and a six-month ski season attract more than 10 million visitors each year. In 1991 a trade agreement with the European Community ended Andorra's tax-haven status, but the country hopes to promote foreign investment and economic development.

Official name: *Principality of Andorra*
Area: *175 sq mi (453 sq km)*
Population: *54,000*
Capital: *Andorra La Vella (pop. 16,150)*
Ethnic groups: *Spanish, Andorran, French*
Language: *Catalan (official), Spanish, French*
Religious groups: *Roman Catholic*
Economy: *tourism, banking, sheep, potatoes, tobacco*
Currency: *Spanish peseta, French franc*

Gibraltar

On a peninsula in southern Spain, the Rock of Gibraltar rises 1,394 feet (425 m) into the sky. It overlooks the Strait of Gibraltar, the narrow link between the Atlantic Ocean and the Mediterranean Sea. The British won Gibraltar from Spain some 300 years ago and administer it as a crown colony. There is talk of autonomy, but so far Gibraltar remains British. Government jobs, tourism, banking, and a shipyard employ most Gibraltarians. On the Rock live some monkeys called Barbary apes. Folklore says that as long as they live there, the British will stay.

Official name: *Gibraltar*
Area: *2.3 sq mi (6 sq km)*
Population: *30,000*
Capital: *Gibraltar*

1 *Spain*

2 *Spain*

3 *Spain*

Spain

1 *Shoppers stroll along Toledo's Calle del Comercio. Building is strictly regulated in this city, a national monument since 1941.*

2 *Farmers stuff pork sausages beneath Torre de Riu castle in Catalonia. The region has its own folkways, language, and cuisine.*

3 *Barcelona's modern stadium hosted the Summer Olympics in 1992. This event and Expo 92, a six-month-long exposition in Seville, focused world attention on Spain.*

Portugal

4 *Across the bay from an Algarve resort, fishermen prepare to launch their boat, its bow painted with protective symbols.*

4 *Portugal*

France is the nearest country in continental Europe to the United Kingdom. Linked by air and English Channel ferries, the two are also now joined by the submarine Channel Tunnel, popularly known as the Chunnel. It is scheduled to open in late 1993.

Linguistic ties unite this continental region. In the west, the Swiss speak French, and in the south, Italian and the local Romansch language. But the native tongue of most Swiss is German, and for everyday conversation they use a dialect called Schwyzerdütsch— Swiss German.

KILOMETERS 0 — 150
STATUTE MILES 0 — 100

For map legend see page 21.

France

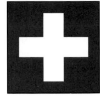

The biggest country in Western Europe, *la belle France* offers the greatest variety of landscapes. Beaches beckon on the English Channel, the Atlantic Ocean, and the Mediterranean Sea. Mountains draw tourists to the Pyrenees on Spain's border; to the Alps and Western Europe's highest peak, Mont Blanc; and to the forested Vosges near Germany. Fishing villages on Brittany's rocky coast attract sightseers. Tourists boost the economy, and the French themselves are enthusiastic travelers.

Most of France is blessed with rich farmland, which has made it the European Community's leading agricultural country. Open-air markets in many towns display fresh farm produce on laden stalls. There are nearly 300 kinds of French cheese alone. In sunny Provence, olives are grown for their oil, and fields of lavender provide essence for perfume. Vineyards flourish everywhere, but the best known wines come from the regions of Bordeaux, Burgundy, and Champagne. France is one of the world's leading producers of wine. The French agricultural lobby is so powerful that in 1992 it managed to stall a trade agreement between the European Community and the United States that involved farm subsidies.

Paris, the capital, on the Seine River in northern France, is by far the biggest city. Sixteen percent of the population lives there. Famous for its broad boulevards and sidewalk cafés, and for monuments such as the Eiffel Tower and the Arc de Triomphe, Paris is the center of French politics, government, and culture. Most major roads, railways, and a network of canals converge there. From Paris barges transport goods by river and canal to Marseille, France's busiest Mediterranean port, and to other countries.

French people take great pride in their culture, which led the way in art, literature, music, and the sciences for centuries. French manners were copied in other countries and French was spoken by diplomats and educated people worldwide until the 20th century, when English became the international language. Majestic Gothic cathedrals rose throughout France in the Middle Ages. Later, kings and nobles built elegant châteaus along the Loire River. King Louis XIV, the Sun King, erected a magnificent palace at Versailles in the 1600s, when France was at a peak of cultural splendor and world power.

The French Revolution of 1789 put an end to monarchy, and France became a republic. Napoléon, an army general, seized control, named himself emperor, and set out to conquer all of Europe. He was defeated in 1815 at Waterloo, Belgium, by British and Prussian forces. Although France later acquired colonies overseas, it never regained its former power. Two world wars fought on French soil weakened it further. Gen. Charles de Gaulle, who led the French resistance to the Nazis during World War II, became president of France in 1958 and helped restore French pride and confidence.

To complement its agricultural strength, France has become an industrial giant. It has forged ahead in high-tech industries such as telecommunications, construction of European Airbus jetliners, and satellite launching—from a base in French Guiana, South America. But the country's top-heavy reliance on nuclear power has come under criticism.

French people today are caught in a conflict between old traditions and new technology, between national pride and international needs. They wonder how to cope with the growing American influence on French culture and how to maintain the purity of their language.

Official name: *French Republic*
Area: *210,026 sq mi (543,965 sq km)*
Population: *56,876,000*
Capital: *Paris (pop. 2,152,000; met. pop. 9,060,000)*
Ethnic groups: *French*
Language: *French*
Religious groups: *Roman Catholic*
Economy: *Agr: livestock, grains, sugar beets, vegetables, fruit. Ind: iron, steel, machinery, transportation equipment, electronics, chemicals, textiles, food processing, wine, tourism, mining, fishing*
Currency: *French franc*

Switzerland

Spectacular mountain scenery and powdery ski slopes have made Switzerland Europe's most famous winter vacation spot. Tourism is one of its biggest businesses. Villages of traditional wooden chalets, their window boxes overflowing with flowers, compete for visitors. Quiet electric trains carry people throughout the country with all the punctuality of Swiss-made watches and clocks.

Many of Europe's highest mountains lie in the Swiss Alps. Their glaciers feed the headwaters of two of the continent's major rivers, the Rhine and the Rhône. The Jura Mountains, lower than the Alps, form a long range on Switzerland's western border. In summertime, lush mountain pastures fatten cows whose rich milk makes cheese and milk chocolate. Villagers give dairy herds a festive send-off each spring.

Between the Alps and the Jura lies a hilly plateau where the main cities are found and where three-fourths of the Swiss people live. Factories in this region turn out machinery, precision instruments, pharmaceuticals, and chemicals.

This small country has four languages: German, French, Italian, and Romansch, a language of Latin origin. Most Swiss speak at least two, and often English as well. In Bern, the capital, and Zürich, the biggest city and chief banking center, German is the primary language. French-speaking Geneva is headquarters for some 150 international organizations.

Switzerland has remained neutral for more than 400 years, refusing to take sides in other countries' wars. However, its big, modern army can mobilize for defense in 48 hours. Swiss men between ages 20 and 50 have had army training and keep their uniforms and firearms at home.

Although staunchly democratic since 1291 when three small cantons formed a union, Switzerland was slow in granting women full voting privileges in its 26 cantons, or states. The seven members of the federal council rotate the role of president by serving terms of one year each.

Official name: *Swiss Confederation*
Area: *15,941 sq mi (41,288 sq km)*
Population: *6,868,000*
Capital: *Bern (pop. 134,400)*
Ethnic groups: *German, French, Italian*
Language: *German, French, Italian, Romansch*
Religious groups: *Roman Catholic, Protestant*
Economy: *Agr: dairy products. Ind: banking, machinery, chemicals, pharmaceuticals, watches, textiles, precision instruments, tourism, metals, foods*
Currency: *Swiss franc*

Liechtenstein

Alpine meadows and terraced vineyards greet visitors to Liechtenstein, one of the smallest, richest countries in the world. Most of its people work in modern factories that produce precision instruments, false teeth, and other goods in an economic union with Switzerland. In 1991 Liechtenstein joined the European Free Trade Association. Low taxes have persuaded upwards of 25,000 foreign companies to establish nominal offices here. A prince heads the conservative government, which first allowed women to vote in 1984. His castle overlooks the capital of Vaduz, situated in a valley between the Alps and the Rhine River.

Official name: *Principality of Liechtenstein*
Area: *62 sq mi (160 sq km)*
Population: *30,000*
Capital: *Vaduz (pop. 4,900)*
Ethnic groups: *Alemannic, Italian*
Language: *German, Alemannic dialect*
Religious groups: *Roman Catholic, Protestant*
Economy: *Agr: livestock, grains, vegetables, grapes. Ind: banking, electronics, metal products, textiles, ceramics, chemicals, tourism, stamps*
Currency: *Swiss franc*

Monaco

Luxurious yachts anchor in Monaco's sunny harbor. The tiny principality on France's southeast coast draws rich visitors to its beaches and to the famous casino in Monte Carlo. Monaco also has some light industry. Low taxes attract foreign businesses, many of them French. And citizens and residents pay no income tax. Tax compromises had to be reached with France, with which Monaco has an economic union. Princes of the Grimaldi family have ruled Monaco off and on for centuries. If a prince should die without a male heir, Monaco would become part of France.

Official name: *Principality of Monaco*
Area: *0.6 sq mi (1.9 sq km)*
Population: *30,000*
Capital: *Monaco*
Ethnic groups: *French, Monégasque, Italian*
Language: *French, Monégasque, Italian*
Religious groups: *Roman Catholic*
Economy: *Ind: tourism, pharmaceuticals, plastics, precision instruments, banking, glass, stamps*
Currency: *French franc*

1 *France*

2 *France*

3 *France*

4 *Switzerland*

5 *Switzerland*

France

1 *Built for Paris's 1889 centennial exposition honoring the French Revolution, the Eiffel Tower arcs above the École Militaire.*

2 *Sleek high-speed trains fill a rail yard. The Trains à Grande Vitesse hurtle from Paris to Lyon at 168 miles (270 km) per hour.*

3 *A cellar master drains Bordeaux wine into a fresh cask. Candlelight helps reveal the presence of unwanted sediment.*

Switzerland

4 *Crowned with flowers and evergreens, a cow returns to her valley home after a summer spent in high Alpine pastures.*

5 *Greenbacks join other foreign currencies in Swiss banks, known worldwide for their dependability and discretion.*

A B C D E F G H J K L M N O P Q R S T U

1 2 3 4 5 6 7 8 9 10 11 12 13 14 15 16 17 18 19

SWITZERLAND

AUSTRIA

Brenner Pass

Bolzano

Udine

+ *Mont Blanc*
15,771 FEET
4,807 METERS

Lake Como

Lake Maggiore

SLOVENIA

Bergamo

Adige R.

Lake Garda

Verona

Venice

Trieste

Novara

Milan

Brescia

Padova

GULF OF VENICE

Turin

Alessandria

Po River

Po River

Parma

Ferrara

FRANCE

LIGURIA

Modena

Genoa

Bologna

Ravenna

GULF OF GENOA

La Spezia

Rimini

⊗ **SAN MARINO**
San Marino

Prato
Florence

Pisa

LIGURIAN SEA

Livorno

Arno River

Ancona

TUSCANY

Tiber River

Siena

Lake Trasimeno

Perugia

Elba

UMBRIA

Lake Bolsena

Terni

ITALY

Pescara

ADRIATIC SEA

CORSICA
(FRANCE)

Civitavecchia

VATICAN CITY ⊗

Rome

ABRUZZI

LATIUM

Campobasso

Foggia

Strait of Bonifacio

Volturno River

Bari

Olbia

Mount Vesuvius
4,203 FEET
1,281 METERS

Sassari

Naples +

Salerno

Potenza

Brindisi

TYRRHENIAN SEA

Herculaneum

Pompeii

SARDINIA

Gulf of Naples

Isle of Capri

Taranto

+ *Punta La Marmora*
6,017 FEET
1,834 METERS

GULF OF TARANTO

Tirso River

Cosenza

IONIAN SEA

Cagliari

Catanzaro

Stromboli

Vulcano

KILOMETERS 15

STATUTE MILES 10

Gozo

Victoria

Comino

Palermo

Messina

Reggio di Calabria

Marfa

Trapani

Strait of Messina

Mount Etna
10,902 FEET
3,323 METERS

MALTA

Sliema

Catania

Rabat

⊗ *Valletta*

SICILY

Strait of Sicily

Salso

Malta

Gela

Syracuse

MEDITERRANEAN SEA

MEDITERRANEAN SEA

0 KILOMETERS 120

0 STATUTE MILES 80

For map legend see page 21.

Active volcanoes contin-
ually threaten the south-
ern part of Italy. One of
the most famous, Mount
Vesuvius near Naples,
erupted in A.D. 79 and
destroyed the towns of
Pompeii and Herculane-
um. Their ruins are pre-
served as tourist sites.
Mount Etna, on the is-
land of Sicily, erupts an
average of once every
ten years. In the Tyrrhe-
nian Sea, the volcanic islands of Stromboli and
Vulcano still smolder.

Italy

Shaped like a high-heeled boot, Italy has one of the most recognizable outlines on the globe. The toe of the boot seems about to touch the Italian island of Sicily, where fruit and olives grow. Another island, sheep-raising Sardinia, lies 140 miles (225 km) offshore, near the knee.

Two great mountain ranges influence Italy's economy. Snowmelt from the Alps on the northern border ensures natural irrigation and hydroelectric power for the Po River Valley, where two-fifths of the population lives. Here farmers grow wheat, corn, and vegetables, and the factories of Milan, Genoa, and Turin turn out goods such as shoes, textiles, computers, and automobiles. Italy's strength lies in manufacturing and fine design; it has to import most raw materials. In the north, employment is high and families live well, owning cars and often vacation homes.

Italy's southern half is less developed. The Apennine mountains that run 840 miles (1,350 km) down the peninsula form part of a rocky, dry landscape. Farmers herd sheep and goats or grow grapes for wine, one of Italy's major exports. In the warmest regions they grow oranges, lemons, and olives. Earning a living is hard. Families live in small villages and enjoy few luxuries. Naples, the south's only big city, suffers from overcrowding and unemployment.

Rome, Italy's capital, sits halfway down the peninsula. Before their empire fell, the ancient Romans controlled all of the Mediterranean region. Around the 12th century, the area north of Rome split into rival city-states.

Chief among these was Venice, built on a cluster of islands. Canals wind through the modern city, and people travel by boat. Among other important city-states, Florence sparked the Renaissance, a period from the 14th to the 17th century when the arts flourished in Europe. Rome, under the control of the Roman Catholic Church, became a center of culture and Christianity. Italy's art, architecture, and ancient history attracted 59 million tourists in 1991.

Unification of the peninsula did not occur until 1870. Thus modern Italy is a young country, and many Italians still put regional loyalties ahead of national feeling. In 1993, however, spurred on by bribery and corruption charges against politicians, voters united in approving a national referendum calling for electoral reform.

Official name: *Italian Republic*
Area: *116,324 sq mi (301,277 sq km)*
Population: *58,026,000*
Capital: *Rome (pop. 2,803,900)*
Ethnic groups: *Italian*
Language: *Italian*
Religious groups: *Roman Catholic*
Economy: *Agr: fruit, vegetables, grains, olives. Ind: machinery, motor vehicles, iron, steel, chemicals, textiles, shoes, food processing, wine, tourism*
Currency: *Italian lira*

San Marino

Wholly surrounded by Italian territory, the tiny Republic of San Marino is a survivor of some 200 city-states that existed before Italy was united in 1870. Its walled capital stands near the top of a 2,425-foot (739 m) peak. Rugged mountain terrain and medieval fortifications attract three million tourists a year. The Sanmarinese, linked to Italy by language, ethnic stock, and treaty, are proud of their separate identity. They support themselves with farming, tourism, light industry, and the sale of postage stamps to foreign collectors. In 1992, San Marino was accepted into the United Nations.

Official name: *Republic of San Marino*
Area: *24 sq mi (61 sq km)*
Population: *24,000*
Capital: *San Marino (pop. 2,400)*
Ethnic groups: *Sanmarinese, Italian*
Language: *Italian*
Religious groups: *Roman Catholic*
Economy: *Agr: wheat, grapes, livestock. Ind: tourism, textiles, wine, olive oil, stamps, cement*
Currency: *Italian lira*

Vatican City

Behind a high stone wall on a hill in Rome lies the world's smallest independent nation. Vatican City is headquarters of the Roman Catholic Church and site of the world's largest church, St. Peter's Basilica. The Pope is the ruler of Vatican City and the spiritual leader of the world's 900 million Roman Catholics. Polish Pope John Paul II, elected in 1978, was the first non-Italian chosen in 456 years. The Vatican has its own coins, stamps, radio station, and newspaper, an army of 100 Swiss Guards, and a superb collection of art treasures. A 1929 treaty with Italy established the state's independence.

Official name: *State of the Vatican City*
Area: *0.2 sq mi (0.4 sq km)*
Population: *1,000*
Ethnic groups: *Italian, other nationalities*
Language: *Italian, Latin*
Religious groups: *Roman Catholic*
Economy: *investments, contributions, tourist mementos, museum fees, stamps, publications*
Currency: *Vatican lira*

Malta

Malta's three major islands lie at the crossroads of the Mediterranean on some of the world's busiest shipping routes. Attracted by its strategic position and deep natural harbors, many nations have controlled Malta since ancient times. As a result, the Maltese people are a mixture of races and cultures.

Today independent and politically neutral, Malta takes advantage of its location. Shipbuilding and repair are major industries. A huge drydock can handle modern supertankers.

Fresh water is scarce and the soil is thin, so farming in the low hills is limited, but a mild climate, prehistoric stone monuments, and historic sites make Malta a tourist's delight.

Official name: *Republic of Malta*
Area: *122 sq mi (316 sq km)*
Population: *361,000*
Capital: *Valletta (pop. 9,200)*
Ethnic groups: *Maltese (mixed Arab, Sicilian, Norman, Spanish, Italian, English)*
Language: *Maltese, English*
Religious groups: *Roman Catholic*
Economy: *Agr: vegetables, fruit, grains, livestock. Ind: tourism, shipbuilding, textiles, electronics*
Currency: *Maltese lira*

1 *Italy*

2 *Italy*

4 *Malta*

3 *Italy*

5 *Vatican City*

Italy

1 *The Roman Colosseum, an amphitheater that opened in A.D. 80, saw gladiators fight each other or men fight wild animals.*

2 *Once the arteries of a powerful maritime republic, Venice's canals are still vital—millions of tourists visit them annually.*

3 *Pasta just wouldn't be the same without parmesan cheese. Some two million wheels come from the Parma region each year.*

Malta

4 *Deep natural harbors and a strategic location led to Malta's shipbuilding industry.*

Vatican City

5 *A Swiss Guard swears allegiance to the Pope, joining the elite force of 100 men that has guarded popes since the early 1500s.*

CZECH REPUBLIC

A
LIECHTENSTEIN   GERMANY   *Inn River*   Krems   *March R.*   SLOVAKIA   UKRAINE

Lake Constance   Danube River   Salgotarjan   **Miskolc**
• Bregenz   Oberndorf   Wels   Steyr   St. Polten   **Vienna** ⊛   *Neusiedler Lake*   Ipoly R.   Eger   • Nyiregyhaza
B   **Salzburg**   *Leitha R.*   • Sopron   **Gyor**   ⊛**Budapest**   **Debrecen**
Hallstatt   **AUSTRIA**   Tatabanya   *Tisza River*
BAVARIAN ALPS   • Kitzbuhel   STYRIA   Szombathely   **Szekesfehervar**   Szolnok
Innsbruck   *Salzach R.*   *Enns River*   • Leoben   Veszprem   Dunaujvaros   Kecskemet   *Koros River*
C   T   I   R   O   L   A   L   P   S   +Grossglockner   *Mur R.*   *Raba River*   **HUNGARY**   *GREAT HUNGARIAN PLAIN*   • Bekescsaba
SWITZERLAND   12,461 FEET   3,798 METERS   CARINTHIA   **Graz**   Zalaegerszeg   *Lake Balaton*   • Hodmezovasarhely
D   *CARNIC ALPS*   *Drau River*   • Klagenfurt   Kaposvar   Szekszard   **Szeged**
ITALY   Villach   *Triglav*   **Maribor**   *Mura River*   Drava   **Pecs**   **Subotica**   ROMANIA
E   *JULIAN ALPS*   +9,393 FEET   2,863 METERS   **SLOVENIA**   *Drava River*   *Danube River*   VOJVODINA
Ljubljana ⊛   *Sava River*   **Zagreb** ⊛   *Tisa River*   • Zrenjanin
F   GULF OF TRIESTE   **CROATIA**   • Karlovac   **Osijek**   **Novi Sad**
G   GULF OF VENICE   **Rijeka**   *Istria*   *Krk*   *Una River*   Slavonski Brod   *Sava River*   **Belgrade** ⊛   Iron Gate Dam
H   Pula   *Gres*   D   I   N   A   R   I   C   **Banja Luka**   *Bosna River*   *Danube River*
Pag   Tuzla   SERBIA   *Morava River*
J   ADRIATIC SEA   *Dugi Otok*   Zadar   **BOSNIA AND**   Zenica   Srebrenica   *Ibar River*
K   Modest in size today,   *HERZEGOVINA*   **Sarajevo** ⊛   Kragujevac   **YUGOSLAVIA**
Austria and Hungary cre-   Sibenik   A   L   **Nis**
ated the great **Austro-**   **Split**   D   M   *Neretva River*
L   **Hungarian Empire** in   *Brac*   A   T   Mostar   P   S
1867. Its territory once   *Hvar*   I   *Drina River*
encompassed Slovenia,   *Vis*   A   MONTENEGRO   • Pec   **Pristina**
M   Croatia, and Bosnia and   *Korcula*   *Mljet*   • Dubrovnik   KOSOVO   BULGARIA
Herzegovina. The Turk-   *Lastovo*   Podgorica
ish Ottoman Empire had   • Bar   *Lake Scutari*
N   formerly controlled all of
the Balkans but had al-   **Skopje** ⊛
most collapsed by the   *Vardar River*
O   late 1800s.   **MACEDONIA**
After World War I, Yu-   ALBANIA
goslavia was united, first   0   KILOMETERS   125   • Ohrid   • Bitola
P   as a kingdom, then as a   0   STATUTE MILES   75   *Lake Ohrid*   *Lake Prespa*   GREECE
socialist federation of re-
publics. Its breakup has   For map legend see page 21.
Q   dominated the region's
politics since 1991. Five
countries replace the six
former republics. Ancient
rivalries have fueled ethnic strife in most of them,
devastating the area.

1   2   3   4   5   6   7   8   9   10   11   12   13   14   15   16   17   18   19

Austria

The towering, snowcapped Alps cover nearly three-quarters of this small republic. Austrians regard their peaks as national assets. Swift mountain streams generate hydroelectric power for factories, found mostly in the eastern lowlands. Forests of spruce and fir supply raw materials for lumber, pulp, and paper.

The tourist industry relies on striking mountain scenery and traditional Alpine villages to draw visitors in all seasons. More than 50 winter resorts such as Innsbruck and Kitzbühel cater to skiers. Strict laws protect parts of the Alps from overdevelopment and pollution.

Historically, Austria's location on heavily used trade routes gave it strategic importance. Mountain passes such as the Brenner Pass link it to countries to the north and south. The Danube River, a navigable waterway that crosses northern Austria, joins Western and Eastern Europe. By 1867, wars and alliances had made Austria the heart of the Austro-Hungarian Empire, a conglomerate nation of 50 million people. Its capital, Vienna, a center of science, art, and music, was noted for its gaiety. But after defeat in World War I, Austria was reduced to a fraction of the size of its former empire.

Since World War II, the Austrian constitution has required neutrality. The country maintains peaceful, profitable relations with its neighbors, acting as a bridge between East and West, and many international agencies have headquarters in Vienna. The end of the Cold War has reinforced that role and led Austria into closer economic cooperation with the European Community. It applied for membership in 1989.

Official name: *Republic of Austria*
Area: *32,377 sq mi (83,856 sq km)*
Population: *7,873,000*
Capital: *Vienna (pop. 1,505,400)*
Ethnic groups: *German*
Language: *German*
Religious groups: *Roman Catholic*
Economy: *Agr: livestock, grains, potatoes, sugar beets. Ind: machinery, iron, steel, tourism, chemicals, textiles, wood and paper products, mining*
Currency: *schilling*

Hungary

Unlike their Slavic and Germanic neighbors, Hungarians are Magyars, descendants of Central Asian nomads who occupied the fertile Danube River basin more than a thousand years ago. Their sense of being different has given Hungarians a strong cultural identity, which they have held on to while often losing their freedom—to the Turks, Austrians, Germans, and, in 1947, to the Soviets.

In 1956 a popular uprising against Soviet control was brutally put down. After that, Hungary sought to forge its own way while not challenging the Soviet Union. Its brand of "goulash communism" (named for Hungary's traditional dish) promoted bold changes. These included limited private enterprise in small businesses and on farms, where less than 20 percent of the work force produces a surplus of food for export.

Since the election of a noncommunist government in 1990, Hungary has pursued its long-range plans to privatize most industries. While progress has been slower than hoped, foreign investment and joint ventures are up.

Cultural ties to large groups of ethnic Hungarians in neighboring Slovakia, Romania, and Serbia have prompted the government to advocate local autonomy for those regions—a move that has angered the host countries.

Official name: *Republic of Hungary*
Area: *35,919 sq mi (93,030 sq km)*
Population: *10,331,000*
Capital: *Budapest (pop. 2,113,600)*
Ethnic groups: *Magyar*
Language: *Hungarian*
Religious groups: *Roman Catholic, Protestant*
Economy: *Agr: grains, potatoes, sugar beets, fruit, livestock. Ind: machinery, engineering, food processing, chemicals, textiles, metals, mining, wine*
Currency: *forint*

Slovenia

Of the new countries struggling to emerge from the former Yugoslavia, Slovenia has made the most promising start. After declaring independence in June 1991, it defeated an attack by the Yugoslav Army that lasted less than two weeks.

Slovenia's terrain features rugged mountains and fertile, densely populated valleys. Until the recent warfare, the Adriatic seacoast as well as the mountains brought in tourist income.

Settled by Slavic tribes 1,400 years ago, Slovenia fell under German control by A.D. 800. Later, Austria held it for centuries. Despite heavy Germanic influence, Slovenian language and culture survived.

An efficient use of labor and industry has made Slovenia more prosperous than the other republics. Unemployment, difficulties in establishing private industry, and ethnic conflicts nearby now challenge independent Slovenia.

Official name: *Republic of Slovenia*
Area: *7,819 sq mi (20,251 sq km)*
Population: *2,000,000*
Capital: *Ljubljana (pop. 323,300)*
Ethnic groups: *Slovene, Croat, Serb*
Language: *Slovenian, Serbo-Croatian*
Religious groups: *Roman Catholic*
Economy: *Agr: livestock, grains, potatoes, sugar beets, fruit. Ind: metals, machinery, textiles, foods*
Currency: *tolar*

Croatia

Croatia's declaration of independence in June 1991 was met with fierce resistance by Serbian residents there, backed by the Yugoslav People's Army. Fighting has ruined cities and towns, disrupted agriculture and industry, left borders in dispute, and wiped out the valuable tourist trade along the Adriatic Coast.

Behind the island-studded coast, known as Dalmatia, mountains rise steeply to a fertile plain, the chief agricultural region. Zagreb, the capital and industrial hub, is situated inland.

The Croats, who migrated to the area in the seventh century, compose more than 75 percent of the population; Serbs make up about 12 percent. The Serbo-Croatian language is written in the Latin alphabet by Croats and in the Cyrillic alphabet by Serbs. Croats are mainly Roman Catholic, while Serbs are Eastern Orthodox.

Until recently, Croatia, along with neighboring Slovenia, fared better economically than the other Yugoslav republics. But the country has received thousands of refugees, and Serbs hold about a third of its territory.

Official name: *Republic of Croatia*
Area: *21,829 sq mi (56,538 sq km)*
Population: *4,400,000*
Capital: *Zagreb (pop. 649,600)*
Ethnic groups: *Croat, Serb*
Language: *Serbo-Croatian*
Religious groups: *Roman Catholic, Orthodox*
Economy: *Agr: grains, fruit, vegetables, livestock. Ind: shipbuilding, chemicals, foods, oil, textiles*
Currency: *Croatian dinar*

Bosnia and Herzegovina

War between Muslims, Croats, and Serbs has ravaged this republic since independence in 1992. Long-held rivalries based mostly upon differing ethnic origin have led to killing, torture, and the "ethnic cleansing" of Muslim populations of entire towns and villages. Much of the capital, Sarajevo, lies in ruins.

Muslims form 44 percent of the population. Their forebears converted to Islam during a long period of Ottoman Turkish rule—an act still viewed as treasonous by many Roman Catholic Croats (17 percent) and Eastern Orthodox Serbs (33 percent). Croatians and Serbians in the neighboring republics have aided the war in the hope of territorial gain. A peace proposal suggests dividing the country into separate regions based on their resident ethnic majorities.

Both Bosnia and Herzegovina are mountainous and poor, with economies based mainly on crops and livestock. Bosnia, in the forested north, has fertile river valleys for grain cultivation. In Herzegovina's warmer climate, fruit and tobacco grow. Chief industries are mining and the production of steel, timber, and textiles.

Official name: *Republic of Bosnia and Herzegovina*
Area: *19,741 sq mi (51,129 sq km)*
Population: *4,000,000*
Capital: *Sarajevo (pop. 526,100)*
Ethnic groups: *Muslim, Serb, Croat*
Language: *Serbo-Croatian*
Religious groups: *Muslim, Christian*
Economy: *Agr: grains, tobacco, fruit, livestock. Ind: steel, mining, textiles, wood products*
Currency: *new Yugoslav dinar*

Yugoslavia

Of the six republics of the former Yugoslav federation, the largest, Serbia, and the smallest, Montenegro, remain united under the name Yugoslavia. They occupy a territory half the size of the former country. Yugoslavia, "the land of the South Slavs," began in 1918 as the Kingdom of Serbs, Croats, and Slovenes, which was renamed the Kingdom of Yugoslavia in 1929. In 1946, it became a federation of six republics under a communist government headed by Josip Broz, who took the name Tito. Marshal Tito died in 1980.

Today's Yugoslavia is mountainous, except in parts of northern Serbia where a fertile plain laced by tributaries of the Danube River yields abundant crops. In Montenegro, the dark-colored mountains that give the region its name drop abruptly to the Adriatic Sea. People there raise crops and livestock or work in forestry.

Ethnic Serbs form about 62 percent of the total population. Mostly Orthodox Christians, they dominate political, military, and economic life, which is centered in the Serbian capital, Belgrade. The Serbs revoked the autonomy of two formerly autonomous provinces. Of these, the first, Vojvodina, has a large Hungarian minority. In the second, Kosovo, a great majority of the residents are Albanian, most of them Muslim. Many of these favor independence or unification of Kosovo with Albania.

Opposed to the declared independence of the other former Yugoslav republics, the "new" Yugoslavia has aided ethnic Serbs in their efforts to unify with Serbia by battling other groups in these countries. The Yugoslav Army, supporting Serbian irregulars known as Chetniks, left Macedonia mostly alone and pulled out quickly from Slovenia, but took over large areas of Croatia and of Bosnia and Herzegovina. The Muslim populations of these countries were a major target. Despite sanctions against their actions, the Serbs have rejected peace initiatives, continuing to push for increased Serbian domination.

Official name: *Federal Republic of Yugoslavia*
Area: *39,450 sq mi (102,173 sq km)*
Population: *9,800,000*
Capital: *Belgrade (pop. 1,087,900)*
Ethnic groups: *Serb, Albanian, Montenegrin, Hungarian*
Language: *Serbo-Croatian, Albanian, Hungarian*
Religious groups: *Eastern Orthodox, Muslim, Roman Catholic*
Economy: *Agr: grains, fruit, vegetables, livestock. Ind: machinery, metals, mining, textiles, foods*
Currency: *new Yugoslav dinar*

Macedonia

For centuries, the former Yugoslav republic of Macedonia was part of a larger region that included sections of present-day Bulgaria and Greece. This was the homeland of Alexander the Great, whose fourth-century B.C. empire stretched from Egypt to India.

A rugged country, Macedonia is the poorest former Yugoslav republic. Most of the people farm along the Vardar River and other valleys. Industry is centered around Skopje, the capital.

Macedonians make up more than two-thirds of the population. Mostly Orthodox Christians, their Slavic language is similar to Bulgarian. A large Albanian minority, chiefly Muslim, lives mainly in the northwest. Since independence in 1991, Macedonia has faced unemployment, serious economic problems, and Greek objections to its name—the same as that of a Greek province.

Official name: *Republic of Macedonia*
Area: *9,928 sq mi (25,713 sq km)*
Population: *2,000,000*
Capital: *Skopje (pop. 458,000)*
Ethnic groups: *Macedonian, Albanian*
Language: *Macedonian, Albanian*
Religious groups: *Eastern Orthodox, Muslim*
Economy: *Agr: grains, tobacco, cotton, fruit, livestock. Ind: mining, steel, chemicals, textiles*
Currency: *denar*

Austria

1 *Hallstatt village, dreaming beside a mountain lake, illustrates the scenery that helps attract millions of tourists each year. Archaeological finds here gave the village's name to an Early Iron Age culture.*

2 *A musician in traditional costume blows his saxhorn on a festive occasion in a valley of the Austrian Tirol.*

Hungary

3 *Dressed like one of his flock, a shepherd on the Great Hungarian Plain sports a warm coat called a suba. His heavy felt hat can be used as a drinking vessel.*

Hungary

4 *Chess devotees at a Budapest bathhouse congregate over a couple of games.*

1 *Austria*

2 *Austria*

3 *Hungary*

4 *Hungary*

1 *Bosnia and Herzegovina*

2 *Yugoslavia*

3 *Croatia*

Bosnia and Herzegovina

1 *In a scene photographed before independence, minarets rise above a 16th-century bridge in the Muslim section of Mostar. Much of the city has since been destroyed in the war between ethnic groups.*

Yugoslavia

2 *Serbian women discuss a length of cloth at an open-air market in peacetime Belgrade. Supplies of many consumer items later dried up under United Nations sanctions.*

Croatia

3 *A Bosnian mother and family breathe easier across the Croatian border in Slavonski Brod. Hundreds of thousands of refugees, mostly Muslims, fled into Croatia from war-torn Bosnia and Herzegovina.*

4 *In days of plenty, farmers lay out their produce on market stalls beneath the spires of Zagreb's medieval cathedral. Private farms grew 75 percent of the food in the former Yugoslav republics.*

Slovenia

5 *At Iskra Telekom near Ljubljana, workers examine circuit boards to be used in the company's communications systems.*

Macedonia

6 *A highland farmer hams it up while milking his sheep to make cheese. Sheep's cheese is a popular delicacy.*

4 *Croatia*

5 *Slovenia*

6 *Macedonia*

UKRAINE

A

Satu Mare
Somes River
Baia Mare
Suceava
MOLDAVIA
Prut River

HUNGARY

Oradea

B

Iasi

MOLDOVA

Cluj-Napoca
Tirgu Mures
Bacau

TRANSYLVANIA
CARPATHIAN MOUNTAINS

C

Arad
• Sighisoara
ROMANIA

Mures River
Siret River

Timisoara
Sibiu
Olt River

D

Resita
TRANSYLVANIAN ALPS
Brasov
Buzau
Braila
Galati
Danube River Delta

Ploiesti
Tulcea

E

Pitesti

Iron Gate Dam

Craiova
Bucharest
Constanta

F

Vidin
Danube River
Ruse

YUGOSLAVIA
Dobrich

G

Iskur River
Pleven
Shumen
Varna

BLACK
SEA

BULGARIA
Gabrovo MOUNTAINS
Sliven

H

BALKAN
Sofia
Pernik
Valley of Roses
Stara Zagora
Burgas

Lake Scutari
Drin R.
Plovdiv
Maritsa River
Tundzha River

J

Shkoder
MACEDONIA
RHODOPE MOUNTAINS
THRACE
Evros River

ADRIATIC
SEA
Struma River

Tirana
Lake Ohrid
Drama

K

Durres
Lake Prespa
Serrai
Komotini

Elbasan
MACEDONIA
Kavala

ALBANIA
Korce
Veroia
Thasos

L

Vlore
Vijose River
Thessaloniki
Samothrace

CHALKIDIKI
Lemnos

Corfu
Ioannina
Mount Olympus +
9,570 FEET
2,917 METERS

M

EPIRUS
PINDUS
THESSALY
Larisa
Volos

AEGEAN
SEA
Lesbos
Mytilini

N

IONIAN
SEA
GREECE
MTS.

Levkas
Agrinion
Chios

O

Cephalonia
Delphi
Euboea
Thebes
Patrai
Marathon
Samos

Zante
Olympia
Corinth
Athens
Andros
Mykonos

P

PELOPONNESUS
Piraeus
CYCLADES
Syros
Naxos
Kos

Q

Kalamai
Sparta
Milos

Cape Matapan
Thira
Rhodes

R

Kithira
DODECANESE
Rhodes

MEDITERRANEAN
SEA
SEA OF CRETE
Karpathos

S

Chania
Iraklion
Knosos

CRETE

T

TURKEY

IONIAN
ISLANDS
SPORADES

Balkans is the name given to the countries of the **Balkan Peninsula** in southeastern Europe. The term applies to the countries on this map, European Turkey and the former Yugoslavia.

Located at the crossroads of Asia, Europe, and Africa, the region has suffered many invasions and much internal conflict. With each conquest, political boundaries were redrawn—and often disputed again. From this, the word "balkanize" was coined, which means to break up a region.

0 KILOMETERS 150
0 STATUTE MILES 100

For map legend see page 21.

1   2   3   4   5   6   7   8   9   10   11   12

Romania

When apple trees grew pears, proclaimed the Romanian dictator Nicolae Ceauşescu, reform would come to Romania. The scornful words prompted student protesters to hang pears on trees in Bucharest, Romania's capital. Tense drama exploded into bloody revolution in the final days of 1989, ending with the execution of Ceauşescu and his wife. A new government has instituted land reforms and begun privatization of industry, but declining production and soaring costs continue to cause unrest.

Although Romania was a former Soviet satellite, it had tried to steer an independent course. Half its trade was with the West. Fertile farmland stretches along its western, eastern, and southern borders. About 30 percent of the work force still farms the land. The country's forested mountains and central plateau contain deposits of oil and minerals. Since the 1950s, Romania has emphasized heavy industries such as steel, chemicals, and machinery, and this has created major air and water pollution problems.

Ceauşescu's harsh measures for reducing the national debt impoverished the citizens. Fuel and farm produce were exported to help repay loans. People suffered shortages of food, electricity, and gasoline. The government has now halted this policy, but supplies remain scarce.

Romanian roots go back to the Romans who colonized the area in the second century, giving the country its name. Its language bears more resemblance to Italian and French than to the Slavic languages of most surrounding nations. It does share a language and ethnic heritage with the majority population of its new neighbor, Moldova, parts of which Romania once owned. Moldovans are divided over reunification.

The Romanian heritage finds expression in traditional folk art, and in music and dancing that enliven outdoor festivals. Vacationers from many countries have long enjoyed these festivities, as well as Romania's mountain scenery and sunny Black Sea resorts.

Official name: *Romania*
Area: *91,699 sq mi (237,500 sq km)*
Population: *23,188,000*
Capital: *Bucharest (pop. 1,989,800)*
Ethnic groups: *Romanian, Hungarian*
Language: *Romanian, Hungarian, German*
Religious groups: *Romanian Orthodox*
Economy: *Agr: corn, wheat, potatoes, sugar beets, oilseeds, livestock, fruit. Ind: machinery, oil, metals, mining, chemicals, lumber, textiles, food processing*
Currency: *Romanian leu*

Bulgaria

Most of the Western world's elegant perfumes are made in France, but chances are the rose oil that forms their base comes from the Valley of Roses in the heart of Bulgaria. Although mountainous, Bulgaria manages to cultivate more than a third of its land. Wheat, corn, and sugar beets grow in the fertile valley that stretches from the Danube River south to the Balkan Mountains. Tobacco, cotton, and fruit thrive in the Maritsa River Valley.

A communist country after World War II, Bulgaria maintained strong ties with the former Soviet Union, and it has continued them with Russia. The Bulgarian language sounds similar to Russian, and both use the Cyrillic alphabet. More important, though, Bulgaria has viewed the Russians as liberators since 1878, when the tsar's troops helped defeat the Ottoman Turks, who had ruled Bulgaria for 500 years.

In the 1950s, Bulgaria turned its small, private farms into huge collectives, where technical advances and greater use of machinery translated into higher productivity. Industrial development encouraged people to move to urban areas, where pollution remains a serious problem. Most Bulgarians now live in towns or cities, many of them in Sofia, the capital.

In 1990, with other communist regimes falling, Bulgaria elected communist officials who promised economic reforms. But in 1991 they were replaced by a democratic government committed to a market economy.

Tourism plays an increasingly important role in Bulgaria's economy. While its resort areas on the Black Sea coast have long been popular with vacationers from East European countries, Bulgaria has recently made an extra effort to attract Western tourists and their hard currency. Modern hotels look out on Black Sea beaches, and ski resorts deck mountain slopes. Bulgarians are also careful to protect many national sites, ranging from a 2,300-year-old Thracian tomb to hundreds of nature reserves.

Official name: *Republic of Bulgaria*
Area: *42,823 sq mi (110,912 sq km)*
Population: *8,866,000*
Capital: *Sofia (pop. 1,141,500)*
Ethnic groups: *Bulgarian, Turk*
Language: *Bulgarian, Turkish*
Religious groups: *Eastern Orthodox, Muslim*
Economy: *Agr: grains, tobacco, fruit, vegetables, livestock, cotton, roses. Ind: machinery, electronics, chemicals, agricultural processing, metals, tourism*
Currency: *lev*

Albania

For about 45 years small, mountainous Albania mistrusted outside influence so much that it placed heavy restrictions on tourism, foreign news, and travel. With a long history of invasion and occupation by foreign powers, Albania guarded its isolation. After German occupation during World War II, a communist regime took power under Gen. Enver Hoxha. Albania remained the most orthodox communist country in Europe until his death in 1985.

Cautious reforms escalated in 1990, when the government announced its desire to resume diplomatic relations with other countries. It lifted the laws against practicing religion and allowed all Albanians to apply for passports. In 1991, boatloads of refugees fled to Italy as riots and strikes brought down the government. A democratic government was voted into office in 1992.

The birthrate is high, and 60 percent of Albanians are under the age of 25. About two-thirds of the people live in the countryside, where they farm along the coastal plain and in river valleys. Reforms included permission for peasants to acquire private plots from collective farms.

But land transfer was held up, chaotic conditions developed, and agricultural production dropped drastically. Industrial production also declined, with Albania's large chromite mines producing only half their potential in 1992. As the government strives to convert to a market economy, large amounts of foreign aid are needed to keep Europe's poorest country going.

Official name: *Republic of Albania*
Area: *11,100 sq mi (28,748 sq km)*
Population: *3,285,000*
Capital: *Tirana (pop. 239,400)*
Ethnic groups: *Albanian*
Language: *Albanian, Greek*
Religious groups: *Muslim, Eastern Orthodox*
Economy: *Agr: grains, vegetables, tobacco, fruit. Ind: mining, oil, food processing, textiles, lumber.*
Currency: *lek*

Greece

The ideals of Western democracy were born in Greece 2,500 years ago, and the word "democracy" comes from the Greek for "power of the people." Ancient Greek scientists foretold the existence of atoms and said the earth orbited the sun. Western civilization grew out of early Greek art, philosophy, and science.

Greek history has seen much turmoil. Conquered by the Macedonians in 338 B.C., Greece suffered many centuries of foreign rule. Not until 1829 did it regain independence. In the 20th century the country was devastated by Nazi occupation, then by a bitter civil war. A conflict with Turkey over the island of Cyprus, begun in the 1950s, remains unresolved. And in 1991, Greece was alarmed by declarations of independence by the former Yugoslav republic of Macedonia. Greece does not want the new state to call itself Macedonia, fearing territorial claims against the Greek province of the same name.

Greece is composed of a group of peninsulas and scattered islands. Mountains that cover about 80 percent of the country further separate regions from one another. The climate is typically Mediterranean, with hot, dry summers and mild, rainy winters. Almost half of the land is suitable for farming, and about a third of the population is employed in agriculture.

Tiny farmsteads, divided up among family descendants, make large-scale agricultural methods impossible. Because of strong family bonds, Greeks have often resisted government efforts to establish farm cooperatives, labor unions, and modern techniques. People who were left without land or jobs have had to seek work in other countries and send earnings home.

Greek industrial growth was strong from the 1940s to 1980. More than half the population now lives in cities. Companies making textiles, chemicals, and other products are concentrated around Athens, the capital, and its port, Piraeus. Air pollution has become a problem there.

The port of Thessaloniki, the largest city after Athens, is the shipping center in the north for the mining industry and for crops grown in Thessaly and Macedonia. Greece has one of the biggest shipping fleets in the world.

Tourism plays a large role in Greece's economy. Some eight million people a year visit the country, lured by its sunny climate, magnificent scenery, and antiquities such as the Athenian Parthenon. The Greek islands, numbering nearly 2,000, also attract vacationers to their historic sites, beach resorts, and fishing villages.

Official name: *Hellenic Republic*
Area: *50,962 sq mi (131,990 sq km)*
Population: *10,064,000*
Capital: *Athens (pop. 885,700)*
Ethnic groups: *Greek*
Language: *Greek*
Religious groups: *Greek Orthodox*
Economy: *Agr: wheat, olives, tobacco, fruit, vegetables, livestock. Ind: shipping, tourism, food processing, textiles, chemicals, metal products, mining, oil*
Currency: *drachma*

1 *Romania*

2 *Bulgaria*

Romania

1 *The painted houses of a Transylvanian village, decorated with ornate wood carvings, are typical of this forest region.*

Bulgaria

2 *A rose picker displays a sample in the Valley of Roses. Bulgaria supplies 40 percent of the world's rose oil used in perfume.*

Greece

3 *A Greek Orthodox church clings to a cliff on the crescent-shaped island of Thíra in the Aegean Sea.*

4 *Greek kefi—high spirits—erupts in dancing near ancient Delphi, as villagers honor their patron saint, St. George.*

Albania

5 *A farm worker in Albania's mountainous north brings in the corn harvest. Two-thirds of the people lead rural lives.*

3 *Greece*

4 *Greece*

5 *Albania*

Asia

When Marco Polo returned to Italy from his 13th-century travels to Asia, people scoffed at the amazing tales he told. His descriptions of the continent—its size, the height of its mountains, its variety of peoples—seemed too fantastic to be real. But most of his stories were not greatly exaggerated. Largest of all the continents, Asia covers nearly one-third of the earth's land surface and is home to more than half of its people in 47 countries. It stretches from the frozen wastes of the Arctic in the north to the sweltering rain forests of Indonesia south of the Equator.

In the west, Asia's boundary with Europe is defined by a line mapmakers trace along the Ural Mountains, through the Caspian and Black Seas, and down the narrow straits that lead into the Aegean and Mediterranean Seas. From there the Suez Canal runs into the Red Sea, and together they set off Asia from the African continent. About 6,000 miles (9,650 km) to the east, Asia ends in the islands of the Western Pacific. The Indian Ocean washes its southern shores.

Earth's highest point is found in Asia. From a Central Asian hub, the continent's greatest mountain ranges radiate like the vanes of a pinwheel. To the southeast curve the Himalaya, the world's loftiest mountains. There Mount Everest soars 29,028 feet (8,848 m), surpassing all other peaks. The Kunlun Mountains stretch eastward; between these mountains and the Himalaya lies the high, vast Plateau of Tibet. To the north sweep the Tian Shan and the Altay Mountains, while the Hindu Kush angles off to the southwest. Asia's mountains and high plateaus have long been barriers to the movement of people and ideas.

Half a continent from Everest, in the region known as the Middle East, the shore of the Dead Sea forms Asia's lowest point, 1,312 feet (400 m) below sea level. Into this salty inland sea flows the Jordan River, one of arid western Asia's life-giving streams. Rising in the mountains of Turkey, the Tigris and Euphrates Rivers drain into the Persian Gulf, supplying water to a wide, fertile plain known since ancient times as Mesopotamia, "the land between the rivers."

Here, some 55 centuries ago, the world's oldest civilization, the Sumerian, took shape. People learned to divert rivers for irrigation and began to harvest surplus food. This supported some people in nonfarming jobs, and cities formed. Other civilizations arose about 2500 B.C. along the Indus River, which flows through modern Pakistan, and 800 years later along China's Yellow River. Asian civilizations gave the world writing, the wheel, astronomy, mechanical printing, and a decimal number system.

Asia also gave birth to all the world's major religions. Hinduism developed in India some 3,500 years ago and remains the primary religion there. Buddhism began in India and spread to East and Southeast Asia, where it is now practiced by many. From the Middle East came Judaism, Christianity, and Islam—three distinct religions that share common roots. Modern Judaism centers on Israel, created in 1948 as a homeland for the world's Jews. Christianity has the largest number of believers worldwide, but only about 10 percent live in Asia. Islam and Hinduism claim very nearly equal numbers of followers in Asia—about 750 million each.

Extreme heat, cold, and lack of water keep at least two-thirds of Asia sparsely inhabited or even unpopulated. Its northernmost expanses consist of bitter cold, treeless tundra where the subsoil is frozen all year. South of this stretches the taiga, a forest belt of hardy evergreens that can survive the long, cold winters and short summers. Vast grasslands called steppes cover much of Central Asia. The steppes are the traditional home of herders, some of whom still live in portable shelters called *yurts* or *gers* and carry their belongings on two-humped camels.

Asia's high mountains and interior plateaus are mostly too dry and cold for human settlement. Interior deserts, such as the Taklimakan and the Gobi, are very thinly populated. In southern desert lands, including the Arabian Peninsula, people have settled along the coasts and at oases—areas made fertile by underground water sources that supply springs and wells. Tent-dwelling nomads still herd livestock in the open desert, though less than in the past.

Most of Asia's population clusters in lowlands along its rivers and coastlines. The valleys of three major rivers that rise in or near the Himalaya—the Indus, Ganges, and Brahmaputra—hold some of the greatest concentrations of people in the world. In China, the world's most populous country, people live chiefly along the

Peaks of the Himalaya, the earth's highest range

Wind-crested dunes in the Gobi, Mongolia

Yellow and Yangtze Rivers. Many Asian rivers, such as Southeast Asia's Mekong, provide new, fertile soil when annual floods recede, and some serve as important transportation routes.

Large numbers of Asians rely on the regular arrival of the summer rainy season. Yearly rains brought by monsoon winds drench South and Southeast Asia and China's southern regions. Farmers plant rice, Asia's most important food crop, in flooded fields and count on the rains to water crops of wheat, millet, and other grains. If the rains fail to arrive, thousands may starve.

Beginning with Genghis Khan, Mongols from the steppes of Central Asia came closer than any other political power to controlling the whole continent. But Asia's diversity of environments, ethnic groups, cultures, and languages has always made unification unlikely. Ethnic and cultural loyalties played a role in the breakup of the former Soviet Union into separate nations. Except for Georgia and the Baltic States, they later joined a new Commonwealth of Independent States. The Soviet empire straddled the physical continents of Europe and Asia, and the Commonwealth still does. Three of its western members are described in the European section of this atlas, but most are found under Asia.

Regardless of their current forms of government, Asian countries face many problems in common. Feeding a continually increasing population is the most pressing challenge. The continent as a whole has made much progress in growing food, but some countries experience severe shortages. Poverty in rural areas forces millions of Asians into already crowded cities. There they live in makeshift shelters without sanitation, the poorest of the poor.

Asia's natural resources, many so far untapped, remain a major strength and hope for the future. Wealth from the immense oil reserves in the Persian Gulf brings improved standards of living to many countries in that region. Hydroelectric power fueled by mighty Asian rivers bolsters the continent's energy supply. Nearly every mineral needed by modern industry can be found in the Asian earth. Powered by human resources, countries such as Japan, Taiwan, Singapore, and Hong Kong have already made giant leaps into industry and modernization—but they still honor their Asian heritage.

Images of the Buddha above an archway join Hindu statuary in the ancient Cambodian temple of Angkor Thom.

Facts About Asia

Area: *17,176,102 sq mi (44,485,900 sq km)
Population: *3,317,800,000
Highest Point: *Mount Everest, China-Nepal, 29,028 ft (8,848 m) above sea level
Lowest Point: Dead Sea, Israel-Jordan, 1,312 ft (400 m) below sea level
Largest Country: *(by area)*
* Russia, excluding European portion, 4,845,580 sq mi (12,550,000 sq km)
Largest Country: *(by population)*
* China 1,165,771,000
Largest Metropolitan Areas: *(by population)*

* Tokyo, Japan	30,421,100
Bombay, India	12,571,700
Shanghai, China	12,495,100

Longest Rivers: *(mi and km)*

Yangtze (Chang Jiang)	3,964	6,380
Yenisey-Angara	3,440	5,536

Largest Lakes: *(sq mi and sq km)*

* Caspian Sea, Asia-Europe	143,244	371,000
Lake Baikal, Russia	12,162	31,500

Largest Desert: *(sq mi and sq km)*

Gobi, China-Mongolia	500,000	1,294,994

*World record

Glossary

Bedouin—a nomadic Arab of the desert.
Buddhism—a religion of Asia that grew from the teachings of Gautama Buddha in the 6th century B.C. He taught salvation through self-purification.
caste—a hereditary social class in Hinduism.
Christianity—a religion based on the teachings of Jesus Christ, who is believed to be the son of God.
dhow—a West Asian boat with a triangular sail.
Hinduism—the major religion of India; it teaches righteous living to achieve a final union with Brahman, the supreme power of the universe.
Islam—a religious belief that there is one God and that Muhammad is the last of the prophets.
Judaism—a religion developed by the ancient Hebrews that teaches belief in one God.
maharaja—a royal Hindu ruler.
monsoons—winds that produce either a dry or a wet season in southern and eastern Asia.
mosque—an Islamic house of worship.
Muslim—a follower of Islam.
pagoda—a tower with several successive roofs, used as a temple or memorial in the Far East.
yurt—a circular tent of felt or animal skins used by nomads in Central Asia; also called a **ger** in Mongolia.

For map legend see page 21.

0 KILOMETERS 600
0 STATUTE MILES 400

Largest of the former Soviet republics and still the largest country in the world, the Russian Federation stretches from the plains of Europe across 11 time zones to an Arctic island in the Bering Strait. The Ural Mountains divide European Russia from its Asian counterpart, called Siberia. Most of the population and the federation's capital, Moscow, are found west of the Urals. Sparsely inhabited Siberia holds the majority of the country's vast natural resources.

For convenience, European and Asian Russia are placed together in this atlas's Asian section.

SWEDEN

NORWAY

POLAND

BALTIC SEA

FINLAND

BARENTS SEA

Franz Josef Land

ARCTIC OCEAN

Kaliningrad

KALININGRAD (RUSSIA)

ESTONIA

Murmansk

LATVIA

LITHUANIA

Lake Ladoga

WHITE SEA

St. Petersburg

Novaya Zemlya

Severnaya Zemlya (North Land)

New Siberian Islands

BELARUS

Lake Onega

Arkhangelsk

KARA SEA

LAPTEV SEA

NORTHERN

Volga R.

EUROPEAN

Northern Dvina River

Pechora R.

TAYMYR PENINSULA

Yaroslavl

PLAIN

Vychegda R.

Khatanga R.

Moscow

Ryazan

Vorkuta

Norilsk

Verkhoyansk

UKRAINE

Don R.

Nizhniy Novgorod

URAL

Yenisey River

CENTRAL

Voronezh

MOUNTAINS

Ob River

Nadym

SIBERIAN

Kotuy

Penza

Kazan

WEST SIBERIAN

River

PLATEAU

Lena River

BLACK SEA

Sea of Azov

Izhevsk

PLAIN

Saratov

TATARSTAN

Perm

Nizhniy Tagil

S I B E R I A

Rostov

Volga River

Samara

Yekaterinburg

Nizhnevartovsk

Lower Tunguska River

Krasnodar

Volgograd

Volga-Don Canal

Ufa

Chelyabinsk

Yakutsk

Mount Elbrus 18,510 FEET 5,642 METERS Highest point in Europe

Orenburg

Irtysh River

Ob River

R U S S I A

Astrakhan

Magnitogorsk

CAUCASUS MOUNTAINS

KAZAKHSTAN

TURKEY

Angara River

GEORGIA

CASPIAN SEA

Ust' Ilimsk

BAIKAL-AMUR MAINLINE R.R.

AZERBAIJAN

Omsk

S I B E R I A

Lena River

TRANS-SIBERIAN RAILROAD

Novosibirsk

Tomsk

Krasnoyarsk

Bratsk

IRAN

KAZAKHSTAN

Kemerovo

Lake Baikal

Barnaul

Novokuznetsk

SAYAN MOUNTAINS

Chita

Ob River

Irkutsk

Shilka R.

CHINA

Ulan Ude

Argun R.

MONGOLIA

Boundary in dispute

A B C D E F G H J K L M N O P Q R

1 2 3 4 5 6 7 8 9 10 11 12 13 14 15 16 17 18 19 20

Russia

The year 1991 saw the momentous breakup of the powerful Soviet Union into 15 independent republics. Of these, the Russian Federation is by far the largest. It stretches halfway around the northern part of the globe and covers nearly half of two continents. European Russia is an extension of the rolling European plain that ends at the Ural Mountains. On the other side of the Urals, Asian Russia—called Siberia—begins as a vast, flat plain, rises to an immense plateau, and finishes as rugged mountain chains in the far east.

Russia ranks sixth in world population, and its 148.5 million people represent more than 80 ethnic groups. Four-fifths of the people are ethnic Russians, descended from Slavs who settled western Russia beginning in the sixth century. Most of them live in cities west of the Urals. Many of the other ethnic peoples live in the federation's 20 autonomous regions. The Tatars form the largest minority—about 3.6 percent of the population. Many live in autonomous Tatarstan. They descend from 13th-century Mongols who conquered Russia and ruled through Russian vassal princes for two centuries.

Russia's Arctic north is a treeless tundra, its permafrost reaching deep beneath the surface. South of the tundra, the taiga—a wide belt of hardy conifers stretching across the country—is succeeded by a mixed forest zone that extends from the Baltic Sea to just beyond the Ural Mountains. Below the forest zone are short-grass plains called steppes. People here grow crops such as wheat, rye, and sugar beets and raise cattle, sheep, and horses.

Some of the mightiest rivers in the world water this vast land. The Volga, Europe's longest river, and many others that drain western Russia empty into the Baltic, Black, and Caspian Seas. The swift rivers of Siberia, such as the Ob and the Yenisey, flow northward to outlets in the Arctic Ocean. They generate hydroelectric power for Siberia's coal and metal mines, oil and gas fields, lumber plants, and industrial cities.

Russia has been ruled by strong and often tyrannical leaders. Prince Ivan III overthrew the Mongols and restored Russian independence in the 15th century. Succeeding rulers expanded their territory. Peter I (the Great) brought Western culture to Russia and built his 18th-century capital, St. Petersburg, in newly acquired Baltic lands.

Centuries of tsarist oppression ended with the Russian Revolution of 1917. Four years of bloody civil war overthrew the tsars and created the communist Soviet Union. The government took over farms and industries, controlled information, and tried to shut out all influence from the West. Under the 30-year leadership of Joseph Stalin, 20 million citizens met their deaths. When Mikhail Gorbachev became head of the Communist Party in 1985, he initiated a move to *glasnost*—openness—and the resulting changes dissolved the Soviet Union in 1991. Russian life has changed dramatically since.

Though many Russians were ready for freedom, they were not prepared for the economic trauma that has accompanied it. Subsidies that controlled food and fuel prices were lifted, causing inflation to zoom to 1,000 percent and more, and unemployment is high. Products previously traded between the former Soviet republics in semi-barter fashion must now be purchased with hard currency, not devalued rubles. Efforts to privatize farms and industries have met with difficulties. Some autonomous republics are clamoring for independence. President Boris Yeltsin, who presided over the events of 1991, has faced much criticism of his leadership.

Official name: *Russian Federation*
Area: *6,592,692 sq mi (17,075,000 sq km)*
Population: *148,543,000*
Capital: *Moscow (met. pop. 9,000,000)*
Ethnic groups: *Russian, Tatar, many others*
Language: *Russian*
Religious groups: *Russian Orthodox, Muslim*
Economy: *Agr: grains, livestock, sugar beets, vegetables, fruit, tobacco. Ind: oil, natural gas, coal, iron ore, other minerals, machinery, wood and paper products, chemicals, motor vehicles, fishing*
Currency: *ruble*

1 *European Russia*

2 *European Russia*

3 *Siberian Russia*

4 *European Russia*

5 *Siberian Russia*

6 *European Russia*

Russia

1 *A long line of customers waits outside one of Moscow's McDonald's in hopes of sampling* big maks *and* chizburgers.

2 *Moscow's 16th-century Cathedral of St. Basil the Blessed was built during the reign of Tsar Ivan IV (the Terrible).*

3 *Children slide on icy Lake Baikal, parts of which remain frozen up to seven months of the year. Baikal is the oldest and deepest lake in the world.*

4 *Russian ballet has long reflected the essence of graceful classical tradition.*

5 *A hunter on the Taymyr Peninsula sets out to find arctic foxes and wild reindeer.*

6 *Sturgeon eggs, carefully washed, strained, and salted, become caviar in Astrakhan, on the Volga River Delta.*

A
A
U
C
A
S
U
S
M
O
U
N
T
A
I
N
S

B   RUSSIA

Gagra

Pitsunda
Gudauta
Sokhumi   ABKHAZIA
C
Tkvarcheli

Ochamchira   Dzhvari
D

Zugdidi
BLACK   **Kutaisi**   Tkibuli
SEA   SOUTH
E   OSSETIA
Poti   Tskhinvali
GEORGIA
F   Telavi
Kobuleti   Borzhomi   ⊗**Tbilisi**
Batumi
L   AJARIA   Akhaltsikhe   **Rustavi**   RUSSIA
G   E   Xacmaz
S   Bolnisi   Saki   Quba
S   *CASPIAN*
H   E   Alaverdi   *SEA*
R   Qazakh   Kura River   Siyazan
Gyumri   Mingacevir
J   Ganca   **AZERBAIJAN**   **Sumqayit**
Kirovakan   Dashkasan
Artyom
K   **ARMENIA**   NAGORNO-   **Baki (Baku)**⊗
Yerevan⊗   *Lake*   KARABAKH   Kazi Magomed
Sevan   Agdam   Sabirabad   Alat
L   C   Xankandi   Ali Bayramli
A   Kura River
U   Fuzuli   Salyan
C   Bilasuvar   Banka
M   NAXCIVAN   A   Masalli   Neftcala
(AZERBAIJAN)   S   Ghapan
U   Lankaran
N   Naxcivan   S
Aras   River   Astara
O   TURKEY
IRAN

P

Q   The soaring peaks of the   federated Soviet republic
Caucasus Mountains de-   called **Transcaucasia,**
fine the northern borders   the three became sepa-
R   of Georgia and Azerbai-   rate Soviet republics in
jan, with the Lesser Cau-   1936. Each now harbors
casus running through   ethnic conflicts that mar
S   northern Armenia to the   the independence
south. These ancient   achieved in 1991.
lands, much prized by
Persians, Turks, Rus-
T   sians, and other powers,
form a cultural bridge between Asia and Europe.
United in 1922 as a

0 KILOMETERS   100
0 STATUTE MILES   50

For map legend see page 21.

U

1   2   3   4   5   6   7   8   9   10   11   12   13   14   15   16   17   18   19   20   21

Georgia

In its days as a Soviet republic, Georgia supplied the rest of the former Soviet Union with nearly all of its tea and citrus fruit and much of its wine and tobacco. The small country's subtropical Black Sea coast and a mild, drier inland region favor the cultivation of these luxury crops.

Mountains and foothills cover most of Georgia. Ranges of the Caucasus rise in the north and south. Fruit and nut trees grow on their forested slopes; sheep and goats graze in summer on lush alpine pastures. Between the mountains lies a high central plateau.

Swift rivers provide hydroelectric power that helps run Georgia's industry, focused around the capital of Tbilisi. Natural resources include manganese, copper, coal, and some oil.

Three thousand years ago, Georgia was the site of a great civilization. The Georgian language, written in a distinct alphabet, belongs to the Caucasian language family, native to the Caucasus region. After converting to Christianity in the fourth century, Georgia was dominated at times by Mongols, Persians, and Turks and turned to Russia for help. It declared independence from the Soviet Union in 1991.

Strong cultural pride fuels many of Georgia's current troubles. There is fighting between the different ethnic groups in its three autonomous regions: Abkhazia, Ajaria, and South Ossetia. South Ossetia is seeking to secede from Georgia and unite with Russia's North Ossetia.

Economic problems include a dramatic plunge in industrial production, unchecked inflation, a severe oil shortage, and the disappearance of tourists from once crowded Black Sea beaches.

Official name: *Republic of Georgia*
Area: *27,027 sq mi (70,000 sq km)*
Population: *5,476,000*
Capital: *Tbilisi (pop. 1,260,000)*
Ethnic groups: *Georgian, Armenian, Russian*
Language: *Georgian, Russian*
Religious groups: *Georgian Orthodox*
Economy: *Agr: tea, fruit, tobacco, livestock. Ind: mining, metals, machinery, wine, tourism*
Currency: *ruble*

Armenia

Smallest of the former Soviet republics, Armenia is a rugged, mountainous land. It has rushing rivers and fertile valleys where fruit, wheat, cotton, and tobacco grow in the warm, dry summers. In the east, huge Lake Sevan covers 525 square miles (1,359 sq km).

In ancient times, Armenia was a large, powerful kingdom, far bigger than its present size. A fourth-century king converted to Christianity and made Armenia the first Christian nation. For much of its later history, Armenia was controlled by others—Arabs, Turks, Persians, and Russians. Early in this century the Ottoman Turks deported or killed many Armenians, causing more than a million deaths.

Armenians make up about 94 percent of the population, with Azeri and Russian minorities. Some 70 percent of the people live in urban areas, where many work in industry. Yerevan, the capital, is the center of industry and culture.

Trouble has plagued Armenia in recent years. A 1988 earthquake killed 25,000 people and left thousands homeless. A dispute with neighboring Azerbaijan over the fate of an Armenian enclave there escalated after Armenia declared freedom from the Soviet Union. With fuel and raw materials cut off by an Azerbaijani blockade, Armenian industry, along with the rest of the economy, barely survives.

Official name: *Republic of Armenia*
Area: *11,583 sq mi (30,000 sq km)*
Population: *3,504,000*
Capital: *Yerevan (pop. 1,199,000)*
Ethnic groups: *Armenian, Azeri, Russian*
Language: *Armenian, Russian*
Religious groups: *Armenian Apostolic*
Economy: *Agr: grains, fruit, cotton, tobacco, livestock. Ind: machinery, mining, chemicals, textiles*
Currency: *ruble*

Azerbaijan

Azerbaijan lies on the western shore of the Caspian Sea. At the beginning of the 20th century, with oil increasingly sought for transportation, industry, and heating, Azerbaijan was one of the world's largest oil producers. Its capital, Baki (Baku), on an oil-rich peninsula, serves as Azerbaijan's chief port and center for its oil refining and petrochemical industries.

The country encompasses a wide variety of terrain. Ranges of the Caucasus Mountains form its northern border, while those of the Lesser Caucasus straddle the border with Armenia in the southwest. Here Armenia's southern region cuts Azerbaijan off from one of its two autonomous regions, Naxcivan.

Lowlands skirt the Kura River and its tributaries. Much of the terrain is steppe or semidesert; where needed, irrigation is used to grow major crops such as cotton and wheat. The southern coastal climate is hot and subtropical. Citrus fruit, grapes, tea, and tobacco grow here. The Caspian Sea yields catches of sturgeon; their eggs, or roe, are prized as caviar.

Muslim Azeris make up 83 percent of the country's population, with Russians and Armenians each accounting for about 6 percent. Azeris, who speak a Turkic language, settled the area in the 11th century. At various times, Persians, Arabs, Mongols, and Russians controlled Azerbaijan. A brief independence after World War I was followed by a Soviet takeover.

Since 1988, a conflict has raged in Azerbaijan's second autonomous region, Nagorno-Karabakh. Its 90 percent Armenian majority wants to unite with Armenia. For five years, Armenians and Azeris have fought an ethnic war and Azerbaijan has blocked the transport of goods into Armenia. The violence has spilled over into the Azeri republic of Naxcivan.

Although oil production has dwindled over time, the promise of plentiful offshore oil may draw foreign investment to independent Azerbaijan. Russia, meanwhile, has aided the embattled country with much needed credit.

Official name: *Republic of Azerbaijan*
Area: *33,591 sq mi (87,000 sq km)*
Population: *7,146,000*
Capital: *Baki (Baku) (pop. 1,150,000)*
Ethnic groups: *Azeri, Armenian, Russian*
Language: *Azeri, Russian*
Religious groups: *Shia Muslim*
Economy: *Agr: cotton, fruit, vegetables, tea, tobacco. Ind: oil and natural gas, chemicals, steel, lumber*
Currency: *ruble*

1 *Armenia*

Armenia

1 *Mount Ararat, 40 miles (64 km) across the border in Turkey, towers above high-rises in Armenia's capital, Yerevan. The peak is the biblical resting place of Noah's ark.*

2 *Alpine meadows in southern Armenia offer ideal summer pasture for sheep and goats. Armenia has been privatizing its agriculture since before independence in 1991.*

2 *Armenia*

3 *Azerbaijan*

4 *Georgia*

5 *Georgia*

Azerbaijan

3 *Village elders congregate in Azerbaijan's rural south, near Lankaran. The warm climate here favors the growth of citrus trees, grapevines, and crops of tea and rice.*

Georgia

4 *In Tbilisi, a Georgian lights church candles to celebrate the 1992 overthrow of the republic's first popularly elected president, considered by many to be tyrannical. A state council later assumed control.*

5 *A bust of the republic's famous native son, Joseph Stalin, occupies the place of honor at the dinner table of one Georgian family.*

A | | | | | | | | | | | | | | | | | | | | | | RUSSIA

Petropavl

Komsomolets • Leninskoye

RUSSIA

Rudnyy **Qostanay** **Kokshetau** Irtyshsk **Pavlodar**

Shchuchinsk Bestobe Kalkaman

Oral Semiyarka Leninogor

Dzhanybek Charsk Zyryan

Aqtobe Ishim R. **Aqmola** **Semey** **Oskemen** **Oktyabrskiy**

Arqalyk KAZAKH Kokpekty Lake

Shakhtinsk Zaysan

Emba Irgiz **Qaraghandy** Ayaguz Zaysan

Caspian Depression Emba R.

Ganyushkino **Atyrau** **KAZAKHSTAN** UPLANDS Aktogay CHINA

Aralsk **Zhezqazghan** Balqash

Komsomolets Bay Saryshagan Lake Druzhba

CASPIAN SEA Beyneu Balkhash Karatal R.

Fort Shevchenko Say Utes ARAL SEA Sarygshagan Lake Balkhash Ili R. **Taldyqorghan**

USTYURT LOWLAND

Aqtau Zhaslyk **Qyzylorda** Chu R.

Kazakhskiy Bay Aksu PLATEAU Muynak Zhuantobe **Almaty (Alma-Ata)**

Bekdash Sarykamyshskoye Lake KYZYL KUM Turkestan Chu MUYUN KUM Narynkol

Nukus **Zhambyl** **Bishkek** Tokmak Przhevalsk

CASPIAN SEA Chagyl **Dashhowuz** TURAN Uchkuduk **Shymkent** KYRGYZ RANGE Talas Ysyk-Kol Lake + Pik Pobedy

Krasnovodsk **Urganch** **Toshkent** Ysyk-Kol 24,406 FEET

Turkmenskiy Bay Nebitdag KARA **UZBEKISTAN** **(Tashkent)** Fergana **KYRGYZSTAN** Naryn R. 7,439 METERS

Nawoiy **Jizzakh** **Angren** Valley **Namangan** Naryn

TURKMENISTAN **Bukhoro** **Khujand** **Andijon** TIAN SHAN CHINA

Gyzylarbat **Charjew** Amu **Qarshi** **Guliston** **Farghona** Osh

Hasan Kuli KOPET MTS. **Ashgabat** Darya R. **Samarqand** Jalal-Abad

Mary **Dushanbe** ZERAVSHAN RANGE **TAJIKISTAN** Rangkul

IRAN Kara Kum Canal **Qarshi** Kulob PAMIRS Shaymak

Sandykachi Termiz Khorugh Pamir R.

AFGHANISTAN

Gushgy

0 KILOMETERS 400

0 STATUTE MILES 200

For map legend see page 21.

Five ex-Soviet republics share a vast **Central Asian** terrain of deserts, steppes, and mountains crossed by two major rivers, the Amu Darya and the Syr Darya. Irrigation by fast-growing populations has depleted the Aral Sea at rivers' end by 60 percent, producing an ecological disaster that affects both climate and human health. Under Soviet planning, the soil was in some places exhausted by agricultural overproduction, and the use of chemical fertilizers caused pollution.

These countries now hope to derive prosperity from their huge reserves of natural gas and oil.

Kazakhstan

Stretching from the Caspian Sea to China, Kazakhstan became Asia's fourth largest country when it gained independence in 1991. Kazakh nomads traditionally herded livestock on the windswept steppes and parched deserts that cover four-fifths of its land. Two of its western lakes—the Caspian and Aral Seas— are salty and Lake Balkhash in the mountainous east is partly so. Precious water from the Syr Darya River in the south is almost all taken for irrigation before it reaches the Aral Sea.

Tsarist Russia absorbed the Kazakhs into its empire in the 18th and 19th centuries. Russian and Ukrainian serfs, freed after 1861, moved east and set up farms on Kazakh grazing lands.

Agriculture was collectivized under the Soviet government, and the nomads were forced to settle. In the process, an estimated one million Kazakhs died of starvation during the 1930s.

After World War II, Russian farmers plowed up the northern steppe and established huge, mechanized wheat farms. More Slavs came to work in mines and industries in the northwest and to run the space launching site and nuclear testing grounds in the east, so that Russians grew nearly as numerous as Kazakhs. Soviet developments in agriculture, space, and nuclear arms left Kazakhstan with long-term ecological and health problems.

Most Kazakhs work in the south as farmers or stock raisers. A nationalist movement arose in the 1980s. By the time independence came, the country's official language was Kazakh; nuclear testing was soon banned. Kazakhstan's economic reforms and its mineral wealth and vast oil fields are now attracting world trade.

Official name: *Republic of Kazakhstan*
Area: *1,049,039 sq mi (2,717,000 sq km)*
Population: *16,947,000*
Capital: *Almaty (Alma-Ata) (pop. 1,128,000)*
Ethnic groups: *Kazakh, Russian, other*
Language: *Kazakh, Russian*
Religious groups: *Muslim, Russian Orthodox*
Economy: *Agr: wheat, livestock, cotton. Ind: oil, mining, metals, machinery, chemicals, textiles*
Currency: *ruble*

Turkmenistan

Turkmenistan, on the east side of the Caspian Sea, is chiefly sandy desert. The people live where there is fresh water, mostly in oases created by mountain streams along the southern border with Iran and Afghanistan.

The capital, Ashgabat, near the Kopet Mountains, is the country's economic and cultural center. Farming in the south and northeast cannot feed the population, so food must be imported. Desalination plants on the shore of the Caspian Sea provide fresh water and electricity to industries in the arid west.

Before Turkmenistan was created in 1924, rival nomadic tribes raised camels and other livestock in the desert. Turkoman rugs and karakul furs are still highly prized. Under Soviet rule the tribes were settled on collective farms.

Construction of the 850-mile-long (1,368 km) Kara Kum Canal, the world's largest irrigation and shipping canal, began in the 1950s. It has tripled the arable land for intensive cotton growing but has also helped to dry up the Aral Sea.

Since independence, a strong, ex-communist president has taken a go-slow path to reform. The world's fourth largest reserve of natural gas lies beneath Turkmenistan's desert, so trade with the energy-hungry world seems assured.

Official name: *Turkmenistan*
Area: *188,418 sq mi (488,000 sq km)*
Population: *3,856,000*
Capital: *Ashgabat (pop. 407,000)*
Ethnic groups: *Turkmen, Russian, Uzbek*
Language: *Turkmen, Russian*
Religious groups: *Sunni Muslim*
Economy: *Agr: cotton, fruit, grains, livestock. Ind: gas, oil, chemicals, textiles, carpets, fishing*
Currency: *ruble*

Uzbekistan

Lying mostly between the Amu Darya and Syr Darya Rivers, Uzbekistan forms the heart of Central Asia. Deserts and steppe cover four-fifths of the land, but a string of fertile oases and the Fergana Valley in the mountainous east support some 21 million people.

Two thousand years ago, the oases of Bukhoro, Samarqand, and Toshkent (now the capital) were busy trade centers on the Silk Road linking China and Europe. After Arabs introduced Islam in the eighth century, the inhabitants built splendid mosaic-covered mosques that became centers of culture and learning.

In the early 16th century, Turkic-speaking nomads called Uzbeks drove out the inhabitants and ruled for 400 years until the area was seized by tsarist Russia in the 1860s. Later, communist rulers drew ethnic and linguistic boundaries in Central Asia, creating five new Soviet republics. Huge state cotton farms were established, and Toshkent grew into Central Asia's biggest, most industrialized city.

Beginning in the 1960s, intensive cotton farming has turned Uzbekistan into the world's third largest producer. Since independence in 1991, Uzbekistan's old communist leaders have resisted reforms. But there is a need to diversify crops and build trade, perhaps by exploiting newly discovered deposits of oil, gas, and gold.

Official name: *Republic of Uzbekistan*
Area: *172,588 sq mi (447,000 sq km)*
Population: *21,301,000*
Capital: *Toshkent (Tashkent) (pop. 2,073,000)*
Ethnic groups: *Uzbek, Russian*
Language: *Uzbek, Russian*
Religious groups: *Sunni Muslim*
Economy: *Agr: cotton, livestock, grains, fruit, vegetables. Ind: natural gas, chemicals, machinery, gold*
Currency: *ruble*

Kyrgyzstan

Kyrgyzstan is shaped like a crab's claw pinching sections of Tajikistan and Uzbekistan. Soviet planners drew boundaries in 1924 that divided the fertile Fergana Valley among the three republics.

Most of Kyrgyzstan is covered by the rugged Tian Shan range whose high crests border China. Lake Ysyk-Kol is one of the world's largest mountain lakes. Hot springs keep it unfrozen.

The Turkic-speaking Kyrgyz were nomadic herders for centuries before tsarist Russia annexed the area in 1876. Under Soviet rule, they were forced onto collective farms, while Slavic immigrants established mines and industries. The population is almost one-fourth Russian.

In 1990, ethnic riots in the Fergana Valley prompted democratic groups to oust their communist leaders and elect a Kyrgyz scientist as president. Broad economic reforms followed. Now seeking hard currency, Kyrgyzstan hopes to attract tourists to its spectacular scenery.

Official name: *Republic of Kyrgyzstan*
Area: *76,834 sq mi (199,000 sq km)*
Population: *4,506,000*
Capital: *Bishkek (pop. 616,000)*
Ethnic groups: *Kyrgyz, Russian, Uzbek, other*
Language: *Kirghiz, Russian*
Religious groups: *Muslim, Russian Orthodox*
Economy: *Agr: livestock, sugar beets, fruit, vegetables, cotton, grains. Ind: machinery, textiles, foods*
Currency: *som*

Tajikistan

Steep mountains cover 90 percent of Tajikistan. The Pamirs, bordering China in the east, contain the highest peaks in Central Asia. People live in southern river valleys and in the northern Fergana Valley. Rushing mountain streams provide electric power and water for irrigating crops of cotton and fruit.

Tajiks are the oldest ethnic group in Central Asia. They speak an Iranian language that stems from early contacts with Persia. Traditionally craftsmen and farmers, their culture survives among rival tribes in the mountains. Despite rich mineral deposits, Tajikistan was the poorest Soviet republic. After independence in 1991, joint Islamic and democratic forces violently challenged a holdover communist government. Bitter civil war broke out in 1992, enhanced by tribal and regional rivalries. Until stability returns, the outlook remains bleak.

Official name: *Republic of Tajikistan*
Area: *55,213 sq mi (143,000 sq km)*
Population: *5,272,000*
Capital: *Dushanbe (pop. 602,000)*
Ethnic groups: *Tajik, Uzbek, Russian*
Language: *Tajik, Russian*
Religious groups: *Sunni Muslim*
Economy: *Agr: cotton, fruit, livestock, perfume oils. Ind: mining, hydroelectric power, textiles, foods*
Currency: *ruble*

1 *Kyrgyzstan-China border*

2 *Turkmenistan*

3 *Turkmenistan*

Kyrgyzstan

1 *Mountaineers climb along a ridge to the 24,406-foot (7,439 m) summit of Pik Pobedy on Kyrgyzstan's border with China.*

Turkmenistan

2 *In a Muslim home in Mary, the hostess preparing green tea for family and guests seated on carpets is following a centuries-old social tradition of Central Asia.*

3 *A bicycle acts as mount for a young herdsman tending camels in the arid Kara Kum. Sturdy beasts of burden, camels are also bred for wool, meat, and milk.*

1 *Uzbekistan*

Uzbekistan

1 *Women in a Bukhoro embroidery factory stitch brilliant designs onto fabric that will be fashioned into traditional clothing.*

2 *Restored to their former beauty, mosaic-covered religious schools for Muslim boys in Samarqand's Registan Square represent architecture of the 15th and 17th centuries.*

Kazakhstan

3 *In Almaty, Shaggies's fast-food restaurant features Western-style uniforms and modern decor. It is a South Korean joint venture in Kazakhstan's boomtown capital.*

Tajikistan

4 *Workers toss cotton bolls with pitchforks to dry them in the sun. Long-staple cotton, requiring extensive irrigation in this arid land, is Tajikistan's most important crop.*

2 *Uzbekistan*

3 *Kazakhstan*

4 *Tajikistan*

BULGARIA

GREECE

GEORGIA

ARMENIA

IRAN

BLACK SEA

Edirne • Kirklareli

• Sinop

Zonguldak

• Karabuk

KUZEY

Samsun

Trabzon

Istanbul ← *Bosporus*

Izmit

Sea of Marmara

Adapazari

ANADOLU

MOUNTAINS

Coruh River

Dardanelles

Bandirma

Bursa

Sakarya River

Ankara ⊛

Kirikkale

Aras River

□ Troy

Balikesir

Kutahya

Eskisehir

Sivas

Erzincan

Erzurum

+ *Mount Ararat*
16,854 FEET
5,137 METERS

A N A T O L I A

Kizil River

TURKEY

Murat River

Van Lake

Manisa

Tuz Lake

Kayseri

Elazig

Van

Izmir

Aksehir Lake

CAPPADOCIA

Malatya

Diyarbakir

Batman

Hakkari

AEGEAN SEA

Denizli

Isparta

Konya

M O U N T A I N S

Maras

Tigris River

K U R D I S T A N

Great Zab River

Antalya

TAURUS

Tarsus

Gaziantep

Urfa

Al Qamishli

Little Zab River

Mersin

Adana

Iskenderun

Aleppo

Euphrates Dam

Mosul

Irbil

Dokan Dam
As Sulaymaniyah

Turkish Cypriots declared the striped area independent in 1983. Only Turkey recognizes this claim.

Nicosia ⊛

Latakia

Ar Raqqah

Lake Assad

Euphrates River

Khabur River

M E S O P O T A M I A

Kirkuk

Diyala River

Famagusta

Hamah

Dayr az Zawr

Tigris River

Tartus

CYPRUS

Limassol

Tripoli

Homs

Orontes River

Palmyra

Tharthar Lake

Khanaqin

LEBANON

Beirut ⊛

LEBANON MTS.

Baalbek

SYRIA

IRAQ

Baghdad ⊛

Sidon

Damascus ⊛

MEDITERRANEAN SEA

Tyre

GOLAN HEIGHTS

Ar Ramadi

Haifa

Sea of Galilee

S Y R I A N

Babylon

Tigris River

Irbid

Karbala

Al Hillah

ISRAEL

Tel Aviv-Yafo

WEST BANK

Az Zarqa

D E S E R T

Euphrates River

Al Amarah

Jerusalem ⊛

Amman

An Najaf

Bethlehem

Jordan River

Dead Sea
−1,312 FEET, −400 METERS

GAZA STRIP

Beersheba

The striped areas show the Israeli-occupied West Bank and Gaza Strip.

JORDAN

An Nasiriyah

Lake Hammar

Shatt al Arab

NEGEV

□ Petra

Basra

The countries on this map, along with Iran, Egypt, and the countries of the Arabian Peninsula, are often called the **Middle East.** There has long been conflict in the Middle East.

The founding of Israel in 1948 as a Jewish state led to war with its neighbors. One major issue is the dispute over the same ancestral lands by Israelis and Palestinian Arabs. A Jordanian-Palestinian delegation is striving to address this problem at Middle East peace talks.

Iraq electrified the world in 1990 by invading Kuwait, giving rise to the Persian Gulf war.

EGYPT

Elat

Aqaba

Gulf of Aqaba

SAUDI ARABIA

KUWAIT

PERSIAN GULF

RED SEA

| 0 | KILOMETERS | 250 |
| 0 | STATUTE MILES | 150 |

For map legend see page 21.

Turkey

East and West meet in Turkey, the country that bridges the continents of Asia and Europe. The European part of Turkey is a small peninsula of rolling grasslands in southeastern Europe. Across a series of waterways linking the Aegean and the Black Seas lies the Asian part of Turkey, a large, mountain-rimmed plateau called Anatolia.

Istanbul, Turkey's largest city, is the only city in the world on two continents. It occupies land on both sides of the Bosporus. Ferries and bridges connect its two halves. Once called Constantinople, Istanbul has been a major seaport for thousands of years.

More than half of Turkey's people are farmers. Many live in the mild coastal areas, where they plant crops such as cotton, tobacco, citrus fruit, and nuts for export, and raise livestock. On the drier and colder plateau, farmers grow mostly wheat and barley for use at home. In mountainous eastern Turkey, farming is more difficult, although people grow grain in the valleys and raise Angora goats for their long, silky hair. Though Turkey has some oil deposits, it must import most of its petroleum needs.

Turkey's rich mineral resources of coal, chromite, copper, and iron, and its cotton crop support major industries. These employ many city dwellers and make Turkey one of the most industrialized countries in the Middle East.

East meets West in Turkey's culture and government as well. Formerly center of the Islamic Ottoman Empire, Turkey became a republic in 1923. The new leader, Kemal Atatürk, abolished many Islamic customs and brought in European ideas and technology. This set the stage for rapid modernization and the adoption of Western systems of law, education, and politics.

Official name: *Republic of Turkey*
Area: *300,948 sq mi (779,452 sq km)*
Population: *59,245,000*
Capital: *Ankara (pop. 2,541,900)*
Ethnic groups: *Turk, Kurd*
Language: *Turkish, Kurdish, Arabic*
Religious groups: *Sunni Muslim*
Economy: *Agr: cotton, tobacco, grains, sugar beets, fruit, nuts, livestock. Ind: textiles, food processing, minerals, steel, oil, construction, lumber, paper*
Currency: *Turkish lira*

Cyprus

A delightful climate that allows a long growing season, golden sandy beaches, and archaeological sites spanning a rich history describe one face of the island nation of Cyprus. Its political climate shows a different one.

Fighting between the Greek-speaking Christian majority and the Turkish-speaking Muslim minority has resulted in a divided country, with the capital, Nicosia, split in the process. Greek Cypriots control the south; there, agriculture, light industry, tourism, and generous doses of foreign aid sustain the economy.

Fearing the imposition of *enosis*—union—with Greece, Turkish troops seized northern Cyprus in 1974 and gave Turkish Cypriots de facto control. In 1983 they claimed independence for the northern third of the island, naming it the **Turkish Republic of Northern Cyprus.** Turkey alone recognizes this claim. Turkish aid and tourism bolster a struggling local economy based mostly on citrus fruit and potatoes.

Negotiations to end the division of the island have been going on for many years. Meantime, a United Nations peacekeeping force patrols a 112-mile-long buffer zone across Cyprus.

Official name: *Republic of Cyprus*
Area: *3,572 sq mi (9,251 sq km)*
Population: *716,000*
Capital: *Nicosia (pop. 210,000)*
Ethnic groups: *Greek, Turk*
Language: *Greek, Turkish*
Religious groups: *Greek Orthodox, Sunni Muslim*
Economy: *Agr: fruit, potatoes, grains, olives. Ind: food processing, textiles, chemicals, tourism, mining*
Currency: *Cypriot pound, Turkish lira*

Lebanon

Tiny Lebanon was once a tourist paradise. Winter visitors could swim in the warm Mediterranean Sea, then ski the slopes of the Lebanon Mountains, all on the same day.

Beirut, the capital, was prosperous and cosmopolitan, the Paris of the Middle East. A center of international banking, trade, and education, Beirut had been a major port since the time of Phoenician traders 3,500 years ago.

Most of the Lebanese live in Beirut and other cities, mainly along the Mediterranean coast. Many are employed in Lebanon's major industries. Rural Lebanese are chiefly farmers. On the humid coastal plain they grow citrus fruit, olives, and grapes. Inland they plant vegetables, fruit, and grains in a fertile valley.

About one-third of Lebanon's people are Christian Arabs, of several different sects, and a majority are Sunni and Shia Muslim Arabs. Civil war among them, lasting from 1975 to 1990, destroyed much of Beirut. Syria and refugee Palestinians living in Lebanon were involved. Palestinian guerrilla strikes into neighboring Israel prompted an Israeli invasion in 1982 and the creation of an Israeli security zone in southern Lebanon. Beirut and the economy are on the mend, but Islamic fundamentalism is growing, especially among the Shia.

Official name: *Republic of Lebanon*
Area: *4,015 sq mi (10,400 sq km)*
Population: *3,439,000*
Capital: *Beirut (met. pop. 1,500,000)*
Ethnic groups: *Arab, Armenian*
Language: *Arabic, French*
Religious groups: *Muslim, Christian*
Economy: *Agr: fruit, wheat, corn, barley, potatoes, tobacco, olives, onions. Ind: banking, food processing, textiles, cement, oil, chemicals, jewelry, metals*
Currency: *Lebanese pound*

Syria

The roots of civilization in Syria reach far back into time. People have lived inside the walls of Damascus, its capital and major center of trade, since 2500 B.C., making it one of the oldest continuously occupied cities in the world.

Behind a narrow, fertile plain along the Mediterranean Sea rise mountain ranges that run south along Lebanon's eastern border. Damascus and other cities lie on a plain east of these mountains. Syria's industry is centered here, and most Syrians live here or on the coast.

While the majority of Syrians now live in urban areas, agriculture is also important. Along the coast farmers grow citrus fruit and vegetables. In the arid land east of the major cities they live in river valleys, using the water to irrigate fields of barley, wheat, and cotton. The latter provides valuable export earnings. In the Syrian Desert, small groups of nomads herd flocks of sheep and goats among the sparse vegetation.

In the 1970s, the Euphrates Dam was built. It created 50-mile-long (80 km) Lake Assad and brought promise of hydroelectric power and new agricultural areas. The Euphrates River has been a source of fertile land since ancient times. But when the irrigation systems from the dam are completed by the end of the century, Syria expects to double its irrigated farmland.

Future conflict over Euphrates water is likely, however, as Syria's upstream neighbor, Turkey, builds its own dams and irrigation projects on its part of the river, while Syria's downstream neighbor, Iraq, demands more water.

Official name: *Syrian Arab Republic*
Area: *71,044 sq mi (184,004 sq km)*
Population: *13,730,000*
Capital: *Damascus (pop. 1,378,000)*
Ethnic groups: *Arab, Kurd, Armenian*
Language: *Arabic, Kurdish, Armenian*
Religious groups: *Muslim, Christian*
Economy: *Agr: cotton, fruit, grains, tobacco, livestock. Ind: textiles, food processing, phosphates, oil*
Currency: *Syrian pound*

Iraq

Scholars locate the biblical Garden of Eden near the port of Basra in southern Iraq. Here the Tigris and Euphrates Rivers join to form the Shatt al Arab waterway. More than 4,000 years ago, the Sumerians built the world's first known cities on the Tigris-Euphrates plain. The rivers provided irrigation for crops that would support urban settlement.

Most of Iraq's people still live on the plain, many clustered in Baghdad, the capital, and other cities. Iraq has the world's second largest oil reserves, and oil income has made Baghdad a modern center of government and industry.

Desert covers southwestern Iraq, the traditional home of nomadic Bedouin herders, though many have now joined settled farmers and herders on the plain. Kurds inhabit the mountainous region that stretches from northern Iraq into neighboring countries. Non-Arab Muslims, the Kurds have long fought the Arab Iraqis for the independence of their homeland, Kurdistan.

For most of the 1980s, Iraq fought a bloody war with Iran that cost thousands of lives and caused billions of dollars in damage to cities, refineries, and shipping terminals in the Persian Gulf. In 1990, partly because of a dispute over oil, Iraq invaded neighboring Kuwait, but was ousted in 1991 by the U. S.-led Desert Storm coalition army. Increased persecution of the Kurds and the majority Shia population by the Iraqi leader, Saddam Hussein, and United Nations sanctions have led to continuing economic difficulties and an unstable political situation.

Official name: *Republic of Iraq*
Area: *169,235 sq mi (438,317 sq km)*
Population: *18,223,000*
Capital: *Baghdad (pop. 5,348,100)*
Ethnic groups: *Arab, Kurd*
Language: *Arabic, Kurdish*
Religious groups: *Shia Muslim, Sunni Muslim*
Economy: *Agr: vegetables, wheat, barley, dates, rice, cotton, livestock. Ind: oil, textiles, cement*
Currency: *Iraqi dinar*

Israel

Sabra, the name Israelis use for a cactus fruit, is the name they also give Jewish people born in Israel. With the creation of modern Israel in 1948, many Jews returned to their historic homeland, lost when the Romans exiled their ancestors some 1,900 years ago. Today, sabras make up about half the population of Israel.

Aside from the fertile Mediterranean coast, most of Israel is desert. To expand farmland, Israelis have mastered water management. One project pipes fresh water from the Sea of Galilee to irrigate *kibbutzim* (collective farms with assets owned in common) and *moshavim* (cooperative farms with some private ownership) as far south as the Negev desert region.

Israel's chiefly urban work force competes worldwide in high-technology industries. But diamond cutting and polishing, centered in the city of Tel Aviv-Yafo, is the most profitable industry. Jerusalem, the capital, contains ancient sites holy to Jews, Christians, and Muslims.

For centuries other native-born inhabitants of the area, Palestinian Arabs, have regarded the land they call Palestine as *their* homeland. In 1987 they began a defiant *intifada*—uprising—in the occupied territories seized by Israel in 1967. Most Palestinians now accept Israel's right to exist. But in the 1990s, dissatisfied with conditions and the continuing absence of statehood, many have turned to Islam and become more militant. Peace talks are trying to resolve the conflicting Israeli and Palestinian claims.

Official name: *State of Israel*
Area: *8,473 sq mi (21,946 sq km)*
Occupied territories: 2,416 sq mi (6,258 sq km)
Population: *5,233,000 (Occupied terr.: 2,043,000)*
Capital: *Jerusalem (pop. 504,100)*
Ethnic groups: *Jewish, Arab*
Language: *Hebrew, Arabic*
Religious groups: *Judaic, Muslim, Christian*
Economy: *Agr: citrus and other fruit, vegetables, cotton, livestock. Ind: food processing, diamond cutting, textiles, chemicals, machinery, electronics*
Currency: *new Israeli shekel*

Jordan

Jordan exports experts, it is said. Since 1962 the education-conscious country has started four major universities, including one in Amman, the capital. Many graduates find jobs in the oil-rich Persian Gulf states; the earnings they send home aid Jordan's economy.

Jordan's eastern desert is the traditional home of the tent-dwelling Bedouin, who herd livestock; many of them have now settled in towns or villages. Meager irrigated farmland lies in the Jordan River Valley. Minerals from the salty Dead Sea and other sites are made into fertilizer at a plant in Aqaba, Jordan's only port.

Jordan became an independent nation in 1946 under King Hussein's grandfather, Abdullah. After the 1948-49 Arab-Israeli war, Abdullah annexed the West Bank of the Jordan River, acquiring a large Palestinian Arab population swelled by refugees. Israel's seizure of the West Bank in 1967 displaced more Palestinians, who now make up nearly half of Jordan's population. Hussein renounced claims to the West Bank in 1988, endorsing Palestinian administration.

Since the Persian Gulf war, Jordan has suffered from a drop in trade with its main partner, Iraq, and from blame for neutrality in the war.

Official name: *Hashemite Kingdom of Jordan*
Area: *35,467 sq mi (91,860 sq km)*
Population: *3,557,000*
Capital: *Amman (pop. 936,300)*
Ethnic groups: *Arab*
Language: *Arabic*
Religious groups: *Sunni Muslim, Christian*
Economy: *Agr: vegetables, fruit, olive oil, wheat, livestock. Ind: chemicals, phosphates, potash*
Currency: *Jordanian dinar*

1 *Turkey*

2 *Turkey*

Turkey

1 *In Istanbul, the only city to straddle two continents, the domes and minarets of the Süleymaniye Mosque overlook waterways that separate Europe from Asia (in the far background).*

2 *Women of Turkey's Anatolia region weave a traditional rug with bold, geometric patterns. Turkish rugs have long been prized around the world.*

1   *Cyprus*

2   *Israel*

Cyprus

1   *Workers harvest grapefruits in a grove in northern Cyprus. The mild climate favors the growth of warm-weather citrus trees.*

Israel

2   *Source of life in a dry land, the Jordan River winds through green orchards and gray fields of cotton on a kibbutz, an Israeli collective farm.*

Jordan

3   *Jordanian women tend thriving cucumber plants in a plastic hothouse. Modern techniques yield big harvests from Jordan's scant fertile land.*

3   *Jordan*

4 *Iraq*

6 *Lebanon*

Iraq

4 An attendant prepares refreshments in a traditional teahouse on Rashid Street in Iraq's capital, Baghdad.

Syria

5 Portraits of President Hafez al-Assad decorate an entrance to the bazaar in the old part of Damascus. Stalls within offer spices and household necessities, as well as fine silks and inlaid wood and copperware.

Lebanon

6 An antiaircraft gun becomes a jungle gym for children in Beirut. Though the civil war in Lebanon is over, the wreckage of warfare still litters the city.

5 *Syria*

JORDAN

ISRAEL

IRAQ

0 KILOMETERS 300
0 STATUTE MILES 200
For map legend see page 21.

KUWAIT
Al Jahrah
⊕ Kuwait

Desert covers much of the **Arabian Peninsula.** As a result, settlement tends to concentrate along coasts or around fertile oases. The discovery of oil brought enormous wealth to the Persian Gulf states— those countries bordering the gulf coast.

Together with other oil-rich countries, some of them formed OPEC (Organization of Petroleum Exporting Countries).
In 1990-91, many of these nations were embroiled, directly or indirectly, in the Persian Gulf war to liberate Kuwait from the Iraqi invasion.

A

B

Gulf of Aqaba

Al Jawf

AN NAFUD

Tabuk

Hail

IRAN

PERSIAN
GULF

Strait of
Hormuz

C

Wadi al Hamd

N

Buraydah

T

Unayzah

Al Qatif

BAHRAIN

Ash Shariqah

Musandam Peninsula
(OMAN)

D

EGYPT

HEJAZ

Wadi ar Rimah

U

Ad Dammam
Dhahran

⊕ Manama

Dubayy

GULF OF OMAN

Medina

Wadi al Jarir

W

Hofuf

Dukhan

⊕ Doha
QATAR

Suhar

Yanbu al Bahr

A

⊕ Riyadh

Abu Dhabi
⊕

Matrah

E

TROPIC OF CANCER

Al Kharj

Y

Harad

Sabkhat
Matti

UNITED ARAB

⊕ Muscat

RED
SEA

Q

SAUDI ARABIA

EMIRATES

Sur

F

A   R   A   B   I   A   N

BOUNDARIES
UNDEFINED

G

Jiddah

Mecca

MTS.

+ Al Hadidah
(meteorite craters)

Umm
as Samim

QUARTER

At Taif

Masira

H

SUDAN

A

Wadi ad Dawasir

E M P T Y

(RUB AL KHALI)

OMAN

Qalat Bishah

J

Al Qunfudhah

P   E   N   I   N   S   U   L   A

K

Abha

S

Khamis Mushayt

BOUNDARY
UNDEFINED

Kuria Muria Islands

Najran

L

Jizan

Sadah

BOUNDARIES
UNDEFINED

Salalah

Wadi al Masilah

ARABIAN SEA

M

Kamaran

Marib

Saywun

Al Hudaydah

⊕ Sanaa

YEMEN

HADHRAMAUT

Ash Shihr

N

ERITREA

Dhamar

Al Bayda

Al Mukalla

Ibb

O

Bab al Mandab

Taizz

Socotra

Aden

GULF OF ADEN

P

DJIBOUTI

INDIAN
OCEAN

Q

SOMALIA

R

1   2   3   4   5   6   7   8   9   10   11   12   13   14   15   16   17   18   19

In 1991, Saudi Arabia became an active participant in the Persian Gulf war to liberate Kuwait, and Saudi territory was used as the operations base for the coalition forces.

Official name: *Kingdom of Saudi Arabia*
Area: *830,000 sq mi (2,149,690 sq km)*
Population: *16,057,000*
Capital: *Riyadh (pop. 1,308,000)*
Ethnic groups: *Arab*
Language: *Arabic*
Religious groups: *Sunni Muslim, Shia Muslim*
Economy: *Agr: wheat, dates, livestock. Ind: oil, petrochemicals, cement, steel, construction, fertilizer*
Currency: *Saudi riyal*

Saudi Arabia

For more than 13 centuries, Muslims all over the world have turned to face western Arabia five times a day. They are directing prayers to the Kaaba in Mecca, Islam's holiest city and birthplace of the Prophet Muhammad. Faithful Muslims hope to make the required hajj, or pilgrimage, to Mecca at least once in their lives.

During those centuries, much of the region's income came from pilgrims who visited Mecca and Medina, Muhammad's burial place. Today, Saudi Arabia's riches come from its east: A quarter of the world's known oil reserves lie beneath the Persian Gulf and the eastern desert.

Desert covers most of Saudi Arabia, harshest in the southeast's sparsely populated Empty Quarter. The country has no rivers or permanent bodies of water. Rainfall irrigates fertile croplands in the southwest, while seasonal wadis or year-round oases provide water for farming elsewhere. For millennia, nomadic Bedouin herders have brought their livestock to graze at desert oases fringed with date palms. Riyadh, the country's capital, sits amid a large oasis.

The modern kingdom of Saudi Arabia did not exist until 1932. Ibn Saud, who united the warring tribes of the Arabian Peninsula, became its first king. Oil, discovered in 1938, propelled Saudi Arabia into the modern world, providing funds for new schools, hospitals, towns, ports, and factories. Yet the country follows conservative Islamic laws. Alcohol is forbidden, and women are subject to many restrictions.

Kuwait

Once dependent on pearling, fishing, and trading, Kuwaiti economy and society were transformed after World War II by oil wealth. The government provided free education, subsidized health care, and other services. Foreign workers poured into Kuwait, making the Kuwaitis a minority in their own country. Desalination plants provided fresh water for industry, limited agriculture, and the expanding urban population.

In 1990 the Kuwaiti dream was shattered by the invasion of Iraqi troops. Although ousted by Desert Storm forces in 1991, the death and destruction they left behind have changed Kuwait forever. The psychological impact has been enormous, and reconstruction costs are currently estimated at about 25 billion dollars.

Official name: *State of Kuwait*
Area: *6,880 sq mi (17,818 sq km)*
Population: *1,379,000*
Capital: *Kuwait (pop. 44,300)*
Ethnic groups: *Arab, South Asian, Iranian*
Language: *Arabic, English*
Religious groups: *Sunni Muslim, Shia Muslim*
Economy: *Ind: oil, petrochemicals, desalination, food processing, salt, construction, fishing*
Currency: *Kuwaiti dinar*

Bahrain

One of the first countries on the Persian Gulf to strike oil may be the first to run out. Bahrain discovered oil in 1932 and soon was transformed from an archipelago of pearl divers to a significant producer of crude oil and natural gas. Of the 35 sand-covered islands that form the

emirate of Bahrain, only 6 are inhabited. Causeways link Bahrain Island, the largest and most heavily populated, with two other islands and with the mainland of Saudi Arabia.

Since their oil reserves may be gone by the year 2000, Bahrainis are developing other industries. Manama, the capital, has become an international banking center, with many foreign banks recycling the gulf region's oil money. Aluminum processing, shipbuilding and repairs, a duty-free port, and satellite communications may also help to ensure a prosperous future.

Official name: *State of Bahrain*
Area: *267 sq mi (691 sq km)*
Population: *531,000*
Capital: *Manama (pop. 151,500)*
Ethnic groups: *Arab, Asian, Iranian*
Language: *Arabic*
Religious groups: *Shia Muslim, Sunni Muslim*
Economy: *Agr: fruit, vegetables. Ind: oil and oil refining, aluminum, banking, ship repair, fishing*
Currency: *Bahraini dinar*

Qatar

A Qatari who wants to complain to the government can go straight to the top. The emir, or ruler, of Qatar will meet in person with any citizen. He makes decisions in consultation with his advisers and within the strict code of Islamic law followed there. Life in this country of stony desert jutting out into the Persian Gulf is still guided by tradition, more so than in some gulf coast countries where oil exports have also brought new prosperity. Qatari women remain heavily veiled. Until recently they were forbidden to drive, even though luxury cars have long been available in Qatar.

Former pursuits of pearl diving and camel herding have given way to jobs in the oil and natural gas industries. Qatar relies on workers from Iran, India, and Pakistan to fill many of these jobs but seeks to replace them with educated, trained Qatari citizens. Today only about a quarter of the population is native Qatari.

Official name: *State of Qatar*
Area: *4,247 sq mi (11,000 sq km)*
Population: *483,000*
Capital: *Doha (pop. 217,300)*
Ethnic groups: *Arab, Indian, Pakistani, Iranian*
Language: *Arabic*
Religious groups: *Sunni Muslim*
Economy: *Ind: oil, fertilizer, petrochemicals, steel, cement, fishing*
Currency: *Qatari riyal*

United Arab Emirates

In the dusty haze of dawn in Sharjah, one of the United Arab Emirates, young boys race their grumbling camels along a six-mile desert course. No betting occurs at these popular contests. It is forbidden by Islamic law in this federation of seven states, each ruled by an emir, or hereditary chieftain.

The discovery of oil in 1958 brought tremendous change to the emirates. Oil derricks drill along a coast once renowned for piracy. Oil money builds roads, ports, schools, and hospitals, and helps expand agricultural land.

When it comes to oil wealth, not all emirates were created equal. Abu Dhabi, which includes the capital, and Dubayy, another trade center, are the wealthiest, with the highest revenues.

Most of the population lives in towns that bear the same names as the emirates. For lack of citizens to fill all the jobs, foreigners form about 85 percent of the work force.

Official name: *United Arab Emirates*
Area: *32,278 sq mi (83,600 sq km)*
Population: *2,522,000*
Capital: *Abu Dhabi (pop. 243,000)*
Ethnic groups: *Arab, Indian, Pakistani, Iranian*
Language: *Arabic*
Religious groups: *Sunni Muslim, Shia Muslim*
Economy: *Agr: dates, alfalfa, vegetables. Ind: oil, fishing, petrochemicals, aluminum, cement*
Currency: *U.A.E. dirham*

Oman

Oil was found in Oman in 1964, but six years later life was little changed. Oman had once had a rich seafaring trade based on sail-driven dhows, but that had declined in the 20th century. Most Omanis still farmed, herded, or fished and had no education or health care. So Qaboos, the sultan's British-educated son, took matters into his own hands: In 1970 he overthrew his father and became sultan himself.

Today, Oman has more than 400 primary schools instead of only three, and 48 hospitals instead of only one, but it remains largely rural. Isolated villages on the Musandam Peninsula overlook the strategic Strait of Hormuz that funnels oil-laden tankers into the Arabian Sea. Fertile areas on Oman's north coast produce mostly dates and on the south coast, livestock.

Mountains in the north and a barren inland plateau complete the picture. Besides oil, great promise lies with an expanding copper industry and the building of deep-water ports.

Official name: *Sultanate of Oman*
Area: *82,030 sq mi (212,457 sq km)*
Population: *1,588,000*
Capital: *Muscat (pop. 85,000)*
Ethnic groups: *Arab, Baluchi, Indian*
Language: *Arabic*
Religious groups: *Ibadhi Muslim, Sunni Muslim*
Economy: *Agr: fruit, dates, grains, cattle, camels. Ind: oil, natural gas, copper, cement, fishing*
Currency: *Omani rial*

Yemen

Arabia Felix, "happy Arabia," the ancient Romans called this region, famed for its rich trade in the precious resins, frankincense and myrrh. Legend says the Queen of Sheba ruled part of it as a wealthy kingdom more than 2,500 years ago. Yemen's capital, the walled city of Sanaa, was once a crossroads for camel caravans bearing goods from as far away as China.

The northern part of Yemen has the greatest share of natural advantages on the Arabian Peninsula. Here high mountains trap the yearly rains. Farmers sow fertile fields in valleys and on terraced hillsides. They grow grains and *qat*, the shrubby plant whose leaves are chewed for their narcotic effect.

By contrast, the south has very little fertile land. Even so, nearly half of the work force is involved in agriculture, growing grains and dates, and raising livestock. The south's economic life centers on the port of Aden, strategically located near the entrance to the Red Sea. A refinery at Aden processes imported crude oil.

From the 1960s to 1990 Yemen was two countries known as the Yemen Arab Republic and the People's Democratic Republic of Yemen. The latter had a socialist government. In May 1990, they united under one flag, fulfilling the old Arab saying, "All Yemen is one."

Official name: *Republic of Yemen*
Area: *203,850 sq mi (527,968 sq km)*
Population: *10,395,000*
Capital: *Sanaa (pop. 427,200)*
Ethnic groups: *Arab*
Language: *Arabic*
Religious groups: *Shia Muslim, Sunni Muslim*
Economy: *Agr: grains, qat, cotton, coffee, fruit, vegetables, livestock. Ind: oil, textiles, leather*
Currency: *Yemeni rial*

1 *United Arab Emirates*

United Arab Emirates

1 *Bedouin keepers haul a balky camel toward the starting line for a race in Sharjah, one of the seven states that make up the United Arab Emirates.*

Saudi Arabia

2 *A swirl of Muslim pilgrims circles the Kaaba—Islam's holiest shrine—in Mecca. Several million come here each year to make the hajj, a pilgrimage aspired to at least once in a devout Muslim's life. Founded by the Prophet Muhammad in the seventh century, Islam is one of the most widely practiced religions in Asia.*

2 *Saudi Arabia*

1 *Oman*

2 *Saudi Arabia*

Oman

1 *A fisherman hauls his catch from coastal waters. Oil industry jobs have lured Omani fishermen away from the sea.*

Saudi Arabia

2 *At a lonely outpost in the Arabian desert, a derrick drills for oil. Saudi Arabia contains the greatest oil reserves in the world.*

3 *Brightly dressed girls swing on a beach at Jiddah. In a few years they will don the veil still worn for modesty by most Saudi women.*

3 *Saudi Arabia*

4 *Kuwait*

5 *Yemen*

Kuwait

4 *An Arab working with the U.S. Army Corps of Engineers confers about a reconstruction project in Kuwait City after the war with Iraq.*

Yemen

5 *An ilb tree stands beside the frankincense trail. The southern part of the Arabian Peninsula supplied frankincense and myrrh to the ancient world.*

0 KILOMETERS 300
0 STATUTE MILES 200

For map legend see page 21.

Iran and Afghanistan formerly shared their northern frontiers with a single superpower—the Soviet Union. Now their neighbors are five newly independent republics. This volatile region has seen recurring waves of political turmoil. Pakistan (including what has since become Bangladesh) was partitioned from India as a separate Muslim nation when India gained independence from the British in 1947. Iran's revolution in 1979 replaced its monarchy with an Islamic theocracy. Afghanistan, freed after a decade of occupation by Soviet troops, remains locked in civil war.

ARMENIA

AZERBAIJAN

Lake Urmia

Khvoy

Tabriz

Ardabil

CASPIAN SEA

TURKMENISTAN

TAJIKISTAN

UZBEKISTAN

Pyandz River

Pamir R.

CHINA

K2 (Godwin Austen)
28,251 FEET
8,611 METERS

TURKEY

Orumiyeh

Rasht

Bandar-e Anzali

Bojnurd

Atrak River

Feyzabad

HINDU KUSH

KARAKORAM RANGE

Zanjan

Qazvin

Mt. Demavend
18,606 FEET
5,671 METERS

Bandar-e Torkman

Quchan

Mazar-e Sharif

Baghlan

Chitral

Sanandaj

ELBURZ MOUNTAINS

Tehran

Mashhad

Meymaneh

K A S H M I R

Hamadan

PAROPAMISUS RANGE

Charikar

Kabul

Mardan

Area claimed by India

Kermanshah

Qom

Torbat-e Heydariyeh

DASHT-E KAVIR
(Salt Desert)

Herat

Harirud River

Khyber Pass

Islamabad

Arak

Kashan

IRAN

Ghazni

Peshawar

Rawalpindi

IRAQ

Dezful

Esfahan

Birjand

AFGHANISTAN

NORTH-WEST FRONTIER

Gujrat

Sialkot

Farah River

Sargodha

Gujranwala

Karun River

Yazd

DASHT-E LUT

Dera Ismail Khan

PUNJAB

Khorramshahr

Ahvaz

Zabol

Qandahar

Faisalabad

Lahore

Abadan

ZAGROS MOUNTAINS

Helmand River

DASHT-E MARGOW

Zhob River

Ravi River

Okara

KUWAIT

Persepolis

Kerman

RIGESTAN

Quetta

Multan

Sutlej River

Shiraz

Dera Ghazi Khan

Bahawalpur

SAUDI ARABIA

Bandar-e Bushehr

Zahedan

Bam

CHAGAI HILLS

PAKISTAN

INDIA

Persian Gulf

BALUCHISTAN

GREAT INDIAN DESERT

BAHRAIN

Bandar-e Abbas

Sukkur

QATAR

Strait of Hormuz

CENTRAL MAKRAN RANGE

SINDH

Hyderabad

Bandar Beheshti

Karachi

Indus River

UNITED ARAB EMIRATES

Gulf of Oman

TROPIC OF CANCER

OMAN

ARABIAN SEA

INDIAN OCEAN

Iran

The stern face of a gray-bearded man dressed in black appeared often in the news in the 1980s. He was the Ayatollah Khomeini, a Muslim religious leader who inspired a revolution in Iran, replacing the monarchy of the shah with a republic based on the teachings of Islam.

Iran consists of a high inland plateau largely covered with desert and salt flats and rimmed by mountains. Most people live in the north and northwest and on the narrow plain bordering the Caspian Sea. At least a third of Iran's cropland must be irrigated, some of it by an ancient technology using hand-dug underground canals called *qanats* to tap groundwater and carry it for miles to irrigate farmland. Wheat is the chief crop. Sheep, some tended by nomads, provide wool for finely woven carpets, known as "Persian" from Iran's former name, Persia.

Iran's people differ from those of other Middle Eastern countries in that they are mostly Persians, not Arabs, descended from Aryan peoples who migrated from Central Asia long ago. Most of them are Shia Muslims. The Shia disagree in certain religious interpretations with the Sunni, who form the Muslim majority worldwide.

Iran drilled the first oil wells in the Middle East in 1908. In the 1960s and 1970s, the shah used oil wealth to modernize his country and expand industry. But discontent mounted, both among conservative Muslims who wanted less influence from the West and liberals who wanted more democratic government.

The shah's regime collapsed in 1979, and Khomeini became the head of a religious form of government called a theocracy. Under Khomeini, Iran promoted the Islamic Revolution worldwide, sometimes through acts of violence.

In 1980 neighboring Iraq, taking advantage of Iran's weakened state and using a dispute over the strategic Shatt al Arab waterway as a pretext, attacked Iran. The war lasted eight years, disrupted agriculture and oil production, and took hundreds of thousands of lives.

Khomeini died in 1989. The new government appears less militant and helped arrange the release of Western hostages held in Lebanon. Yet Iran is slow in reestablishing contact with the West, and much anti-West sentiment remains.

Official name: *Islamic Republic of Iran*
Area: *636,296 sq mi (1,648,000 sq km)*
Population: *59,651,000*
Capital: *Tehran (pop. 6,042,600)*
Ethnic groups: *Persian, Azeri Turk, Kurd, other*
Language: *Persian, Turkic languages, Kurdish*
Religious groups: *Shia Muslim, Sunni Muslim*
Economy: *Agr: wheat, barley, rice, sugar, cotton, dates, grapes, sheep, goats, tea, tobacco, pistachios. Ind: oil, petrochemicals, textiles, cement, carpets*
Currency: *Iranian rial*

Afghanistan

A crossroads of Central Asia, Afghanistan has been invaded throughout its history. Successive groups have sought to attach this landlocked territory to their empires or to penetrate through the Khyber Pass to regions beyond. Those who came—Persians, Greeks, Arabs, Mongols, and others—left settlers who added to Afghanistan's ethnic diversity.

Most of Afghanistan is covered with mountains and desert. A plain in the north provides good farmland. The people are chiefly subsistence farmers and herders, members of a variety of tribal and ethnic groups. Less than 25 percent of them can read.

In Afghanistan, tribal and ethnic loyalties come first, which makes national unity a problem. But when the former Soviet Union sent troops to Afghanistan in 1979 to support the failing Marxist government there, they met fierce resistance from Muslim guerrillas known as *mujahidin*—holy warriors—united by their religious beliefs. During the ten years of Soviet occupation, millions of Afghans fled the country. Thousands more left their bombed-out villages and crowded into Kabul, the capital. With foreign troops now gone, strife among rival factions delays the task of rebuilding the country.

Official name: *Islamic State of Afghanistan*
Area: *251,773 sq mi (652,090 sq km)*
Population: *16,862,000*
Capital: *Kabul (pop. 1,424,400)*
Ethnic groups: *Pathan, Tajik, Hazara, Uzbek, other*
Language: *Pushtu, Dari (Persian), many others*
Religious groups: *Sunni Muslim, Shia Muslim*
Economy: *Agr: livestock, wheat, fruit, nuts. Ind: textiles, soap, furniture, shoes, cement, carpets*
Currency: *afghani*

Pakistan

The cradle of one of the world's oldest civilizations forms the heartland of modern Pakistan. About 4,500 years ago, planned cities with household water supplies and public sewer systems flourished on the Indus River Plain. Today that plain is the agricultural core of Pakistan, a Muslim nation created when India was partitioned in 1947. The Islamic faith unites the Pakistani people, who are otherwise divided by differences in language and cultural heritage.

Towering mountains occupy most of northern and western Pakistan. K2 (Godwin Austen), the world's second highest peak, rises 28,251 feet (8,611 m) in the Karakoram Range. Desert covers the southeast region, while a dry tableland ridged with low mountains spans the southwest.

About half of Pakistan's people are farmers. Wheat, the main food crop, and cotton, an important export crop and the basis for a growing textile industry, benefit from the world's largest integrated irrigation system. Much manufacturing is centered in Karachi, a populous port on the Arabian Sea.

In the 1990s, increased privatization of agriculture and industry has helped strengthen the economy. But Pakistan's rapidly growing population, swelled by Afghan refugees, many of whom remain in the northwestern border area, is straining the country's food resources.

Official name: *Islamic Republic of Pakistan*
Area: *307,374 sq mi (796,095 sq km)*
Population: *121,665,000*
Capital: *Islamabad (pop. 204,400)*
Ethnic groups: *Punjabi, Sindhi, Pathan, Baluchi*
Language: *Urdu, Punjabi, Sindhi, Pushtu*
Religious groups: *Sunni Muslim, Shia Muslim*
Economy: *Agr: wheat, rice, cotton, sugarcane. Ind: textiles, steel, food processing, cement, fertilizer, oil and natural gas*
Currency: *Pakistan rupee*

1 *Iran*

Iran

1 *In a fish factory on the Caspian Sea, women workers fill cans with caviar taken from sturgeon caught there. Their conservative dress is required by law in Iran.*

2 *Tehran clings to the southern slopes of the Elburz Mountains. Modern buildings here in the northern part of the capital give way to bazaars and poor housing in the south.*

Afghanistan

3 *The blue-domed mosque in Mazar-e Sharif, almost obscured by a flock of sacred white doves, stands at the reputed burial site of Ali, the Prophet Muhammad's son-in-law. The shrine is a center of pilgrimage.*

Pakistan

4 *Young women look out from a bus in Lahore. Pakistani women traditionally wear a scarf over their head and shoulders when appearing in public.*

5 *Bobbing in rowboat-like howdahs, women and children of western Pakistan ride camels to a wedding in traditional style.*

2 *Iran*

3 *Afghanistan*

4 *Pakistan*

5 *Pakistan*

A B C D E F G H J K L M N O P Q R S T

1 2 3 4 5 6 7 8 9 10 11 12 13 14 15 16 17

KILOMETERS 0 — 400
STATUTE MILES 0 — 200
For map legend see page 21.

Once a separate land-mass, the Indian subcontinent began to collide with continental Asia some 40 to 60 million years ago. It has rammed 1,250 miles (2,000 km) into Asia, pushing up the Himalaya, parts of which continue to rise about 1 inch (2.54 cm) every 5 years.

India owns three island groups in the surrounding seas, but the biggest island, Sri Lanka, and the Maldives are independent countries.

CHINA

KASHMIR
Srinagar
Indus River
Jammu
Amritsar
PUNJAB
Ludhiana
Chandigarh
Haridwar
Delhi
New Delhi ⊕
Yamuna River
Jaipur
Jodhpur
Ajmer
Gwalior
Kota
Udaipur
GREAT INDIAN DESERT
Luni River
PAKISTAN

Nanda Devi
25,645 FEET
7,817 METERS +
HIMALAYA
GANGES
Lucknow
Agra
Kanpur
Allahabad
Varanasi
Ganges
NEPAL
Kathmandu ⊕
Patan
Gorakhpur
PLAIN
Patna
River

Mount Everest
29,028 FEET
8,848 METERS
Highest point in the world
Kanchenjunga
28,208 FEET
8,598 METERS
SIKKIM
Gangtok
Darjiling
Biratnagar
Saidpur
Rangpur
BHUTAN
⊕ Thimphu
ASSAM
Brahmaputra River
HIMALAYA
Guwahati
Dibrugarh
Imphal
Sylhet

Meghna River
Rajshahi
BENGAL
Dhaka ⊕
BANGLADESH
TROPIC OF CANCER
Khulna
Chittagong
MYANMAR

Rann of Kutch
Ahmadabad
Rajkot
Bhavnagar
Indore
Vadodara
Bhopal
RANGE
CHOTA NAGPUR
Jabalpur
VINDHYA
Narmada River
INDIA
Jamshedpur
PLATEAU
Calcutta
Bilaspur
Mouths of the Ganges

Gulf of Khambhat
Surat
Akola
Amravati
Nagpur
Tapi River
Godavari River
Chandrapur
Mahanadi River
Cuttack
BAY OF BENGAL

Bombay
WESTERN
Pune
DECCAN
Sholapur
Warangal
GHATS
Vishakhapatnam
ARABIAN SEA
PLATEAU
Hyderabad
Kolhapur
Krishna River
Belgaum
Kurnool
Hubli
Bellary
EASTERN GHATS
Nellore
GHATS
Bangalore
Madras
Mangalore
Pondicherry
Coimbatore
Madurai
Palk Strait
Cochin
Jaffna
SRI LANKA
Trincomalee
Trivandrum
GULF OF MANNAR
Anuradhapura
Mahaweli River
Cape Comorin
Colombo ⊕
Kandy
Galle

INDIAN OCEAN

INDIA
BAY OF BENGAL
Lakshadweep (INDIA)
Andaman Islands (INDIA)
ANDAMAN SEA
LACCADIVE SEA
Nicobar Islands (INDIA)
⊕ Male
MALDIVES
EQUATOR
INDIAN OCEAN
Chagos Archipelago (BRITISH INDIAN OCEAN TERRITORY)

KILOMETERS 0 — 1000
STATUTE MILES 0 — 600

Area claimed by China

India

From the high wall of the Himalaya to the tip of Cape Comorin, the subcontinent of India reveals an enormous diversity of peoples, languages, and terrain. Tibetan-speaking herdsmen tend yaks and sheep in the western Himalaya. Hindi-speaking farmers live in mud-walled villages on the Ganges Plain. From Gypsies in the western desert to fishermen on the southwest coast, people converse in different languages. Hindi is the national one, but 17 other languages are recognized as official.

India's population adds up to more than 882 million—second in size only to China's. Nearly 40 percent of these people live on the fertile Ganges Plain. To the south stretches the Deccan Plateau, bordered by mountain ranges that drop to narrow coastal plains.

In this polyglot country, English serves as the chief language of government and business. This is a heritage from the years before 1947 when India was part of the far-flung British Empire and prized for its textiles, jute, indigo, and spices. The British represented the last of a number of conquerors.

Aryan herders from Central Asia arrived about 1500 B.C. Their religion blended with practices of the local people to form Hinduism, which is followed by more than 80 percent of Indians. Hinduism supports the organization of society into groups called castes. A person is born into a caste, which traditionally defines occupation, the groups one can eat with, and the groups into which one can marry. Groups with a very low status, such as latrine cleaners, were formerly called untouchables. The caste system still operates in India, although modern law makes discrimination illegal.

There are about 100 million Muslims in India, despite the fact that millions left in 1947, when the separate Muslim nation of Pakistan was partitioned off at the time of India's independence. Millions of Hindus and Sikhs also fled into India from the two areas designated as Pakistan, producing the largest mass migration of people in history—and perhaps the bloodiest, as Muslims and non-Muslims slaughtered each other.

More than 7 out of 10 Indians live in villages, and farming supports about two-thirds of the work force. Much of the land is fertile, but most farmers own merely a few acres and many none at all. They cannot afford fertilizer, good seed, or machinery, and most rely on the annual monsoon rains to provide water for their crops.

At least half of all Indians live in grinding poverty. In crowded cities, squatters' shacks spring up to house landless migrants from the countryside. More than 12 million people jam Bombay, India's largest metropolitan area, and Calcutta is not far behind. Industry is important in the cities. Cotton textiles are a major export, with huge factories located in Bombay. Calcutta manufactures jute, and the iron and steel mills of nearby Jamshedpur rank among Asia's largest. India also has a strong electronics industry.

With an electorate of more than 400 million, India is the world's largest democracy. Politicians campaign briskly in rural areas, where villagers who cannot read recognize the different political parties by their symbols. About half the people are illiterate, but the government is trying to improve this through village schools.

Hindus and Muslims still clash in India, as do Hindus and Sikhs, members of a militant offshoot of Hinduism, many of whom want their own independent state. Violence, poverty, and a skyrocketing population likely to exceed one billion by the year 2000 provide the most serious challenges to the future of this diverse country.

Official name: *Republic of India*
Area: *1,269,346 sq mi (3,287,590 sq km)*
Population: *882,575,000*
Capital: *New Delhi (pop. 294,100)*
Ethnic groups: *Indo-Aryan, Dravidian*
Language: *Hindi, English, many other languages*
Religious groups: *Hindu, Sunni Muslim, other*
Economy: *Agr: rice, wheat, sorghum, millet, legumes, oilseeds, cotton, jute, sugarcane, rubber, tobacco, tea, coffee. Ind: textiles, steel, machinery, motor vehicles, electronics, chemicals, mining, gems*
Currency: *Indian rupee*

Nepal

Nestled under the eaves of the lofty Himalaya, landlocked Nepal forms a steep staircase to the earth's highest mountain realm. Along its border with India, a flat region called the Terai lies only about 250 feet (75 m) above sea level. To the north, swift rivers lash the lower ranges of the Himalaya, shaping fertile valleys. On Nepal's border with China stand many of the world's highest peaks, with Everest topping the rest.

The average per capita income in Nepal is only $170 a year. About 80 percent of the people are subsistence farmers. They plant grain and tend livestock in the Terai and the central region, where most Nepalese live. Yak herders inhabit the northern high mountain zone.

Nepal is the world's only officially Hindu country, but Buddhism flourishes there as well. Temples and monuments of both faiths abound, especially in the Kathmandu Valley, site of the capital, Kathmandu. Festivals of either religion draw the whole community to celebrate.

Wood provides 70 percent of the country's fuel, and deforestation is rampant. Rapid population growth also drives farmers up mountain slopes to clear new fields. When the slopes are stripped of trees, erosion results, destroying fields and clogging rivers with mud. Villagers are planting new trees, and hydroelectric power may one day provide an energy alternative.

Official name: *Kingdom of Nepal*
Area: *54,362 sq mi (140,797 sq km)*
Population: *19,851,000*
Capital: *Kathmandu (pop. 235,200)*
Ethnic groups: *Indo-Nepalese, Tibeto-Nepalese*
Language: *Nepali, many others*
Religious groups: *Hindu, Buddhist*
Economy: *Agr: rice, corn, wheat, sugarcane, oilseeds, jute, livestock. Ind: tourism, textiles, cement*
Currency: *Nepalese rupee*

Bhutan

Money is new to the Bhutanese, as are roads and tourists. After centuries of self-imposed isolation under the feudal rule of Buddhist lords, the tiny Himalayan Kingdom of Bhutan, the Land of the Thunder Dragon, is entering the modern world slowly and cautiously.

Most Bhutanese grow grain and raise livestock on remote mountain slopes and in valleys cut by rivers flowing north to south. Fortress-like *dzongs*, massive stone religious and administrative centers, dominate the valleys. Above the tree line, herders pasture yaks in the summer. In southern Bhutan, farmers cultivate rice and fruit amid tropical vegetation.

Bhutan is ruled by a king under a treaty with India, whereby the latter provides foreign policy advice. To protect its cultural traditions, Bhutan limits tourists to a few thousand a year.

Official name: *Kingdom of Bhutan*
Area: *18,147 sq mi (47,000 sq km)*
Population: *800,000*
Capital: *Thimphu (pop. 20,000)*
Ethnic groups: *Bhotia, Nepalese*
Language: *Dzongkha (a Tibetan dialect), Nepali*
Religious groups: *Mahayana Buddhist, Hindu*
Economy: *Agr: grains, potatoes, fruit, cardamom. Ind: lumber, cement, chemicals, food processing*
Currency: *ngultrum*

Bangladesh

Water defines Bangladesh, the low delta country born of the silt carried by two major river systems, the Ganges and the Brahmaputra. They merge with the Meghna shortly before reaching the Bay of Bengal; there the combined streams drop their remaining load to form lacy fingers of land.

The river channels constantly shift course, and monsoon rains cause them to flood their banks. So rural Bangladeshis—about 85 percent of the population—must build their houses on mud platforms built from earth collected during the dry season. Boats provide most transportation; roads often wash out at the river's edge.

Fertile soil, the country's chief resource, and ample water enable Bangladeshi farmers to harvest as many as three rice crops a year. This is often not enough, though, to feed the inhabitants of the world's most densely populated agricultural nation. Farmers earn money by planting jute, Bangladesh's chief export. Cash crops of tea grow in hilly regions in the east.

The rainy season is a crucial time. Raging monsoon floods often combine with runoff from deforested slopes upriver in Nepal and northern India to drown the land, causing thousands of deaths and leaving millions of people homeless. At monsoon's end, cyclones may strike, followed by deadly tidal waves that surge up from the Bay of Bengal. When the rains come late, too, poor harvests cause widespread hunger.

Bangladesh was formerly East Pakistan, the smaller part of a two-part nation split off from India in 1947; West Pakistan lay 1,000 miles (1,600 km) away. The two had little in common besides the Muslim faith, and the East fought a civil war to gain independence in 1971. Bangladesh depends on foreign aid for survival. Its leaders strive against huge odds to improve the economy and to provide health, education, and employment for the ever-growing population.

Official name: *People's Republic of Bangladesh*
Area: *55,598 sq mi (143,998 sq km)*
Population: *111,445,000*
Capital: *Dhaka (met. pop. 5,731,000)*
Ethnic groups: *Bengali*
Language: *Bengali*
Religious groups: *Sunni Muslim, Hindu*
Economy: *Agr: rice, jute, tea, sugarcane. Ind: textiles, food processing, leather, fertilizer, shrimp, steel*
Currency: *taka*

Maldives

The Maldives archipelago, located in the Indian Ocean about 400 miles (644 km) southwest of India, consists of more than a thousand small coral islands. They form 19 atolls—groups of islands encircling a lagoon. Only 200 or so of the islands are inhabited. The original Maldivians probably arrived there from southern India and Sri Lanka several thousand years ago.

The islands' position near major sea routes brought traders of many nationalities. Legend says one traveler, a Muslim holy man, converted the people to Islam, now the sole religion.

Many Maldivians are poor and fish for a living, casting from boats for tuna. Some of the catch, boiled and smoked, becomes "Maldive fish," a delicacy exported to Japan, India, and Sri Lanka. Tourism also brings in much revenue. The government rents out some 60 islands as resorts—visited mostly by Europeans and Japanese drawn to the white sand beaches, colorful coral formations, and abundant marine life.

Official name: *Republic of Maldives*
Area: *115 sq mi (298 sq km)*
Population: *222,000*
Capital: *Male (pop. 55,100)*
Ethnic groups: *Maldivian*
Language: *Divehi*
Religious groups: *Sunni Muslim*
Economy: *Agr: coconuts, grains, root crops, vegetables, fruit. Ind: fishing, tourism, shipping, clothing*
Currency: *rufiyaa*

Sri Lanka

Sri Lanka has had various names over the centuries. Arab traders called this spice-growing island off the southeastern tip of India Serendib. This led to the word "serendipity," which means finding something valuable or pleasant by accident.

The moist, green highlands of Sri Lanka's southern interior *are* pleasant—and valuable, too. Tea, introduced by the British, who called the island Ceylon, flourishes there on well-tended plantations. Sri Lanka is the second largest tea exporter in the world. India comes first.

Flat or gently rolling plains cover the rest of Sri Lanka. Coconut and rubber plantations sprawl across the wet areas of the southwest. Spices are still cultivated but are now of little economic importance. Rice, the chief food crop, grows all over but must often be irrigated.

Sri Lanka's beautiful parks protect elephants and other wildlife. Inland, Buddhist monuments reflect the faith of 70 percent of the population. About nine out of ten Sri Lankans over age five can read, a very high literacy rate for Asia.

But Sri Lanka has its dark side. Since 1983 the Hindu Tamil minority in the north and east has been engaged in a civil war with the Buddhist Sinhalese majority. The Tamils claim discrimination and demand an independent homeland. Thousands of people have lost their lives in the fighting. India, concerned about the 50 million Tamils in its southernmost state, sent troops in 1987 to try to disarm the Sri Lankan Tamils, but withdrew them in 1990. Sri Lankans have discussed federation as a possible solution.

Official name: *Democratic Socialist Republic of Sri Lanka*
Area: *25,332 sq mi (65,610 sq km)*
Population: *17,632,000*
Capital: *Colombo (pop. 609,000)*
Ethnic groups: *Sinhalese, Tamil, Moor*
Language: *Sinhala, Tamil, English*
Religious groups: *Theravada Buddhist, Hindu*
Economy: *Agr: rice, tea, coconuts, rubber, sugarcane, livestock. Ind: textiles, cement, gems*
Currency: *Sri Lankan rupee*

India

1 *In royal splendor, the former Maharaja of Banaras leads a procession during a religious festival. Banaras, a holy city on the Ganges, draws millions of faithful Hindus who come to bathe in the sacred waters. The city's official name is Varanasi, but it is also widely known as Banaras.*

1 *India*

India

1 *Trucks, carts, bicycles, and rickshas vie for space on a crowded Delhi street. The old city and the capital, New Delhi, together form India's third largest urban area.*

2 *Village girls swing and sing to celebrate the coming of the monsoon season. Most Indian farmers depend on the regular arrival of the rains to water their crops.*

Sri Lanka

3 *A stroll along an ancient reservoir takes these children of Anuradhapura to school. Their town was once the capital of a long succession of Sinhalese kings.*

Nepal

4 *To curb erosion on this mountain slope, a boy plants pine seedlings near Kathmandu. Nepal now seeks to replenish forests cleared for farmland, firewood, and fodder.*

Bangladesh

5 *Bundles of jute, the country's main export, sail upstream from the Ganges Delta. Rivers transport goods and people in this watery land.*

1 *India*

2 *India*

3 *Sri Lanka*

4 *Nepal*

5 *Bangladesh*

China occupies the heart of **East Asia** in the region still often called the **Far East**, particularly by Europeans. Home to more than one-fifth of earth's people, China overshadows two tiny territories: Portugal's Macau and the United Kingdom's Hong Kong. Both are scheduled to be returned to China by the end of this century.

Taiwan is a part of China but has its own government, formed by Nationalist Chinese who fled the mainland in 1949 after the communist takeover. China is still trying to induce Taiwan to return to the control of the Beijing government.

RUSSIA

KAZAKHSTAN

Youyi Feng
14,350 FEET
4,374 METERS

Dund-Us

Uvs Lake

Hovsgol Lake

Uliastay

Darhan

Orhon River

Choybalsan

GREATER KHINGAN RANGE

Amur River

Qiqihar

Songhua River

Harbin

MANCHURIA

Altay

Bayanhongor

Ulaanbaatar

Herlen River

Changchun

Jilin

MONGOLIA

KYRGYZSTAN

Shihezi

Urumqi

ALTAY MOUNTAINS

Buyant-Uhaa

INNER MONGOLIA

Liao River

Shenyang

Fushun

TIAN   SHAN

GOBI

Anshan

NORTH KOREA

Dandong

Kashi

XINJIANG

Turpan Depression
-505 FEET
-154 METERS

Beijing

Hohhot

Baotou

Datong

Tianjin

Tangshan

Dalian

TAJIKI-STAN

Tarim River

Lop Nur

NORTH

SOUTH KOREA

AFGHANI-STAN

Shache

Kongur Shan
25,325 FEET
7,719 METERS

TAKLIMAKAN DESERT

Yumen

Jiayuguan

Great Wall

Yinchuan

Yellow River

Taiyuan

CHINA

Shijiazhuang

PLAIN

Qingdao

PAKISTAN

KUNLUN

Muztag
22,923 FEET
6,987 METERS

Qinghai Lake

Jinan

YELLOW SEA

Area claimed by India

MOUNTAINS

Golmud

Xining

Lanzhou

Wei River

Luoyang

Zhengzhou

Grand Canal

INDIA

Indus R.

PLATEAU OF TIBET

CHINA

Xi'an

Huainan

Wuxi

Yellow River

QIN   LING

Nanjing

Shanghai

TIBET

Yangtze River

Salween River

Mekong River

Yangtze River

Suzhou

Hangzhou

Ningbo

H I M A L A Y A

Brahmaputra River

Lhasa

Wuhan

Dongting Lake

Poyang Lake

Nanchang

EAST CHINA SEA

NEPAL

Xigaze

Chengdu

Changsha

Fuzhou

Taiwan Strait

Mount Everest
29,028 FEET
8,848 METERS
Highest point in the world

BHUTAN

Chongqing

Hengyang

Taipei

INDIA

Guiyang

Guilin

Xiamen

Taichung

TAIWAN

Kunming

Shantou

Tainan

TROPIC OF CANCER

Guangzhou

Kaohsiung

PACIFIC OCEAN

MYANMAR

Nanning

Xi River

HONG KONG (UNITED KINGDOM)

MACAU (PORTUGAL)

Victoria

LAOS

VIETNAM

Gulf of Tonkin

Haikou

SOUTH CHINA SEA

HAINAN

0   KILOMETERS   500

0   STATUTE MILES   300

For map legend see page 21.

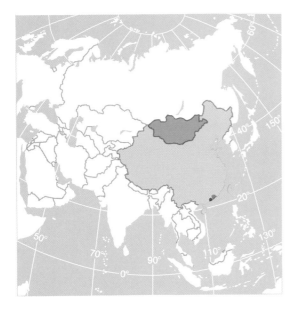

Mongolia

Genghis Khan, ruler of the Mongols, led an army of swift, fierce horsemen out of Central Asia around A.D. 1200 and founded a huge empire. Today, Mongolia is about twice the size of Texas, a high, dry plateau situated between China and Russia. For many years, most Mongolians were nomads who rode horseback to herd sheep and lived in round tents called *gers* or *yurts*. Camels and yaks provided transport for trade. Trucks and motorbikes are now taking over, and most people live in rural settlements or in towns.

A Chinese province known as Outer Mongolia for more than 200 years, Mongolia declared itself the Mongolian People's Republic in 1924. In 1992 it changed its official name to Mongolia and dropped the communist star from its flag.

The country was a buffer state between the former Soviet Union and China. Both vied in giving Mongolia economic aid to build up its industry, but animal husbandry remains the chief economic activity. Mongolia now is striving to convert to an independent market economy.

Official name: *Mongolia*
Area: *604,250 sq mi (1,565,000 sq km)*
Population: *2,252,000*
Capital: *Ulaanbaatar (pop. 548,400)*
Ethnic groups: *Mongolian, Kazakh*
Language: *Khalkha Mongolian*
Religious groups: *Lamaistic Buddhist*
Economy: *Agr: livestock, wheat, oats, barley, hay. Ind: animal products, building materials, mining*
Currency: *tugrik*

China

The Great Wall of China, snaking from the Yellow Sea to the desert lands of the west, was the Chinese Empire's defense against invaders from the north. Begun more than 2,200 years ago, it was rebuilt over the centuries. On its other borders, China was already protected by nature's barriers: seas, tropical forests, the world's highest mountains, and a vast desert.

For 4,000 years the Chinese shunned outside influence and built a great civilization in the country they called the Middle Kingdom. Foreign influence in politics, economics, and technology began to encroach in the mid-19th century, and in the 20th century China took its place as one of the world's great powers.

More than a billion people live in China—more than four times as many as in the United States, although China is only slightly bigger. Because much of the country is covered with mountains, arid steppe, or desert, 90 percent of the people crowd into the low-lying eastern third of China. Many cities such as the capital, Beijing, and Shanghai, China's largest city, hold millions of people, but most Chinese live in the countryside. Beijing is a northern city and Mandarin, a northern tongue, is the national language.

Chinese civilization began in the north along the Yellow River, or Huang He in Chinese. The population is still densest in fertile valleys where great rivers cross China. About 70 percent of Chinese farm the land. In the north they grow wheat for steamed bread and noodles. The Qin Ling Mountains divide the dry, cool north from the warm, moist south. Here the Yangtze River, China's longest waterway, flows 3,964 miles (6,380 km) from the Tibetan border to the East China Sea. Its Chinese name, Chang Jiang, means simply "long river." The south is called "China's rice bowl" because it supplies much of the country with its staple food, rice.

China's cold northeast, sometimes called Manchuria, has large deposits of oil, coal, and iron, as well as great forests for timber. Industry is strong there and the people enjoy one of the highest standards of living in China.

Western China consists of two regions rich in minerals and other resources that together make up about one-third of China's territory. Most people there belong to ethnic minorities. Xinjiang, a region of mountains and deserts, is inhabited chiefly by Central Asian peoples who are Muslims. Tibet, just to the south on the world's highest plateau, is often called "the roof of the world." Tibetans are devout Buddhists.

China has 55 ethnic minorities, many with their own customs, dress, and languages. The majority group, however, the Han Chinese, makes up about 93 percent of the population.

China was ruled by emperors until this century. A single family called a dynasty would hold power until it weakened and was overthrown. Then a new leader would start a new dynasty. Around 500 B.C., a philosopher named Confucius created a social philosophy that taught people to respect authority and seek harmony within both family and nation. This outlook prevailed throughout most of China's long history.

In the 19th century, European powers broke through China's isolation. Seeking trade in tea, silk, porcelain, and ivory, they introduced opium, which undermined Chinese society. By superior military power, they forced the Chinese to let them set up enclaves along the coast.

In 1911, Chinese revolutionaries overthrew the last emperor and made China a republic. After a decade or so of political disorder, the Nationalist Party ruled until 1949. A Chinese Communist Party formed in the 1920s, and after World War II civil war escalated between the two. In 1949 the Communists routed the Nationalists and established the People's Republic of China under Mao Zedong. The Nationalists fled to Taiwan and set up a rival government.

The Communists completely changed China. All land was claimed by the government. Peasants were organized into communes, and women joined the work force. Floods and famine, China's eternal scourges, were eased by new dams and improved agriculture. Many plans went wrong, though, and the cost of economic progress was lack of freedom. After Mao Zedong died in 1976, a new government under Deng Xiaoping brought reforms and offered signs that China was becoming a more open society. But a harsh crackdown in 1989 followed student-led protests in Beijing's Tiananmen Square.

In recent years, however, China's moves toward a market economy have brought unparalleled growth. Perhaps prosperity will lead to democracy, as it has in other Eastern nations.

Official name: *People's Republic of China*
Area: *3,705,407 sq mi (9,596,961 sq km)*
Population: *1,165,771,000*
Capital: *Beijing (pop. 7,000,000; met. pop. 9,879,700)*
Ethnic groups: *Han Chinese, 55 minorities*
Language: *Mandarin Chinese, many others*
Religious groups: *Confucian, Buddhist, Taoist*
Economy: *Agr: rice, wheat, corn, other grains, oilseeds, fruit, vegetables, sugarcane, cotton, livestock. Ind: steel, iron, coal, machinery, electronics, textiles, chemicals, food processing, paper, oil, fishing*
Currency: *yuan*

Taiwan

Two governments claim to rule China: the Communist Party government on the mainland and the Nationalist Party government on the island of Taiwan, which its leaders call the Republic of China. Neither government, in fact, has any control over the other's territory, yet both agree that Taiwan is a province of China.

Communists overthrew the Nationalist government in China in 1949. More than one million refugees fled to Taiwan. Their leaders set up the Nationalist government there, hoping to regain control of the mainland. Until 1971 Taiwan represented China in international affairs. That year the United Nations recognized the People's Republic of China instead.

Dynamic Taiwan, humming with industry, has one of the world's great trading economies, with many exports going to the United States. Most people live modern lives in Taiwan's crowded cities, but farmers also grow enough food to create a surplus for export.

Political reforms have loosened the hold of the former one-party system, and democrats are demanding an independent Taiwan. Some ruling party members suggest two Chinas with equal status, while China proposes autonomy under its rule. Taiwan's future remains unclear.

Official name: *Taiwan*
Area: *13,900 sq mi (36,000 sq km)*
Population: *20,830,000*
Capital: *Taipei (pop. 2,681,900)*
Ethnic groups: *Taiwanese, Chinese*
Language: *Mandarin Chinese, Taiwanese, Hakka*
Religious groups: *Buddhist, Confucian, Taoist*
Economy: *Agr: sugarcane, rice, vegetables, fruit. Ind: machinery, electronics, textiles, plastics, food processing, plywood, cement, shipbuilding*
Currency: *new Taiwan dollar*

Macau

Macau, a tiny enclave on China's south coast, has been a Portuguese trading center since 1557 and is now a "Chinese territory under Portuguese administration." Gambling has long been an important source of income, but Macau relies also on tourism and the manufacture of textiles, fireworks, and other goods for export. The capital city's architecture, customs, and official language are Portuguese, but most of its people are Chinese. In 1999, Macau will revert to China.

Official name: *Macau*
Area: *6.5 sq mi (16.9 sq km)*
Population: *474,000*
Capital: *Macau*

Hong Kong

Machinery whirs and business bustles around the clock. Hong Kong never sleeps. One of the world's greatest trading centers, the small British colony on China's south coast handles a huge volume of international trade through its deep, modern harbor surrounded by tall buildings.

Though Hong Kong is administered by a British governor, nearly all of its 5.7 million people are Chinese. It is one of the most densely populated places on earth. With little farmland, it must import most food and water from China.

The colony consists of several adjacent areas. The United Kingdom forced China to give up Hong Kong Island in 1842, then took another island and Kowloon Peninsula on the mainland in 1860. In 1898 the British leased a neighboring area called the New Territories for 99 years.

The United Kingdom has agreed to give the colony back to China in 1997. And China has promised to let Hong Kong keep its capitalist system and free life-style for 50 years. But the governor's efforts to push ahead democratic reforms in 1992 brought an angry Chinese response that alarmed the people about their fate.

Official name: *Hong Kong*
Area: *413 sq mi (1,071 sq km)*
Population: *5,748,000*
Capital: *Victoria*
Ethnic groups: *Chinese*
Language: *Chinese, English*
Religious groups: *Buddhist, Confucian, Taoist*
Economy: *Agr: rice, vegetables, livestock. Ind: textiles, electronics, finance, trade, tourism, shipping*
Currency: *Hong Kong dollar*

China

1 *Winding nearly 4,000 miles (6,437 km) from east coast to western desert, the Great Wall, begun more than 22 centuries ago, guarded ancient China's northern border.*

2 *Silkworms seek vacant compartments in a cocoon "condo." When settled, they spin the strong filaments used in thread and fabric.*

3 *Shoulder-harnessed trackers pull a junk upstream against the Yangtze's current.*

4 *China's largest city and major seaport, Shanghai is home to 12.5 million people.*

5 *Toy trucks destined for the United States take shape on assembly lines in one of China's Special Economic Zones. Low taxes and other bargains draw foreign investors.*

1 *China*

2 *China*

3 *China*

4 *China*

5 *China*

1 *Tibet, China*

China

1 *Horses graze beneath the Potala, the former palace of the Dalai Lama in Lhasa, Tibet. The Buddhist leader fled to India in 1959 after China crushed a Tibetan revolt.*

Hong Kong

2 *Night-lit skyscrapers illumine Hong Kong's thriving business district. Its magnificent harbor has made it one of East Asia's most successful trading centers.*

Mongolia

3 *A Mongolian horse breeder poses proudly with his stock. Mounted on swift steeds, his forebears conquered much of Asia in the 13th century.*

4 *Round felt tents called* yurts or gers *house nomad families. Many nomads have now settled on state farms or in urban areas.*

2 *Hong Kong*

3 *Mongolia*

4 *Mongolia*

0 KILOMETERS 250
0 STATUTE MILES 150

For map legend see page 21.

North and South Korea share a peninsula that for more than a thousand years held a unified country. Japan controlled Korea from 1910 until the end of World War II. Japan's defeat in 1945 resulted in the present north-south division.

Across the Korea Strait sprawls the 2,000-mile-long (3,220 km) archipelago of Japan, industrial giant of East Asia. Most of Japan's people share the same ethnic background, and this island nation shows a unique degree of cultural unity.

A
B
C
D
E
F
G
H
J
K
L
M
N
O
P
Q
R

1 2 3 4 5 6 7 8 9 10 11 12 13 14 15 16 17 18

RUSSIA

Teshio River

KITAMI MTS.

Asahikawa

Ishikari River

Sapporo

Tomakomai *HIDAKA RANGE*

Kushiro

HOKKAIDO

Uchiura Bay

Hakodate

SEIKAN TUNNEL

Tsugaru Strait

Aomori

Hachinohe

Akita

Morioka

HONSHU

Kitakami River

OU RANGE

Ishinomaki

Yamagata

Sendai

Sado

Niigata

Shinano River

ABUKUMA MTS.

JAPAN

Iwaki

MIKUNI RANGE

Toyama

Nagano

Utsunomiya

PACIFIC OCEAN

Kanazawa

Maebashi

RYOHAKU MTS.

AKAISHI RANGE

Tokyo
Yokohama

Gifu

Wakasa Bay

Lake Biwa

Mount Fuji 12,388 FEET 3,776 METERS

Nagoya

Kyoto

Shizuoka

CHUGOKU MTS.

Himeji

Kobe

Hamamatsu

Okayama

Osaka

Hiroshima

Sakai

Inland Sea

Wakayama

Takamatsu

MTS.

Matsuyama

Kochi

SHIKOKU

Kitakyushu

Suo Sea

Fukuoka

Beppu **Oita**

Sasebo

Kumamoto

KYUSHU MTS.

Nagasaki

+ Mount Aso 5,223 FEET 1,592 METERS

EAST CHINA SEA

Miyazaki

Kagoshima

KYUSHU

Osumi Islands

Tokara Islands

RYUKYU ISLANDS

SEA OF JAPAN

Oki Islands

KOREA STRAIT

Tsushima Islands

PHILIPPINE SEA

Cheju Island •Cheju

Goto Islands

Amami Islands

Naze

R Y U K Y U   I S L A N D S

Okinawa Islands

Naha

Okinawa

PHILIPPINE SEA

Sakishima Islands

R Y U K Y U

RUSSIA

CHINA

Paektu 9,003 FEET 2,744 METERS

Tu man River

Chongjin

Manpo

Yalu River

MOUNTAINS

NANGNIM

Kimchaek

NORTH KOREA

Sinuiju

Hamhung
Hungnam

Taedong River

Pyongyang

Wonsan

Korea Bay

Nampo

Kosong

Haeju

Sokcho

TAEBAEK

Seoul **Chunchon**

Inchon

Wonju

Suwon

Han River

YELLOW SEA

MTS.

SOUTH KOREA

Chongju

Naktong River

Taejon

Chonju

Pohang

Taegu

Ulsan

Kwangju

Masan

Mokpo

Pusan

Yosu

South Korea

South Korea occupies the lower 45 percent of the rugged Korean peninsula. Forested mountains cover its central region, rising to their highest in the east. Lowlands stretch along the south and west coasts, where most people live. A humid climate often allows two crops a year. People of both Koreas share the same language and ethnic heritage. They eat rice daily with their national dish, *kimchi*, a fiery mixture of cabbage, white radish, and red pepper.

South Korea encourages free enterprise and attracts many foreign investors. In the past 30 years the country has had strong economic growth. Much industry is centered around Seoul, the capital, only 25 miles (40 km) from the border with North Korea. In 1991, the two Koreas signed a mutual nonaggression pact.

South Korea has vigorously pursued export markets for its manufactures. In 1992 it restored normal relations with China—interrupted during the Korean War—thus expanding an already lucrative trade relationship.

Official name: *Republic of Korea*
Area: *38,230 sq mi (99,016 sq km)*
Population: *44,284,000*
Capital: *Seoul (pop. 10,628,000)*
Ethnic groups: *Korean*
Language: *Korean*
Religious groups: *Buddhist, Christian, Confucian*
Economy: *Agr: grains, vegetables, fruit. Ind: textiles, steel, electronics, ships, motor vehicles, fishing*
Currency: *South Korean won*

North Korea

The Korean peninsula lies between Japan and China. Japan controlled it from 1910 to the end of World War II. The Japanese defeat resulted in a division—meant to be temporary—that endures today. North Korea, then occupied by Soviet troops, became a communist state, and U. S.-occupied South Korea became a democracy.

North Korea has abundant resources of coal and iron ore but little farmland, because three-fourths of its mountainous terrain is forested. Even so, about a third of the people are farmers, organized into large collectives and state farms. Industry, a major income earner, suffers from aging equipment and power shortages.

In 1950, North Korea invaded South Korea. An armistice was signed in 1953, but North Korea still maintains a large army. Recent Korean unification talks were held up by concern over North Korea's nuclear program and its reluctance to comply with international regulations.

Official name: *Democratic People's Republic of Korea*
Area: *46,540 sq mi (120,538 sq km)*
Population: *22,227,000*
Capital: *Pyongyang (pop. 2,000,000)*
Ethnic groups: *Korean*
Language: *Korean*
Religious groups: *Buddhist, Confucian, Chondogyo.*
Economy: *Agr: rice, corn, vegetables. Ind: machinery, chemicals, mining, metals, textiles, cement*
Currency: *North Korean won*

Japan

Pop a tape into your VCR, turn on your TV, play a cassette on your boom box, boot your computer, or snap a picture with your camera. Each time you do one of these things, chances are you are using a product made in Japan. In little more than a hundred years, Japan has transformed itself from an isolated, feudal island empire to one of the world's leading manufacturers of electronic goods, cars, and ships.

This industrial miracle has been accomplished in a country that crowds 124 million people into a space about the size of California. Japan's four major and many smaller islands are spread out in a 2,000-mile-long (3,220 km) arc, but the extremely steep, forested terrain tends to limit settlement to narrow coastal plains and river valleys. Most crowded is the area from Kobe to Tokyo in the southern part of Honshu island. More than 50 percent of the people live there.

Japan is dangerously earthquake-prone. It experiences more than 10,000 tremors a year. Hundreds of volcanoes, at least 40 of them active, rise on the Japanese landscape. The most famous is Japan's highest mountain and national symbol, Mount Fuji, an almost perfect cone.

Japan has few mineral resources and must import fuel and nearly all the raw materials it needs for industry. Less than one-fifth of the land is suitable for cultivation. Remarkably, Japanese farmers grow about three-fourths of the country's food. They use modern farming technologies and have developed improved varieties of rice, the main food crop. Japan's fishing fleet, one of the largest in the world, provides another staple of the Japanese diet.

The country's chief resources are its people and a culture that allows for change. Early in its history, Japan borrowed heavily from China, adopting Chinese writing as well as ideas about art, music, and religion, especially Buddhism. Most Japanese today observe Buddhism along with Shintoism, Japan's own ancient religion.

Two centuries of isolation under the rule of military governors called shoguns ended in the 1860s. Japan sought out Western ideas and technologies in order to modernize the country and establish Japanese industry. The desire for raw materials spurred Japan to conquer countries in the Pacific and fueled its militancy in World War II. Japan emerged from defeat to become within a few decades an industrial giant. In the 1990s, complaints of unfair trade practices have led Japan to consider greater *kyosei*—symbiosis—with its chief partners, the U. S. and Europe.

Japanese life today blends the old with the new. The ancient sport of sumo wrestling competes with *beisuboru*, or baseball. Centuries-old dramas called No and Kabuki thrive alongside an enormous film industry. And no matter how busy their lives or how crowded their cities, Japanese seek inspiration in nature's beauty and simplicity, an aspect of their Shinto heritage.

Official name: *Japan*
Area: *145,875 sq mi (377,815 sq km)*
Population: *124,366,000*
Capital: *Tokyo (pop. 11,855,600; met. pop. 30,421,100)*
Ethnic groups: *Japanese*
Language: *Japanese*
Religious groups: *Shinto, Buddhist*
Economy: *Agr: rice, sugar, wheat, vegetables, fruit. Ind: metals, machinery, electrical products, electronics, motor vehicles, textiles, chemicals, cement, fishing, shipbuilding*
Currency: *yen*

1 *Japan*

2 *Japan*

3 *Japan*

4 *Japan*

Japan

1 *The snowcapped cone of Mount Fuji rises above the haze on Honshu. The volcano is sacred to members of the Fujiko sect, who seek harmony with nature by climbing it.*

2 *A computerized locator map in this Honda helps a driver navigate city streets. Japan exports about four million cars each year.*

3 *A monk rakes pebbles in a Zen garden near Kyoto. In this form of Buddhism, doing such a simple, mechanical task can bring the mind enlightenment.*

4 *Aspiring sumo wrestlers try to topple a professional who probably outweighs each boy six to one. Though popular, the ancient sport has lost many fans to baseball.*

South Korea

5 *The heavy traffic of modern Seoul circles the city's old South Gate. One in four South Koreans now lives in the teeming capital.*

North Korea

6 *In a factory in Nampo, a worker uses a lathe to polish glassware to a smooth finish.*

5 *South Korea*

6 *North Korea*

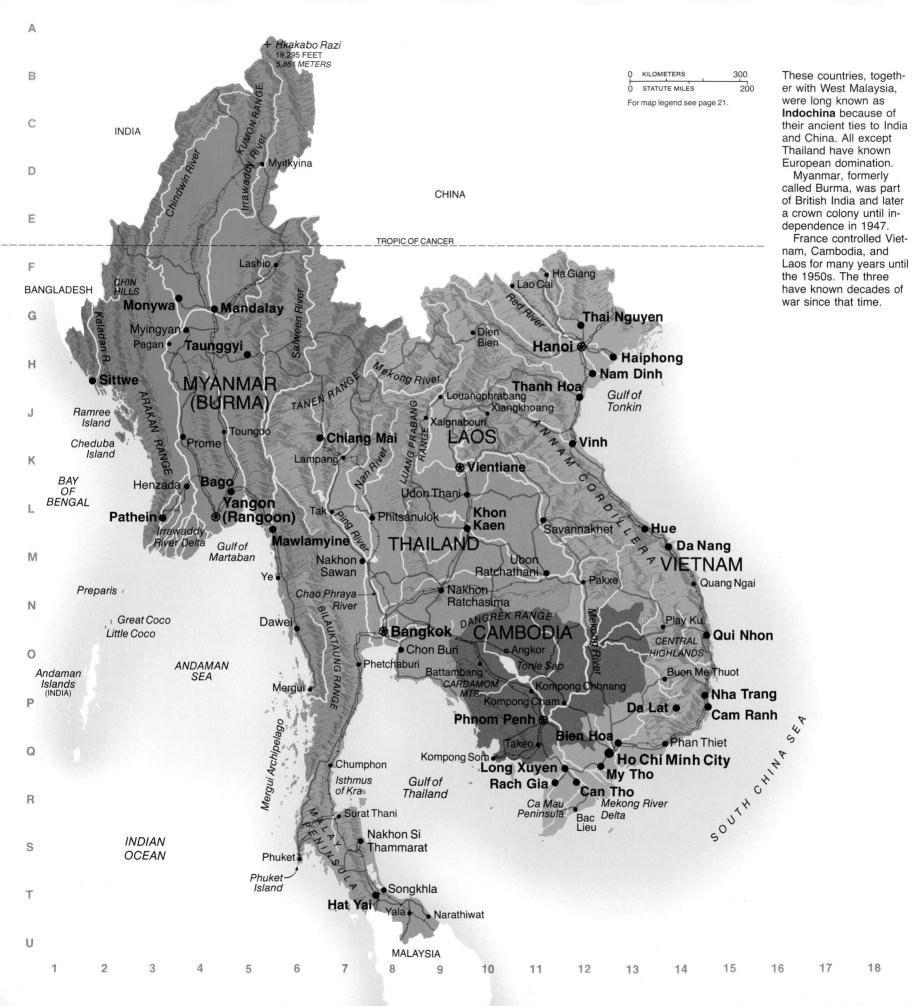

These countries, together with West Malaysia, were long known as **Indochina** because of their ancient ties to India and China. All except Thailand have known European domination.

Myanmar, formerly called Burma, was part of British India and later a crown colony until independence in 1947.

France controlled Vietnam, Cambodia, and Laos for many years until the 1950s. The three have known decades of war since that time.

0 KILOMETERS 300
0 STATUTE MILES 200
For map legend see page 21.

A
B
C
D
E
TROPIC OF CANCER
F
G
H
J
K
L
M
N
O
P
Q
R
S
T
U

1 2 3 4 5 6 7 8 9 10 11 12 13 14 15 16 17 18

Hkakabo Razi
19,295 FEET
5,881 METERS

INDIA

CHINA

Myitkyina

KUMON RANGE

Chindwin River

Irrawaddy River

BANGLADESH

CHIN HILLS

Lashio

Ha Giang
Lao Cai

Monywa   Mandalay

Myingyan
Pagan   Taunggyi

Salween River

Dien Bien

Thai Nguyen

Red River

Hanoi

Haiphong
Nam Dinh

Sittwe

MYANMAR
(BURMA)

Mekong River

Thanh Hoa

Gulf of
Tonkin

Kaladan R.

TANEN RANGE

Louangphrabang
Xiangkhoang

LAOS

Vinh

Ramree
Island

Xaignabouri

Cheduba
Island

Toungoo
Prome

Chiang Mai

LUANG PRABANG RANGE

Vientiane

ARAKAN RANGE

Lampang

Nan River

Udon Thani

ANNAM CORDILLERA

Hue

BAY
OF
BENGAL

Henzada   Bago

Ping River

Phitsanulok

Khon
Kaen

Savannakhet

Da Nang

Pathein

Yangon
(Rangoon)

Tak

THAILAND

VIETNAM

Irrawaddy
River Delta

Mawlamyine

Gulf of
Martaban

Nakhon
Sawan

Ubon
Ratchathani

Quang Ngai

Ye

Chao Phraya
River

Pakxe

Preparis

Nakhon
Ratchasima

Play Ku

Great Coco
Little Coco

Dawei

BILAUKTAUNG RANGE

DANGREK RANGE

CAMBODIA

CENTRAL
HIGHLANDS

Qui Nhon

ANDAMAN
SEA

Bangkok

Angkor

Mekong River

Buon Me Thuot

Andaman
Islands
(INDIA)

Chon Buri

Tonle Sap

Phetchaburi

Battambang

Kompong Chhnang

Nha Trang

Da Lat

CARDAMOM
MTS.

Kompong Cham

Cam Ranh

Mergui

Phnom Penh

Bien Hoa

Phan Thiet

INDIAN
OCEAN

Chumphon

Kompong Som

Takeo

Long Xuyen

Ho Chi Minh City

My Tho

Isthmus
of Kra

Gulf of
Thailand

Rach Gia

Can Tho

Mekong River
Delta

Mergui
Archipelago

Surat Thani

Ca Mau
Peninsula

Bac
Lieu

SOUTH CHINA SEA

MALAY PENINSULA

Nakhon Si
Thammarat

Phuket

Phuket
Island

Songkhla

Hat Yai   Yala   Narathiwat

MALAYSIA

Myanmar

Until 1989 Myanmar was known as Burma, a name that referred only to the Burmans, the nation's largest ethnic group. But many other groups share this country, the largest on the Southeast Asian mainland, so its name was changed to one that the people use for their country.

A horseshoe of mountains and a high plateau rim Myanmar on three sides. Through the center flows the Irrawaddy River, the country's lifeline, providing transportation and fertile soil. Two-thirds of the population lives in the Irrawaddy Valley; the delta yields abundant crops of rice, one of the chief exports. Yangon (Rangoon), the capital, also serves as the major port.

Myanmar has ample mineral deposits and forests that provide 75 percent of the world's teak, but the economy suffers from poor planning, a thriving black market, and an illegal opium trade. The military-ruled government has virtually abolished democratic law, and ethnic minorities lack representation. Such problems keep Myanmar one of Asia's poorest countries.

Official name: *Union of Myanmar (Burma)*
Area: *261,218 sq mi (676,552 sq km)*
Population: *42,502,000*
Capital: *Yangon (Rangoon) (pop. 2,458,700)*
Ethnic groups: *Myanmar (Burman, Shan, Karen)*
Language: *Myanmar (Burmese), Shan, Karen*
Religious groups: *Theravada Buddhist*
Economy: *Agr: rice, legumes, oilseeds, sugarcane, peanuts. Ind: food processing, textiles, teak, mining*
Currency: *kyat*

Thailand

Thailand is shaped like an elephant's head. Mountains in the north and west form the long forehead. A dry eastern plateau marks the ear. The mouth cuts into the fertile central plain, the country's "rice bowl," while the trunk snakes down the narrow, tin-rich peninsula that connects Thailand with Malaysia.

Established as a kingdom in the 13th century, the country was named Siam in 1782. Unlike its Southeast Asian neighbors, Siam was never ruled by a Western country. In 1939 it changed its name to Thailand—"land of the free."

Most Thai are farmers who live in villages where the *wat*, or Buddhist temple, is the social and religious focus for the community. Many young Thai men shave their heads and eyebrows and don yellow robes for at least several months of life as a Buddhist monk.

Thailand is prosperous, with a growing economy. Bangkok, the capital, is the chief port and industrial center. Tourists visit the city's many temples, as well as the island resort of Phuket and the uplands around Chiang Mai. But Thailand faces many problems. Higher incomes in the city have drawn an influx of rural poor, causing overcrowding and pollution. Of concern, too, are refugee groups on the Cambodian border and a rebellious Muslim minority in the south.

Official name: *Kingdom of Thailand*
Area: *198,457 sq mi (514,000 sq km)*
Population: *56,340,000*
Capital: *Bangkok (met. pop. 5,876,000)*
Ethnic groups: *Thai, Chinese*
Language: *Thai*
Religious groups: *Theravada Buddhist*
Economy: *Agr: rice, sugarcane, corn, rubber, cassava, pineapples. Ind: tourism, textiles, tin, fishing*
Currency: *baht*

Laos

Geographically, politically, and economically, Laos is truly a land caught in the middle. Five countries hem in this nation covered with mountains and rain forest. During the Vietnam War, North Vietnamese Communists used Laos as a supply route to South Vietnam. With no access to the sea, Laos depends on Thailand and Vietnam to help get its exports to market.

About half the people are ethnic Lao. Most of them live in villages on the fertile floodplain of the Mekong River and its tributaries, which also form the main transportation network. Nearly all Lao are farmers who grow sticky rice. Tribal peoples such as the Hmong live in the highlands, supplementing their income from slash-and-burn agriculture by planting opium poppies.

Laos has known little peace since its independence from France in 1953. Two decades of civil war ended in 1975 with a communist takeover aided by North Vietnam. To improve the economy, the government now allows more private enterprise and foreign trade and investment.

Official name: *Lao People's Democratic Republic*
Area: *91,429 sq mi (236,800 sq km)*
Population: *4,440,000*
Capital: *Vientiane (pop. 377,400)*
Ethnic groups: *Lao, tribal Thai, Hmong*
Language: *Lao*
Religious groups: *Theravada Buddhist, tribal*
Economy: *Agr: rice, corn, vegetables, fruit, coffee, cotton. Ind: tin, gypsum, lumber, electricity, fishing*
Currency: *new kip*

Cambodia

A large, fertile basin watered by the Mekong River system forms the heart of Cambodia. The basin also contains Tonle Sap, a lake that quadruples in size during the rainy season. The annual flooding enriches the soil with sediment, and farmers plant rice. Mountains and forested hills surround the basin on three sides.

Nine out of ten Cambodians are Khmer, descendants of a people who controlled Southeast Asia from the 9th to the 13th century. The Khmer built magnificent stone and brick temples at Angkor. Angkor lies now in partial ruin, victim of the invading forest and of nearly ceaseless civil wars since 1970. Cambodia suffered greatly under a radical communist regime that destroyed the economy and caused the deaths of more than a million people. Some of the refugees who fled to Thailand have returned. But United Nations efforts to unite rival political groups have not yet restored peace and stability.

Official name: *Cambodia*
Area: *69,898 sq mi (181,035 sq km)*
Population: *9,054,000*
Capital: *Phnom Penh (met. pop. 800,000)*
Ethnic groups: *Khmer, Chinese*
Language: *Khmer*
Religious groups: *Theravada Buddhist*
Economy: *Agr: rice, rubber, corn, cassava, pepper. Ind: rice milling, textiles, fishing, lumber, cement*
Currency: *riel*

Vietnam

Vietnamese describe their country as "two rice baskets dangling from opposite ends of a carrying pole." In the north lies the fertile delta of the Red River. Dikes and irrigation channels enable its farmers to harvest two crops of rice each year. The south contains the wide, swampy delta of the Mekong River, one of the world's most productive rice-growing areas. The "pole" is the Annam Cordillera, a mountain chain covering two-thirds of the country. To the east of that range lies a narrow coastal plain.

The Vietnamese, who came from China more than 2,000 years ago, remained in the north for centuries. There Vietnamese culture took shape with many Chinese influences, including Buddhism. Gradually the Vietnamese moved south.

Vietnam was controlled by France for about 70 years before nationalists drove the French out in 1954. Independence resulted in a divided country. Communist North Vietnam's desire to control non-communist South Vietnam led to the ten-year-long Vietnam War. More than three million United States troops were sent to help fight the Communists. Saigon, the capital of South Vietnam, fell to the North in 1975. All of Vietnam was united under a communist government based in Hanoi, the North's capital, and Saigon was renamed Ho Chi Minh City.

Today Vietnam is gradually recovering from wartime damage that undermined its economy. But this recovery effort has been hurt by huge cuts in aid from the former Soviet Union. Offshore oil exploration has begun to attract considerable foreign investment. More is expected if the Vietnamese cooperate fully in accounting for U. S. servicemen missing in action (MIAs) and normal political relations between the two countries can be reestablished.

Under new, liberal policies, a market economy is gaining strength, and many consumer goods are now available. The south, especially Ho Chi Minh City, has adapted faster than the north to this economic dynamism.

Official name: *Socialist Republic of Vietnam*
Area: *127,242 sq mi (329,556 sq km)*
Population: *69,212,000*
Capital: *Hanoi (pop. 1,088,900)*
Ethnic groups: *Vietnamese*
Language: *Vietnamese*
Religious groups: *Mahayana Buddhist, Taoist*
Economy: *Agr: rice, rubber, fruit, vegetables, corn, sugarcane. Ind: food processing, oil, cement, metals, chemicals, paper, machinery, textiles, fishing*
Currency: *dong*

1 *Myanmar*

2 *Laos*

3 *Vietnam*

4 *Thailand*

5 *Cambodia*

Myanmar

1 Worth nearly its weight in gold, Shwe Dagon Pagoda in Yangon glistens with 90 million dollars' worth of the metal. Legend says eight hairs of the Buddha rest within.

Laos

2 Laotians pan for gold in the mud of the Mekong River. The small amounts extracted provide farmers with extra income.

Vietnam

3 Imposing buildings and tree-lined boulevards give Hanoi a French air. The French controlled Vietnam for some 70 years.

Thailand

4 Before dawn, a tapper slits a rubber tree to start the flow of latex into a cup below. The sap runs heaviest early in the day.

Cambodia

5 Making one of the 2,000 gestures she needs to qualify, this student of Khmer ballet hopes to join the national dance troupe.

Island archipelagoes form Indonesia and the Philippines. This southeastern region of Asia is dotted with volcanoes, part of the Pacific Ring of Fire. Here, the Philippine plate slides under the Eurasian plate. Friction and heat result in volcanic eruptions.

Along with Indochina, these scattered island countries are referred to as **Southeast Asia.** The countries on this map and Thailand have joined in the Association of Southeast Asian Nations, known as ASEAN.

0 KILOMETERS 500
0 STATUTE MILES 300

For map legend see page 21.

Batan Islands

Babuyan Islands

Baguio • Banaue

PHILIPPINE SEA

LUZON

Mount Pinatubo
Angeles **Quezon City**
Manila

MINDORO

PHILIPPINES

Calbayog *SAMAR*

PANAY **Tacloban**
Iloilo *CEBU* *LEYTE*

Bacolod **Cebu**

PALAWAN *NEGROS*

• Butuan

SULU SEA

MINDANAO

Zamboanga

Kinabalu
13,455 FEET
4,101 METERS • Kudat

Mount Apo
9,692 FEET
2,954 METERS **Davao**

PACIFIC

Kota Kinabalu • Sandakan

OCEAN

SOUTH CHINA SEA

Banda Aceh

George Town **Kota Baharu**

Kuala Terengganu

Ipoh MALAYSIA

Medan

Pematangsiantar

MALAY PENINSULA

THAILAND

SABAH *Sulu Archipelago*

BRUNEI **Bandar Seri Begawan**
Miri •

MALAYSIA

CELEBES SEA

Manado

Strait of Malacca

Kuala Lumpur

Sibu • SARAWAK *Kayan River*

Gorontalo Ternate • *HALMAHERA*

Dumai •

Johor Baharu

SINGAPORE Kuching •

BORNEO

Kapuas River

Samarinda

Pekanbaru

Pontianak • Sintang

INDIAN OCEAN

Padang *Hari River*

SUMATRA

KALIMANTAN

Balikpapan **Palu**

Kerinci
12,467 FEET
3,800 METERS

Jambi

Barito River

CELEBES

Makassar Strait • Mamuju *Malili Lake Towuti*

MOLUCCAS (SPICE ISLANDS)

Sorong •

Palembang

BANGKA

GREATER SUNDA ISLANDS

BILLITON

INDONESIA

Banjarmasin

BURU *CERAM*

Bandar Lampung

JAVA SEA

Ujungpandang

BANDA SEA

Ambon

Jakarta

Bogor **Cirebon** **Semarang** *Madura*
Bandung **Surabaya**
Surakarta
Borobudur □
Yogyakarta **Malang** *BALI* *SUMBAWA* *FLORES* *ALOR*
Banyuwangi • • Raba • Ruteng • Dili

JAVA **Denpasar**

Mount Agung
10,308 FEET
3,142 METERS

LESSER SUNDA ISLANDS

SUMBA • Waingapu

TIMOR

Kupang

TANIMBAR ISLANDS

TIMOR SEA

Philippines

Described as "a piece of Latin America in the Pacific," the Philippines is unique in Southeast Asia. This sprawling archipelago encompasses 7,100 islands spread across 500,000 square miles (1,295,000 sq km). Claimed for Spain in 1521 by Ferdinand Magellan and named after King Philip II, the Philippines spent 333 years as a Spanish colony. Because of this heritage, about 85 percent of the people are Roman Catholic.

The islands are tropical and mountainous with narrow coastal plains. They lie at the mercy of nature's often destructive forces. Typhoon season can bring storms packing winds of 185 miles an hour (298 kmph). Volcanoes erupt, creating havoc. In 1991, Mount Pinatubo, 55 miles (89 km) northwest of Manila, erupted, killing nearly 900 people and destroying the livelihood of some 650,000 more.

The archipelago's first inhabitants are thought to have crossed by land bridges from mainland Asia some 30,000 years ago. Later, groups of Malays, ancestors of most modern Filipinos, arrived by boat in a succession of migrations. One group of Malays, the Ifugao, built extensive, irrigated rice terraces on Luzon like those still cultivated there.

Today about 700 islands are inhabited. Most people live on Luzon or Mindanao, which make up two-thirds of the country. Agriculture, fishing, and forestry employ about half the work force. The Philippines is the largest exporter of coconuts and coconut oil. The products of its vast but dangerously depleted hardwood forests are major exports, too; Philippine mahogany is famous throughout the world. Industry, centered around Manila, the capital, employs about 10 percent of the working population, but power shortages hinder full-scale production.

Filipino is the official language, but English is widely spoken and is used in all the schools. The United States controlled the Philippines from 1898 until the Japanese occupation in World War II. In 1946 the Philippines set up a U. S.-inspired democratic system. The present leader, President Fidel Ramos, succeeded Corazon Aquino, who had peacefully forced out dictator Ferdinand Marcos. Ramos now faces the huge task of improving the neglected economy and initiating a land reform program.

Official name: *Republic of the Philippines*
Area: *115,831 sq mi (300,000 sq km)*
Population: *63,667,000*
Capital: *Manila (pop. 1,876,000)*
Ethnic groups: *Malay*
Language: *Filipino, English*
Religious groups: *Roman Catholic, Muslim*
Economy: *Agr: rice, corn, coconuts, sugarcane, fruit. Ind: food processing, textiles, chemicals, wood products, electronics, minerals, oil refining, fishing*
Currency: *Philippine peso*

Malaysia

Malaysia owes much of its economic success to some rubber seeds that a 19th-century British explorer smuggled out of Brazil. The British took some seedlings to their protectorate on the Malay Peninsula and established rubber plantations there in the 1890s. Today, Malaysia is the world's leading producer of natural rubber.

Only half of Malaysia occupies the lower peninsula. The other half lies 400 miles (644 km) across the South China Sea on the island of Borneo. Both sections have mountainous interiors and swampy coastal plains. Heat and abundant rainfall promote dense rain-forest vegetation, including about a thousand varieties of orchids.

Nearly half the people are descendants of Malays who came from southern China about 4,000 years ago. Most Malays today farm or fish for a living. In the 19th century, the British recruited Indian workers for the rubber plantations, where most of their descendants have stayed. Chinese also came to mine tin, another export. Many Chinese took their earnings to the cities and started businesses. Tribal groups such as the Iban live in the rain forests of East Malaysia.

An independent federation since 1963, rich in resources that include timber and petroleum, Malaysia is booming. The country is now emphasizing industrial development. Manufacturing is centered around densely populated Kuala Lumpur, the capital, and the busy port of Pinang. A literate work force, low wages, and political stability attract foreign investors, but the government encourages Malay business ownership.

Official name: *Malaysia*
Area: *127,317 sq mi (329,749 sq km)*
Population: *18,742,000*
Capital: *Kuala Lumpur (pop. 919,600)*
Ethnic groups: *Malay, Chinese, Indian, other*
Language: *Malay, many other languages*
Religious groups: *Muslim, Buddhist, Hindu*
Economy: *Agr: rubber, oil palm, rice, cacao, pepper. Ind: electronics, oil, tin, textiles, lumber, fishing*
Currency: *ringgit or Malaysian dollar*

Singapore

Located off the tip of the Malay Peninsula, the tiny country of Singapore is made up of 58 islands. The country, chief island, and capital are all called Singapore. Established by the British in 1819 on the site of a Malay fishing village, Singapore was valued for its deep-water harbor and strategic position along the narrow sea routes connecting the Indian and Pacific Oceans. It quickly became an important free port and entrepôt—a distribution center—for goods traveling between Asia and the West.

Since independence in 1965, Singapore has concentrated on industrial development. The per capita income is one of the highest in Asia. Most people live in self-contained "new towns," complete with high-rise apartments, shopping centers, and recreational facilities, but a strict government limits personal freedom. Singapore

EQUATOR

• Mogoi

Mamberamo River

Jayapura

IRIAN JAYA

Jaya Peak +
16,500 FEET
5,029 METERS

MAOKE MOUNTAINS

NEW GUINEA

ARU ISLANDS

PAPUA NEW GUINEA

Digul River

DOLAK

ARAFURA SEA

AUSTRALIA

21   22   23   24   25   26   27   28   29   30   31   32

must import most of its food and even its water, which is piped in from Malaysia.

Official name: *Republic of Singapore*
Area: *239 sq mi (618 sq km)*
Population: *2,765,000*
Capital: *Singapore*
Ethnic groups: *Chinese, Malay, Indian*
Language: *English, Malay, Chinese, Tamil*
Religious groups: *Buddhist, Muslim, Hindu*
Economy: *Agr: poultry, vegetables, fruit, orchids. Ind: oil refining, electronics, shipbuilding, finance*
Currency: *Singapore dollar*

Brunei

The Sultan of Brunei rules his tiny Islamic kingdom with a firm hand, but most people don't seem to mind. Wealth from oil and natural gas provides Brunei's citizens with free education and medical care, and low-cost housing, fuel, and food.

Brunei consists of two separate wedges of land in northern Borneo. Most people live along the coast near the offshore oil fields or in the capital, Bandar Seri Begawan. Like other towns and villages in the swampy lowlands, part of the capital is built on stilts. Most Bruneians work for the government or in the oil industry. The country must import the bulk of its food. Brunei is the newest member of ASEAN, the regional economic and political union.

Official name: *State of Brunei Darussalam*
Area: *2,226 sq mi (5,765 sq km)*
Population: *275,000*
Capital: *Bandar Seri Begawan (pop. 52,300)*
Ethnic groups: *Malay, Chinese, other*
Language: *Malay, English, Chinese*
Religious groups: *Sunni Muslim, Buddhist*
Economy: *Agr: rice, cassava, fruit, vegetables. Ind: oil, natural gas, construction, fishing*
Currency: *Brunei dollar*

Indonesia

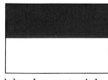

"Unity in diversity" is the national motto of Indonesia. Some 300 ethnic groups speaking more than 250 languages inhabit this 13,677-island equatorial archipelago that extends for 3,200 miles (5,150 km). Indonesia has the largest population in the world after China, India, and the United States.

Less than half of the mountainous islands are inhabited. Sixty percent of the huge population lives on Java, an island about the size of Alabama. Java also contains most of the archipelago's active volcanoes, whose ash often creates fertile farmland. Rain forest and swamps cover much of neighboring Sumatra, a site of rich offshore deposits of oil and natural gas.

The Moluccas, known as the Spice Islands, have supplied the world with cloves, nutmeg, and pepper for centuries. Drawn by the spice trade, Portuguese, Spanish, British, and Dutch adventurers sailed to Indonesia in the 1500s. The Dutch eventually controlled most of the islands as a colony. Independence came in 1949.

Irian Jaya occupies the western half of the island of New Guinea. Only decades ago, headhunting and cannibalism were practiced by the tribes living among its remote rain forests. Irian Jaya and Kalimantan today are Indonesia's frontier, with valuable mineral resources, vast stands of hardwoods, and spare land for resettling people from overcrowded islands in a program known as "transmigration."

Many centuries ago, rival Buddhist and Hindu kingdoms vied for control of the archipelago with its vital waterways that link the Pacific and Indian Oceans. Later, Muslim traders brought Islam, which spread throughout the islands except for Bali. Today Indonesia has more followers of Islam than any other country.

On Bali, Hindu beliefs still hold fast. Combined with spirit and ancestor worship, they guide all aspects of life. Here and on Java, graceful dancers perform the precise movements of ancient dances to the exotic strains of a gamelan orchestra. Instruments include metal gongs, drums, and the xylophonelike *gambang.*

Most Indonesians farm, growing rice and other food crops on small plots of land. They also work on plantations that supply cash crops such as rubber. Industry, including tourism, draws many would-be workers to cities like Jakarta, the capital, on densely packed Java. There the less successful live in makeshift housing and earn a meager living selling food or operating foot-driven pedicabs. Indonesia's major need is to create new jobs for its growing population.

Official name: *Republic of Indonesia*
Area: *741,101 sq mi (1,919,443 sq km)*
Population: *184,475,000*
Capital: *Jakarta (met. pop. 8,254,000)*
Ethnic groups: *Some 300 groups, mostly Malay*
Language: *Bahasa Indonesia, Javanese, other*
Religious groups: *Muslim*
Economy: *Agr: rice, cassava, corn, oil palm, rubber, cacao, coffee, sugarcane, coconuts, tea, tobacco. Ind: oil, natural gas, lumber, minerals, textiles, fishing*
Currency: *rupiah*

1 *Philippines*

2 *Philippines*

3 *Philippines*

Philippines

1 *Flooded terraces on Luzon provide ample rice harvests thanks to the "green revolution." This agricultural research program produced high-yield varieties of grain.*

2 *In a sterile environment, workers assemble circuits at a factory in Manila. The delicate components are then shipped to foreign electronics firms.*

3 *This 11-year-old boy mines gold in the hills of Mindanao. Laws prohibiting child labor are often ignored by poor Filipinos.*

1 *Malaysia*

2 *Singapore*

3 *Singapore*

4 *Indonesia*

5 *Indonesia*

6 *Indonesia*

Malaysia

1 *An orangutan, a "person of the forest" in Malay, seems to ponder its future. Protected by law, orangutans still face hunting, and destruction of their rain forest habitat.*

Singapore

2 *The luxury goods of the world await shoppers at Singapore's Lucky Plaza, where duty-free imports draw local people and tourists alike.*

3 *Fast-food, Singapore style: Street hawkers like these have been moved into food centers, where they conform to strict laws of cleanliness, recently imposed.*

Indonesia

4 *Children in a Java village gather to watch cartoons on a TV set provided by the government. A state-owned educational channel broadcasts for five or six hours a day.*

5 *A Buddha gazes out over the temple complex of Borobudur in central Java. In 1983 an international team completed restoration of the ninth-century monument.*

6 *In the remote highland jungles of Irian Jaya, a Dani tribesman uses friction to start a fire with dried grasses.*

Africa

Until the 19th century, most of Africa was a mystery to the Western world. Its impenetrable forests, rivers blocked by falls, vast deserts, and diseases had stymied explorers' attempts to penetrate the interior. Little was known about the hundreds of different groups of people who lived south of the Sahara in communities ranging from small villages to sprawling kingdoms. Nor was it guessed that, some four million years ago, our ancestors took their first upright steps in Africa's heartland. Africa, home of the lion and elephant, the tall Watusi and diminutive Pygmy, the longest river and largest desert, was also the birthplace of humanity.

Africa is a huge continent, second in size only to Asia, but it has fewer of the geographic features found on other continents. Its coastline has a relatively small number of inlets and peninsulas. Most of the continent consists of a large, high plateau that drops steeply to narrow coastal plains. Few mountain regions mark Africa, and those that do, like the Atlas Mountains in the northwest, are small ranges compared to those on other continents or are isolated volcanic mountains, such as Mount Kilimanjaro. In addition, Africa's major rivers follow very irregular courses. Africa's unique geologic history explains these features.

On a world map, Africa's west coast and South America's east coast look as if they could fit together. That's because they once did. About 200 million years ago, the continents were part of a supercontinent called Pangaea. Africa lay at the center of the southern half, known as Gondwana. Some 180 million years ago, Gondwana broke away from Pangaea. Later, continent-size chunks broke off from Gondwana and drifted away on tectonic plates. Some pieces collided with other plates and crumpled along their edges, forming long mountain chains. The African plate moved very little, so it has no collision-caused ranges like the Andes or the Himalaya.

Sharp land drops called escarpments formed at the continent's edges where the other plates broke away. At the same time, Africa's rivers, which had once emptied into vast inland seas and lakes, carved new channels as lakes and rivers drained toward the new coasts. Rivers such as the Nile, the Niger, and the Zambezi changed their courses, sometimes drastically.

The Great Rift Valley is a currently active plate tectonics zone. Here the earth's crust is pulling apart, forming a long, wide depression. Erosion has uncovered fossils buried for millions of years. At Olduvai Gorge and other sites, archaeologists have found the remains of ancestral humans and long-extinct species of animals.

Africa is centered on the Equator. A large part of the land is desert. The Kalahari and Namib Deserts blanket much of southern Africa; in the north the Sahara, the earth's largest desert, covers more than a quarter of the continent. The desert is chiefly the domain of nomadic herders. Settlement is possible, though, around oases.

Severe droughts in combination with unwise land use are leading to desertification, particularly in the Sahel, the arid region of short grasses on the Sahara's southern edge. In the 1980s, the Sahel was the site of extreme human misery. Millions of people starved or became refugees.

In contrast to the desert countries, central African countries along the Equator are among the wettest places on earth. Here rain falls nearly every day on dense rain forest. Away from the urbanized coast, the forest remains sparsely settled. In West Africa, however, large populations and long settlement have greatly changed the environment.

Between forest and desert lie savanna grasslands, home to wildebeests, zebras, lions, and other animals. In East Africa, the rapidly growing human population is encroaching on the savanna, placing many species in danger. To save its wildlife, some African nations are setting aside huge tracts of land for national parks. Much of the Serengeti Plain in Kenya and Tanzania is now a wildlife sanctuary. But poachers still endanger the survival of elephants and rhinoceroses, which they kill for their valuable tusks and horns.

Culturally and historically, there are two Africas, roughly divided by the Sahara. In ancient times, the Egyptian Empire spread civilization along the Nile. Later, North African peoples were influenced by the Greek and Roman Mediterranean civilizations. In the seventh century, an Arab invasion swept the region. Today the Islamic religion is one of the most important influences in North African society, and Arabic is the primary language. The area is commonly

Tanzania's snowcapped Mount Kilimanjaro

Victoria Falls on the Zambezi River

EUROPE

MEDITERRANEAN SEA

ATLAS MOUNTAINS

ASIA

Ahaggar
Mountains

Libyan Desert

Nile

TROPIC OF CANCER

S   A   H   A   R   A

Tibesti
Mountains

Nubian
Desert

RED SEA

Lake Assal
512 FEET
156 METERS
Lowest point in
Africa

Cape Verde Islands

S   A   H   E   L

Senegal
River

Lake Chad

ETHIOPIAN

GULF OF ADEN

Niger River

S   U   D   A   N

HIGHLANDS

AFRICA

Zaire (Congo) River

INDIAN
OCEAN

EQUATOR

Congo
Basin

Lake Victoria

Great Rift Valley

Mount Kilimanjaro
19,340 FEET
5,895 METERS
Highest point in
Africa

ATLANTIC
OCEAN

Lake
Tanganyika

Seychelles

Lake Malawi

Comoro
Islands

St. Helena

Zambezi River

MOZAMBIQUE CHANNEL

Victoria Falls

Madagascar

Namib Desert

TROPIC OF CAPRICORN

Kalahari
Desert

Orange River

Cape of Good Hope

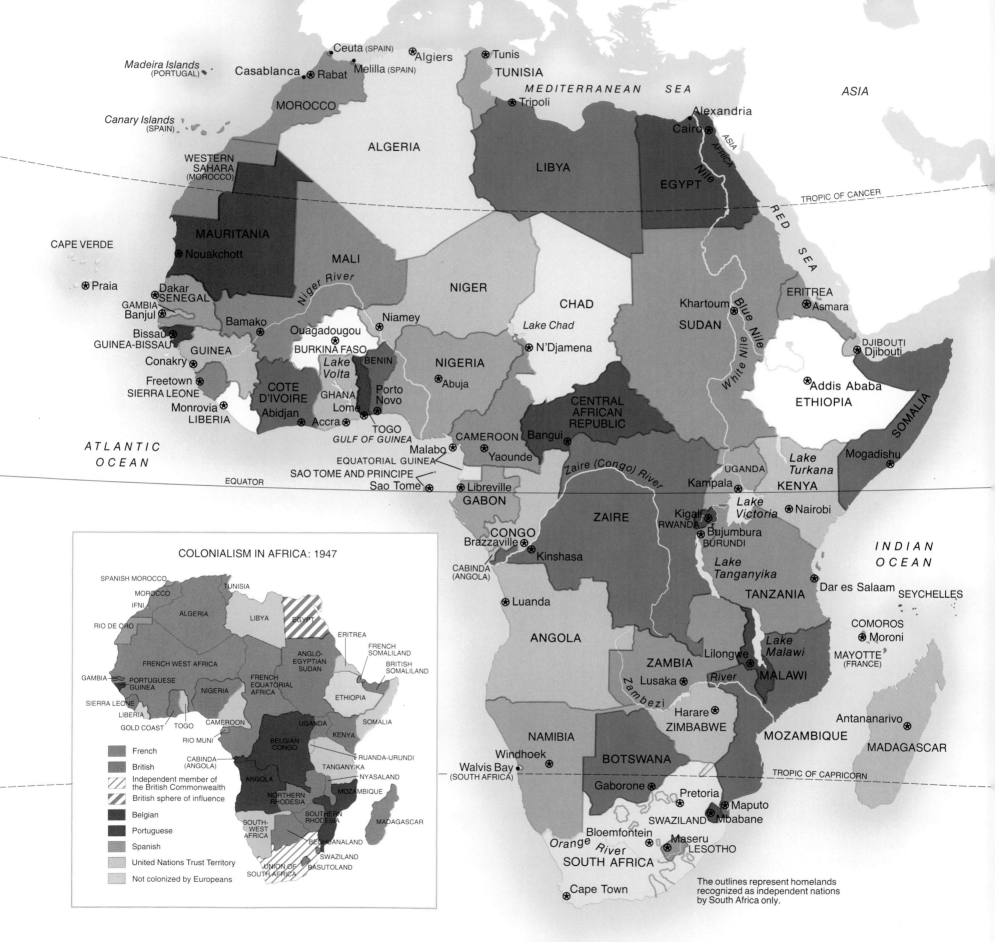

EUROPE

ASIA

Madeira Islands
(PORTUGAL)

Ceuta (SPAIN)
⊛ Algiers
⊛ Tunis

Casablanca
⊛ Rabat
Melilla (SPAIN)

TUNISIA

MEDITERRANEAN SEA

Tripoli

⊛ Alexandria
Cairo ⊛

MOROCCO

Canary Islands
(SPAIN)

ALGERIA

LIBYA

EGYPT

Nile

TROPIC OF CANCER

WESTERN
SAHARA
(MOROCCO)

RED SEA

CAPE VERDE

MAURITANIA

⊛ Nouakchott

MALI

NIGER

Khartoum
⊛

ERITREA
⊛ Asmara

⊛ Praia

Niger River

SUDAN

Blue Nile

DJIBOUTI
⊛ Djibouti

Dakar
⊛ SENEGAL

CHAD

Lake Chad

White Nile

GAMBIA
Banjul ⊛

Bamako
⊛

Niamey
⊛

Ouagadougou
⊛
BURKINA FASO

N'Djamena
⊛

⊛ Addis Ababa

Bissau
GUINEA-BISSAU

GUINEA

*Lake
Volta*

BENIN

NIGERIA

Abuja
⊛

CENTRAL
AFRICAN
REPUBLIC

ETHIOPIA

Conakry ⊛

Freetown ⊛
SIERRA LEONE

COTE
D'IVOIRE

GHANA
Lome

Porto
Novo

SOMALIA

Monrovia
LIBERIA

Abidjan
⊛

Accra
⊛

TOGO

CAMEROON
⊛ Bangui

Bangui

⊛ Mogadishu

GULF OF GUINEA

Malabo
⊛

Yaounde
⊛

Zaire (Congo) River

UGANDA

*Lake
Turkana*

*ATLANTIC
OCEAN*

EQUATORIAL GUINEA

SAO TOME AND PRINCIPE

Sao Tome
⊛

⊛ Libreville

Kampala
⊛

KENYA

EQUATOR

GABON

ZAIRE

Kigali
RWANDA

*Lake
Victoria*

⊛ Nairobi

CONGO
Brazzaville
⊛

⊛ Kinshasa

⊛ Bujumbura
BURUNDI

CABINDA
(ANGOLA)

*Lake
Tanganyika*

*INDIAN
OCEAN*

⊛ Luanda

TANZANIA

⊛ Dar es Salaam

SEYCHELLES

ANGOLA

COMOROS
⊛ Moroni

ZAMBIA

Lilongwe
⊛

*Lake
Malawi*

MAYOTTE
(FRANCE)

Lusaka
⊛

River

MALAWI

Zambezi

NAMIBIA

Harare
⊛
ZIMBABWE

MOZAMBIQUE

⊛ Antananarivo

MADAGASCAR

Windhoek
⊛

BOTSWANA

TROPIC OF CAPRICORN

Walvis Bay
(SOUTH AFRICA)

Gaborone
⊛

Pretoria
⊛

⊛ Maputo
Mbabane

Bloemfontein
⊛

SWAZILAND

Maseru
⊛
LESOTHO

Orange River

SOUTH AFRICA

The outlines represent homelands
recognized as independent nations
by South Africa only.

⊛ Cape Town

COLONIALISM IN AFRICA: 1947

SPANISH MOROCCO

MOROCCO

IFNI

TUNISIA

ALGERIA

LIBYA

EGYPT

ERITREA

FRENCH
SOMALILAND

RIO DE ORO

ANGLO-
EGYPTIAN
SUDAN

BRITISH
SOMALILAND

GAMBIA

FRENCH WEST AFRICA

PORTUGUESE
GUINEA

NIGERIA

FRENCH
EQUATORIAL
AFRICA

ETHIOPIA

SIERRA LEONE

LIBERIA

GOLD COAST

TOGO

CAMEROON

UGANDA

SOMALIA

RIO MUNI

BELGIAN
CONGO

KENYA

CABINDA
(ANGOLA)

RUANDA-URUNDI

ANGOLA

TANGANYIKA

NORTHERN
RHODESIA

NYASALAND

MOZAMBIQUE

SOUTH-
WEST
AFRICA

SOUTHERN
RHODESIA

MADAGASCAR

BECHUANALAND

SWAZILAND

UNION OF
SOUTH AFRICA

BASUTOLAND

■	French
■	British
▨	Independent member of the British Commonwealth
▨	British sphere of influence
■	Belgian
■	Portuguese
■	Spanish
■	United Nations Trust Territory
■	Not colonized by Europeans

grouped with Middle Eastern Arab countries.

South of the Sahara lies a land of tremendous human diversity, where hundreds of black ethnic groups live, many with different languages and cultures. Traditional beliefs have been overlaid with Muslim and Christian ones, but many Africans still practice traditional religions that emphasize the power of ancestors and of spirits that inhabit the natural world.

Great kingdoms and empires developed here thousands of years ago. By the 14th century, Timbuktu in present-day Mali was a thriving center of commerce and Islamic learning. Zimbabwe in the southeast flourished as a political and trading center. Ruins uncovered there contained coins from China and beads from India.

Extensive contact with Europeans began in the 1440s, when Portuguese sailors began exploring Africa's west coast. Soon slaves became a major item of trade. Over the next three centuries, more than 25 million Africans, most of them captured in raids by other Africans, were sold into slavery. By the late 1800s, European colonization was in full swing. In 1885, European leaders carved the continent into colonies, setting borders without regard to ethnic boundaries. Those decisions still haunt Africa, even though most African countries won independence in the 1960s. In recent years, civil wars have taken an enormous toll in human lives.

Today, poverty plagues much of Africa. The continent includes 21 of the world's 30 poorest countries. Most people depend on farming for survival. Recurrent droughts, such as the severe 1992 one in southern Africa, bring malnutrition or famine. Diseases—malaria, sleeping sickness, and AIDS—attack millions.

African countries are striving to improve health, education, and agricultural development. Many are overly dependent on a single cash crop or commodity whose value may fluctuate and are seeking to diversify their economies. There are other signs, too, of change. In South Africa, where the government policy of apartheid long made discrimination against nonwhites legal, black Africans have won new rights. And in many African countries, one-party regimes are being replaced by democratic multiparty governments—a promising omen for Africa's political future.

A mountain of ivory tusks confiscated by Kenyan officials in 1989 represents 1,500 elephants killed by poachers.

Facts About Africa

Area: 11,687,187 sq mi (30,269,680 sq km)
Population: 654,600,000
Highest Point: Mount Kilimanjaro, Tanzania, 19,340 ft (5,895 m) above sea level
Lowest Point: Lake Assal, Djibouti, 512 ft (156 m) below sea level
Largest Country: *(by area)* Sudan 967,500 sq mi (2,505,813 sq km)
Largest Country: *(by population)* Nigeria 90,122,000
Largest Metropolitan Areas: *(by population)*

Cairo, Egypt	13,000,000
Lagos, Nigeria	5,000,000
Kinshasa, Zaïre	3,700,000

Longest Rivers: *(mi and km)*

* Nile	4,145	6,671
Zaïre (Congo)	2,900	4,667
Niger	2,590	4,169

Largest Desert: *(sq mi and sq km)*

* Sahara	3,500,000	9,064,958

Largest Lakes: *(sq mi and sq km)*

Victoria	26,834	69,500
Tanganyika	12,703	32,900

*World record

Glossary

apartheid—a former government policy of racial segregation and discrimination in South Africa.

cacao—a tropical tree bearing seeds called cacao or cocoa beans, used to make cocoa and chocolate.

CFA franc—Communauté Financière Africaine franc (African Financial Community).

desertification—deterioration of land within deserts and along their moister margins, caused by a combination of human use and drought conditions.

drought—a long period without rain.

homeland—an area set aside for a people of a particular national, racial, or cultural origin.

nomads—livestock herders who migrate seasonally with their herds according to pasture and water.

Pygmies—groups of central African peoples who usually stand less than five feet tall.

rift valley—a trough-shaped valley formed when the earth's crust sinks between parallel faults.

Sahel—the semiarid grassland directly south of the Sahara in western and central Africa.

savanna—a tropical grassland with scattered trees.

Sudan—the largest country in Africa, in the northeast; also the name given by Arabs to the region in north-central Africa between the Sahara and the equatorial forests. It includes the Sahel.

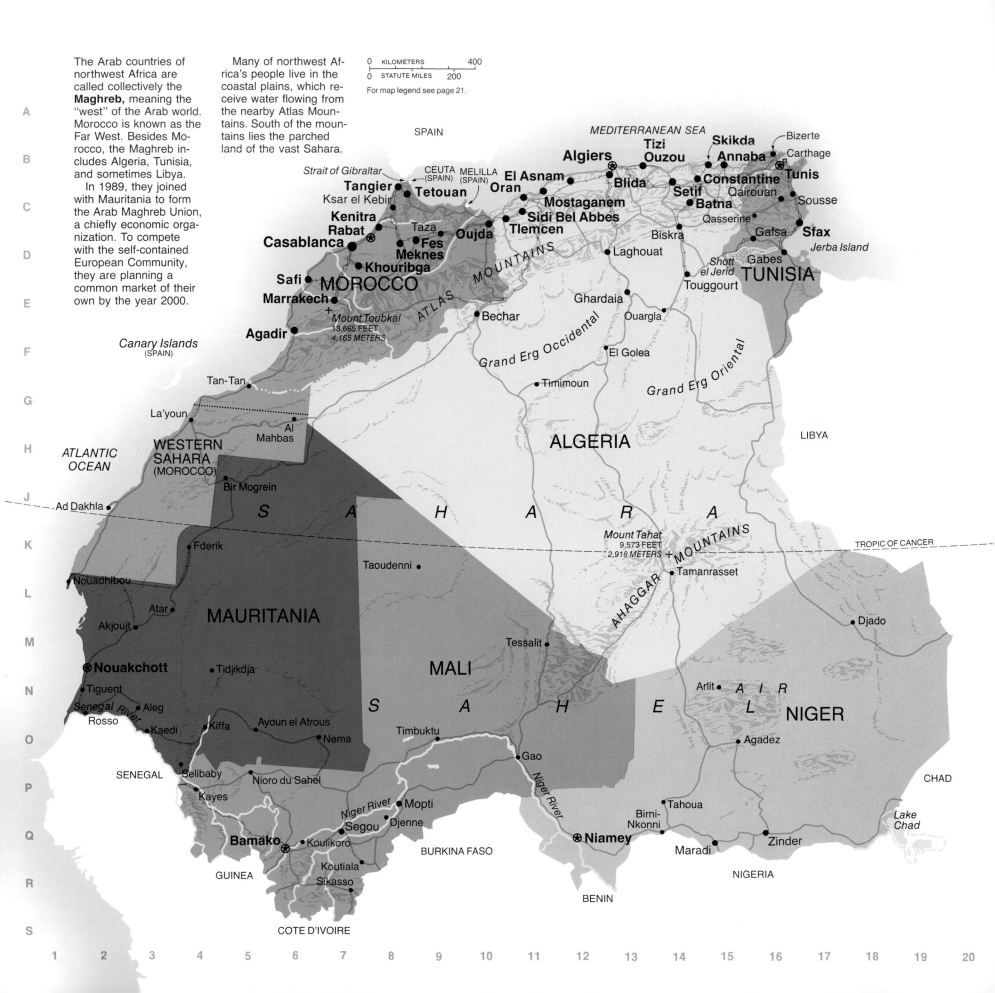

The Arab countries of northwest Africa are called collectively the **Maghreb,** meaning the "west" of the Arab world. Morocco is known as the Far West. Besides Morocco, the Maghreb includes Algeria, Tunisia, and sometimes Libya.

In 1989, they joined with Mauritania to form the Arab Maghreb Union, a chiefly economic organization. To compete with the self-contained European Community, they are planning a common market of their own by the year 2000.

Many of northwest Africa's people live in the coastal plains, which receive water flowing from the nearby Atlas Mountains. South of the mountains lies the parched land of the vast Sahara.

KILOMETERS 400
STATUTE MILES 200
For map legend see page 21.

SPAIN
MEDITERRANEAN SEA
Bizerte
Carthage
Tizi
Ouzou
Skikda
Annaba
Tunis
Algiers
Blida
Constantine
El Asnam
Setif
Qairouan
Sousse
Oran
Mostaganem
Batna
Sidi Bel Abbes
Qasserine
Tetouan
Taza
Tlemcen
Sfax
Strait of Gibraltar
CEUTA (SPAIN)
MELILLA (SPAIN)
Tangier
Ksar el Kebir
Oujda
Biskra
Gafsa
Jerba Island
Kenitra
Rabat
Fes
Meknes
Laghouat
Shott el Jerid
Gabes
Casablanca
Khouribga
TUNISIA
Touggourt
Safi
MOROCCO
Ghardaia
Marrakech
Mount Toubkal
13,665 FEET
4,165 METERS
Bechar
Ouargla
Agadir
ATLAS MOUNTAINS
El Golea
Grand Erg Occidental
Canary Islands
(SPAIN)
Tan-Tan
Timimoun
Grand Erg Oriental
La'youn
Al Mahbas
WESTERN SAHARA
(MOROCCO)
ATLANTIC OCEAN
ALGERIA
LIBYA
Bir Mogrein
Ad Dakhla
S   A   H   A   R   A
Mount Tahat
9,573 FEET
2,918 METERS
TROPIC OF CANCER
Fderik
Taoudenni
Tamanrasset
Nouadhibou
Djado
Atar
MAURITANIA
AHAGGAR MOUNTAINS
Akjoujt
Tessalit
AIR
Nouakchott
MALI
Arlit
NIGER
Tiguent
Senegal River
Aleg
Tidjikdja
S   A   H   E   L
Rosso
Kaedi
Kiffa
Ayoun el Atrous
Timbuktu
Agadez
SENEGAL
Nema
Gao
Selibaby
Nioro du Sahel
Tahoua
Kayes
Niger River
Mopti
Birni-Nkonni
CHAD
Segou
Djenne
Lake Chad
Bamako
Koulikoro
Niger River
Niamey
Koutiala
BURKINA FASO
Maradi
Zinder
GUINEA
Sikasso
NIGERIA
BENIN
COTE D'IVOIRE

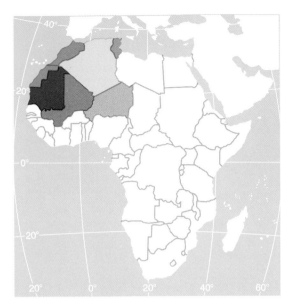

The discovery of phosphates in the desert region of **Western Sahara** (formerly Spanish Sahara) to the southwest helped fuel a costly war between Morocco and the Polisario, a guerrilla organization fighting for Western Saharan independence. Morocco has claimed sovereignty over this onetime Spanish colony, and Moroccan troops have occupied much of the region since 1976. In 1988 the United Nations proposed a referendum allowing inhabitants to vote for autonomy or to remain part of Morocco, but disputes over who should vote and other procedural matters have prevented it from taking place.

Official name: *Kingdom of Morocco*
Area: *275,117 sq mi (712,550 sq km)*
Population: *26,167,000*
Capital: *Rabat (met. pop. 1,287,000)*
Ethnic groups: *Arab, Berber, Moor*
Language: *Arabic, Berber, French*
Religious groups: *Sunni Muslim*
Economy: *Agr: livestock, wheat, barley, fruit, sugar beets, vegetables, olives. Ind: phosphates, food processing, textiles, tourism, leather, fishing*
Currency: *Moroccan dirham*

plateaus, home to herders of sheep and goats. Beyond the Saharan range of the Atlas Mountains stretches the barren desert that blankets more than 85 percent of the country.

Official name: *Democratic and Popular Republic of Algeria*
Area: *919,595 sq mi (2,381,741 sq km)*
Population: *26,041,000*
Capital: *Algiers (pop. 1,507,200)*
Ethnic groups: *Arab, Berber*
Language: *Arabic, Berber, French*
Religious groups: *Sunni Muslim*
Economy: *Agr: wheat, barley, fruit, olives, vegetables, livestock. Ind: iron, steel, oil, natural gas, mining, motor vehicles, cement, textiles, wine, chemicals*
Currency: *Algerian dinar*

Morocco

Africa draws closest to Europe at Morocco's northern tip. Spain lies only nine miles (14 km) away, across the Strait of Gibraltar, yet Morocco is a world as well as a continent apart. In the teeming main square of Marrakech, vendors in hooded robes called djellabas offer wares made of tooled leather or copper and brass. Dentists advertise their trade with samples of extracted molars. Snake charmers and fire-eaters vie for attention.

From fertile plains along the Atlantic coast, Morocco's terrain rises to the Atlas Mountains, snowcapped in winter. Beyond stretches the Sahara. Originally inhabited by Berbers, whose descendants still herd and farm in the highlands, Morocco was invaded by Arabs in the seventh century. The following century, an alliance of Arabs and Berbers conquered Spain. Their descendants, known as Moors, ruled parts of the Iberian Peninsula until finally driven out in 1492 by a Christian campaign. Spain and Portugal seized lands in northern Morocco, and Spain still controls the coastal towns of Ceuta and Melilla.

Today about half of Moroccans live by farming, chiefly on the Atlantic plains. Fishing off the Atlantic coast is also important. But Morocco's economy relies most heavily on its mineral resources. With the world's largest known phosphate reserves, it has become the leading exporter of phosphate rock. Casablanca, the largest city and chief port, handles most export trade, and is also the main industrial center.

Algeria

There's a strong French flavor to Algeria. People in its cities speak French as well as Arabic. Vintners in its coastal hills produce fine wines, and French dishes are enjoyed along with local favorites such as couscous, a savory stew of semolina and lamb.

From 1834 to 1962, Algeria was a possession of France. A French elite owned much of the farmland and ran business and government. The legendary French Foreign Legion patrolled the Sahara. In 1954 a bloody civil war erupted. When it ended in 1962, Algeria won independence, but it lost many professionals and skilled workers as French citizens fled back to France.

Large deposits of oil and natural gas helped revive its economy and fuel industrialization, making Algeria one of the most developed Arab countries. But Algiers, the capital, and other cities suffer unemployment and housing shortages. Lately, Islamic fundamentalist groups have increased in importance. When it seemed, in the early 1990s, that they would gain power through democratic elections, the army took over the government, which canceled the elections, precipitating riots, arrests, and deaths.

Most Algerians live along the coastal plain, a fertile strip that slopes up to a northern range of the Atlas Mountains. South of this range lie high

Tunisia

Smallest and northernmost of the North African countries, Tunisia has an extensive coastline along the Mediterranean Sea. More than three million visitors a year come to resorts on these sunny shores. Tourism makes a significant contribution to the country's income.

Besides tourism, Tunisia's economy relies on oil, mining, and agriculture. Dates grow in isolated areas including the desert, but most farming takes place in the country's fertile northern half. Olive groves flourish along the east coast, and Tunisia is a leading exporter of olive oil.

Strategically located at the Strait of Sicily, Tunisia controlled many of the major trade routes of the ancient world. The Carthaginian Empire was founded here some 2,800 years ago. Rome grew into a powerful rival empire and, in 146 B.C., completely destroyed Carthage.

Governed by France from 1881 to 1956, Tunisia after independence adopted a progressive outlook. Under the leadership of Habib Bourguiba, whose poor health forced his retirement in 1987, women were freed from the veil and won the right to vote. The government now faces a growing Islamic fundamentalist movement.

Official name: *Republic of Tunisia*
Area: *63,170 sq mi (163,610 sq km)*
Population: *8,424,000*
Capital: *Tunis (pop. 596,700)*
Ethnic groups: *Arab*
Language: *Arabic, French*
Religious groups: *Sunni Muslim*
Economy: *Agr: wheat, barley, olives, grapes, citrus fruit, dates, vegetables. Ind: phosphates, oil, tourism, cement, steel, textiles, food processing, fishing*
Currency: *Tunisian dinar*

Mauritania

For centuries nomads herded livestock in the Sahel, the semiarid grassland that runs across Mauritania's southern region. But the land was overgrazed and stripped of trees for fuel. Mauritanians now plant trees there, but the impact of droughts and desertification has left much of the Sahel region devastated.

Refugees jam camps of tents and shacks, their animals dead and farmlands exhausted. Nouakchott, the capital since 1960 when this French colony won independence, was built for a few thousand residents but now holds nearly 400,000. Rich coastal fishing and iron ore mining offer the greatest hope for this stricken country.

In 1991, a new Islamic constitution allowing multiparty elections was approved, but contested election results proclaimed the head of the former military government president.

Official name: *Islamic Republic of Mauritania*
Area: *397,955 sq mi (1,030,700 sq km)*
Population: *2,103,000*
Capital: *Nouakchott (pop. 393,300)*
Ethnic groups: *Moor, Fulani, Wolof, other*
Language: *Arabic, French, Fula, Wolof, other*
Religious groups: *Sunni Muslim*
Economy: *Agr: livestock, millet, vegetables, dates, gum arabic. Ind: fishing, iron ore, gypsum, copper*
Currency: *ouguiya*

Mali

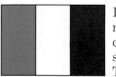

In the 11th century, Tuareg nomads founded a seasonal camp at a West African oasis. From this camp grew Timbuktu, a caravan post trading in gold, salt, and slaves. Also a center of Islamic learning, it became the pearl of the Mali and Songhai Empires, which ruled from the 13th to the 16th century.

In recent decades, droughts in the Sahel have plagued Mali, a country of small farmers and nomadic herders, forcing many of the Tuareg nomads to settle in towns. Tuareg rebellions have erupted in northern Mali and in Niger and Algeria, prompting Mali's new civilian government to join the others in seeking solutions.

Mali reaches north into the Sahara. The Niger River waters the best croplands in the south, where most people live. Cotton rules a farm-based economy. Fishing is centered in Ségou and Mopti, northeast of the capital, Bamako.

Mali is landlocked. Steamboats on the Niger, a few roads, and a single railroad link it to neighboring nations. Poor transportation hinders most exploitation of minerals, although gold mining shows promise. Formerly a colony called French Sudan, Mali has taken back its old, imperial name. It gained full independence in 1960.

Official name: *Republic of Mali*
Area: *478,841 sq mi (1,240,192 sq km)*
Population: *8,538,000*
Capital: *Bamako (pop. 658,300)*
Ethnic groups: *Bambara, Fulani, Tuareg, other*
Language: *French, Bambara, Fula, other*
Religious groups: *Sunni Muslim, traditional*
Economy: *Agr: millet, rice, corn, cotton, peanuts, sugarcane, livestock. Ind: food processing, fishing*
Currency: *CFA franc*

Niger

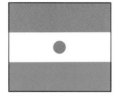

The landlocked nation of Niger is shaped somewhat like a fish, its tail pointing to the southwest. The country's northern half reaches into the searing Sahara. Much of the south is part of the Sahel, a thirsty belt along the desert's edge, where droughts periodically turn sparse grasslands to dust and wipe out nomads' cattle, goats, and sheep.

A five-year drought struck in 1968; by the time the June-to-September rains returned, 90 percent of the livestock had died. Thousands of people fled to neighboring countries or crowded into Niger's few cities, seeking food and jobs. Anti-desertification is now urgently explored.

Niger's mountains yield uranium; one of the world's top producers, the country was hard hit in the early 1980s by falling world prices. Most people, though, live on Niger's southern edge, where they herd livestock or tend crops of peanuts, sorghum, and millet. In the southwest, the Niger River that gave the country its name also gives it its best farmland. Here villagers raise rice, cotton, and other crops. Once a French colony, Niger won independence in 1960. An interim government replaced military-backed rule in 1991 and held free elections in 1993.

Official name: *Republic of Niger*
Area: *489,191 sq mi (1,267,000 sq km)*
Population: *8,319,000*
Capital: *Niamey (pop. 398,300)*
Ethnic groups: *Hausa, Djerma-Songhai, Fulani*
Language: *French, Hausa, Djerma, Fula, other*
Religious groups: *Sunni Muslim*
Economy: *Agr: grains, cassava, peanuts, cotton, cowpeas, livestock. Ind: uranium, cement, textiles*
Currency: *CFA franc*

1 *Tunisia*

Tunisia

1 *Modern buildings flank a divided avenue in Tunisia's capital, Tunis. Trees shade traditional market stalls that line the center of the avenue.*

Niger

2 *Young Wodaabe herdsmen use elaborate makeup and facial contortions to charm girls. The courtship rituals of these nomads of the Sahel are centuries old.*

3 *Women near Tahoua file past a steeply sloped field of crops. Rainfall here is so sparse that farmers may have to plant 100 seeds for every one that sprouts.*

2 *Niger*

3 *Niger*

1 *Mali*

2 *Morocco*

3 *Morocco*

Mali

1 *Calabashes strew the market ground in Djénné beneath the walls of its famous mud-brick mosque. Protruding studs help workmen scale the walls to make repairs.*

Morocco

2 *In crowded Fès, only one street is open to motor traffic. People use mules to carry goods through narrow passageways.*

3 *Gleaming brass and copper brighten a corner in a suq, or marketplace, in Marrakech. Many Moroccan women veil their faces when going out in public.*

4 *Mauritania*

Mauritania

4 *Villagers shovel encroaching desert dunes away from their schoolhouse. Caused partly by deforestation, creeping sands have buried whole towns in the Sahel region, which is subject to desertification.*

Algeria

5 *Traders haggle over sheep in the marketplace at Ghardaia, a desert town known for centuries for this "stock exchange." The arched colonnade behind holds shops.*

5 *Algeria*

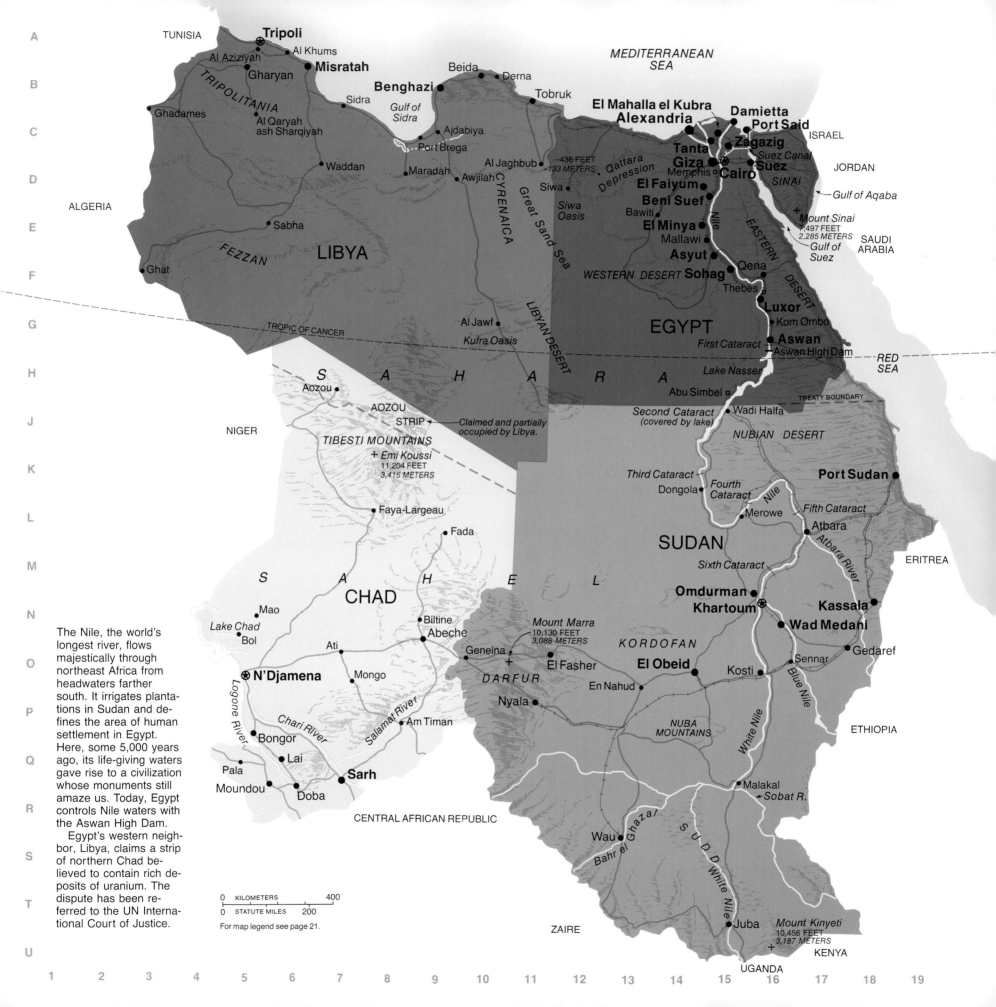

A TUNISIA
Tripoli ✴
Al Aziziyah • Al Khums
Gharyan **Misratah**
TRIPOLITANIA
Ghadames
Al Qaryah
ash Sharqiyah

MEDITERRANEAN
SEA

Beida • Derna
B **Benghazi** • Tobruk
Sidra
*Gulf of
Sidra*

Ajdabiya
C • Port Brega
El Mahalla el Kubra
Alexandria **Damietta**
Port Said
Tanta **Zagazig** ISRAEL
Giza *Suez Canal*
Al Jaghbub −436 FEET Qattara Memphis **Cairo** ✴ **Suez** JORDAN
Al Jaghbub −133 METERS Depression **El Faiyum** *SINAI*
D Waddan Maradah Awjilah Siwa • **Beni Suef** *Gulf of Aqaba*
ALGERIA *CYRENAICA* *Siwa* Bawiti • + *Mount Sinai*
Oasis **El Minya** 7,497 FEET SAUDI
FEZZAN Mallawi • 2,285 METERS ARABIA
E Sabha *Great Sand Sea* *Gulf of
Suez*
Asyut Qena •
• Ghat *WESTERN DESERT* **Sohag** *EASTERN*
F *Libyan Desert* Thebes • *DESERT*
Luxor
EGYPT • Kom Ombo
G TROPIC OF CANCER Al Jawf • **Aswan**
Kufra Oasis *First Cataract* Aswan High Dam *RED
SEA*
H *S   A   H   A   R   A* *Lake Nasser*
Abu Simbel ▫ TREATY BOUNDARY
Aozou • *Second Cataract* • Wadi Halfa
J AOZOU *(covered by lake)* *NUBIAN   DESERT*
NIGER STRIP → *Claimed and partially
occupied by Libya.*
TIBESTI MOUNTAINS
+ *Emi Koussi* *Third Cataract* **Port Sudan** •
K 11,204 FEET Dongola • *Fourth
3,415 METERS Cataract* *Fifth Cataract*
Merowe • Atbara •
L • Faya-Largeau *Nile*
• Fada *SUDAN* *Atbara River*
M ERITREA
Sixth Cataract
Omdurman • **Kassala** •
N • Mao Biltine • Mount Marra **Khartoum** ✴
Lake Chad Abeche • 10,130 FEET **Wad Medani** •
Bol • 3,088 METERS *KORDOFAN* Gedaref •
O Ati • Geneina • El Fasher • **El Obeid** • Kosti • Sennar •
✴ **N'Djamena** + En Nahud • *NUBA* White Nile
CHAD Mongo • *DARFUR* Nyala • *MOUNTAINS* ETHIOPIA
P *Chari River* Blue Nile
Bongor • *Salamat River*
Q Lai • • Am Timan
Pala •
Moundou • Doba • **Sarh** Malakal •
R *Sobat R.*
CENTRAL AFRICAN REPUBLIC
S *Bahr el Ghazal* *S U D D*
Wau • *White Nile*
T 0   KILOMETERS   400
0   STATUTE MILES   200
Juba • *Mount Kinyeti*
ZAIRE 10,456 FEET
For map legend see page 21. 3,187 METERS
U KENYA
UGANDA

The Nile, the world's longest river, flows majestically through northeast Africa from headwaters farther south. It irrigates plantations in Sudan and defines the area of human settlement in Egypt. Here, some 5,000 years ago, its life-giving waters gave rise to a civilization whose monuments still amaze us. Today, Egypt controls Nile waters with the Aswan High Dam.

Egypt's western neighbor, Libya, claims a strip of northern Chad believed to contain rich deposits of uranium. The dispute has been referred to the UN International Court of Justice.

Logone River

1 2 3 4 5 6 7 8 9 10 11 12 13 14 15 16 17 18 19

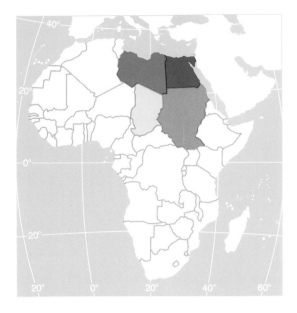

Libya

Part of the world's largest desert, the Sahara, dominates Libya. Only two strips of land 50 miles (80 km) wide along the Mediterranean Sea receive enough rainfall for farming. One fertile region surrounds Tripoli, the capital, in the northwest, while the other includes the city of Benghazi in the northeast. Most Libyans live in these coastal lowlands.

At one time, farmers in the north produced enough food to make the country self-sufficient, but with the discovery of oil in 1959, many left farming for higher-paying oil-field jobs. Despite lower oil prices in recent years, petroleum remains a mainstay of Libya's economy.

During spring and fall, hot, dust-laden winds called ghiblis blow from the desert. When the ghibli blows, temperatures in coastal centers can reach 110°F (43°C). There are no permanent rivers in Libya, but huge underground reservoirs of water have been found in the desert. In 1991 the government inaugurated the Great Man-made River project that aims to carry water thousands of miles through a 13-foot (4 m) pipeline from the desert to coastal regions.

Libya has a young population: More than half its people are under 18 years old. Most are of Arab or Berber descent, but nomadic Tuaregs herd goats and camels in the desert, and Tebu tribesmen live in the Tibesti Mountains.

Since 1969 Col. Muammar Qaddafi has ruled Libya through a socialist government. His backing of terrorism led to a U. S. air raid in 1986. The United Nations imposed limited sanctions in 1992, after Qaddafi's refusal to turn over Libyans accused of bombing passenger jetliners.

Official name: *Socialist People's Libyan Arab Jamahiriya*
Area: *679,362 sq mi (1,759,540 sq km)*
Population: *4,485,000*
Capital: *Tripoli (pop. 591,100)*
Ethnic groups: *Arab, Berber*
Language: *Arabic, Berber*
Religious groups: *Sunni Muslim*
Economy: *Agr: wheat, barley, olives, vegetables, fruit, livestock. Ind: oil, food processing, textiles*
Currency: *Libyan dinar*

Egypt

Egypt was known in ancient times for its engineering wonders. Beginning about 2650 B.C., stone masons and laborers built huge pyramids on the western bank of the Nile. They were tombs for Egypt's rulers. In the largest, the Great Pyramid of Khufu, some 2 million stones averaging more than 2.5 tons each (2.3 metric tons) were hauled into place.

In the 1960s, Egyptian and Soviet engineers constructed a modern wonder: the Aswan High Dam on the Nile, 364 feet (111 m) high and 2.3 miles (3.7 km) wide. Lake Nasser, stretching behind the dam from Egypt into Sudan, is the largest freshwater lake in either country. The High Dam tamed the Nile's annual floods and provided a year-round supply of water for irrigation and hydroelectric power. Though the dam has blocked the flow of alluvial silt that once enriched the soil, its benefits are considerable.

An ancient Greek historian called Egypt "the gift of the Nile" because the river is Egypt's lifeblood. The Nile Valley and its delta, which make up only 4 percent of Egypt's land, support most of the country's agriculture and 99 percent of its population. In the Western Desert, which covers two-thirds of the country, rain has not fallen in some areas for years. But underground water reservoirs are being explored, and in fertile oases date palms grow.

Along the Nile, cotton, sugarcane, fruit, and vegetables are cultivated for export. Fellahin—peasant farmers—raise food crops such as corn and rice, as well as sheep and goats. Farm families usually live in houses made of mud bricks that have been dried in the sun.

Egypt's population has increased enormously, and the nation must now import more than half of its food. Cairo, which holds 13 million people in its greater metropolitan area, is the largest city in Africa and the Arab world. Rapid urban growth has created major problems for this capital city, whose inhabitants suffer from poverty, unemployment, and severe housing shortages. An earthquake in 1992 damaged thousands of homes and killed about 600 people.

Industry is concentrated in Cairo and in Alexandria, the chief port and second largest city. Cairo's prestige in the Arab world, eroded by the signing of a peace treaty with Israel in 1979, is growing again. At the same time, a militant Islamic movement is striving to replace the secular government with a theocracy.

Official name: *Arab Republic of Egypt*
Area: *386,662 sq mi (1,001,449 sq km)*
Population: *55,680,000*
Capital: *Cairo (pop. 6,052,800; met. pop. 13,000,000)*
Ethnic groups: *Egyptian, Nubian*
Language: *Arabic*
Religious groups: *Sunni Muslim, Coptic Christian*
Economy: *Agr: corn, rice, wheat, cotton, sugarcane, vegetables, citrus fruit, livestock. Ind: food processing, textiles, tourism, oil, fertilizers, cement, fishing*
Currency: *Egyptian pound*

Chad

The Sahara already covers nearly all of Chad's mountainous northern half. Desertification has now affected much of the semiarid Sahel region where nomads graze cattle, bringing with it famine and desolation. Chad's only good agricultural land lies in the south, around Lake Chad and between the Chari and Lagone Rivers. Here farmers raise livestock, food crops, and cash crops of cotton on small farms. Lions, elephants, and leopards living in the wooded savanna are major tourist attractions.

The people of Chad are among the world's poorest. The country has few roads and no railroad, and there is little manufacturing. Civil war between the Muslim north, supported by Libya, and the non-Muslim south has devastated Chad's frail economy. Continuing disputes delay the possibility of democratic reform.

Official name: *Republic of Chad*
Area: *495,755 sq mi (1,284,000 sq km)*
Population: *5,239,000*
Capital: *N'Djamena (pop. 500,000)*
Ethnic groups: *Sara, many others*
Language: *French, Arabic, African languages*
Religious groups: *Muslim, traditional, Christian*
Economy: *Agr: millet, sorghum, peanuts, cassava, yams, dates, cotton, livestock. Ind: textiles, fishing*
Currency: *CFA franc*

Sudan

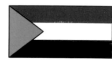

The next time you toast a marshmallow or pop a gumdrop into your mouth, you may be eating a bit of Sudan. Sticky goodies such as these contain gum arabic, the sap of the acacia tree that grows in Sudan, the largest and most diverse country in Africa. More than 50 different ethnic groups live within its borders, which encompass savannas, deserts, mountains, and rain forests.

In the south lies the Sudd, one of the world's largest swamps. It drains into the White Nile, which joins the Blue Nile at Khartoum, the capital, to form the main course of the Nile. Farmers grow cotton, an important export crop, in the irrigated region between the two rivers. Sugarcane grows between the Sudd and Khartoum on one of the world's biggest sugar plantations.

The Sahara covers the northern third of Sudan. Here Arab nomads raise camels and goats. Hills along the Red Sea trap enough rain to nourish pastures where Beja nomads graze camels and flocks of sheep.

Most Sudanese are small farmers, living off sorghum and millet crops. Women use stones to grind the grains into a flour from which they make a flat bread. This is eaten with a spicy vegetable soup that may also contain meat or eggs. The different cultures that make up Sudan meet in town markets called suqs, where Arab merchants sell clothing and imported goods, while tribal people peddle food and handicrafts.

Sudan has plenty of good farmland. Yet millions of people in the south face starvation because, for decades, farming has been disrupted by a civil war between the mostly Arab central government located in the north and the black Africans who live in the south. Drought has taken its toll as well. Floods of refugees from neighboring countries also afflicted by war and famine have added their numbers to the masses of displaced Sudanese. Its problems aggravated by economic difficulties and the policies of an Islamic fundamentalist government, Sudan in the 1990s is a country in crisis.

Official name: *Republic of the Sudan*
Area: *967,500 sq mi (2,505,813 sq km)*
Population: *26,477,000*
Capital: *Khartoum (pop. 476,200)*
Ethnic groups: *Arab, Nilotic groups, Beja, other*
Language: *Arabic, African languages, English*
Religious groups: *Muslim, traditional, Christian*
Economy: *Agr: sorghum, millet, wheat, cotton, gum arabic, sesame, peanuts, sugarcane, livestock. Ind: food processing, textiles, oil, cement, mining, fishing*
Currency: *Sudanese pound*

Egypt

1 *Pyramids rise from the desert sands at Giza. These huge stone structures were built about 4,500 years ago as tombs for the kings of Egypt.*

2 *Boys guide straw-laden donkeys through palm-shaded fields in the Nile Valley.*

3 *Cairo, Africa's largest city, holds 13 million people in its metropolitan area. Tall apartment complexes and overcrowded housing create a high population density.*

Chad

4 *A goatherd drives his flock across the Sahara. About half of Chad is desert.*

Libya

5 *At a factory in Gharyan, workers turn out ceramic tableware.*

Sudan

6 *Forehead scars of a woman carrying a water pot identify her as one of the Mondari people. Many different ethnic groups inhabit Sudan, Africa's largest country.*

1 *Egypt*

2 *Egypt*

3 *Egypt*

5 *Libya*

4 *Chad*

6 *Sudan*

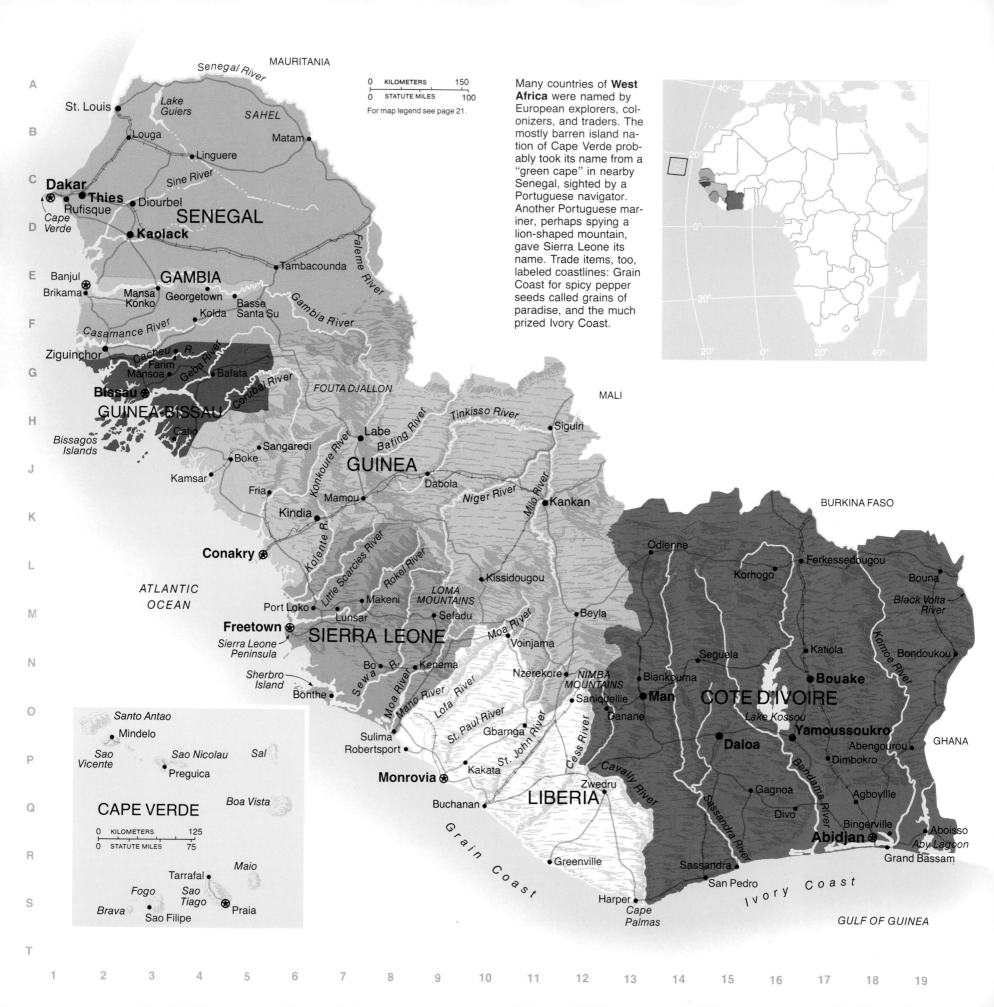

MAURITANIA

A

B

C

Senegal River

St. Louis

Lake
Guiers

SAHEL

Louga

Matam

Linguere

Sine River

Dakar

Thies

Rufisque

Diourbel

*Cape
Verde*

SENEGAL

D

Kaolack

Tambacounda

E

Banjul

GAMBIA

Brikama

Mansa
Konko

Georgetown

Basse
Santa Su

Faleme River

F

Kolda

Casamance River

Gambia River

Ziguinchor

Cacheu   *R.*

Farim

Mansoa

Geba River

Bafata

G

Bissau

Corubal River

FOUTA DJALLON

MALI

GUINEA-BISSAU

H

*Bissagos
Islands*

Catio

Sangaredi

Labe

Bafing River

Tinkisso River

Siguiri

Boke

GUINEA

J

Kamsar

Fria

Mamou

Dabola

Niger River

Milo River

Kankan

K

Kindia

Konkoure River

BURKINA FASO

L

Conakry

Kolente R.

Kissidougou

Odienne

Korhogo

Ferkessedougou

Bouna

*ATLANTIC
OCEAN*

Little Scarcies River

Rokel River

*LOMA
MOUNTAINS*

Beyla

*Black Volta
River*

M

Port Loko

Makeni

Sefadu

Moa River

Lunsar

Freetown

*Sierra Leone
Peninsula*

SIERRA LEONE

Seguela

Katiola

Bouake

Komoe River

Bondoukou

N

Bo   *R.*

Kenema

Voinjama

Nzerekore

*NIMBA
MOUNTAINS*

Biankouma

Man

COTE D'IVOIRE

Sewa R.

Moa River

*Sherbro
Island*

Saniquellie

Lake Kossou

O

Bonthe

Mano River

Lofa River

Danane

Bandama River

Sulima

St. Paul River

Gbarnga

St. John River

Cess River

Daloa

Yamoussoukro

Abengourou

P

Robertsport

Kakata

Cavally River

GHANA

Dimbokro

Monrovia

Zwedru

Sassandra River

Gagnoa

Agboville

Q

Buchanan

LIBERIA

Divo

Bingerville

Abidjan

Aby Lagoon

Grand Bassam

R

Greenville

Sassandra

San Pedro

Ivory Coast

S

Harper

*Cape
Palmas*

Grain Coast

GULF OF GUINEA

T

For map legend see page 21.

0   KILOMETERS   150
0   STATUTE MILES   100

Many countries of **West
Africa** were named by
European explorers, col-
onizers, and traders. The
mostly barren island na-
tion of Cape Verde prob-
ably took its name from a
"green cape" in nearby
Senegal, sighted by a
Portuguese navigator.
Another Portuguese mar-
iner, perhaps spying a
lion-shaped mountain,
gave Sierra Leone its
name. Trade items, too,
labeled coastlines: Grain
Coast for spicy pepper
seeds called grains of
paradise, and the much
prized Ivory Coast.

CAPE VERDE

Santo Antao

Mindelo

*Sao
Vicente*

Sao Nicolau

Sal

Preguica

Boa Vista

Maio

Tarrafal

Fogo

*Sao
Tiago*

Brava

Sao Filipe

Praia

0   KILOMETERS   125
0   STATUTE MILES   75

1   2   3   4   5   6   7   8   9   10   11   12   13   14   15   16   17   18   19

Cape Verde

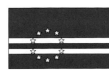

Drought has defined Cape Verde from the time of its first Portuguese settlement in 1462 to the present. This chain of 15 volcanic islands 400 miles (644 km) west of Senegal is mostly barren and mountainous. A devastating drought that began in 1968 cut crop yields by 90 percent and sent thousands of people abroad to find work. Many of them now send money home.

Of those who remain, some continue to farm. Others have found jobs as fishermen, salt miners, or laborers digging water wells, planting drought-resistant trees, and building dams.

Cape Verde became an independent country in 1975. Its struggling economy, however, has been dependent on foreign aid. In the 1990s, the government began trying to improve the economy by encouraging greater private investment in industries such as tourism and fishing.

Official name: *Republic of Cape Verde*
Area: *1,557 sq mi (4,033 sq km)*
Population: *403,000*
Capital: *Praia (pop. 61,700)*
Ethnic groups: *Creole, African*
Language: *Portuguese, Crioulo*
Religious groups: *Roman Catholic*
Economy: *Agr: corn, beans, sweet potatoes, sugarcane, cassava, bananas, coffee. Ind: fishing, salt*
Currency: *Cape Verde escudo*

Senegal

In Senegal, local singer-storytellers called *griots* tell tales of history and tradition. They are keepers of the cultural heritage in this land of low, rolling plains—a land occupied for centuries by France before Senegal achieved independence in 1960.

The French favored Senegal above their other African colonies, making Dakar the headquarters for their West African empire. Today Dakar is Senegal's capital and one of the continent's leading ports, well equipped to handle supertankers and other large oceangoing ships.

French roots hold fast in Senegal. French is the official language, and many French citizens hold key jobs in commerce and industry. Still, the nation retains its African character. Most Senegalese speak a native language called Wolof. Most farm or raise cattle, sheep, and goats.

Senegal benefits from a sizable amount of industry, chiefly in food processing, textiles, and chemicals, with factories centered around Dakar. It also has successful fishing, tourism, and phosphate-mining operations. But it suffers from disastrous droughts. When these occur, crops fail, including one of the chief export crops, peanuts. With the help of foreign aid, Senegal and neighboring countries hope to solve the water-shortage problem by building irrigation canals and damming rivers.

In 1981, Senegal instituted a multiparty system of government—one of a growing number of African countries to follow this political route.

Official name: *Republic of Senegal*
Area: *75,955 sq mi (196,722 sq km)*
Population: *7,947,000*
Capital: *Dakar (pop. 1,500,000)*
Ethnic groups: *Wolof, Fulani, Serer, other*
Language: *French, Wolof, other African languages*
Religious groups: *Sunni Muslim*
Economy: *Agr: grains, peanuts, cassava, cotton, livestock. Ind: fishing, textiles, chemicals, mining*
Currency: *CFA franc*

The Gambia

A narrow ribbon of land 200 miles (322 km) long, The Gambia snakes into the western edge of the African continent. Except for its coastline, this country is entirely surrounded by Senegal, with which it shares many ethnic and religious ties. A former British colony, The Gambia gained independence in 1965.

In 1889, Great Britain and France fixed the country's unusual boundaries, which follow the Gambia River as it winds through dense mangrove swamps and grass-covered flats. Back from the river lie rolling savanna lands, where Gambians grow upland crops such as the nation's principal cash crop, peanuts.

Saltwater and freshwater fishing bring in additional income, as does tourism. But most Gambians live in poverty, struggling against drought and insect infestation to raise enough corn, rice, and millet to feed themselves. Life expectancy here is low, only 44 years.

Official name: *Republic of The Gambia*
Area: *4,361 sq mi (11,295 sq km)*
Population: *909,000*
Capital: *Banjul (pop. 44,200)*
Ethnic groups: *Malinke, Fulani, Wolof, Jola*
Language: *English, Mandinka, Fula, Wolof*
Religious groups: *Sunni Muslim*
Economy: *Agr: grains, peanuts, cotton, livestock. Ind: food processing, tourism, textiles, fishing*
Currency: *dalasi*

Guinea-Bissau

Small groups of courageous villagers spearheaded the struggle for liberation in Guinea-Bissau in the early 1960s. Scrambling through thickets and rice fields, they battled the well-equipped army of their Portuguese colonial rulers. Soon thousands of their countrymen joined them in a war that would last more than ten years.

The Portuguese fought hard to keep this land with its navigable rivers, its tropical rain forests, its many coastal islands where coconut palms grow. When they finally gave it up, they left ruined crops and widespread poverty.

The country's new socialist leaders tried to rebuild the economy. Faced with food shortages in the 1980s, they produced a four-year plan targeting agricultural development. The food situation improved, but the country remained one of the world's poorest. In 1991, political reforms began, and single-party rule came to an end.

Most of the people grow only enough food for themselves. On the coast, the Balante grow rice in irrigated paddies. In the interior, the Malinke farm and the Fulani raise livestock. Their herds survive despite the presence of the tsetse fly, which transmits disease. Fishing has become a major economic activity. Fish and shellfish abound off the coast and in deep estuaries.

Official name: *Republic of Guinea-Bissau*
Area: *13,948 sq mi (36,125 sq km)*
Population: *1,003,000*
Capital: *Bissau (pop. 125,000)*
Ethnic groups: *Balante, Fulani, Malinke, other*
Language: *Portuguese, Crioulo, African languages*
Religious groups: *traditional, Muslim*
Economy: *Agr: rice, oil palm, root crops, peanuts, coconuts, fruit. Ind: food processing, fishing, lumber*
Currency: *Guinea-Bissau peso*

Guinea

The Fouta Djallon region—high plateaus cut by rivers, deep valleys, and plunging waterfalls—helps Guinea earn its reputation for scenic beauty. The country is a treasure-house of natural resources, including one-quarter of the world's bauxite. Huge deposits of iron ore lie in the mountains near the Liberian border. Most of the land is well watered and fertile.

Despite these resources, Guinea remains poor and undeveloped. More than 80 percent of its people make a bare living from farming. In the swampy soil along the coast, they grow staple crops of cassava and rice, and in upland valleys, vegetables and fruit. Herders on the Fouta Djallon plateau and eastern savanna graze small, humpless cattle called N'dama. On the forested hills of the southeast, farmers grow cash crops of coffee.

Guinea's first leader after independence from France in 1958 was a dictator, Ahmed Sekou Touré. "We prefer poverty in liberty to wealth in slavery," he proclaimed. During most of Touré's 25-year regime, the country turned its back on the West and on policies that might have helped to develop its resources. Many people were imprisoned for their political beliefs. Nearly two million fled abroad. Since Touré's death in 1984, Guinea has tried to improve foreign relations and to speed up economic development.

Official name: *Republic of Guinea*
Area: *94,926 sq mi (245,857 sq km)*
Population: *7,784,000*
Capital: *Conakry (pop. 705,300)*
Ethnic groups: *Fulani, Malinke, Susu, 15 others*
Language: *French, African languages*
Religious groups: *Muslim, traditional*
Economy: *Agr: cassava, rice, fruit, vegetables, oil palm, peanuts, coffee. Ind: bauxite, diamonds*
Currency: *Guinea franc*

Sierra Leone

A 15th-century Portuguese explorer named this West African region. Sierra Leone means "lion mountain" and may describe the shape of a mountain on the Sierra Leone Peninsula. Here, in 1787, British philanthropists established Freetown as a settlement for liberated slaves. After the British government outlawed slavery in 1807, it made Sierra Leone a colony. British Navy ships patrolled the coast, intercepting slave ships bound for the New World. Freetown became a refuge for thousands of former slaves.

The descendants of those slaves, the Creoles, today make up barely 2 percent of the population of the now independent nation, but their mother tongue, Krio, is spoken throughout the country. The Creoles once were prominent in Sierra Leone's political and commercial life. Since independence in 1961, leaders from larger ethnic groups have replaced them.

More and more of Sierra Leone's people are moving to cities in search of jobs. But almost three-quarters still live in rural areas, from the coastal belt of beaches and swampland to the inland forests, plains, and mountains. Crop yields are low, so many farmers work part of the year as miners. Diamond mining is important to the economy, but the resource is dwindling and smugglers may be taking as much as 95 percent of production out of the country. Fishing is significant along the coast, where a fleet of canoes hauls in several thousand tons of fish a year.

Official name: *Republic of Sierra Leone*
Area: *27,699 sq mi (71,740 sq km)*
Population: *4,436,000*
Capital: *Freetown (pop. 469,800)*
Ethnic groups: *Mende, Temne, Creole, other*
Language: *English, Krio, Mende, Temne*
Religious groups: *traditional, Muslim*
Economy: *Agr: rice, cassava, cacao, coffee, oil palm, livestock. Ind: diamonds, rutile, bauxite, fishing*
Currency: *leone*

Liberia

Freed black slaves left the United States in the early 1800s to found a new nation in West Africa. They settled along a sandy coastline dotted with lagoons and bordered by thick rain forest. Here the newcomers mingled with local fishermen, farmers, and traders. Liberia became Africa's first independent republic in 1847, with a constitution modeled after that of the United States and a capital named after President Monroe.

Descendants of the American settlers make up about 5 percent of Liberia's population today. These Americo-Liberians once ran the country, but a revolt in 1980 brought a purely African group to power.

A bloody civil war broke out a decade later, killing an estimated 20,000 people, sending hundreds of thousands of refugees into neighboring countries, and devastating the economy. Monrovia, the capital, lost much of its business community. Of the Liberians who remain in the country, most live in villages scattered throughout the forests. They grow only enough cassava, rice, fruit, and vegetables to feed their families.

Official name: *Republic of Liberia*
Area: *43,000 sq mi (111,369 sq km)*
Population: *2,777,000*
Capital: *Monrovia (pop. 421,100)*
Ethnic groups: *Kpelle, Bassa, Grebo, other*
Language: *English, many African languages*
Religious groups: *traditional, Muslim, Christian*
Economy: *Agr: rice, cassava, rubber, oil palm, coffee, cacao. Ind: iron ore, diamonds, lumber, fishing*
Currency: *Liberian dollar*

Côte d'Ivoire

A century ago, Abidjan was a sleepy coastal fishing village of about 700 people. Today 1.8 million Ivoirians live and work in this cosmopolitan city with its high-rise office buildings and wide avenues. It remains the seat of government, although Yamoussoukro, some 137 miles (220 km) northwest, has been designated the new capital.

Abidjan continues to grow. Each year roughly 10,000 people, mainly farmers from the dry northern savanna and laborers from neighboring countries, move to the city. They seek work in government, and in the automobile assembly plant, aluminum factory, and small manufacturing firms. Many Ivoirians, however, live in traditional villages in the humid, forested southern half of the country. Some grow export crops such as cacao and coffee that provide income for the developing nation.

Félix Houphouët-Boigny, president after independence was gained from France in 1960, increased economic growth by encouraging foreign investment, improving farming methods, and expanding the range of exports.

Côte d'Ivoire, known in English as the Ivory Coast, takes its name from the elephant ivory trade that began in the 1400s and flourished through the late 1800s and early 1900s. Today ivory trade is illegal, and the nation protects its elephants and other wildlife in game reserves.

Official name: *Republic of Côte d'Ivoire*
Area: *124,504 sq mi (322,463 sq km)*
Population: *12,951,000*
Capital: *Abidjan (met. pop. 1,850,000)*
Ethnic groups: *More than 60 groups*
Language: *French, African languages*
Religious groups: *traditional, Muslim, Christian*
Economy: *Agr: yams, cassava, rice, corn, millet, cacao, coffee, oil palm, fruit, cotton, rubber, sugarcane. Ind: food processing, lumber, oil refining, textiles*
Currency: *CFA franc*

Côte d'Ivoire

1 *With daggers drawn to heighten the drama, dancers of the Dan ethnic group toss a young girl back and forth. Girls selected to learn the ritual acrobatic dances begin training at the age of four. The government hopes to preserve such customs while melding some 60 ethnic groups into one nation.*

1 *Côte d'Ivoire*

1 *Sierra Leone*

2 *Senegal*

Sierra Leone

1 *At an open-air market in Freetown, many women run their own small businesses, selling goods and foodstuffs.*

Senegal

2 *Window-shopping in Senegal's capital, Dakar, elegantly dressed women study the latest fashions from Paris.*

3 *Spacious boulevards and plazas mark Dakar. Founded as a colonial outpost in 1857, today it blends French chic with African zest.*

3 *Senegal*

5 *Cape Verde*

The Gambia

4 *A boat on the Gambia River takes on a cargo of peanuts. The river is a national lifeline, The Gambia's main avenue of trade, travel, and communication.*

Cape Verde

5 *Islanders gather fresh coconuts to eke out food supplies. Thin soil and frequent droughts limit farming; Cape Verdeans import much of their food.*

4 *The Gambia*

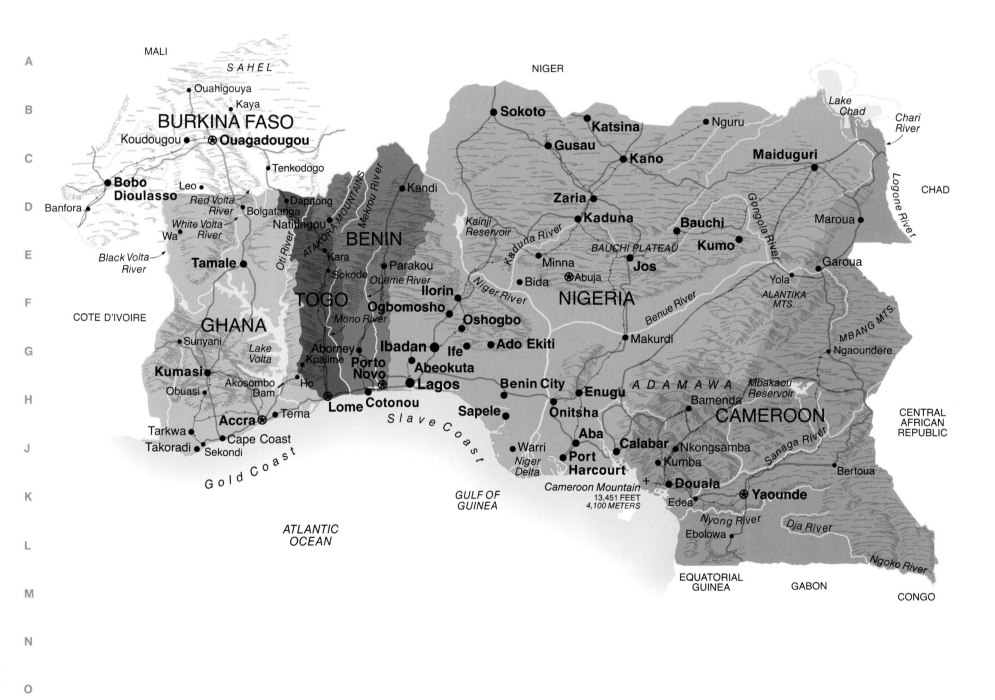

Europeans called Ghana the Gold Coast. Copious amounts of the precious metal were mined or panned from rivers and carried overland to the Mediterranean. The Portuguese established a

West African sea route in the 15th century, trading goods for gold with local African nations. They built a great castle called Elmina (from "the mine") that warded off competitors for nearly a century.

Between the 16th and 19th centuries, Elmina became a staging post for the trading activity that gave the Slave Coast its name. The region was a center for the West African slave trade.

0 KILOMETERS 250
0 STATUTE MILES 150

For map legend see page 21.

A

B

MALI

SAHEL

• Ouahigouya

• Kaya

BURKINA FASO

Koudougou • ⊕ Ouagadougou

C

• Tenkodogo

NIGER

Sokoto

Katsina

• Nguru

Lake Chad

Chari River

Gusau

Kano

Maiduguri

CHAD

D

Bobo Dioulasso

Banfora

Leo •

Dapaong •

Natitingou •

Bolgatanga •

Red Volta River

White Volta River

Zaria

Kaduna

Bauchi

Kumo

Maroua

Kandi

BAUCHI PLATEAU

Gongola River

Logone River

Kaduna River

Kainji Reservoir

E

Wa •

Black Volta River

Tamale

Kara

Sokode •

BENIN

Parakou •

Oueme River

Minna •

Bida •

Jos

⊕ Abuja

Garoua

Yola •

ALANTIKA MTS.

COTE D'IVOIRE

TOGO

Ilorin

NIGERIA

F

GHANA

Ogbomosho

Mono River

Niger River

Benue River

MBANG MTS.

Sunyani •

Lake Volta

Oshogbo

G

Kumasi

Obuasi •

Akosombo Dam

Abomey • Kpalime

Ife

Ado Ekiti

Makurdi •

ADAMAWA

Mbakaou Reservoir

Ngaoundere •

H

Accra ⊕

Tarkwa •

Takoradi •

Sekondi •

Cape Coast

Tema •

Ho •

Porto Novo

Lome Cotonou

Ibadan

Abeokuta

Lagos

Benin City

Sapele •

Enugu

Onitsha

Bamenda •

CAMEROON

CENTRAL AFRICAN REPUBLIC

J

Gold Coast

Slave Coast

Warri •

Niger Delta

Port Harcourt

Aba

Calabar

Nkongsamba •

Kumba •

Sanaga River

Bertoua •

K

ATLANTIC OCEAN

GULF OF GUINEA

Cameroon Mountain
13,451 FEET
4,100 METERS

Douala

Edea •

Yaounde ⊕

L

Nyong River

Ebolowa •

Dja River

Ngoko River

M

EQUATORIAL GUINEA

GABON

CONGO

N

O

P

1 2 3 4 5 6 7 8 9 10 11 12 13 14 15 16 17 18 19

Burkina Faso

In 1984, Upper Volta chose a new name, Burkina Faso, which, loosely translated, means "land of honest men" in the local languages. The country's main ethnic group is called the Mossi.

The nation is one of the poorest in the world. More than 80 percent of the families scratch out a living growing sorghum, millet, and corn, or raising livestock. About one in five people can read. One in four children goes to school.

Burkina Faso lies on an inland plateau cut by three major south-flowing rivers. Part of the northern region is in the arid Sahel. All over the country too much grazing and cultivation have exhausted already poor soil. Droughts cause food shortages and even famine. Each year about 500,000 Burkinabe leave home to find seasonal work in countries to the south.

Some hope for Burkina Faso lies in its mineral deposits, especially manganese in the northeast. But mining requires roads and railways, both inadequate in this struggling nation.

Official name: *Burkina Faso*
Area: *105,869 sq mi (274,200 sq km)*
Population: *9,567,000*
Capital: *Ouagadougou (pop. 441,500)*
Ethnic groups: *More than 50 groups, including Mossi, Mande, Fulani, Lobi, Bobo*
Language: *French, African languages*
Religious groups: *traditional, Muslim, Christian*
Economy: *Agr: grains, livestock, peanuts, cotton, shea nuts, sesame. Ind: food processing, textiles*
Currency: *CFA franc*

Ghana

Ghana's local chieftains oversee festivals marking birth and death, puberty, marriage, and harvest. By doing so, they hope to preserve traditional Ghanaian culture despite the pressures of modernization.

In 1957, Ghana became the first black African colony to win independence. Rich in gold and diamonds, in fertile land, and in fish-laden waters, the nation seemed ready to follow its visionary leader, Kwame Nkrumah, into a bright future.

Ghana had only one harbor: Nkrumah built a second, modern port at Tema. Ghana needed more electricity: Nkrumah raised the giant Akosombo Dam on the Volta River, creating a steady source of energy and the world's largest artificial lake in terms of surface area—3,500 square miles (9,065 sq km). But Nkrumah gradually transformed his government into a dictatorship. Unwise spending and mismanagement led to economic and political chaos. A military coup toppled him in 1966, but the situation improved little under succeeding regimes. In the 1990s, some progress was made as Ghana began a move toward democracy.

About a quarter of the people live in poverty, in areas ranging from the dry rolling northern savanna to the humid forests of the southwest. Most Ghanaians farm, raising their own food on small plots. Many who live in the forest belt produce cocoa beans, Ghana's largest export.

Official name: *Republic of Ghana*
Area: *92,100 sq mi (238,537 sq km)*
Population: *16,009,000*
Capital: *Accra (met. pop. 949,100)*
Ethnic groups: *Ashanti, Ewe, Fante, Ga, other*
Language: *English, Akan, Dagomba, Ewe, Ga*
Religious groups: *traditional, Christian, Muslim*
Economy: *Agr: cassava, yams, corn, sorghum, millet, rice, plantains, cacao, cotton, coffee. Ind: mining, lumber, fishing, food processing, aluminum*
Currency: *cedi*

Togo

Long and narrow, measuring only 100 miles (160 km) across at its widest, Togo stretches 360 miles (580 km) north from the Gulf of Guinea. Highlands extend southwest to northeast through grassy plains, where coffee, cacao, and cotton are raised. Forests of teak, mahogany, and bamboo grow on southern plateaus.

Togo's main ethnic group, the Ewe, live near the coast, where French colonial rule provided schooling and jobs until independence in 1960. Today many Ewe farm, the traditional livelihood of most Togolese; some are merchants or government workers. Southern Togolese also mine phosphates, an ingredient of fertilizers and the country's leading export.

The hill people of the north include the Kabye, whose ancestors settled northern Togo from the West African savanna. Skilled farmers, they cultivate millet, sorghum, and beans for food, and peanuts as a cash crop.

Official name: *Republic of Togo*
Area: *21,925 sq mi (56,785 sq km)*
Population: *3,814,000*
Capital: *Lomé (pop. 366,500)*
Ethnic groups: *37 groups, including Ewe, Kabye*
Language: *French, Ewe, Kabye, Dagomba*
Religious groups: *traditional, Christian, Muslim*
Economy: *Agr: cassava, yams, corn, sorghum, millet, beans, livestock, coffee, cacao, cotton, peanuts, oil palm. Ind: phosphates, food processing, textiles*
Currency: *CFA franc*

Benin

Formerly called Dahomey, Benin established its national palm-oil trade in the 1800s under an African kingdom of that name. Later a French colony, it won independence in 1960.

Benin has fertile soil and some forest cover; a grassy landscape reaches nearly to its seacoast. In lagoon villages on the marshy southern shore, fishermen and their families live in bamboo huts built on stilts, and children ferry to school in dugout canoes. Beyond the lagoons, on a fertile plateau, farmers clear the land to grow crops for their own use and cotton and oil palms for income. Herders of cattle and sheep live in the Atakora Mountains of the northwest.

Under French rule, many citizens attended school, but in recent years there have not been enough skilled jobs for these people. In 1989, the government renounced Marxism. Soon after, newly elected leaders began economic reforms.

Official name: *Republic of Benin*
Area: *43,484 sq mi (112,622 sq km)*
Population: *4,995,000*
Capital: *Porto Novo, official (pop. 208,000)*
  Cotonou, de facto (pop. 487,000)
Ethnic groups: *Fon, Adja, Yoruba, Bariba, other*
Language: *French, Fon, other African languages*
Religious groups: *traditional, Christian, Muslim*
Economy: *Agr: cassava, yams, corn, beans, sorghum, peanuts, cotton, oil palm. Ind: food, textiles*
Currency: *CFA franc*

Nigeria

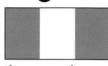

One of every four black Africans is Nigerian. Known as the giant of West Africa, Nigeria has more people than any other country on the continent. It is also one of the most populous nations in the world. But in size it only ranks 14th among African countries.

Nigeria is Africa's leading oil producer. It also has rich deposits of natural gas. The discovery of oil in the 1950s generated enormous income. Nigeria's leaders invested much of this wealth in roads, railways, and schools, as well as in manufacturing and communications systems. In recent years the nation has relied on oil for 90 percent of its export earnings, which makes it vulnerable to the rise and fall of world oil prices.

Urban life has a long history here. Some cities, such as Kano, a Muslim cultural center in the north, and Ibadan, a regional capital in the south, date back several centuries. Others grew up during the oil boom, when people moved from country to city in search of jobs. The nation's new capital, Abuja, is a planned city that was begun in the 1980s. Today, a third of Nigeria's people are city dwellers. The Lagos metropolitan area has about five million residents.

Many Nigerians, however, dwell in mud-and-thatch houses in small villages, where they farm, fish, or herd. Their loyalties to extended family and to village are strong. So are their ethnic allegiances. More than 300 ethnic groups live in Nigeria. The variety of languages, customs, artistic traditions, and styles of dress give the nation its great cultural richness.

The largest groups include the Hausa and Fulani, who dominate the broad expanse of the sandy northern plains bordering the Sahara. Though the region receives little rain, these people manage to grow sorghum, millet, peanuts, and cotton, and to raise livestock.

Other major groups are the Yoruba of the southwest and the Ibo of the southeast. Nigeria's moist southern regions support dense tropical forest—much of which southern farmers have cleared to plant cacao, rubber, and oil palm trees. On the coast, amid a maze of creeks and lagoons, people grow coconut and oil palms.

After achieving independence from British colonial rule in 1960, Nigeria divided sharply along ethnic and regional lines. A bitter and bloody civil war erupted in 1967 when the Ibo formed the Republic of Biafra along the southeastern coast. About a million civilians died, primarily from starvation, before the war ended in 1970. Nigeria's present leaders continue to struggle for stability and unity among the 30 states that make up this diverse nation.

Official name: *Federal Republic of Nigeria*
Area: *356,669 sq mi (923,768 sq km)*
Population: *90,122,000*
Capital: *Abuja (pop. 369,000)*
Ethnic groups: *More than 300 groups*
Language: *English, Hausa, Ibo, Yoruba*
Religious groups: *Muslim, Christian, traditional*
Economy: *Agr: yams, cassava, sorghum, millet, corn, rice, cacao, peanuts, oil palm, rubber, cotton, livestock. Ind: oil, natural gas, minerals, steel, textiles, food processing, lumber, car assembly, fishing*
Currency: *naira*

Cameroon

Diverse lands and peoples meet in Cameroon. The landscape ranges from coastal rain forest to inland savanna, from palm-lined beaches to mountain forests. The people include about 200 ethnic groups, many with their own arts, traditions, and languages.

The most dominant group economically are the Bamileke of the western mountains, who grow coffee for export. They also hold about 70 percent of the nation's professional jobs. On the northern and central savannas, farmers raise millet, peanuts, and rice; nearby the Fulani herd horses, cattle, sheep, and goats.

Isolated bands of Pygmies hunt small game and gather food in the southeastern forests. On the southern coastal plain live the Douala, for whom the nation's major port is named. They are the most educated people in the country.

From 1970 until 1985, oil production and manufacturing boosted economic growth, but then prices fell and export earnings dropped. Today, agriculture is the chief source of income. Varied crops grow on the lush hillsides of Cameroon Mountain. At 13,451 feet (4,100 m), this volcano is the highest mountain in West Africa and one of the wettest places on earth, receiving more than 30 feet (9 m) of rain a year.

Official name: *Republic of Cameroon*
Area: *183,569 sq mi (475,442 sq km)*
Population: *12,658,000*
Capital: *Yaoundé (pop. 712,100)*
Ethnic groups: *About 200 groups*
Language: *French, English, African languages*
Religious groups: *Christian, traditional, Muslim*
Economy: *Agr: root crops, grains, cacao, coffee, cotton, bananas, rubber, oil palm, sugarcane, livestock. Ind: agricultural processing, oil, lumber, aluminum*
Currency: *CFA franc*

1 *Benin*

2 *Nigeria*

3 *Burkina Faso*

4 *Ghana*

5 *Cameroon*

Benin

1 *Wooden pilings hold bamboo houses above the high tide mark in Ganvié, a village built on a tidal lagoon near Cotonou. Canoes are used for fishing and ferrying.*

Nigeria

2 *Known as the "go-slow," rush hour clogs a street in Lagos. Five million people live in and around Nigeria's former capital.*

Burkina Faso

3 *Bella men go to great lengths to protect themselves from desert sun; their white head wraps reflect sunlight. Cotton veils shield faces from windblown sand.*

Ghana

4 *Country women near Sunyani fill pots and pails with water for the day's chores. Missionaries helped build the village well.*

Cameroon

5 *Cupped in a volcanic crater, Lake Bambili is slowly drying up, like the already swampy lake beyond. Someday the volcanic soil here will be fertile farmland.*

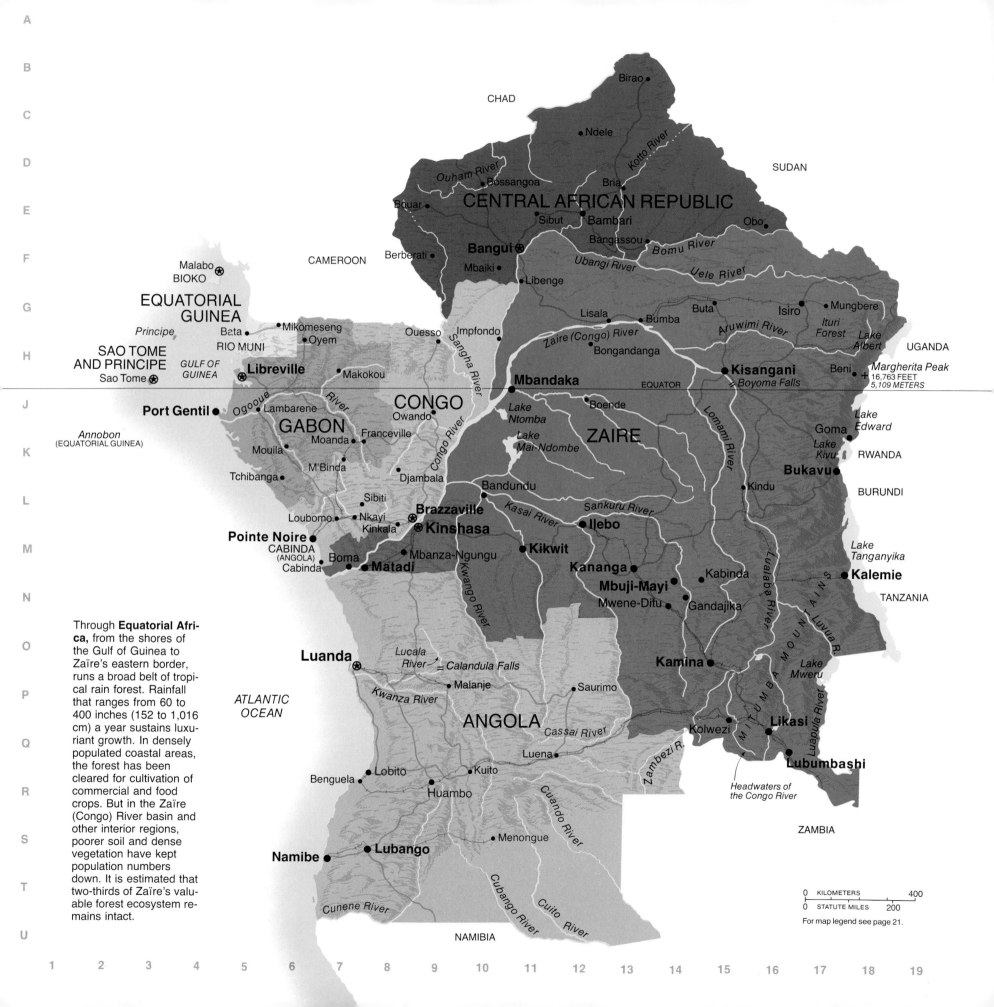

A B C D E F G H J K L M N O P Q R S T U

CHAD

Birao

Ndele

CENTRAL AFRICAN REPUBLIC

SUDAN

Ouham River

Bossangoa

Bria

Kotto River

Bouar

Sibut   Bambari

Bangassou   Obo

CAMEROON

Berberati

Bangui ⊗

Mbaiki

Bomu River

Ubangi River

Libenge

Uele River

Malabo ⊗
BIOKO

Principe

Bata   •Mikomeseng

RIO MUNI   Oyem

Ouesso   Impfondo

Lisala   Bumba   Buta

Isiro   •Mungbere

*Ituri
Forest*

*Lake
Albert*

UGANDA

**EQUATORIAL
GUINEA**

SAO TOME
AND PRINCIPE

*GULF OF
GUINEA*

Sao Tome ⊗

⊗ **Libreville**

•Makokou

Sangha River

Mbandaka

Zaïre (Congo) River

Bongandanga

EQUATOR

Kisangani
Boyoma Falls

Beni   *Margherita Peak*
+ 16,763 FEET
5,109 METERS

Annobon
(EQUATORIAL GUINEA)

Port Gentil •

*Ogooue
River*

•Lambarene

Owando

GABON

Franceville

Congo River

*Lake
Ntomba*

Boende

*Lake
Mai-Ndombe*

ZAIRE

Lomami River

*Lake
Edward*

Goma

*Lake
Kivu*

RWANDA

Mouila

Moanda

M'Binda

Djambala

Bukavu

BURUNDI

Tchibanga

Sibiti

Loubomo   Nkayi
Kinkala

Brazzaville ⊗
⊗ **Kinshasa**

Bandundu

Kasai River

Sankuru River

Kindu

*Lake
Tanganyika*

Pointe Noire •

CABINDA
(ANGOLA)

Boma   Mbanza-Ngungu

Cabinda   **Matadi**

Kwango River

Kikwit

Ilebo

Kananga

Mbuji-Mayi
Mwene-Ditu

Kabinda

Gandajika

Lualaba River

Kalemie

TANZANIA

Luanda ⊗

*Lucala
River*   = *Calandula Falls*

Malanje

Kwanza River

ANGOLA

Saurimo

Kamina

*Lake
Mweru*

Luapula River

Luvua R.

MITUMBA MOUNTAINS

*ATLANTIC
OCEAN*

Through **Equatorial Africa,** from the shores of
the Gulf of Guinea to
Zaïre's eastern border,
runs a broad belt of tropical rain forest. Rainfall
that ranges from 60 to
400 inches (152 to 1,016
cm) a year sustains luxu-
riant growth. In densely
populated coastal areas,
the forest has been
cleared for cultivation of
commercial and food
crops. But in the Zaïre
(Congo) River basin and
other interior regions,
poorer soil and dense
vegetation have kept
population numbers
down. It is estimated that
two-thirds of Zaïre's valuable forest ecosystem re-
mains intact.

Cassai River

Luena

Benguela   Lobito

Kuito

Huambo

Cuando River

Zambezi R.

Kolwezi

Likasi

Lubumbashi

*Headwaters of
the Congo River*

ZAMBIA

Menongue

Namibe •   **Lubango**

Cunene River

Cubango River

Cuito River

NAMIBIA

0   KILOMETERS   400
0   STATUTE MILES   200

For map legend see page 21.

1 2 3 4 5 6 7 8 9 10 11 12 13 14 15 16 17 18 19

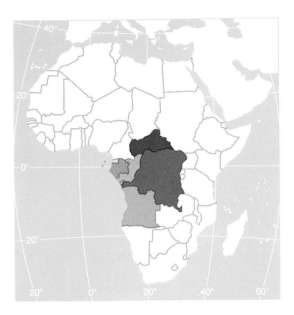

Central African Republic

At the heart of Africa lies the Central African Republic. Most of this landlocked nation consists of a rolling plateau of grassland drained by two river systems, one flowing north, the other flowing south. The country's southwestern corner dips into Africa's rain-forest belt; its northeastern tip is semidesert. About 80 ethnic groups live along the rivers and across the countryside.

Since winning independence from France in 1960, the republic has suffered political instability and economic hardship. One ruler declared himself emperor and got rich at the country's expense before being deposed. Now the government is moving slowly toward democracy.

Today, four out of five people farm. Many grow food crops on small plots. Others raise cotton for export or labor on European-owned coffee plantations. Some workers mine diamonds, but deposits of uranium remain unexploited.

Official name: *Central African Republic*
Area: *240,535 sq mi (622,984 sq km)*
Population: *3,154,000*
Capital: *Bangui (pop. 596,800)*
Ethnic groups: *80 groups, including Banda, Baya*
Language: *French, Sango*
Religious groups: *traditional, Christian*
Economy: *Agr: cassava, yams, peanuts, millet, sorghum, corn, rice, bananas, livestock, cotton, coffee, sesame, tobacco. Ind: diamonds, lumber, textiles*
Currency: *CFA franc*

São Tomé and Príncipe

Off the west coast of Equatorial Africa two volcanic islands rise from the sea, São Tomé and smaller Príncipe. A former Portuguese colony, the mountainous islands and several islets were united as an independent country in 1975. In 1991 the government turned from Marxism to democracy. Most of the people dwell on São Tomé, where they farm or fish for tuna and shark. The country specializes in cacao and other cash crops—so much so that it has to import most of its food.

Official name: *Democratic Republic of São Tomé and Príncipe*
Area: *372 sq mi (964 sq km)*
Population: *127,000*
Capital: *São Tomé (pop. 35,000)*
Ethnic groups: *mixed African, Portuguese-African*
Language: *Portuguese*
Religious groups: *Roman Catholic*
Economy: *Agr: cacao, coconuts, coffee, oil palm, bananas. Ind: food processing, textiles, soap, fishing*
Currency: *dobra*

Equatorial Guinea

Violent storms often strike Equatorial Guinea, lashing the rain forest of Río Muni, its mainland region, and battering the shores of its five islands. Political storms, too, struck the nation after it won independence from Spain in 1968. The first ruler of Africa's only Spanish-speaking country ruined its economy and created a reign of terror. He was overthrown in 1979, but economic recovery is slow.

Today nearly all workers in this poor republic are farmers. Some grow cacao, the major export crop, on the boot-shaped island of Bioko. Here and on the less fertile mainland, where most Equatorial Guineans live, small-scale farmers grow coffee. Lumbermen harvest trees for plywood from the thick tropical woodlands.

Official name: *Republic of Equatorial Guinea*
Area: *10,831 sq mi (28,051 sq km)*
Population: *367,000*
Capital: *Malabo (pop. 30,400)*
Ethnic groups: *Fang, Bubi*
Language: *Spanish, Fang, Bubi, other*
Religious groups: *Roman Catholic*
Economy: *Agr: yams, cassava, bananas, cacao, coffee, oil palm, livestock. Ind: lumber, fishing*
Currency: *CFA franc*

Gabon

Dense equatorial forest, lush with more than 3,000 species of vegetation, blankets most of Gabon. The huge *okoumé* tree, used for making plywood, once supplied much of the nation's income. Now oil does, though forestry is still important. Rich deposits of manganese and uranium also help to give Gabon one of the highest per capita incomes in Africa.

The government allocates a lot of money to roads, railways, and large agricultural projects such as banana and oil palm plantations. Many Gabonese don't benefit from these programs. Half the people live in villages on the coast or along the rivers, where they grow cassava, yams, and taro on small family plots.

Gabon is known to many as the onetime home of Albert Schweitzer, the Nobel Prize-winning physician and philosopher who founded a missionary hospital near Lambaréné in 1913.

Official name: *Gabonese Republic*
Area: *103,347 sq mi (267,667 sq km)*
Population: *1,534,000*
Capital: *Libreville (pop. 352,000)*
Ethnic groups: *about 40 Bantu groups*
Language: *French, Fang, other Bantu languages*
Religious groups: *Christian, traditional*
Economy: *Agr: root crops, bananas, cacao, coffee, oil palm. Ind: oil, lumber, mining, food processing*
Currency: *CFA franc*

Congo

The northern part of Congo is a world of green intensity. Dense vine thickets and tropical trees create a thick blanket of vegetation.

Most Congolese live south of this deeply forested region, on the coastal plains and in river valleys between the capital, Brazzaville, and the sea. Here lie most of the country's farmlands and industries. About a third of the people are farmers, populating the thousands of small settlements clustered along the Congo River and its tributaries. Many plant cassava, fruit, and peanuts on family plots or tend cash crops such as sugarcane on modern plantations.

The nation's city dwellers hold jobs in government, commerce, or industry. Most live in Brazzaville on the Congo, or in the port city of Pointe Noire, linked to the capital by the Congo-Ocean Railway. This railroad and the Congo's many waterways make the nation central Africa's door to the Atlantic for trade and transport. Though lumber provides the country with a steady income, oil has driven its economy since rich offshore oil fields began to produce in 1978.

Official name: *Republic of the Congo*
Area: *132,047 sq mi (342,000 sq km)*
Population: *2,377,000*
Capital: *Brazzaville (pop. 760,300)*
Ethnic groups: *BaKongo, Sangha, Teke, Mboshi*
Language: *French, Lingala, Kikongo, other*
Religious groups: *Christian, traditional*
Economy: *Agr: cassava, other root crops, fruit, sugarcane, peanuts, corn, rice, livestock, oil palm, coffee, cacao. Ind: oil, lumber, food processing, mining*
Currency: *CFA franc*

Zaïre

In the dense tropical rain forests of Zaïre, a haunting yodel at times breaks the deep silence and resonates among the trees. It is the song of Pygmy women who make their homes in this hot, humid region. Pygmies have lived here ever since their ancestors settled the land in prehistoric times.

Zaïre is a huge country lying at the heart of the Zaïre River basin. It is 75 times the size of Belgium, its former ruler, which granted Zaïre independence in 1960. Central Africa's largest nation in population as well as land area, Zaïre counts more than 200 ethnic groups among its diverse peoples.

Many of Zaïre's people are poor farmers. They live in houses of mud bricks or dried mud and sticks in villages that hold from a few dozen to a few hundred people. There they grow cassava, corn, and rice, and some catch fish in the rivers. More and more Zaïrians are moving to Kinshasa, the capital, and other big cities to look for jobs. Most can't find work and end up living in crowded squatters' villages outside the cities.

Zaïre has the potential for great wealth. Some of the world's largest reserves of copper, cobalt, and diamonds are found in the south. The Zaïre River system also offers rich promise for transportation and hydroelectric power. And, with farmland ranging from tropical lowlands to cool, dry highlands, Zaïre can grow valuable cash crops of coffee, oil palm, rubber, tea, and cotton.

Since independence, however, civil war, corruption, and mismanagement have devastated the economy. Falling export earnings and rising import prices have made matters worse. In the 1990s, the inflation rate approached 8,000 per-

cent, and people were demanding that the government make economic and political changes.

Official name: *Republic of Zaïre*
Area: *905,568 sq mi (2,345,409 sq km)*
Population: *37,928,000*
Capital: *Kinshasa (met. pop. 3,700,000)*
Ethnic groups: *More than 200 groups, mostly Bantu*
Language: *French, many African languages*
Religious groups: *Christian, traditional*
Economy: *Agr: cassava, bananas, root crops, corn, peanuts, rice, coffee, oil palm, rubber, tea, cotton. Ind: mining, food processing, textiles, cement, oil*
Currency: *zaïre*

Angola

Thirty years of war have made life harsh for Angolans. The country is well endowed with rich farmland and valuable minerals, such as diamonds, iron ore, and copper. But war has disrupted the economy and devastated the land, from the narrow coastal plain to the hilly central plateau, the nation's breadbasket.

The conflict began in the 1960s, when three rebel groups fought for independence from the Portuguese. When Portugal finally withdrew in 1975, one group seized power. Fierce fighting continued, this time between the ruling Marxist party and other rebels. In 1991, a United Nations-sponsored peace accord brought an end to the war. But fighting resumed after longtime rebel leader Jonas Savimbi failed to win the presidency in 1992 elections.

Few Angolans—most of them farmers, herders, traders, or miners—have escaped the effects of war. Hundreds of thousands have been killed or displaced. Many rural families have left their farms for urban-area shantytowns. Once a major exporter of several cash crops, Angola now exports less and imports most of its food.

One bright spot in the economy is oil. Big reserves lie off the shore of Cabinda, a forested sliver of land separated from the rest of Angola by a strip of coastal territory belonging to Zaïre.

Official name: *People's Republic of Angola*
Area: *481,354 sq mi (1,246,700 sq km)*
Population: *8,902,000*
Capital: *Luanda (pop. 1,544,400)*
Ethnic groups: *Ovimbundu, Kimbundu, other*
Language: *Portuguese, Bantu languages*
Religious groups: *traditional, Christian*
Economy: *Agr: cassava, corn, millet, bananas, sugarcane, vegetables, sweet potatoes, coffee, cotton, sisal. Ind: oil, mining, food processing, textiles*
Currency: *kwanza*

1 *Angola*

Angola

1 *The swift Kwanza River rushes over a scenic waterfall. A dam on the Kwanza southeast of the capital, Luanda, produces a third of Angola's hydroelectric power.*

2 *Drillers work on an oil rig off the Cabinda coast, where Angola is developing a rich petroleum field.*

2 *Angola*

1 *Zaïre*

2 *Zaïre*

3 *Zaïre*

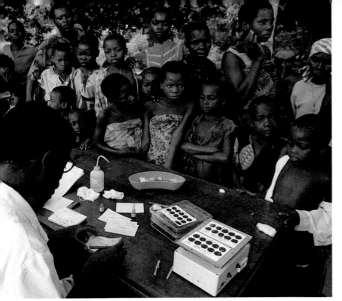

4 *Congo*

Zaïre

1 *In the Ituri Forest, seminomadic Efe Pygmy women cook while men prepare to hunt. When the clan moves, women build new huts of saplings and leaves.*

2 *Tidy mud houses with thatched roofs give a storybook look to Luotu, a farming village on the Equator south of Beni.*

3 *Balancing amid rapids on the Zaïre River, an Enya tribesman prepares to place a trumpet-shaped fish trap.*

Congo

4 *At Brazzaville, children line up to have blood tests for parasitic infections. Health programs fight tropical diseases such as sleeping sickness and malaria.*

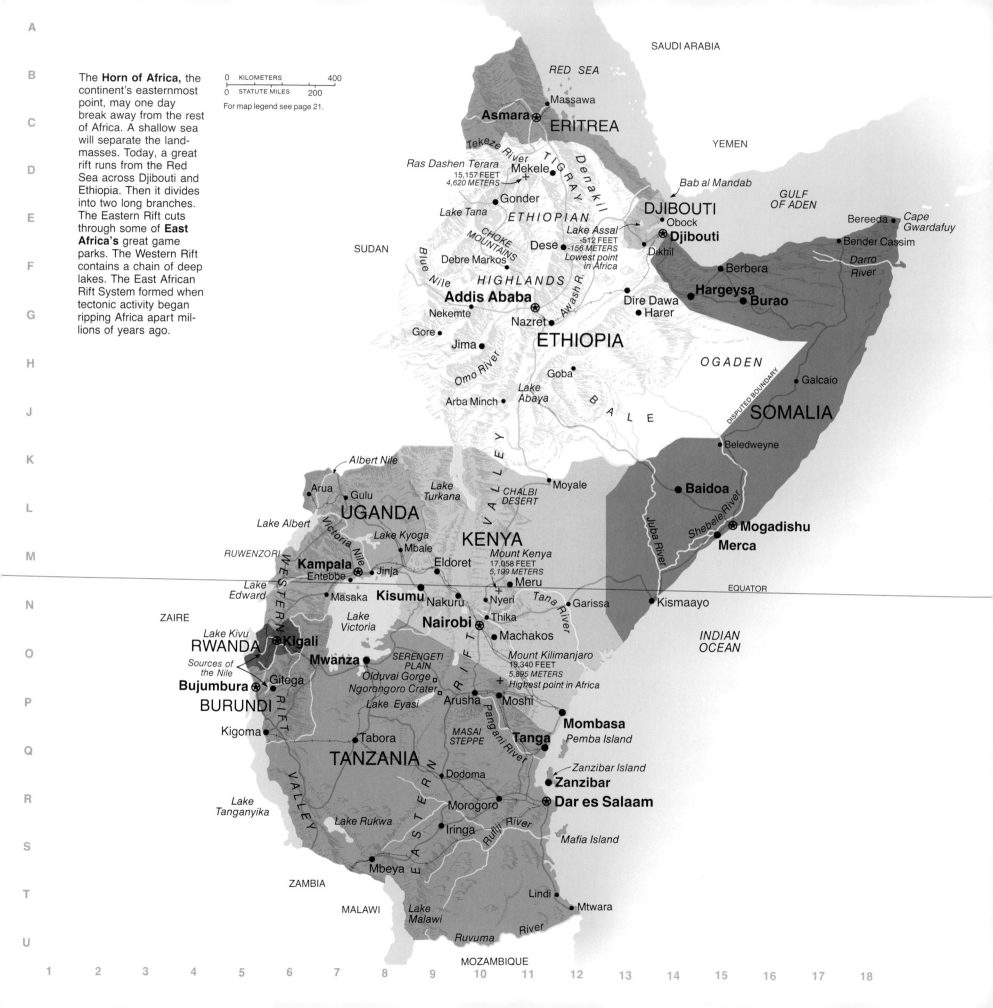

The **Horn of Africa,** the continent's easternmost point, may one day break away from the rest of Africa. A shallow sea will separate the land-masses. Today, a great rift runs from the Red Sea across Djibouti and Ethiopia. Then it divides into two long branches. The Eastern Rift cuts through some of **East Africa's** great game parks. The Western Rift contains a chain of deep lakes. The East African Rift System formed when tectonic activity began ripping Africa apart millions of years ago.

0 KILOMETERS 400
0 STATUTE MILES 200
For map legend see page 21.

SAUDI ARABIA

RED SEA

Massawa

Asmara ⊗ ERITREA

Tekeze River

YEMEN

Ras Dashen Terara
15,157 FEET Mekele
4,620 METERS +

TIGRAY Denakil

Bab al Mandab

GULF OF ADEN

DJIBOUTI

Obock

⊗ **Djibouti**

Bereeda • Cape Gwardafuy

• Bender Cassim

Gonder •

Lake Tana

ETHIOPIAN

Lake Assal
-512 FEET
-156 METERS
Lowest point
in Africa

Dikhil

Darro River

Dese •

Berbera •

SUDAN

Debre Markos •

HIGHLANDS

Addis Ababa ⊗

Dire Dawa •

Hargeysa

Burao

Blue Nile

Nekemte •

Nazret •

Harer •

Gore •

Jima •

ETHIOPIA

Awash R.

OGADEN

• Galcaio

Goba •

Omo River

BALE

Arba Minch •

Lake Abaya

DISPUTED BOUNDARY

SOMALIA

Albert Nile

• Beledweyne

Arua •

Gulu •

Lake Turkana

• Moyale

CHALBI DESERT

Baidoa

VALLEY

Mogadishu ⊗

Lake Albert

UGANDA

Juba River

Shebele River

RUWENZORI

Victoria Nile

Lake Kyoga

• Mbale

KENYA

Merca

WESTERN

Kampala

Entebbe • Jinja •

Eldoret •

Mount Kenya
17,058 FEET
5,199 METERS

EQUATOR

Lake Edward

Masaka •

Kisumu

Nakuru •

Meru •
+

INDIAN OCEAN

ZAIRE

Lake Victoria

Nyeri •

Tana River

Garissa •

Kismaayo •

Lake Kivu

Nairobi ⊗

• Thika

Kigali ⊗

RWANDA

Mwanza

SERENGETI PLAIN

• Machakos

Sources of the Nile

Olduvai Gorge

Mount Kilimanjaro
19,340 FEET
5,895 METERS
Highest point in Africa

Bujumbura ⊗ Gitega •

Ngorongoro Crater

Arusha •

Moshi •

RIFT

BURUNDI

Lake Eyasi

Pangani River

Kigoma •

MASAI STEPPE

Mombasa

Pemba Island

Tanga

Tabora •

TANZANIA

Dodoma •

Zanzibar Island

Lake Tanganyika

EASTERN

Morogoro •

Zanzibar

Dar es Salaam ⊗

Lake Rukwa

VALLEY

Iringa •

Rufiji River

Mafia Island

ZAMBIA

Mbeya •

RIFT

Lindi •

MALAWI

Lake Malawi

Mtwara •

Ruvuma River

MOZAMBIQUE

Ethiopia

Famine brought Ethiopia to world attention in the 1980s, when drought struck the land and fields once rich in crops turned to seas of dust. Despite food aid, more than one million Ethiopians died.

Were it not for recurring drought, poor crop management, and a long-running war, Ethiopia might be one of the most prosperous agricultural countries in Africa. Its land varies from hot lowlands to rugged mountains. Two-thirds of the country is made up of a high, temperate, fertile plateau. A range of crops can thrive in this diverse terrain, including the coffee tree, which grows wild in the southwestern highlands.

For more than 2,000 years, emperors and kings ruled Ethiopia. The last emperor, Haile Selassie, was overthrown in 1974 and replaced by a socialist government. Strife plagued the nation as Eritrea and Tigray provinces waged war against the government. In 1991, the socialists fell, and new leaders, mostly from Tigray, promised autonomy for Eritreans until they could hold a referendum on independence.

Official name: *People's Democratic Republic of Ethiopia*
Area: *423,778 sq mi (1,097,580 sq km)*
Population: *51,000,000*
Capital: *Addis Ababa (pop. 1,739,100)*
Ethnic groups: *Oromo, Amhara, Tigre, other*
Language: *Amharic, Orominga, Tigrinya, Arabic*
Religious groups: *Ethiopian Orthodox, Muslim*
Economy: *coffee, grains, textiles, oil refining*
Currency: *birr*

Eritrea

Armed rebellion against Ethiopia and years of drought ravaged this land but united its people. In April 1993, nearly 100 percent of Eritrea's registered voters chose independence from Ethiopia. Their new country is mountainous, with a narrow coastal plain that stretches some 600 miles (965 km) along the Red Sea. Most of the people are farmers, but only 5 percent of the land is currently being cultivated.

Official name: *Eritrea*
Area: *48,000 sq mi (124,320 sq km)*
Population: *3,500,000*
Capital: *Asmara (pop. 400,000)*

Djibouti

One of the hottest, driest spots on earth, Djibouti is a land of rocky desert dotted with salt lakes and rare patches of pastureland. Its location, wrapped around a natural harbor at the southern end of the Red Sea, has made its capital, also called Djibouti, an international port crucial to the country's economy. Half the people live in the port city; the rest are nomadic herders of sheep, goats, and camels.

Official name: *Republic of Djibouti*
Area: *8,958 sq mi (23,200 sq km)*
Population: *433,000*
Capital: *Djibouti (pop. 290,000)*
Ethnic groups: *Somali (Issas), Afar, French, Arab*
Language: *French, Somali, Afar, Arabic*
Religious groups: *Sunni Muslim*
Economy: *transshipment, livestock, vegetables*
Currency: *Djibouti franc*

Somalia

Most people in Somalia belong to one ethnic group and share a common descent and culture. They believe that places with large Somali populations, such as parts of Djibouti, Kenya, and Ethiopia, should belong to Somalia, and they have fought—unsuccessfully—to gain these territories. Of the country's workers, two-thirds are nomadic herders on the dry scrubby plateaus. Drought is a perennial problem.

In the early 1990s, clan-based warfare escalated into anarchy and starvation. A UN effort helped restore order and distribute food, but sporadic violence continued to afflict the nation.

Official name: *Somali Democratic Republic*
Area: *246,201 sq mi (637,657 sq km)*
Population: *8,325,000*
Capital: *Mogadishu (pop. 500,000)*
Ethnic groups: *Somali*
Language: *Somali, Arabic*
Religious groups: *Sunni Muslim*
Economy: *Agr: grains, sugarcane, livestock, bananas. Ind: sugar, hides, textiles, oil refining*
Currency: *Somali shilling*

Uganda

"The pearl of Africa," Winston Churchill called this green land of mountains, lakes, and wild animals. That was in colonial days, before the civil war that raged for two decades.

Uganda draws together people from many different linguistic and cultural backgrounds. Most trace their roots to one of 40 ethnic groups who have lived in this region for hundreds of years, farming the fertile plateau and uplands.

The plateau lies just north of Lake Victoria, the world's third largest lake, and is rimmed by mountains in the east and west. In the far west, the sharp white tops of the Ruwenzori range, known as the Mountains of the Moon, soar up to 16,763 feet (5,109 m). Like their forebears, most Ugandans still raise food crops and livestock—in the east on mountain slopes, in the southwest, and on Lake Victoria's shores.

Uganda's future seemed bright at independence in 1962. Cash crops earned money for schools, hospitals, and roads. But in 1971, Idi Amin Dada rose to power and instituted a reign of terror. The following years brought violence, fear, and economic ruin. Uganda's present government has worked to restore peace and economic stability. Now the country faces a new threat: AIDS. Thousands have died from it.

Official name: *Republic of Uganda*
Area: *91,134 sq mi (236,036 sq km)*
Population: *17,477,000*
Capital: *Kampala (pop. 773,000)*
Ethnic groups: *40 groups: Bantu, Nilotic, other*
Language: *English, KiSwahili, Luganda*
Religious groups: *Christian, traditional*
Economy: *Agr: plantains, cassava, sweet potatoes, grains, coffee, cotton, tea, sugarcane; tobacco, livestock. Ind: food processing, textiles, cement, fishing*
Currency: *Uganda shilling*

Kenya

The world as it was in the beginning. That is how people describe the great grasslands and plains of Kenya, which still teem with huge herds of wild animals despite heavy poaching in recent years. In the mid-1900s, the government set aside 6 million acres (2.4 million ha) to protect its lions, elephants, rhinoceroses, and other wildlife. Today, 15 national parks and 23 game reserves, besides Indian Ocean beaches, make tourism a vital industry.

Kenya, though poor, is East Africa's most prosperous country. Good farmland is found only in the southwestern highlands, which occupy barely 10 percent of the land. Here, amid drought, farmers struggle to grow enough crops to feed the nation. They raise corn and other food, as well as cash crops of coffee, tea, sisal, and pyrethrum, used to make pesticides. About 75 percent of the people crowd within this small area. The dry inland plain that extends across 60 percent of Kenya is only sparsely inhabited by nomadic herders of cattle and camels.

Most Kenyans descend from Africans, but many coastal people have Arab roots. Of the 32 ethnic groups that live in Kenya, the largest is the Kikuyu. The country has one of the world's fastest growing populations; many families have six or more children. This booming growth hinders Kenya's economic progress, creating unemployment as well as land shortages that threaten the nation's parklands.

Official name: *Republic of Kenya*
Area: *224,961 sq mi (582,646 sq km)*
Population: *26,164,000*
Capital: *Nairobi (pop. 1,200,000)*
Ethnic groups: *Kikuyu, Luhya, Luo, Kamba, Kalenjin, Kisii, Meru, other*
Language: *English, KiSwahili, Kikuyu, other*
Religious groups: *traditional, Christian*
Economy: *Agr: grains, cassava, sugarcane, fruit, coffee, tea, sisal, pyrethrum, cotton, livestock. Ind: tourism, food processing, oil refining, cement*
Currency: *Kenya shilling*

Rwanda

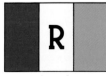

In the steep, grassy hills of this tiny nation, one is rarely out of sight of people. Rwanda, one of Africa's most densely populated countries, has more than a thousand people sharing each square mile of farmland. Some 90 percent of Rwandans work plots that dot the hillsides. They raise export crops of coffee and tea—also vegetables and grains, though barely enough to feed their growing numbers.

Of the three ethnic groups in Rwanda, the Hutu, the Tutsi, and the Pygmy Twa, the Hutu make up about 90 percent of the population. Farmers by tradition, they were dominated for centuries by the Tutsi, a cattle-herding people who migrated to the region some 500 years ago from the Horn of Africa. In 1959, the Hutu seized power from the Tutsi. Fighting resumed in 1990 when exiles invaded from Uganda.

Official name: *Republic of Rwanda*
Area: *10,169 sq mi (26,338 sq km)*
Population: *7,718,000*
Capital: *Kigali (pop. 300,000)*
Ethnic groups: *Hutu, Tutsi, Twa*
Language: *Kinyarwanda, French, KiSwahili*
Religious groups: *Christian, traditional*
Economy: *Agr: bananas, root crops, grains, livestock, coffee, tea, pyrethrum. Ind: tin, other mining*
Currency: *Rwanda franc*

Burundi

Like neighboring Rwanda, Burundi is a small, densely populated, landlocked nation. Ethnic conflict often flashes through these rolling highlands to the northeast of Lake Tanganyika. Since independence from Belgium in 1962, surges of violence have erupted between the minority Tutsi and the majority Hutu. The worst clash occurred in 1972, when more than 100,000 Hutu were killed. Though outnumbered by the Hutu six to one, the Tutsi control the government, army, and businesses.

Burundi has a pleasant climate but hardly any flat land. Most people live on family farms in clusters of houses that sit atop the many hills. From these farms come enough bananas, vegetables, and other food crops to feed the people and small crops of coffee, tea, and cotton for export. The country has deposits of nickel and other ores, which it plans to mine.

Official name: *Republic of Burundi*
Area: *10,747 sq mi (27,834 sq km)*
Population: *5,821,000*
Capital: *Bujumbura (pop. 226,600)*
Ethnic groups: *Hutu, Tutsi, Twa*
Language: *Kirundi, French, KiSwahili*
Religious groups: *Christian, traditional*
Economy: *Agr: bananas, root crops, grains, livestock, coffee, tea, cotton. Ind: textiles, hides*
Currency: *Burundi franc*

Tanzania

Tanzania shows the many faces of Africa within the bounds of a single nation. It encompasses the varied physical terrain of a continent—wide, lion-colored plains and snowcapped mountains, coastal beaches and highland lakes. It also embraces more than 120 ethnic groups and a spectrum of religions, from Christianity and Islam to traditional African beliefs.

No single ethnic group dominates the country. One group, though small, is known worldwide: the nomadic Masai, some of whom still herd humped cattle in the grassy northern plains. The mighty Serengeti and other great game parks draw tourists eager to see the elephants, lions, giraffes, and immense herds of gazelles, wildebeests, and zebras.

One of Africa's most stable nations, Tanzania was created in 1964 when mainland Tanganyika joined with the island state of Zanzibar. From this union came the name TAN-ZAN-IA. Soon after, under the presidency of Julius Nyerere, the country launched a program of African socialism called *ujamaa*, which translates as "familyhood" in KiSwahili.

Most Tanzanians live in far-flung homesteads and villages near the country's borders—on the narrow coastal plain, on lake shores, and on fertile mountain slopes, such as those of Mount Kilimanjaro. Few inhabit the interior, a desolate plateau covering much of the country.

Through ujamaa the government encouraged people to live and farm together, sharing work, resources, health care, and schooling. Under the program, the nation's literacy rate jumped from 28 percent in 1967 to nearly 80 percent in 1985. Life expectancy rose from 38 years to 52.

But farm production fell short of government hopes. Most farmers still grow only enough food crops for their own use, and, in spite of their efforts, food is a leading import. In very fertile areas, some farmers grow export crops of coffee, cotton, tea, and on Zanzibar, cloves.

Official name: *United Republic of Tanzania*
Area: *364,900 sq mi (945,087 sq km)*
Population: *27,432,000*
Capital: *Dar es Salaam (pop. 1,360,900)*
Ethnic groups: *More than 120 groups, mostly Bantu, including Sukuma, Makonde, Chaga, Nyamwezi*
Language: *KiSwahili, English, African languages*
Religious groups: *traditional, Christian, Muslim*
Economy: *Agr: cassava, grains, vegetables, fruit, coffee, cotton, tea, sisal, tobacco, cloves, cashew nuts. Ind: food processing, textiles, oil refining, tourism*
Currency: *Tanzanian shilling*

1 *Tanzania*

Tanzania

1 *A mother cheetah and four cubs enjoy a protected life in a national park on the Serengeti Plain. Outside such preserves, their chances of survival would be slim.*

2 *Young Masai women and girls gather to celebrate the birth of a child in a village near the rim of Ngorongoro Crater. Some 15,000 Masai herders live in this area.*

2 *Tanzania*

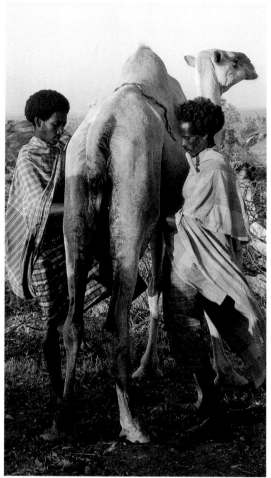

1 *Somalia*

2 *Uganda*

3 *Ethiopia*

Somalia

1 *Nomads share in milking a camel. Desert life depends on camels; they supply milk, meat, hides, and wool, and are prized as pack or riding animals.*

Uganda

2 *City workers catch rides home during Kampala's afternoon rush hour. Many commute from the countryside, where they grow crops to supplement their salaries.*

Ethiopia

3 *Flat-topped acacia trees provide shade for cattle grazing on government grasslands. Socialist leaders gave peasant families the right to farm on nationalized rural lands.*

4 *Rwanda*

5 *Djibouti*

6 *Kenya*

Rwanda

4 *A mountain gorilla munches wild celery in the Virunga Mountains west of Kigali. Only about 600 members of this endangered subspecies survive in the wild.*

Djibouti

5 *An 11-year-old Afar girl tends goats for her family. The Afar nomads eke out a living by raising animals for food and mining salt for sale.*

Kenya

6 *Nairobi's high-rise city-center serves as the commercial and communications hub of East Africa.*

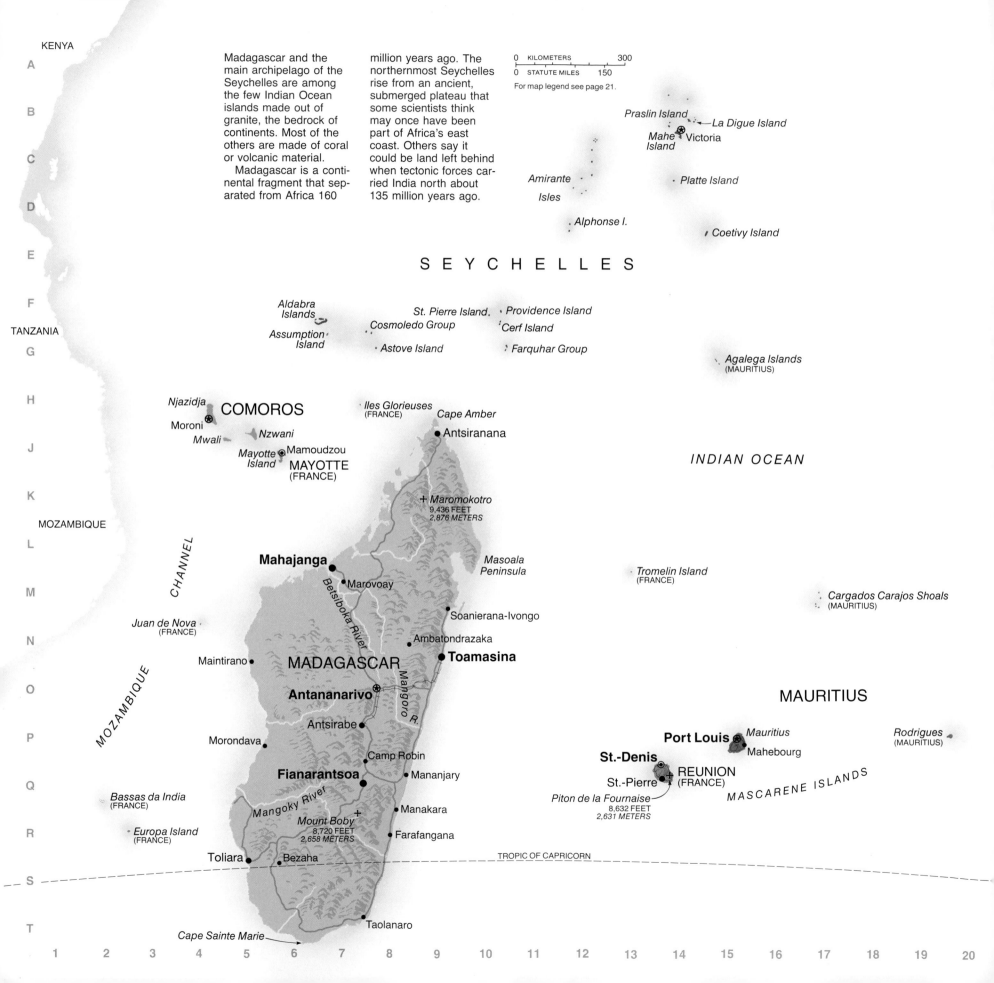

SOMALIA

KENYA

Madagascar and the main archipelago of the Seychelles are among the few Indian Ocean islands made out of granite, the bedrock of continents. Most of the others are made of coral or volcanic material.

Madagascar is a continental fragment that separated from Africa 160 million years ago. The northernmost Seychelles rise from an ancient, submerged plateau that some scientists think may once have been part of Africa's east coast. Others say it could be land left behind when tectonic forces carried India north about 135 million years ago.

0   KILOMETERS   300

0   STATUTE MILES   150

For map legend see page 21.

Praslin Island
← La Digue Island
Mahe ⊕ Victoria
Island

Amirante
Isles

Platte Island

Alphonse I.

Coetivy Island

S E Y C H E L L E S

TANZANIA

Aldabra Islands
St. Pierre Island.
Cosmoledo Group
Providence Island
Cerf Island
Assumption Island
Astove Island
Farquhar Group

Agalega Islands
(MAURITIUS)

Njazidja COMOROS
Moroni ⊕
Mwali   *Nzwani*
Iles Glorieuses
(FRANCE)
Cape Amber
• Antsiranana

INDIAN OCEAN

Mayotte ⊚ Mamoudzou
Island   MAYOTTE
(FRANCE)

+ *Maromokotro*
9,436 FEET
2,876 METERS

MOZAMBIQUE

CHANNEL

Masoala Peninsula

Tromelin Island
(FRANCE)

Mahajanga •
• Marovoay

Cargados Carajos Shoals
(MAURITIUS)

Betsiboka River

• Soanierana-Ivongo

Juan de Nova
(FRANCE)

• Ambatondrazaka

MOZAMBIQUE

Maintirano •   **MADAGASCAR**

Toamasina

MAURITIUS

Antananarivo ⊕

Mangoro R.

• Antsirabe

Port Louis ⊚ *Mauritius*

• Mahebourg

Rodrigues
(MAURITIUS)

Morondava •

St.-Denis ⊚

Fianarantsoa
• Camp Robin

• Mananjary

Bassas da India
(FRANCE)

Mangoky River

St.-Pierre
REUNION
(FRANCE)

MASCARENE ISLANDS

• Manakara

Piton de la Fournaise
8,632 FEET
2,631 METERS

Europa Island
(FRANCE)

Mount Boby
8,720 FEET
2,658 METERS

+ • Farafangana

Toliara • • Bezaha

TROPIC OF CAPRICORN

Cape Sainte Marie → • Taolanaro

1 2 3 4 5 6 7 8 9 10 11 12 13 14 15 16 17 18 19 20

A B C D E F G H J K L M N O P Q R S T

Comoros

Early travelers called the Comoros "Islands of the Moon" because of the magical gleam of moonlight on their shores. Mostly mountainous and volcanic, the three main islands of the Comoros support tropical vegetation but few crops. They lie between Africa and Madagascar in the Mozambique Channel of the Indian Ocean.

Most Comorans share Arab, African, and Malagasy origins, practice the Islamic religion, and speak a Swahili dialect. Their traditional dwellings are made of banana and coconut leaves or of lava cemented with sand and chalk.

Almost all Comorans farm. Many raise food crops, but yields are poor and the country must import more than half its food. Occupying much of the scarce land are foreign-owned plantations that cultivate cash crops: vanilla, cloves, copra, and plants that provide oils for perfume. The country is the leading producer of ylang-ylang.

The Comoros formerly belonged to France but declared its independence in 1975. Since then it has faced poverty despite foreign aid and has suffered from turbulent politics.

Official name: *Federal Islamic Republic of the Comoros*
Area: *719 sq mi (1,862 sq km)*
Population: *494,000*
Capital: *Moroni (pop. 22,000)*
Ethnic groups: *Comoran (Bantu, Arab, Malagasy)*
Language: *Arabic, French, Shaafi Islam (Swahili)*
Religious groups: *Sunni Muslim*
Economy: *Agr: cassava, rice, corn, yams, bananas, coconuts, vanilla, cloves, ylang-ylang. Ind: perfume*
Currency: *Comoros franc*

Mayotte

Coral reefs surround this tropical island in the Comoro archipelago. The reefs enclose a large lagoon, whose sheltered waters protect shipping and Mayotte's lobster and shrimp industry. Vanilla and coffee beans, coconut palms, and ylang-ylang trees, used to make perfume, grow in the volcanic island's fertile soil.

In 1975, Mayotte chose to remain linked to France when the rest of the Comoro Islands declared independence. The Comoran government still claims Mayotte as part of its territory.

Official name: *Territorial Collectivity of Mayotte*
Area: *144 sq mi (373 sq km)*
Population: *87,000*
Capital: *Mamoudzou (pop. 7,325)*

Seychelles

Isolated in the Indian Ocean, the islands of Seychelles have evolved a variety of unique species, such as the jellyfish plant, whose fruit with winged seeds resembles a jellyfish, and the *coco-de-mer*, a giant palm bearing a nut that weighs up to 40 pounds (18 kg).

The nation of Seychelles is made up of more than 90 widely scattered islands. It includes about 40 large granite islands with high green peaks and some 50 small coral islets, flat and unpopulated. Nearly 90 percent of the people live on Mahé, the largest island, which is also the site of the capital, Victoria.

Uninhabited until the mid-1700s, Seychelles was ruled first by the French, then by the British. It gained independence in 1976. Most Seychellois have mixed African, European, and Asian ancestry. On the larger islands they grow coconuts and cinnamon, the chief cash crops. Fish is important, too, as a food and an industry. The plant and animal life draw tourists, as do the clear seas, white beaches, and tropical climate.

Official name: *Republic of Seychelles*
Area: *175 sq mi (453 sq km)*
Population: *71,000*
Capital: *Victoria (pop. 23,300)*
Ethnic groups: *Creole*
Language: *Creole, English, French*
Religious groups: *Roman Catholic*
Economy: *Agr: coconuts, bananas, cinnamon, vanilla, tea. Ind: tourism, food processing, fishing*
Currency: *Seychelles rupee*

Madagascar

Earth's fourth largest island, after Greenland, New Guinea, and Borneo, Madagascar lies 250 miles (400 km) east of the African coast. A high central plateau rises steeply from the narrow, densely populated east coast, then slopes gradually down to the drier grasslands of the western plains.

Madagascar was under French control before independence in 1960. The Malagasy, as the inhabitants are called, are Afro-Asian. They are thought to descend from Indonesian seafarers who migrated to Madagascar 1,500 to 2,000 years ago, possibly by way of Africa. Later groups, too, arrived from Asia and Africa.

The central highlands are home to the largest, most powerful group, the Merina, who once ruled Madagascar. Here they and the Betsileo cultivate rice, the island's chief staple, and work in government and commerce in urban areas. The second largest group, the Betsimisaraka, live on the east coast, where they raise valuable export crops of coffee, vanilla, and cloves.

Once part of the African mainland, the island of Madagascar broke away about 160 million years ago. Its plants and animals, isolated from outside species, evolved into unique varieties, including some 40 species of lemurs, 200 species of butterflies, half the world's chameleon species, and 1,000 types of orchids. Since humans arrived, many species have become extinct.

Today Madagascar faces environmental disaster. After centuries of misuse, four-fifths of the island is bare and eroded, burned over by the Malagasy who must farm and herd to survive. Rain washes the red clay soil into rivers that carry it far out to sea. Only a fraction of the island's forests remains. Madagascar's leaders are taking steps toward conservation. In recent years, for example, they have increased the amount of government-protected forestland. They realize that halting the damage is vital to the nation's economy—and to the survival of the island once called "the naturalist's promised land."

Official name: *Democratic Republic of Madagascar*
Area: *226,658 sq mi (587,041 sq km)*
Population: *11,942,000*
Capital: *Antananarivo (pop. 802,400)*
Ethnic groups: *Merina, Betsimisaraka, other*
Language: *French, Malagasy*
Religious groups: *traditional, Christian*
Economy: *Agr: rice, cassava, bananas, beans, livestock, coffee, vanilla, cloves, sugarcane, peanuts, sisal. Ind: food processing, textiles, mining, fishing*
Currency: *Malagasy franc*

Réunion

Often called the twin sister of Mauritius, nearby Réunion shares its sugar-based economy, volcanic origin, and climate, but sugar production lags far behind its sister island. Réunion has less favorable conditions. Level farmland is scarce, and torrential rains strip the soil from steep slopes. Volcanoes dominate the landscape; Piton de la Fournaise erupts almost every year.

Réunion's population traces its descent to French settlers, African slaves, and Asian laborers. Once a French colony, the island became a French overseas department in 1946.

Official name: *Department of Réunion*
Area: *969 sq mi (2,510 sq km)*
Population: *618,000*
Capital: *Saint-Denis (pop. 142,000)*
Ethnic groups: *mixed French, African, Malagasy, Chinese, Pakistani, Indian*
Language: *French, Creole*
Religious groups: *Roman Catholic*
Economy: *Agr: sugarcane, corn, cassava, fruit, vegetables, vanilla, tea. Ind: rum, perfume oils, tourism*
Currency: *French franc*

Mauritius

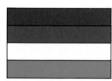

The smell of molasses pervades this oyster-shaped volcanic island in the Indian Ocean. Cane sugar and its by-products, rum and molasses, have dominated the economy of Mauritius for more than a century. Of late, export processing—the making of export goods such as clothing from imported material—and tourism have gained importance. But sugar still reigns.

Coral reefs surround the island, which has natural harbors and fine beaches. From the coast, the land rises to a misty central plateau rimmed by dramatic black peaks. Rodrigues Island and two island groups are dependencies.

Mauritius averages more than 1,300 people per square mile. The Creoles descend from African slaves and Europeans, but most islanders trace their roots to Indians who came to work the cane fields after slavery was abolished.

Official name: *Mauritius*
Area: *788 sq mi (2,040 sq km)*
Population: *1,094,000*
Capital: *Port Louis (pop. 142,000)*
Ethnic groups: *Indo-Mauritian, Creole*
Language: *English, Creole, French, Hindi, Urdu*
Religious groups: *Hindu, Roman Catholic, Muslim*
Economy: *Agr: sugarcane, tea, tobacco. Ind: food processing, textiles, tourism, electronics, jewelry*
Currency: *Mauritian rupee*

1 *Madagascar*

2 *Seychelles*

3 *Mauritius*

Madagascar

1 *Vendors offer a variety of goods, including clothes, rice, and French-style bread, a colonial legacy, at a market in Camp Robin.*

Seychelles

2 *With wooden spears, weekend fishermen on La Digue Island search for octopuses, which they can sell for extra cash.*

Mauritius

3 *Pins, skewers, and hooks pierce a Tamil penitent during a Hindu religious ceremony called Cavadee. Many inhabitants of Mauritius trace their ancestry to India.*

Réunion

4 *A fiery pit and flowing lava attract tourists and scientists as Réunion's only active volcano, Piton de la Fournaise, puts on one of its frequent displays of natural fireworks.*

4 *Réunion*

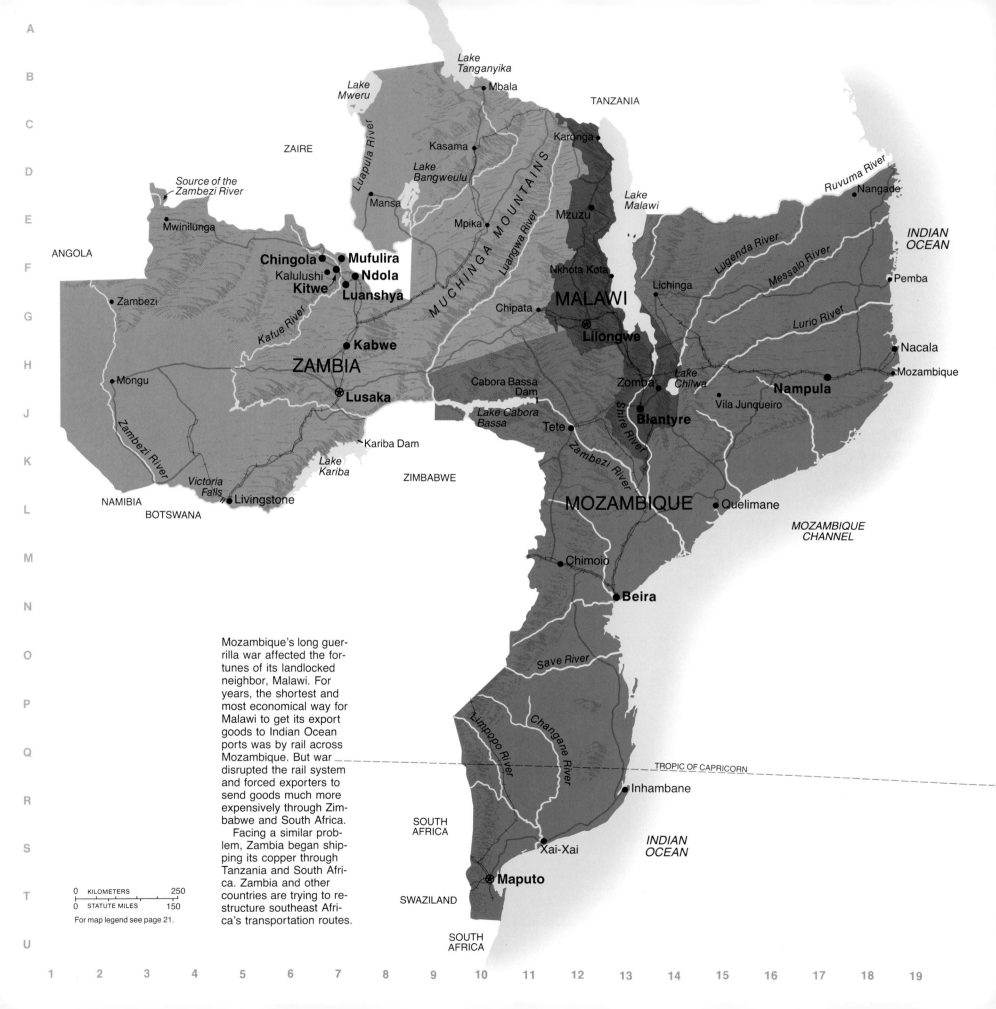

A B C D E F G H I J K L M N O P Q R S T U

ZAIRE

ANGOLA

Source of the Zambezi River

Lake Tanganyika

Lake Mweru

● Mbala

TANZANIA

Luapula River

● Kasama

Lake Bangweulu

● Karonga

● Mwinilunga

● Mansa

● Mpika

Luangwa River

Mzuzu

Lake Malawi

Ruvuma River

Nangade ●

INDIAN OCEAN

Chingola ● ● **Mufulira**

Kalulushi ● ● **Ndola**

Kitwe **Luanshya**

● **Zambezi**

Kafue River

MUCHINGA MOUNTAINS

Nkhota Kota

Lugenda River

Lichinga ●

Messalo River

Pemba ●

Chipata ●

MALAWI

Kabwe ●

ZAMBIA

● Mongu

✠ **Lusaka**

⊕ **Lilongwe**

Lurio River

Nacala ●

Zomba ●

Lake Chilwa

Mozambique ●

Nampula

Cabora Bassa Dam

Shire River

Vila Junqueiro ●

Zambezi River

Blantyre

Tete ●

Lake Cabora Bassa

↙ Kariba Dam

Lake Kariba

ZIMBABWE

Zambezi River

Victoria Falls ⋙

⋙ Livingstone

NAMIBIA

BOTSWANA

MOZAMBIQUE

Quelimane ●

MOZAMBIQUE CHANNEL

Chimoio ●

Beira

Mozambique's long guerrilla war affected the fortunes of its landlocked neighbor, Malawi. For years, the shortest and most economical way for Malawi to get its export goods to Indian Ocean ports was by rail across Mozambique. But war disrupted the rail system and forced exporters to send goods much more expensively through Zimbabwe and South Africa.
    Facing a similar problem, Zambia began shipping its copper through Tanzania and South Africa. Zambia and other countries are trying to restructure southeast Africa's transportation routes.

Save River

Limpopo River

Changane River

TROPIC OF CAPRICORN

Inhambane ●

SOUTH AFRICA

INDIAN OCEAN

0   KILOMETERS   250
0   STATUTE MILES   150

For map legend see page 21.

SWAZILAND

Xai-Xai ●

⊕ **Maputo**

SOUTH AFRICA

1 2 3 4 5 6 7 8 9 10 11 12 13 14 15 16 17 18 19

Zambia

Some say that Zambia was born with a copper spoon in its mouth. Along the nation's border with Zaïre runs a "copperbelt" that holds one of the world's richest copper deposits.

Though mining provides jobs and government income, farming remains the backbone of Zambia's economy. Grassy plateaus offer fertile farmland. Water resources are plentiful. The Luangwa and Kafue Rivers run like blue threads through the landscape, crossing two large national parks that are home to leopards, elephants, and other wildlife. The great Zambezi River forms the border with Zimbabwe. On its way east, the river spills over mile-wide Victoria Falls, cascading 354 feet (108 m) into a misty gorge. Downstream, the river enters Lake Kariba, formed by the huge Kariba Dam and power station, a major energy source.

Eight out of ten Zambian workers are farmers. Most tend their own land, using hand hoes to cultivate corn and other food crops on village plots. Others work on the big foreign-owned farms along the railroad lines between Kabwe and Livingstone, where they grow cash crops such as corn, cotton, peanuts, and tobacco.

Each year, hundreds of Zambians leave this way of life to seek better jobs and housing in the cities. The nation has become highly urbanized. About half its people are crowded into the copperbelt cities and the capital, Lusaka.

Zambia's economy has suffered from a decline in world copper prices that began in the 1970s.

Also, copper reserves are dwindling and could be gone within a few decades. The government has been encouraging city dwellers to return to farming. At present, only about one-fifth of the country's arable land is cultivated.

Official name: *Republic of Zambia*
Area: *290,586 sq mi (752,614 sq km)*
Population: *8,385,000*
Capital: *Lusaka (pop. 870,000)*
Ethnic groups: *More than 70 groups, mainly Bantu*
Language: *English, many Bantu languages*
Religious groups: *Christian, traditional*
Economy: *Agr: corn, millet, cassava, sugarcane, cotton, peanuts, tobacco, coffee. Ind: mining, food processing, textiles, chemicals, cement, fishing*
Currency: *Zambian kwacha*

Malawi

The widespread burning of grass to plant crops turns Malawi into a land of fire each October. Agriculture dominates the economy of this small country. Farmers raise rice on the hot, humid shores of Lake Malawi, which forms the landlocked nation's eastern border and occupies a fifth of its territory. The sparkling lake, famed for its sandy beaches, is home to hundreds of fish species. From the lake the land rises steeply to cooler plateaus where tobacco thrives, an important export crop. Another is tea, grown on mountain slopes to the south.

Ninety percent of all Malawians till small plots of farmland near their mud-hut villages. Many of them are members of large families of nine or ten people. In a country with few natural resources and little industry, population growth is a major problem. Jobs are scarce. Many thousands of men seek work in South Africa, Zambia, and Zimbabwe. Malawi also suffers under the burden of some one million refugees from the guerrilla war in neighboring Mozambique.

After gaining independence from the British in 1964, Malawi enjoyed a long period of peace and stability. Recent years, however, have brought political protests and labor unrest.

Official name: *Republic of Malawi*
Area: *45,747 sq mi (118,484 sq km)*
Population: *8,709,000*
Capital: *Lilongwe (pop. 234,000)*
Ethnic groups: *Chewa, Nyanja, Tumbuka, Yao*
Language: *Chichewa, English, other African*
Religious groups: *Christian, traditional, Muslim*
Economy: *Agr: corn, root crops, sugarcane, tobacco, tea, peanuts, cotton. Ind: food processing, fishing*
Currency: *Malawi kwacha*

Mozambique

Mozambique forms a Y 1,556 miles (2,504 km) long on the southeast coast of Africa. The Zambezi River splits the nation. In the south, a broad coastal plain gives way to grassy plateaus in the west. North of the river, a narrow shoreline yields to low plateaus and rugged highlands cloaked in tropical vegetation.

War, too, has divided the country. Mozambique won independence from Portuguese rule in 1975. Soon after, rebels supported by South Africa began guerrilla warfare against Mozambique's socialist government. Some 600,000 people died in the conflict, including 100,000 civilians killed by the rebels. More than four million Mozambicans fled, many seeking refuge in neighboring countries. A lingering drought devastated family food plots, so half of those who remained endured severe food shortages and survived on food supplied by other countries. Finally, in the fall of 1992, both sides agreed to a cease-fire, and a few months later United Nations peacekeeping forces entered the country.

For foreign income, Mozambique has long relied on fees paid by nearby landlocked nations that used its railroads and ports. During the war, guerrillas disrupted these transport routes by blowing up bridges and rails. In the fertile north-central provinces, cash crops once grew in abundance: coconuts, cotton, tea, and the leading export, cashews. Now much of the land lies fallow and deserted.

Mozambique has great potential for wealth, with good farmland and large mineral deposits. One of the world's largest dams, the Cabora Bassa on the Zambezi River, supplies electricity and water for irrigation. Lake Malawi and the Indian Ocean offer rich fishing opportunities. During their long rule, the Portuguese exploited the nation's natural resources but left its economy underdeveloped. Their departure caused the exodus, too, of skilled managers and technicians. War and natural calamities have hindered Mozambique's rebuilding process.

Official name: *Republic of Mozambique*
Area: *308,642 sq mi (799,380 sq km)*
Population: *16,617,000*
Capital: *Maputo (pop. 1,069,700)*
Ethnic groups: *Makua, Tsonga, Malawi, Shona*
Language: *Portuguese, many African languages*
Religious groups: *traditional, Christian, Muslim*
Economy: *Agr: cassava, coconuts, corn, sorghum, peanuts, bananas, cashews, sugarcane, cotton, tea, sisal. Ind: food processing, mining, textiles, shrimp*
Currency: *metical*

1 *Zambia*

2 *Mozambique*

3 *Malawi*

4 *Malawi*

5 *Malawi*

Zambia

1 *Under watchful eyes, workers at a state-controlled emerald mine remove debris from rough stones and sort them into piles.*

Mozambique

2 *A woman in the northeastern port city of Mozambique wears powder made from ground bark to protect her skin.*

Malawi

3 *Highland timber plantations await harvesting. To conserve trees, Malawians turn wood into charcoal, a slow-burning fuel.*

4 *Men capture cichlids in Lake Malawi, home to some 500 to 1,000 species found nowhere else in the world.*

5 *Aquarium owners prize colorful cichlids such as this speckled specimen.*

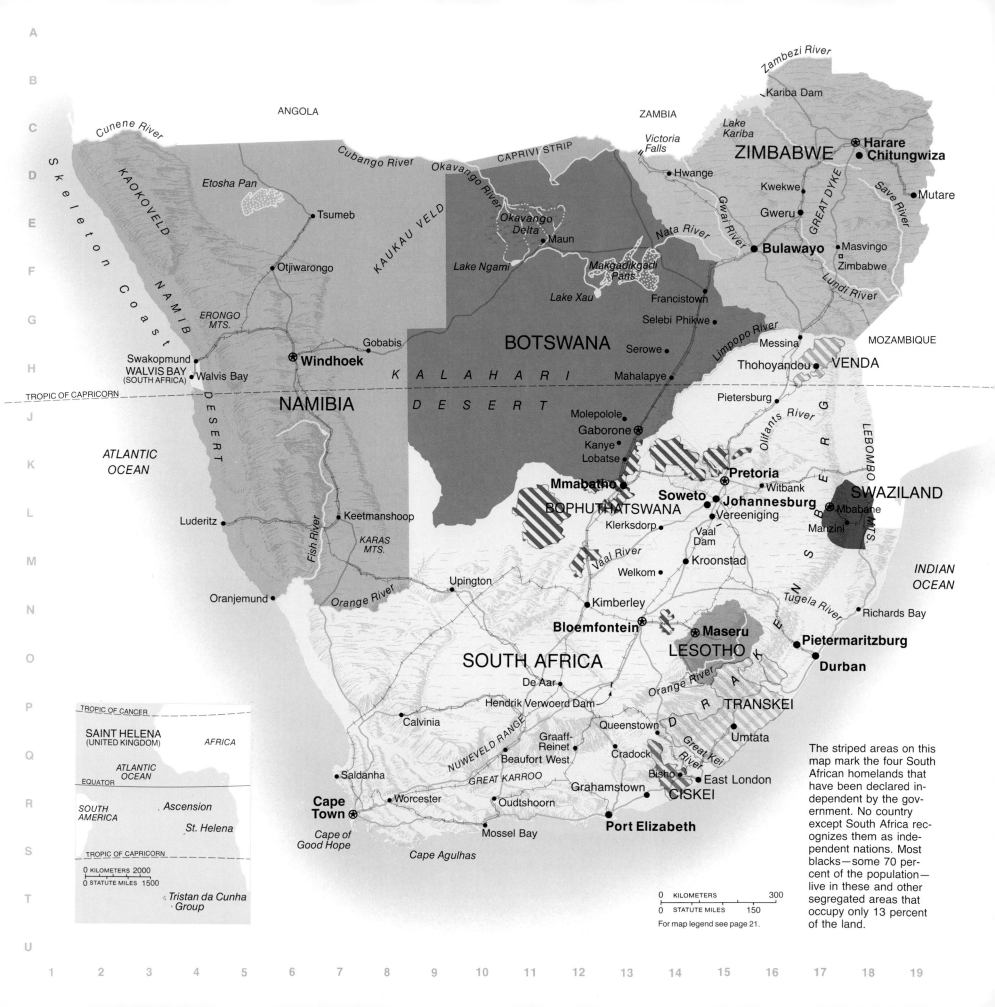

A B C D E F G H J K L M N O P Q R S T U

ANGOLA

Cunene River

Zambezi River

ZAMBIA

Kariba Dam

Lake Kariba

Victoria Falls

ZIMBABWE

⊛ **Harare** ● **Chitungwiza**

● Hwange

Kwekwe ●

GREAT DYKE

Save River

● Mutare

Cubango River

Okavango River

CAPRIVI STRIP

KAOKOVELD

Etosha Pan

● Tsumeb

KAUKAU VELD

Okavango Delta

● Maun

Lake Ngami

Makgadikgadi Pans

Lake Xau

Gweru ●

● **Bulawayo**

Gwai River

Nata River

Masvingo ●

□ Zimbabwe

Lundi River

S k e l e t o n   C o a s t

N A M I B

ERONGO MTS.

● Otjiwarongo

● Gobabis

Lake Ngami

Francistown ●

Selebi Phikwe ●

BOTSWANA

Serowe ●

Limpopo River

Messina ●

MOZAMBIQUE

Thohoyandou ● VENDA

Swakopmund ●
WALVIS BAY
(SOUTH AFRICA) ● Walvis Bay

⊛ **Windhoek**

K A L A H A R I

Mahalapye ●

Pietersburg ●

TROPIC OF CAPRICORN

NAMIBIA

D E S E R T

Olifants River

ATLANTIC OCEAN

D E S E R T

Molepolole ●

Gaborone ⊛

Kanye ●

Lobatse ●

LEBOMBO MTS.

● Luderitz

● Keetmanshoop

KARAS MTS.

Fish River

Mmabatho

BOPHUTHATSWANA

⊛ **Pretoria** ● Witbank

Soweto ● ● **Johannesburg**
Vereeniging ●

SWAZILAND

⊛ Mbabane
Manzini ●

Klerksdorp ●

Vaal River

Vaal Dam

● Kroonstad

Welkom ●

INDIAN OCEAN

● Upington

Orange River

● Kimberley

Bloemfontein ⊛

Tugela River

● Richards Bay

● Oranjemund

⊛ **Maseru**

LESOTHO

Pietermaritzburg

Durban

SOUTH AFRICA

De Aar ●

Hendrik Verwoerd Dam

Orange River

D R A K E N S B E R G

TRANSKEI

● Calvinia

Queenstown ●

Umtata ●

Graaff-Reinet ●

Cradock ●

Great Kei River

● East London

NUWEVELD RANGE

Beaufort West ●

CISKEI

Bisho ●

● Saldanha

Grahamstown ●

GREAT KARROO

Worcester ●

Oudtshoorn ●

Cape Town ⊛

Cape of Good Hope

Mossel Bay ●

Port Elizabeth

Cape Agulhas

TROPIC OF CANCER

SAINT HELENA
(UNITED KINGDOM)   AFRICA

ATLANTIC OCEAN

EQUATOR

SOUTH AMERICA   · Ascension

· St. Helena

TROPIC OF CAPRICORN

0 KILOMETERS 2000
0 STATUTE MILES 1500

· *Tristan da Cunha Group*

0 KILOMETERS 300
0 STATUTE MILES 150

For map legend see page 21.

The striped areas on this map mark the four South African homelands that have been declared independent by the government. No country except South Africa recognizes them as independent nations. Most blacks—some 70 percent of the population—live in these and other segregated areas that occupy only 13 percent of the land.

1 2 3 4 5 6 7 8 9 10 11 12 13 14 15 16 17 18 19

Namibia

In the language of the Nama, *namib* means "the land without people." Namibia's sparse population, which includes the Nama and nine other ethnic groups, inhabits a harsh land. The Namib Desert, a narrow ribbon of towering dunes and rock outcrops, extends along the Atlantic coast. Inland, desert sands rise to a plateau of patchy grassland where herders vie for grazing range. The east belongs to the sand and scrub of the Kalahari Desert.

Namibia was ruled for 74 years by South Africa, despite a long rebellion by black nationalist groups and criticism from the United Nations. In 1990, Namibia became a democracy and elected as its first president Sam Nujoma, a leader of the 23-year guerrilla war against South African rule. Nujoma's government seeks to heal ethnic divisions with a strong multiparty system and to encourage agriculture and the fishing and mining industries. Large deposits of diamonds, uranium, and other minerals promise a bright future for one of Africa's newest nations.

Official name: *Namibia*
Area: *318,261 sq mi (824,292 sq km)*
Population: *1,452,000*
Capital: *Windhoek (pop. 114,500)*
Ethnic groups: *Ovambo and others, white, mixed*
Language: *English, Afrikaans, African, German*
Religious groups: *Christian, traditional*
Economy: *Agr: livestock, grains. Ind: mining (diamonds, uranium, other ores), meat-packing, fishing*
Currency: *South African rand*

Botswana

Botswana's national emblem has a one-word motto: "Pula." Rain. There is never enough of it. The rolling red sands and low thorny scrub of the Kalahari Desert cover most of this country. From May to October, the sun bakes the land to dust. Droughts strike often, with searing sun and hot winds. Many years can pass before the rains fall again.

Botswana has a flourishing democracy and little strife. Poor at independence in 1966, it now has one of Africa's fastest growing economies. The discovery of diamonds in 1967 fueled its growth. At heart, though, this remains a cattle country. Most people make a living through farming and livestock. Because crop yields are often low, thousands of men migrate to South Africa and Zimbabwe to work mines and farms.

Northern Botswana holds the great inland delta of the Okavango River, a fertile, watery world of shifting streams and abundant wildlife. Rising in the west, the river fans out across a vast marshland before being swallowed by the sands of the Kalahari, the Land of Thirst.

Official name: *Republic of Botswana*
Area: *231,805 sq mi (600,372 sq km)*
Population: *1,360,000*
Capital: *Gaborone (pop. 133,800)*
Ethnic groups: *Batswana, Kalanga, Basarwa*
Language: *English, seTswana, other African*
Religious groups: *traditional, Christian*
Economy: *Agr: corn, sorghum, millet, beans, livestock. Ind: mining, meat-packing, tourism*
Currency: *pula*

Zimbabwe

An ancient hilltop city gave this nation its name, which means "houses of stone." Built between the 8th and 15th centuries in southeastern Zimbabwe, the sprawling city was the center of a flourishing gold and ivory trade for the Shona people. Most of Zimbabwe occupies a high, rolling plateau studded with rock outcrops. At its core lies the Great Dyke, a geological formation that holds rich deposits of gold, silver, chromite, and other minerals.

The Ndebele warrior people, arriving from South Africa in the 1830s, conquered the Shona. The abundant natural resources also brought white settlers, the cause of a turbulent history. For more than 80 years a tiny white minority controlled the country, then called Rhodesia. When white leaders declared the nation independent from the United Kingdom in 1965, guerrilla war ensued, as blacks fought for a government based on majority rule. The United Nations imposed sanctions forbidding trade with Rhodesia. In 1980 the white government gave in, and Zimbabwe was born.

Most Zimbabweans depend on farming for a living. But much of the country, including the best farmland, still belongs to whites, who own large commercial farms that produce tobacco, wheat, and other export crops. The government is trying to redistribute land, but progress has been slow. Zimbabwe is also one of the major manufacturing nations in Africa.

Famous for its beauty, Zimbabwe has national parks that are home to elephants, zebras, lions, and hippos. In the west are the spectacular Victoria Falls, whose African name translates as "the smoke that thunders."

Official name: *Republic of Zimbabwe*
Area: *150,804 sq mi (390,580 sq km)*
Population: *10,339,000*
Capital: *Harare (pop. 681,000)*
Ethnic groups: *Shona, Ndebele*
Language: *English, Shona, SiNdebele*
Religious groups: *traditional, Christian*
Economy: *Agr: corn, millet, wheat, tobacco, cotton, sugarcane, soybeans, coffee, tea, cattle. Ind: mining, food processing, metals, textiles, chemicals, wood*
Currency: *Zimbabwe dollar*

South Africa

South Africa occupies a huge swath of land at the continent's southernmost tip, where the Atlantic and Indian Oceans meet. Few African nations have such a range of terrain. At the heart of South Africa sprawls a vast inland plateau, much of it prairielike. A string of mountain ranges, including the Drakensberg, skirts the east and south. Desert dominates the west.

South Africa has enormous deposits of gold, diamonds, chromite, platinum, and coal. The income from mining these resources has generated cities, industrial centers, huge cattle and sheep ranches, and mechanized farms. Orchards cloak rolling hills, and there are great fields of corn, wheat, and sugarcane. Johannesburg, center of gold mining, is South Africa's largest urban area, followed by Cape Town, one of three capitals.

For all its wealth and beauty, South Africa is a

troubled land, struggling with the legacy of *apartheid*—the name given to the policy of racial segregation enforced by the white-minority government from 1948 to 1991. The word means "apartness." Under apartheid, blacks had virtually no political rights, though they outnumbered whites five to one. They could not freely choose where to live or work or go to school. Good land and good jobs were reserved for whites. The policy brought fierce rebellion at home and condemnation from abroad.

Apartheid was created by Afrikaners—South Africans descended from Dutch settlers—who came to power in 1948 after years of British domination. The Afrikaners divided South Africans into four major groups and governed each by a separate set of laws. These groups are whites, coloreds (people of mixed race), Asians, and Africans. The last group, the largest by far, numbers more than 25 million.

Under its policy of separateness, the government established racially based states or "homelands," one for each of the ten major black ethnic groups. It set aside only 13 percent of the nation's total area for black Africans and forced many blacks to move to these scattered fragments of rural land. Here the poor soil makes it hard to raise sufficient crops and livestock. With no natural resources and few jobs, the homelands have become islands of poverty.

Four of the homelands were declared independent countries by the South African government: **Transkei** on the Indian Ocean in 1976; a collection of seven separate enclaves called **Bophuthatswana** in 1977; **Venda** in the far north in 1979; and **Ciskei,** a small wedge of dry land in the south, in 1981. Only South Africa recognizes them as independent countries.

Today most black South Africans still live in these homelands or in townships, huge segregated suburbs and shantytowns on the outskirts of cities. Homelands and townships serve as pools of cheap labor, which keep South Africa's mines, industries, and commercial farms going.

Beginning early in the 1900s, black South Africans founded the African National Congress (ANC) and other groups, aiming to achieve majority rule in South Africa. The ANC's efforts included strikes and demonstrations, often brutally suppressed by the South African police. Thousands of blacks died in the clashes. Many were imprisoned, including Nelson Mandela, the best known leader of the ANC and a symbol of black resistance.

In 1990, Mandela was released from prison by South Africa's newly elected president, F. W. de Klerk. More changes soon came: Laws that had been the basis for apartheid policy were repealed, and a longstanding ban on black political groups was lifted. In 1993, the country took an enormous step forward on the road to a post-apartheid society. Black and white political leaders agreed to hold the country's first-ever free elections in April 1994 and declared that every citizen would have the right to vote.

Official name: *Republic of South Africa*
Area: *471,445 sq mi (1,221,037 sq km)*
Population: *41,688,000*
Capital: *Pretoria, administrative (pop. 443,100)*
Cape Town, legislative (pop. 776,600)
Bloemfontein, judicial (pop. 104,400)
Ethnic groups: *black, white, mixed, Asian*
Language: *Afrikaans, English, Bantu languages*
Religious groups: *Christian, Hindu, Muslim*
Economy: *Agr: corn, wheat, sugarcane, tobacco, fruit, cattle, sheep. Ind: gold, diamonds, iron, coal, and other mining, steel, machinery, motor vehicles, chemicals, textiles, food processing, fishing*
Currency: *South African rand*

Swaziland

A king called the Ngwenyama, or Lion, rules this mountainous nation, one of Africa's three remaining monarchies, the others being Lesotho and Morocco. Almost surrounded by South Africa, tiny, landlocked Swaziland fits like a handkerchief in the breast pocket of its giant neighbor, and is tightly bound to its economy. More than 95 percent of Swazi imports come from South Africa or travel through it.

Swaziland has valuable deposits of coal and diamonds, large forests, and well-watered farmland, but the king and his subjects reap few benefits from this wealth. They own less than two-thirds of their nation's land. The rest belongs to Europeans, who mine all the minerals and raise most of the export crops: sugarcane, citrus fruit, and timber grown on plantations.

Most Swazis are farmers who raise corn and cattle on lands that suffer from erosion and overgrazing. The people regard their animals as prize possessions and measures of their wealth.

Official name: *Kingdom of Swaziland*
Area: *6,704 sq mi (17,364 sq km)*
Population: *825,000*
Capital: *Mbabane (pop. 38,600)*
Ethnic groups: *Swazi, Zulu*
Language: *English, siSwati*
Religious groups: *Christian, traditional*
Economy: *Agr: corn, rice, livestock, sugarcane, cotton, fruit. Ind: food processing, wood pulp, mining*
Currency: *lilangeni*

Lesotho

The name Lesotho means "place of the Sotho tribe" to the Basotho, the people of this country. Their tiny kingdom of high plateaus and spectacular snow-clad mountains is surrounded by South Africa. Lesotho has few resources and little farmland—just a narrow strip in the western lowlands, where most people live. The land suffers from erosion and overgrazing by cattle and by sheep and goats raised for their wool and mohair.

Though Lesotho has been strongly opposed to South Africa's racial policies, it has relied heavily on its neighbor for trade and jobs. About a third of Basotho men leave their country for three to nine months a year to work in South Africa, chiefly in the gold and coal mines. These miners can earn as much as ten times what their countrymen make working on farms at home.

A new project may help Lesotho's economy. A network of dams, tunnels, and canals is being built to take water from the Orange River and divert it northward for sale to South Africa.

Official name: *Kingdom of Lesotho*
Area: *11,720 sq mi (30,355 sq km)*
Population: *1,880,000*
Capital: *Maseru (pop. 109,400)*
Ethnic groups: *Basotho*
Language: *Sesotho, English*
Religious groups: *Christian, traditional*
Economy: *Agr: corn, sorghum, wheat, legumes, fruit, livestock. Ind: tourism, wool, mohair*
Currency: *loti*

St. Helena

The British colony of St. Helena is a tiny volcanic island in the Atlantic Ocean 1,200 miles (1,930 km) from Africa. Its main claim to fame is that French emperor Napoleon Bonaparte lived in exile there from 1815 until his death in 1821.

Though much of the land is bare, St. Helena has diverse plant life, including 40 unique species. The islanders fish, raise livestock and crops on the scarce arable land, and make lace or wood carvings, which they sell to passengers on ships that stop at Jamestown, the only village.

The colony includes the Tristan da Cunha island group and Ascension Island, famous as a nesting ground for sea turtles and sooty terns.

Official name: *St. Helena*
Area: *158 sq mi (410 sq km)*
Population: *7,000*
Capital: *Jamestown (pop. 1,332)*

1 *Namibia*

2 *Namibia*

Namibia

1 *Like a great sand sea, the 1,300-mile-long (2,100 km) Namib Desert rises from the Namibian coast and reaches into neighboring Angola and South Africa.*

2 *Uncut diamonds mined near Oranjemund range in color from blue-white to pink to chartreuse. Such gem-quality diamonds are a leading Namibian export.*

1 *Lesotho*

Lesotho

1 *Toting saddle and baggage, a miner arrives home on a visit from his job in South Africa. Many men of Lesotho seek work there because jobs are scarce at home.*

Botswana

2 *Water-lily pads up to 16 inches (40 cm) across cover a lagoon in the Okavango River Delta. This inland swamp is a refuge for hippos, crocodiles, and other wildlife.*

2 *Botswana*

3 *South Africa*

4 *South Africa*

South Africa

3 *Cape Town sprawls near the cloud-covered Cape of Good Hope. Rounding the cape in 1488, Portuguese explorers found a long-sought sea route from Europe to India.*

4 *Balancing her heavy load, a Zulu woman carries home a bucket of precious water from a distant well.*

Zimbabwe

5 *Shaking off its colonial past, Zimbabwe (formerly Rhodesia) changed its capital's name from Salisbury to Harare. Renamed avenues now honor African heroes.*

5 *Zimbabwe*

Oceania

Nothing on earth is bigger than the Pacific Ocean. It covers a third of the globe, more than all the land areas lumped together. It reaches from the Arctic Ocean to Antarctica and includes 21 seas within its borders. At its widest, near the Equator, the Pacific Ocean extends more than 11,000 miles (17,700 km)—almost halfway around the world. It touches every continent but Europe and Africa.

The Pacific is also the world's deepest ocean, with an average depth of 12,925 feet (3,940 m). The deepest point, Challenger Deep in the Mariana Trench, lies 35,827 feet down (10,920 m)—nearly 7 miles (11 km) below the surface.

More than 25,000 islands (not counting the many islands of Japan, the Philippines, and Indonesia) are spread across the Pacific. They range in size from New Guinea's 305,986 square miles (792,500 sq km) to tiny reefs and atolls that barely rise above the waves. This part of the world is known as Oceania.

Oceania's high islands have greater resources than its low ones. Many high islands are volcanic, made up of mountains tall enough to wring out moisture from offshore breezes. As rain, the moisture provides abundant water for plants or crops to grow in the rich volcanic soil. High islands such as New Zealand, Tahiti, and Hawaii can support heavily concentrated populations because of their large size and varied resources. Many high islands have copper, nickel, gold, and other valuable mineral deposits.

By contrast, many of the low islands are covered only with thin, sandy soil and suffer from periodic droughts. Only small, widely scattered groups of people can live on them. Very often they depend on fish from the sea and on coconuts or coconut products for a livelihood.

Most of the low islands are atolls—coral islands surrounding lagoons. An atoll begins as a reef built around a volcano by countless tiny sea creatures called coral polyps. The reef is formed by the hard outer skeletons that protect their soft bodies. In time, the volcano wears away or sinks beneath the sea, but the reef continues to grow. Finally it breaks the surface, forming a ring-shaped island or chain of islets.

Geographers divide Oceania into four regions. Melanesia means "black islands." Melanesians generally are short and dark-skinned, much like Australia's Aborigines. Micronesia means "little islands" and Polynesia means "many islands." The people of these regions usually are lighter skinned and taller than Melanesians. Many have some European or Asian ancestors in their family trees. Australia and New Zealand, settled largely by British colonists, have predominantly white populations.

Most Pacific islands lie in the tropics and so are warm year-round and have adequate rainfall. But much of Australia is hot and dry. Its only major river system is the Murray-Darling, which has headwaters in the Great Dividing Range. Australia's climate is influenced by the mountains, as well as by a globe-circling high-pressure system that dominates the region.

Mount Cook, highest mountain in New Zealand

Desert oaks in Australia's Simpson Desert

Facts About Oceania

Population: 27,588,000
Largest Country: Australia, area 2,966,153 sq mi (7,682,300 sq km); pop. 17,782,000
Highest Point: Mount Wilhelm, Papua New Guinea, 14,793 ft (4,509 m) above sea level.
Lowest Point: Lake Eyre, Australia, 52 ft (16 m) below sea level
Largest Metropolitan Area: Sydney, pop. 3,623,600
Longest River: Murray-Darling, Australia, 2,310 mi (3,717 km)
Longest Reef: *Great Barrier Reef, Australia, 1,250 mi (2,012 km)
Largest Lake: Eyre 3,600 sq mi (9,323 sq km)

*World record

Glossary

archipelago—a group or chain of islands.
atoll—a coral island or islets encircling a lagoon.
the Commonwealth—a voluntary association of independent countries that maintains ties of friendship, cooperation, and assistance. The British monarch is the symbolic head.
copra—dried coconut meat that yields oil.
coral—hard outer skeletons of tiny marine animals, called coral polyps, which form reefs and islands.
outback—the remote backcountry of Australia.
pidgin—simplified speech consisting of words adapted from other languages; used between people who speak different languages.
taro—a plant raised throughout the tropics for its edible, starchy root.

Great Barrier Reef off Australia's northeast coast

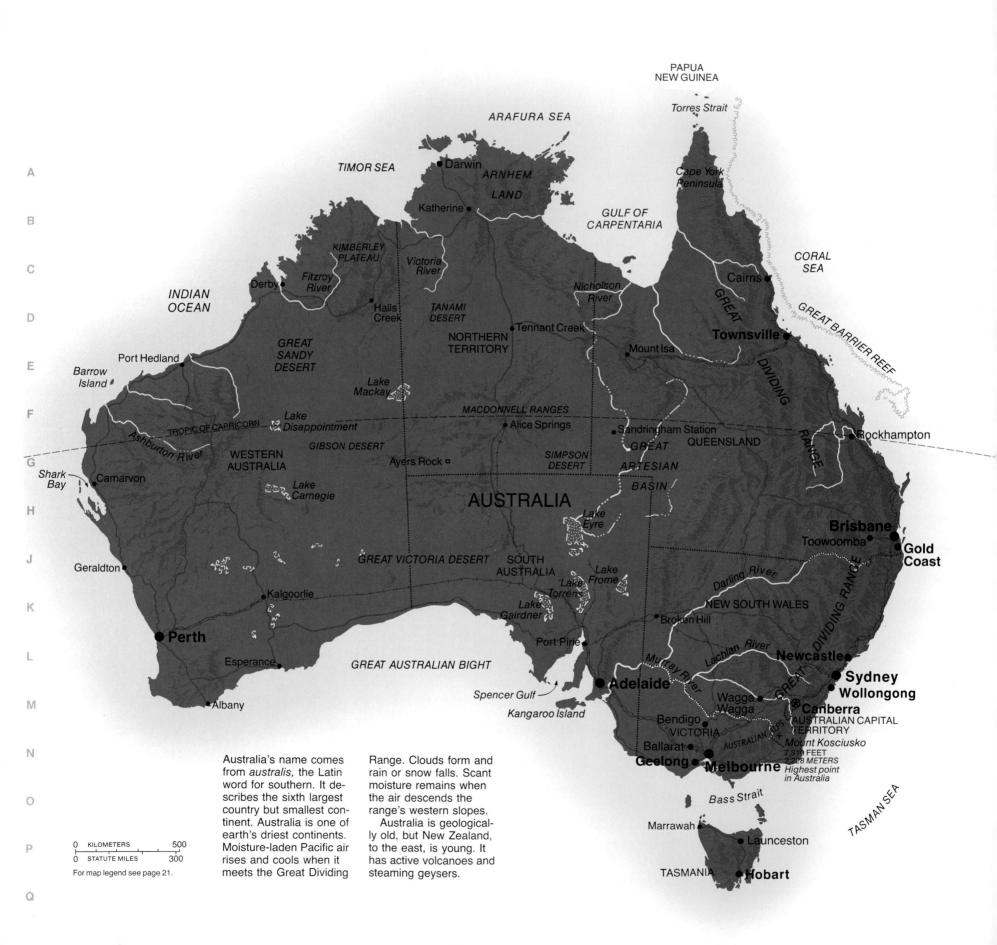

A B C D E F G H J K L M N O P Q

PAPUA
NEW GUINEA

Torres Strait

ARAFURA SEA

TIMOR SEA

●Darwin

*ARNHEM
LAND*

Cape York
Peninsula

*GULF OF
CARPENTARIA*

*CORAL
SEA*

Katherine

*KIMBERLEY
PLATEAU*

*Victoria
River*

*Nicholson
River*

Cairns●

GREAT

GREAT BARRIER REEF

Derby●   *Fitzroy
River*

Halls
Creek●

*TANAMI
DESERT*

*INDIAN
OCEAN*

*Barrow
Island*

Port Hedland●

*GREAT
SANDY
DESERT*

NORTHERN
TERRITORY

●Tennant Creek

Mount Isa●

DIVIDING

Townsville

Lake
Mackay

Rockhampton●

MACDONNELL RANGES

Lake
Disappointment

TROPIC OF CAPRICORN

●Alice Springs

Sandringham Station●

RANGE

Ashburton River

GIBSON DESERT

WESTERN
AUSTRALIA

Ayers Rock □

*GREAT
ARTESIAN*

GREAT

QUEENSLAND

*Shark
Bay*

Carnarvon●

*SIMPSON
DESERT*

Lake
Carnegie

AUSTRALIA

Lake
Eyre

BASIN

Brisbane

Toowoomba●   ●**Gold
Coast**

GREAT VICTORIA DESERT

SOUTH
AUSTRALIA

Lake
Frome

Darling River

Geraldton●

Lake
Torrens

NEW SOUTH WALES

Kalgoorlie●

Lake
Gairdner

Broken Hill●

Lachlan River

Newcastle

Perth●

Port Pirie●

Murray River

Esperance●

GREAT AUSTRALIAN BIGHT

Wagga
Wagga●

Sydney
Wollongong

Albany●

Adelaide

Spencer Gulf

Bendigo●

VICTORIA

Canberra
AUSTRALIAN CAPITAL
TERRITORY

Kangaroo Island

Ballarat●

AUSTRALIAN ALPS

*Mount Kosciusko
7,310 FEET
2,228 METERS
Highest point
in Australia*

Geelong

Melbourne

Bass Strait

TASMAN SEA

Marrawah●

●Launceston

TASMANIA

Hobart

Australia's name comes
from *australis,* the Latin
word for southern. It de-
scribes the sixth largest
country but smallest con-
tinent. Australia is one of
earth's driest continents.
Moisture-laden Pacific air
rises and cools when it
meets the Great Dividing

Range. Clouds form and
rain or snow falls. Scant
moisture remains when
the air descends the
range's western slopes.
   Australia is geologically old, but New Zealand,
to the east, is young. It
has active volcanoes and
steaming geysers.

0 KILOMETERS 500
0 STATUTE MILES 300

For map legend see page 21.

Australia

Australia is the only country to occupy an entire continent. And because all of it lies south of the Equator, people sometimes call it Down Under. It is an ancient land whose highlands have been worn down into broad plains and plateaus. The longest and highest mountain chain, the Great Dividing Range, runs the entire length of the east coast and reaches its greatest height—7,310 feet (2,228 m)—on top of Mount Kosciusko.

Australia is a thinly populated land. It is also prosperous, thanks to productive farms, extensive sheep and cattle ranches, and large deposits of coal, bauxite, iron ore, and gold. Most Australians live about as well as Americans and Canadians do. More than 80 percent of the nation's 17.8 million people live in large, modern cities located mostly along the southeast coast. Here the climate is moderate, rain is reliable, and the soil is fertile.

West of the Great Dividing Range lies a region of wheat farms and livestock ranches. And farther west spread the great plains and deserts of central and western Australia—the outback, as Australians call it. Here, amid the sparse vegetation, blistering heat, and dust sprawl enormous sheep and cattle ranches, called stations. One of them in South Australia covers more than 12,000 square miles (31,080 sq km). In the great empty reaches of the outback, children get their lessons by mail and radio, doctors visit their patients by plane, and stockmen use helicopters to help round up cattle.

Australia's long isolation from other continents has given it many unusual animals; these include kangaroos, koalas, wombats, and wallabies—mammals called marsupials because they carry their young in pouches. The dingo, a wild dog, roams the outback, and the platypus, a mammal hatched from an egg, swims the rivers.

Extending along the Queensland coast for 1,250 miles (2,012 km) is the Great Barrier Reef. Built by tiny coral polyps over millions of years, it is the biggest structure built by living creatures and is home to 1,500 fish species, 400 kinds of coral, and countless other marine animals.

Australia's earliest inhabitants, the Aborigines, came from Asia via Indonesia about 40,000 years ago. Now most of them live in poverty, outcasts in their own land. Capt. James Cook made England's first claim on the continent in 1770. After a long period of colonization, Australia became an independent country in 1901. Today Australia is a self-governing member of the Commonwealth. The country is made up of six states, one of which is the island of Tasmania. It also has two federal territories: Northern Territory and the Australian Capital Territory, which contains the capital city, Canberra.

Official name: *Commonwealth of Australia*
Area: *2,966,153 sq mi (7,682,300 sq km)*
Population: *17,782,000*
Capital: *Canberra (pop. 310,000)*
Ethnic groups: *European, Asian, Aborigine*
Language: *English*
Religious groups: *Protestant, Roman Catholic*
Economy: *Agr: livestock, wheat, sugarcane, barley, fruit, vegetables, cotton. Ind: iron, coal, other mining, wool, oil, food processing, machinery, motor vehicles, chemicals, textiles, electronics, tourism*
Currency: *Australian dollar*

New Zealand

"God's own country," an early prime minister called New Zealand. He referred to the island nation's spectacular scenery, lush pastures, mild climate, and pristine beaches. Though only about the size of the British Isles, New Zealand's two main islands enjoy all the geographical diversity of an entire continent.

North Island, where three-quarters of the nation's three and a half million people live, has fertile fields, as well as active volcanoes, geysers, and major ski resorts amid snow-clad mountains. Lake Taupo, near the middle of the island, is famous for its trout. Auckland, the island's largest city, presides as a center of commerce and manufacturing for textiles and wood products. The nation's capital, Wellington, lies near Cook Strait, which separates the two islands.

South Island is a land of mountains and forests and glaciers and lakes. The Southern Alps, rising abruptly from the sea, create spectacular fjords and waterfalls along the southwest coast. New Zealand's highest mountain, Mount Cook, rises 12,349 feet (3,764 m) above sea level. On fertile plains and pastures along the east coast, New Zealanders grow cereal grains and graze immense flocks of sheep and herds of cattle. The world's largest exporter of lamb and dairy products, New Zealand ranks second behind Australia as an exporter of wool.

Most New Zealanders are descendants of 19th-century British settlers or of Maori explorers who arrived from Polynesia about a thousand years ago.

Official name: *New Zealand*
Area: *103,883 sq mi (269,057 sq km)*
Population: *3,433,000*
Capital: *Wellington (pop. 150,301)*
Ethnic groups: *European, Maori, Pacific Islander*
Language: *English, Maori*
Religious groups: *Protestant, Roman Catholic*
Economy: *Agr: livestock, fodder, fruit, vegetables. Ind: food processing, wool, wood and paper products, metals, textiles, chemicals, motor vehicles, fishing*
Currency: *New Zealand dollar*

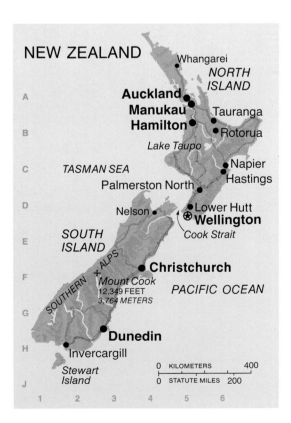

Australia

1 *Soap, soda pop, and spears combine old and new ways of life in the north. Father and daughter have just visited a truck that supplies their Aboriginal community.*

2 *Oscar the camel noses into a lesson transmitted by two-way radio to a girl living at Sandringham Station, an isolated cattle ranch in Queensland.*

3 *Ferryboats churn the waters of Sydney Harbour in an annual Ferrython race. The finish line lies beyond the white, curved roofs of the city's Opera House.*

4 *A koala youngster hitches a ride from its mother. Australia's isolation from other continents helped produce koalas, kangaroos, and other pouched marsupials.*

New Zealand

5 *Workers check sliced kiwifruit at a cannery on North Island. The fuzzy fruit takes its name from the flightless kiwi, New Zealand's national bird.*

6 *A Maori boy, his face decorated with a felt-tip pen, recalls the custom of tattooing—a warrior's reward for bravery in battle.*

1 *Australia*

3 *Australia*

2 *Australia*

5 *New Zealand*

4 *Australia*

6 *New Zealand*

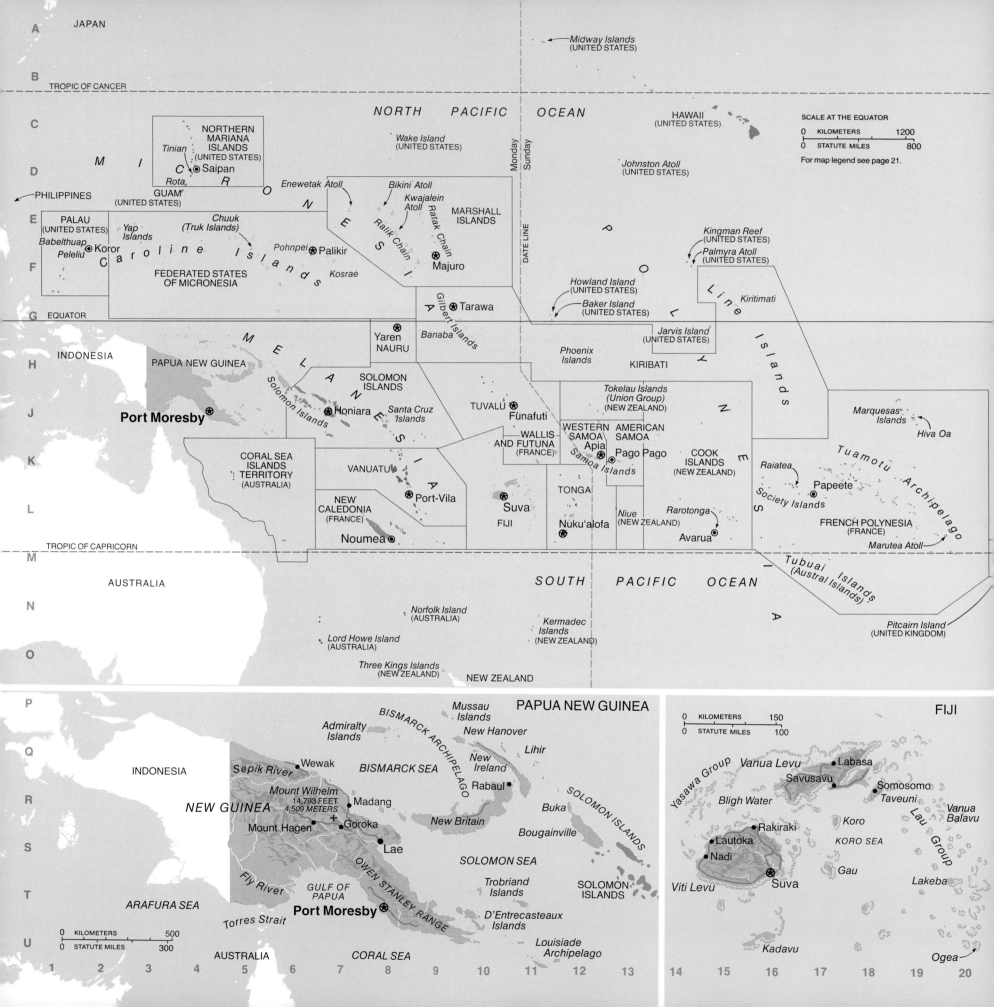

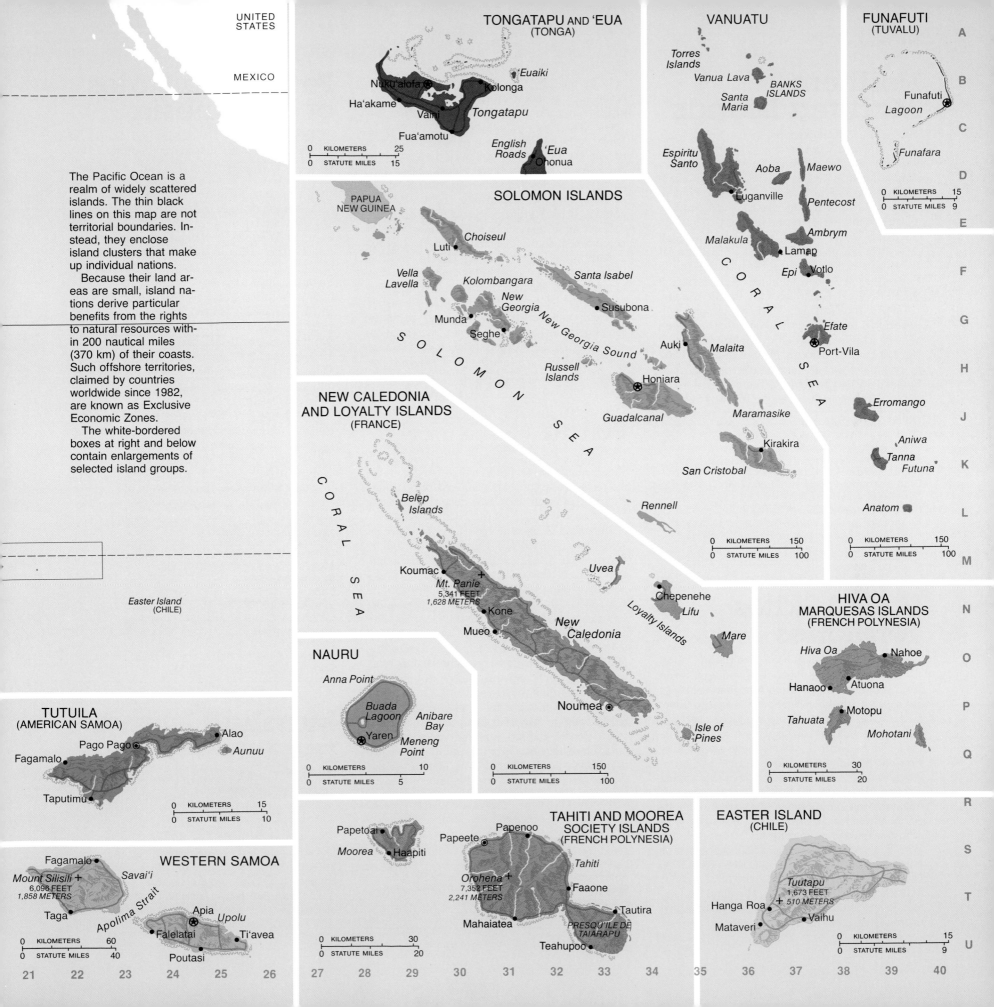

UNITED STATES

MEXICO

The Pacific Ocean is a realm of widely scattered islands. The thin black lines on this map are not territorial boundaries. Instead, they enclose island clusters that make up individual nations.

Because their land areas are small, island nations derive particular benefits from the rights to natural resources within 200 nautical miles (370 km) of their coasts. Such offshore territories, claimed by countries worldwide since 1982, are known as Exclusive Economic Zones.

The white-bordered boxes at right and below contain enlargements of selected island groups.

Easter Island (CHILE)

TONGATAPU AND 'EUA (TONGA)

'Euaiki
Nuku'alofa ⊛
Kolonga
Ha'akame
Vaini
Tongatapu
Fua'amotu
English Roads
'Eua
Ohonua

| 0 KILOMETERS 25 |
| 0 STATUTE MILES 15 |

VANUATU

Torres Islands
Vanua Lava
BANKS ISLANDS
Santa Maria
Espiritu Santo
Aoba
Maewo
Luganville
Pentecost
Malakula
Ambrym
Lamap
Epi
Votlo
Efate
⊛ Port-Vila
Erromango
Aniwa
Tanna
Futuna
Anatom

C O R A L   S E A

FUNAFUTI (TUVALU)

Funafuti ⊛
Lagoon
Funafara

| 0 KILOMETERS 15 |
| 0 STATUTE MILES 9 |

SOLOMON ISLANDS

PAPUA NEW GUINEA
Choiseul
Luti
Vella Lavella
Kolombangara
Santa Isabel
New Georgia
Susubona
Munda
Seghe
New Georgia Sound
Auki
Malaita
Russell Islands
Honiara ⊛
Guadalcanal
Maramasike
Kirakira
San Cristobal
Rennell

S O L O M O N   S E A

| 0 KILOMETERS 150 |
| 0 STATUTE MILES 100 |

NEW CALEDONIA AND LOYALTY ISLANDS (FRANCE)

Belep Islands
Koumac
Mt. Panie 5,341 FEET 1,628 METERS
Kone
Mueo
New Caledonia
Uvea
Chepenehe
Lifu
Loyalty Islands
Mare
Noumea ⊚
Isle of Pines

C O R A L   S E A

| 0 KILOMETERS 150 |
| 0 STATUTE MILES 100 |

NAURU

Anna Point
Buada Lagoon
Anibare Bay
Yaren ⊛
Meneng Point

| 0 KILOMETERS 10 |
| 0 STATUTE MILES 5 |

HIVA OA MARQUESAS ISLANDS (FRENCH POLYNESIA)

Hiva Oa
Nahoe
Hanaoo
Atuona
Tahuata
Motopu
Mohotani

| 0 KILOMETERS 30 |
| 0 STATUTE MILES 20 |

TUTUILA (AMERICAN SAMOA)

Alao
Pago Pago ⊚
Fagamalo
Aunuu
Taputimu

| 0 KILOMETERS 15 |
| 0 STATUTE MILES 10 |

WESTERN SAMOA

Fagamalo
Mount Silisili 6,096 FEET 1,858 METERS
Savai'i
Taga
Apolima Strait
Apia
Upolu
Falelatai
Ti'avea
Poutasi

| 0 KILOMETERS 60 |
| 0 STATUTE MILES 40 |

TAHITI AND MOOREA SOCIETY ISLANDS (FRENCH POLYNESIA)

Papetoai
Papenoo
Papeete ⊚
Moorea
Haapiti
Tahiti
Orohena 7,352 FEET 2,241 METERS
Faaone
Mahaiatea
PRESQU'ILE DE TAIARAPU
Tautira
Teahupoo

| 0 KILOMETERS 30 |
| 0 STATUTE MILES 20 |

EASTER ISLAND (CHILE)

Tuutapu 1,673 FEET 510 METERS
Hanga Roa
Mataveri
Vaihu

| 0 KILOMETERS 15 |
| 0 STATUTE MILES 9 |

A B C D E F G H J K L M N O P Q R S T U

21 22 23 24 25 26 27 28 29 30 31 32 33 34 35 36 37 38 39 40

Northern Mariana Islands

This string of 16 islands—some large, some small—forms a 500-mile-long (805 km) arc in the western Pacific Ocean. The northernmost islands, small and volcanic, are mostly uninhabited. At the southern end of the chain, Saipan, Tinian, and Rota are the largest, most populated islands in the Northern Mariana group.

During World War II, these onetime Japanese strongholds suffered some of the fiercest fighting in the Pacific. After the war, the United States took over their administration as part of the U. S. Trust Territory of the Pacific Islands.

In 1978 the Northern Marianas became self-governing, but with continued ties to the United States. The islanders enjoy rights and privileges of U. S. citizenship. Most of them are Chamorros, people of mixed Micronesian and Spanish ancestry. Many of them work for the government or in the booming tourist trade.

Official name: *Commonwealth of the Northern Mariana Islands*
Area: *184 sq mi (477 sq km)*
Population: *43,345*
Capital: *Saipan (pop. 38,896)*
Ethnic groups: *Chamorro, Micronesian*
Language: *English, Chamorro*
Religious groups: *Roman Catholic*
Economy: *Agr: coconuts, fruit, vegetables, cattle, pigs. Ind: tourism, copra, handicrafts, fishing*
Currency: *U. S. dollar*

United States Territories

A handful of territories belonging to the United States dots the blue Pacific—islands scattered from **Midway** in the north to **American Samoa** in the south, from **Jarvis Island** in the east to **Guam** in the west. These holdings range in size from 209-square-mile (541 sq km) Guam, a volcanic island rising 1,332 feet (406 m) above sea level, to **Howland Island,** a mile-and-a-half-long (2.4 km) coral strip that barely pokes above the waves.

Baker, Howland, and Jarvis Islands, as well as **Palmyra Atoll** and **Kingman Reef,** are uninhabited. Scientists visit them from time to time to study seabirds and marine life. During World War II, some of them served as military bases or staging areas. Palmyra, a collection of about 50 islets, is covered with dense growths of coconut and other trees. In the 1800s, Howland, Baker, and Jarvis Islands were mined for guano, bird droppings used as fertilizer.

U. S. military forces maintain bases on islands such as **Johnston Atoll,** the site of high-altitude nuclear tests during the 1950s and 1960s. The Navy administers the Midway Islands, scene of a World War II naval battle that turned the tide of war against Japan. And the Air Force is in charge of **Wake Island,** three coral islets clustered around a lagoon. Once used as a refueling stop for transpacific flights, Wake is now a weather station and a small military base.

Guam and American Samoa, the most heavily populated of the U. S. Pacific islands, are self-governing territories. Their people, most of them island natives, enjoy modern conveniences from shopping malls to discotheques, cars to television sets. Fishing, fish processing, tourism, and subsistence crops of coconuts, sweet potatoes, bananas, and corn are the mainstays of American Samoa's economy. On Guam, most islanders earn salaries from jobs in stores or on U. S. military installations.

Palau

Westernmost of the Caroline Islands, Palau stands on the threshold of independence. It remains the last island group under United States administration in what was once the far-flung U. S. Trust Territory of the Pacific Islands.

More than 200 islands make up Palau, which is sometimes called Belau. In hope of eventual independence, a new capital is planned for mountainous Babelthuap, largest of the islands. The present capital, Koror, is a cinder-block and tin-roof town on the nearby island of the same name. Tourism and U. S. aid are the chief sources of income for the islands.

Palau is famed as a scuba diver's paradise. Many of its green-clad limestone islands, surrounded by reefs and translucent water, bulge from the sea like mushroom caps. On some islands, shrimp and jellyfish live in marine lakes fed by seeping seawater. And the wreckage of World War II, rusting ships and airplanes, rests in sapphire lagoons. On one island, Peleliu, more than 13,000 people died as U. S. Marines struggled to wrest the island from Japan.

Official name: *Palau*
Area: *177 sq mi (458 sq km)*
Population: *15,122*
Capital: *Koror (pop. 10,501)*
Ethnic groups: *Palauan*
Language: *Palauan, English*
Religious groups: *Roman Catholic*
Economy: *Agr: coconuts, cassava, sweet potatoes. Ind: tourism, handicrafts, fishing*
Currency: *U. S. dollar*

Federated States of Micronesia

The Federated States of Micronesia celebrated a big event in 1986: After decades as a United States trust territory, the islands had become a sovereign, self-governing country. In 1989, the country dedicated a new capital, Palikir, on the island of Pohnpei (or Ponape, as it used to be called). The states in the federation are island clusters named Yap, Chuuk (formerly Truk), Pohnpei, and Kosrae.

But the country also has problems. It is very small. The total land area, about four times the size of Washington, D. C., is broken into some 600 tropical islands and atolls scattered across 1,800 miles (2,900 km) of open ocean. This gives the islanders wonderful vistas of sea and sky, but makes communications difficult and provides few natural resources.

The islands have little industry besides tourism and are heavily dependent on aid from the United States. To keep U. S. aid flowing after independence, the Federated States signed a compact of free association that allows the U. S. to set up military bases in the event of an emergency. Most of the nation's 115,000 people either work for the government or grow coconuts, cassava, and sweet potatoes.

Official name: *Federated States of Micronesia*
Area: *271 sq mi (702 sq km)*
Population: *115,000*
Capital: *Palikir*
Ethnic groups: *Micronesian, Polynesian*
Language: *English, indigenous languages*
Religious groups: *Protestant, Roman Catholic*
Economy: *Agr: coconuts, cassava, sweet potatoes, fruit, pigs, poultry. Ind: copra, tourism, fishing*
Currency: *U. S. dollar*

Marshall Islands

Paradise lost. That's the story of the Marshall Islands, a double chain of low-lying atolls and islands reaching some 800 miles (1,285 km) across the western Pacific Ocean. Governed by the United States since the end of World War II, islanders in 1986 became a self-governing nation in free association with the United States—and largely supported by continuing U. S. aid.

The Marshall Islands are best known for two of their remotest atolls, Bikini and Enewetak (Eniwetok). Between 1946 and 1958 the atolls were rocked by 66 nuclear blasts. One of them was more powerful than the combined power of all the explosives ever used in war. Enewetak islanders have since returned to their atoll, but Bikini is still too radioactive. Today most Bikinians live on a distant island, far from the palm-fringed lagoon of their old home.

Kwajalein, the world's largest atoll, has a 60-mile-long lagoon that is used as a target for unarmed missiles launched from California. The atoll's biggest island, also named Kwajalein, is the site of a large, modern U. S. Army base. Many Marshallese work on the island, commuting daily from the neighboring isle of Ebeye.

Official name: *Republic of the Marshall Islands*
Area: *70 sq mi (181 sq km)*
Population: *50,000*
Capital: *Majuro (pop. 19,664)*
Ethnic groups: *Micronesian*
Language: *English, Malayo-Polynesian*
Religious groups: *Christian*
Economy: *Agr: coconuts, taro, fruit, pigs, poultry. Ind: tourism, copra, fishing, handicrafts*
Currency: *U. S. dollar*

Nauru

Europeans first saw Nauru in 1798 and named it Pleasant Island. Today, the lush tropical vegetation of the coastal areas is pleasing to the eye, but a landscape scarred by phosphate mining lies beyond.

The fertilizer deposits make up 80 percent of the island. Mining them has caused extensive environmental damage, but selling them has made Nauruans wealthy. In the 1980s, per capita income reached $20,000 annually; it has since fallen to $10,000 a year. Citizens, however, pay no taxes, and education, housing, and health care are available free or at rock-bottom prices. The islanders import most of their food, drinking water, and energy supplies. Unfortunately, the rich, imported food has created health problems: obesity, heart disease, and diabetes.

The phosphate deposits are expected to run out by the year 2000, so Nauru is investing in a long-term trust fund and in properties overseas.

Official name: *Republic of Nauru*
Area: *8 sq mi (21 sq km)*
Population: *9,000*
Capital: *Yaren (pop. 600)*
Ethnic groups: *Nauruan, other Pacific Islanders*
Language: *Nauruan, English*
Religious groups: *Protestant, Roman Catholic*
Economy: *Agr: coconuts. Ind: phosphates, finance*
Currency: *Australian dollar*

Kiribati

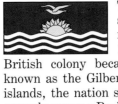

The country's name is spelled Kiribati but pronounced Kir-uh-bas. Until 1979, when this former British colony became independent, it was known as the Gilbert Islands. Made up of 33 islands, the nation straddles the Equator and sprawls across a Pacific Ocean area almost two-thirds the size of the contiguous United States. Lumped together, the land area of its scattered islands totals only 277 square miles (717 sq km).

Most of Kiribati's islands are low-lying and studded with palm and pandanus trees. Islanders fish, harvest coconuts, and grow bananas, taro, breadfruit, and papaya. One island, Banaba, or Ocean Island, earned income through exports of phosphate. But now the deposits are exhausted and the citizens of Kiribati rely on aid from Australia, New Zealand, and the United Kingdom. The island of Tarawa, where Kiribati's capital is, was the scene of some of the bloodiest fighting in the Pacific during World War II.

Official name: *Republic of Kiribati*
Area: *277 sq mi (717 sq km)*
Population: *75,000*
Capital: *Tarawa (pop. 25,200)*
Ethnic groups: *Micronesian*
Language: *English, Gilbertese*
Religious groups: *Roman Catholic, Protestant*
Economy: *Agr: coconuts, root crops, vegetables, fruit, pigs, poultry. Ind: fishing, copra, handicrafts*
Currency: *Australian dollar*

Papua New Guinea

Papua New Guinea occupies the eastern half of New Guinea, the world's second largest island (after Greenland). An Australian territory until it won independence in 1975, the country today numbers about four million people. The capital, Port Moresby, is home to more than 170,000 and is a major shipping center for coffee, cocoa, copra, palm oil, and timber. Minerals are also an important export. The island of Lihir is said to contain the world's largest gold deposit outside of Africa.

Papua New Guinea is a rugged, tropical country swept by monsoon rains and covered with thick rain forests. Here live the brilliant birds of paradise and a butterfly species with an 11-inch (28 cm) wingspread. The nation's southwestern lowlands include one of the world's largest swamps, and giant crocodiles called *pukpuks*.

Inland, the volcanic peaks and sharp limestone ridges of the central highlands rise nearly 15,000 feet (4,570 m). In places the terrain is so jagged that explorers called it "broken bottle country." Valleys and forests tucked amid the crags were home to tribes unknown to the outside world or even to each other until the 1930s.

Some tribes practiced head-hunting. Others were cannibals. All led traditional lives, hunting, gathering, raising pigs, and cultivating plots of taro and yams. Many now wear modern trappings such as T-shirts and plastic beads, and groups entertain tourists with their dances. Even today some villages can be reached only on foot or by air. Although few paved roads connect the nation's towns and villages, more than 400 airstrips serve the backcountry.

Altogether, Papua New Guinea's people speak more than 700 languages. Many speak pidgin English, or a variation called "police motu," and refer to their monarch, Queen Elizabeth II, as "Misis Kwin." For although Papua New Guinea is an independent nation, it is also a member of the Commonwealth.

Official name: *Papua New Guinea*
Area: *178,260 sq mi (461,691 sq km)*
Population: *3,860,000*
Capital: *Port Moresby (pop. 173,500)*
Ethnic groups: *Papuan, Melanesian*
Language: *English, Papuan and Melanesian languages, pidgin English*
Religious groups: *Christian, traditional*
Economy: *Agr: coconuts, root crops, cacao, coffee, oil palm, pigs. Ind: copper, gold, lumber, fishing*
Currency: *kina*

Solomon Islands

When the fighting was over, 25,000 men—mostly Japanese and American troops—lay dead. And the ocean floor east of Guadalcanal, largest of the Solomon Islands, was so littered with sunken ships that the area became known as "Iron Bottom Sound."

Today, the guns of war are silent. But the wreckage of World War II still rusts on many of the beaches of this nation, a British protectorate until it won independence in 1978.

The Solomons got their name from a wily Spanish explorer who sought to recruit settlers by linking the islands to the fabled riches of King Solomon. The islands themselves form a double chain of volcanic peaks and low-lying atolls in the Solomon Sea. The six biggest islands are rugged, with razor-backed ridges slashed by deep valleys and matted with dense forests. Equatorial rains drench them much of the year.

Most of the islanders are Melanesians. Many live along the shore in simple houses with thatched roofs. They harvest crops of coconuts for themselves and for export. From the coconuts comes copra, the dried meat that provides oil for cooking and for making soap and candles. The islanders also sell fish, timber, and seashells used for buttons. They speak some 80 different languages, and they also speak pidgin English.

Honiara, the capital and largest city, is on the island of Guadalcanal.

Official name: *Solomon Islands*
Area: *10,985 sq mi (28,450 sq km)*
Population: *360,000*
Capital: *Honiara (pop. 30,500)*
Ethnic groups: *Melanesian*
Language: *English, Melanesian languages*
Religious groups: *Protestant, Roman Catholic*
Economy: *Agr: coconuts, taro, oil palm, cacao, rice, fruit, vegetables. Ind: fishing, lumber, copra*
Currency: *Solomon Islands dollar*

Tuvalu

In the local tongue, Tuvalu means "eight standing together." Although nine atolls make up this nation, almost all of the people live on eight of them. Each of these has a local government called an island council, and one, Funafuti, is also the site of the national capital. Fewer than a hundred people live on the smallest atoll. Until 1978, Tuvalu was a British colony known as the Ellice Islands.

Most of the coral islands encircle lagoons and are shaded by coconut palms and breadfruit and pandanus trees. The islanders live in thatched-roof houses, and fish and cultivate their gardens for a living. The country exports copra and handicrafts, but most of its income is derived from selling coins and stamps to collectors, and from aid sent by foreign nations, including other members of the Commonwealth.

Official name: *Tuvalu*
Area: *10 sq mi (26 sq km)*
Population: *9,000*
Capital: *Funafuti (pop. 2,800)*
Ethnic groups: *Polynesian*
Language: *Tuvaluan, English*
Religious groups: *Protestant*
Economy: *coconuts (copra), fishing, stamps, coins*
Currency: *Tuvaluan and Australian dollars*

Western Samoa

"Home is the sailor, home from the sea. . . ." So read the words on the mountaintop tomb of Robert Louis Stevenson, author of *Treasure Island* and other tales of adventure. He died in 1894 on his beloved island of Upolu, one of the two largest reef-fringed, volcanic islands in Western Samoa. His house still stands near Apia, the capital and only major town of this South Sea island nation.

The words on Stevenson's grave are fitting. According to legend, it was from the Samoa Islands that Polynesians launched their giant, double-hulled canoes more than a thousand years ago and began to spread their culture across the unexplored Pacific.

Today, Western Samoa, unlike the neighboring islands of American Samoa, still clings to traditional Polynesian ways. Most of its 195,000 people live along the shore in *fale*, thatched-roof shelters with no walls. Each person lives in a large family group presided over by a *matai*, or chief. Samoans fish, raise pigs and chickens, and grow coconuts, bananas, and taro.

Official name: *Independent State of Western Samoa*
Area: *1,093 sq mi (2,831 sq km)*
Population: *195,000*
Capital: *Apia (pop. 33,200)*
Ethnic groups: *Samoan*
Language: *Samoan, English*
Religious groups: *Protestant, Roman Catholic*
Economy: *Agr: coconuts, taro, bananas, papayas. Ind: lumber, tourism, food processing, fishing*
Currency: *tala*

Vanuatu

Most of Vanuatu's people live in thatched houses, as they always have. They raise pigs and cultivate taro, yams, and bananas for themselves. To earn money, they export copra, cocoa, beef, and timber cut from tropical rain forests.

Once known as New Hebrides, Vanuatu was ruled jointly by Britain and France until 1980. That year the Y-shaped string of 80 coral and volcanic islands became an independent nation. Its capital, Port-Vila, is a whitewashed town of about 19,000 people on the island of Efate. It is also a tax haven. Some 100 banks shelter millions of dollars sent from Hong Kong, Singapore, and other overseas money centers.

But traditional beliefs still shape life on these South Pacific islands. On the island of Tanna, for example, one group of people awaits the second coming of John Frum. The group belongs to a cargo cult. They believe in a god who will someday return to their island, bringing gifts of trucks, jeeps, radios, and other goods the way American soldiers did in World War II. They have built piers to receive the cargoes.

And on Pentecost Island, young "land divers" hurl themselves from towers up to 90 feet (27 m) high to assure a good yam harvest. Vines tied to the divers' ankles break their fall.

Official name: *Republic of Vanuatu*
Area: *5,700 sq mi (14,760 sq km)*
Population: *175,000*
Capital: *Port-Vila (pop. 19,400)*
Ethnic groups: *Melanesian, French*
Language: *Bislama, English, French*
Religious groups: *Protestant, Roman Catholic*
Economy: *Agr: coconuts, taro, yams, fruit, cacao, coffee, livestock. Ind: tourism, food, fishing, lumber*
Currency: *vatu*

Fiji

In Fiji there is a legend about a fisherman who one day caught an eel. The eel, fearing for its life, pleaded to be put back in the water. The fisherman obliged and, in return, he and his descendants were granted the ability to walk barefoot across hot stones without burning their feet. To this day, Fijian fire walkers entertain tourists by strolling unharmed across hot stones—feats that defy scientific explanation.

Fiji is a nation of some 320 islands in the South Pacific Ocean, only about 100 of which are inhabited. Some are volcanic peaks rising abruptly out of the ocean. Others are coral strips or flat, sandy isles. In size the islands range from mere rocks to 4,010-square-mile (10,386 sq km) Viti Levu, the larger of the group's two main islands.

Most of Fiji's 750,000 people live near the coast on Viti Levu. Here, too, stands the nation's capital, Suva, a busy metropolis that combines colorful parks and gardens with Indian, Melanesian, and European architectural styles.

Native Fijians, a mixture of Melanesian and Polynesian, only slightly outnumber the descendants of workers brought from India in the late 1800s and early 1900s to work on sugarcane plantations. Today, as businessmen, farmers, doctors, lawyers, and teachers, Indians control much of Fiji's economy, while native islanders own most of the land. The situation has caused tension between the two groups and in 1987 led to the takeover of the government by Fijians.

A British colony from 1874 until 1970, Fiji once was known as the Cannibal Islands. Today it is a republic with one of the best developed economies in the region. Visitors from around the world come to relax on its sunny beaches and are assured of a warm *Ni sa bula*—Welcome.

Official name: *Republic of Fiji*
Area: *7,056 sq mi (18,274 sq km)*
Population: *750,000*
Capital: *Suva (pop. 69,700)*
Ethnic groups: *Indian, Fijian*
Language: *English, Fijian, Hindi*
Religious groups: *Christian, Hindu*
Economy: *Agr: sugarcane, coconuts, cassava, rice, ginger. Ind: tourism, gold mining, fishing, lumber*
Currency: *Fiji dollar*

Tonga

Capt. James Cook, the English navigator, visited Tonga in 1773 and 1777 and was so cordially welcomed he named this cluster of 170 South Sea islands the "Friendly Islands." Little did he know the local chiefs planned to kill him during his second visit. But Cook sailed away unaware of his narrow escape, and the island nation, ruled a thousand years by Polynesian kings, later became a British protectorate.

Today, Tonga is again an independent kingdom, the only monarchy remaining in Polynesia. It is also a member of the Commonwealth. Two-thirds of the people live on Tongatapu, Tonga's largest island and site of its capital, Nuku'alofa.

Many of Tonga's islands are fertile and have plenty of rainfall. Some are forest covered. Low-lying islands are made of coral; higher ones are volcanic, some with active volcanoes.

Most Tongans live in small villages, where they raise pigs and grow vegetables and fruit. They harvest coconuts, vanilla beans, and bananas for sale overseas. Many migrants work in New Zealand for a while and send money home, thus boosting Tonga's economy.

Official name: *Kingdom of Tonga*
Area: *270 sq mi (699 sq km)*
Population: *103,000*
Capital: *Nuku'alofa (pop. 21,400)*
Ethnic groups: *Tongan*
Language: *Tongan, English*
Religious groups: *Protestant, Roman Catholic*
Economy: *Agr: coconuts, yams, taro, vegetables, bananas, vanilla, spices. Ind: tourism, fishing*
Currency: *pa'anga*

New Zealand Territories

Scattered like confetti across the Pacific Ocean south of the Equator are the islands that make up New Zealand's overseas territories.

The 15 **Cook Islands** are self-governing in free association with New Zealand. Half the population of 18,000 lives on lush, volcanic Rarotonga. Most grow coconuts, citrus fruit, and pineapples or work in the tourist and clothing industries.

Niue (pronounced New-way), a limestone plateau, rises sheer from the sea west of the Cook Islands. Niue takes its name from *Niu*, a Polynesian word for coconut tree, and *e*, meaning "behold." It is one of the world's largest coral islands. Many of its cliffs have been carved by pounding waves into a wonderworld of caves, pools, and grottoes. Self-governing since 1974, Niue earns income through exports of copra, passion fruit, honey, limes, and handicrafts.

North of Niue, close to the Equator, lies **Tokelau,** a trio of low-lying atolls. Tokelau has thin soil and few natural resources aside from fish and shellfish. In 1990 a typhoon wiped out all of the banana trees and most of the coconut palms.

New Zealand's three Pacific territories support small Polynesian populations. Most of the people live on crops of coconuts, taro, and yams, and they raise pigs and poultry. The islanders depend on aid from New Zealand, as well as on money sent home by relatives who have moved away to better their lives.

French Territories

On the highest slopes of Raiatea Island in **French Polynesia** lives one of the world's unusual plants. It is a slender-leaved gardenia with five white petals that look like the outstretched fingers of a hand. The plant grows only on Raiatea. Islanders say that its flower is the hand of a princess who died of a broken heart when forbidden to marry a young man from another island.

A delightfully romantic tale, of course. But how fitting that such a story should come from these lush, tropical islands that long have inspired artists, writers, and adventurers to thoughts of earthly paradise. Even the crusty William Bligh, captain of the *Bounty* and its mutineering crew, thought one of the islands, Tahiti, "the finest island in the world."

Located halfway between South America and Australia, French Polynesia is made up of some 120 islands grouped into four archipelagoes. Altogether the islands cover an ocean area about

half the size of the United States. But the land part is tiny—about the size of Rhode Island. Some islands are volcanic, with cloud-wreathed peaks rising straight out of the sea. Others are coral atolls covered with coconut palms.

A French protectorate since the 1800s, French Polynesia became one of France's Pacific territories in 1957. The others are the **Wallis and Futuna Islands** and mineral-rich **New Caledonia,** a major producer of high-quality nickel.

Tahiti, the largest and most heavily populated of the French Polynesian islands, earns much of its income from tourism. Its biggest city, Papeete, is a busy port for shipping coconut oil and serves as the capital for all of French Polynesia.

But even paradise has problems. Between 1966 and 1992, France tested nearly 200 atomic weapons on remote atolls in French Polynesia. In New Caledonia, a drive for independence has brought violence and bloodshed.

Pitcairn Island

In 1789, Fletcher Christian and his fellow mutineers took over H.M.S. *Bounty* and cast its captain, William Bligh, adrift in an open boat. Then they sailed away to one of the world's most remote islands—Pitcairn. It and three uninhabited isles are now a British colony lying 1,350 miles (2,170 km) from the nearest commercial port. Pitcairn's cliffs rise from the sea like walls of a fortress. Volcanic soil supports crops for a dwindling population of *Bounty* descendants.

Official name: *Pitcairn Islands (3 uninhabited)*
Area: *18 sq mi (47 sq km)*
Population: *52*
Capital: *Adamstown*

Easter Island

Great stone figures known as *moai* mystify visitors to this remote volcanic island owned by Chile. Carved with stone tools, the giant statues may have symbolically linked the natural and cosmic worlds for ancient worshipers.

The Easter Islanders, mostly descendants of the Polynesians who settled here 1,600 years ago, fish, farm, or raise livestock for a living. Dutch explorers discovered the island on Easter Sunday, 1722, hence its name.

Official name: *Easter Island*
Area: *47 sq mi (122 sq km)*
Population: *2,100*
Capital: *Hanga Roa*

2 *Tahiti, French Polynesia*

3 *Marutea, French Polynesia*

1 *Fiji*

Fiji

1 *Damp leaves laid on hot rocks release clouds of vapor as Fijian fire walkers demonstrate their ability to walk barefoot across the stones.*

French Polynesia

2 *Legendary beauty of Tahitian women reflects a blend of several nationalities and has inspired painters and photographers from around the world.*

3 *Rare black pearls, cultivated in the warm waters of a lagoon, take several years to grow and may be worth thousands of dollars when harvested.*

4 *The island of Moorea rises from a reef-fringed lagoon, an unspoiled retreat within sight of its sister island, Tahiti.*

4 *Moorea, French Polynesia*

5 *Kwajalein Atoll, Marshall Islands*   6 *Western Samoa*

7 *Easter Island*

Marshall Islands

5 *Americans shop for groceries at a super-market on Kwajalein Atoll. Some 3,000 civilians and U. S. Army personnel live on the atoll, and many of them work at its missile-testing facility.*

Western Samoa

6 *Paddling his outrigger canoe, a fisherman from Savai'i Island preserves seamanship skills prized by his Polynesian ancestors.*

Easter Island

7 *Stone heads jut from a grassy slope as Halley's Comet soars above them in this double exposure. The island's stone figures weigh as much as 89 tons (81 metric tons).*

1 *Upolu, Western Samoa*

2 *Papua New Guinea*

3 *Federated States of Micronesia*

Western Samoa

1 *Thatched-roof houses called* fale *have open-wall air-conditioning in a village on the island of Upolu. Palm mats can be let down to keep out rain and sun.*

Papua New Guinea

2 *Daubed with clay body paint, Gimi story-tellers of the Eastern Highlands dramatize tribal myths and legends—in this case part of a boys' initiation ceremony.*

Federated States of Micronesia

3 *A farmer of Kosrae displays his produce. Easternmost of Micronesia's four federated states, Kosrae is known locally for its fine limes, oranges, tangerines, and bananas.*

Palau

4 *Diver in a bubble bath? No, these are the jellyfish that swarm in some of the 80 or so salt lakes that dot these South Pacific isles.*

4 *Palau*

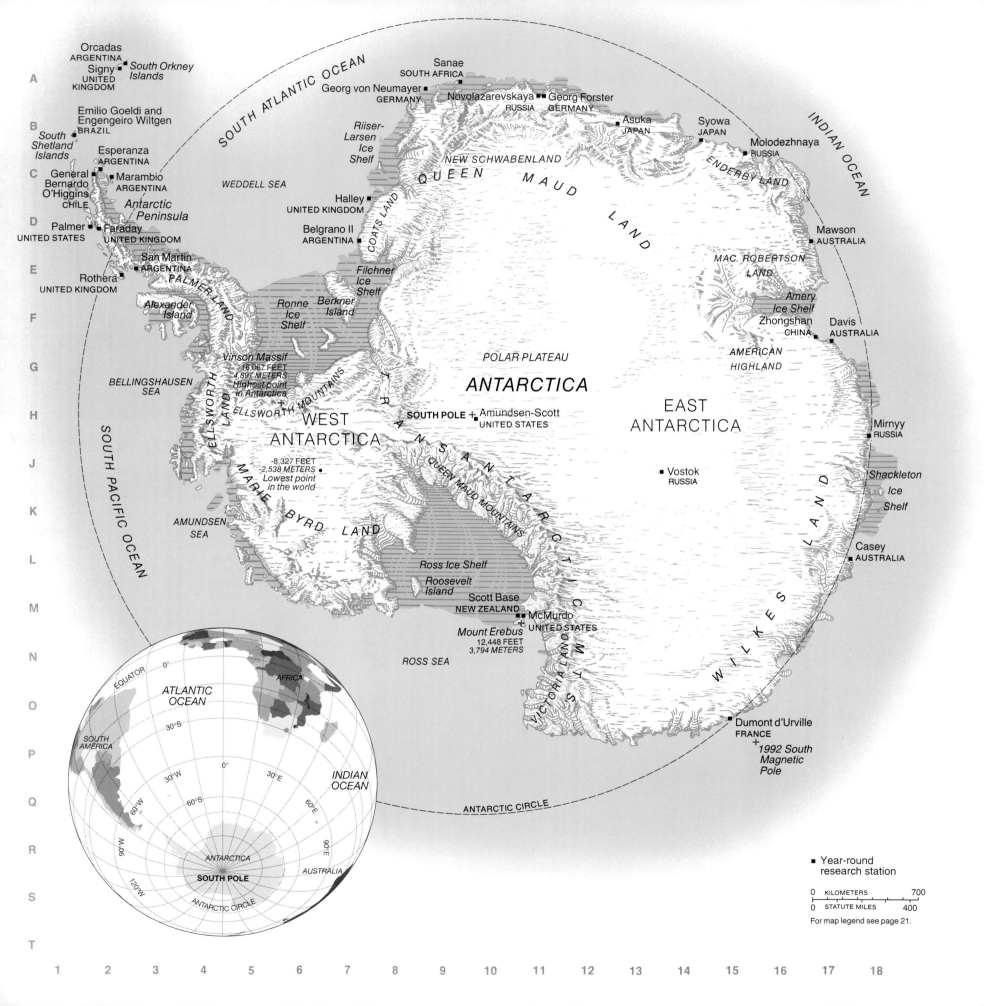

A
Orcadas
ARGENTINA
Signy *South Orkney*
UNITED *Islands*
KINGDOM

SOUTH ATLANTIC OCEAN

Sanae
SOUTH AFRICA

Georg von Neumayer
GERMANY

Novolazarevskaya Georg Forster
RUSSIA GERMANY

Asuka
JAPAN

Syowa
JAPAN

INDIAN OCEAN

B
Emilio Goeldi and
Engengeiro Wiltgen
BRAZIL
*South
Shetland
Islands*

*Riiser-
Larsen
Ice
Shelf*

Molodezhnaya
RUSSIA

C
Esperanza
ARGENTINA
General
Bernardo
O'Higgins Marambio
CHILE ARGENTINA

NEW SCHWABENLAND

QUEEN MAUD LAND

ENDERBY LAND

WEDDELL SEA

Halley
UNITED KINGDOM

COATS LAND

D
Palmer *Antarctic
Peninsula*
UNITED STATES Faraday
UNITED KINGDOM

Belgrano II
ARGENTINA

Mawson
AUSTRALIA

E
San Martin
ARGENTINA
Rothera *PALMER LAND*
UNITED KINGDOM

*Filchner
Ice
Shelf*

*MAC. ROBERTSON
LAND*

*Amery
Ice
Shelf*

F
*Alexander
Island*

ELLSWORTH LAND

*Ronne
Ice
Shelf*

*Berkner
Island*

Zhongshan
CHINA

Davis
AUSTRALIA

POLAR PLATEAU

*AMERICAN
HIGHLAND*

G
*BELLINGSHAUSEN
SEA*

Vinson Massif
16,067 FEET
4,897 METERS
Highest point
in Antarctica

ELLSWORTH MOUNTAINS

ANTARCTICA

H
SOUTH PACIFIC OCEAN

WEST
ANTARCTICA

SOUTH POLE Amundsen-Scott
UNITED STATES

EAST
ANTARCTICA

Mirnyy
RUSSIA

J
-8,327 FEET
2,538 METERS
Lowest point
in the world

TRANSANTARCTIC

QUEEN MAUD MOUNTAINS

Vostok
RUSSIA

*Shackleton
Ice
Shelf*

K
MARIE BYRD LAND

*AMUNDSEN
SEA*

WILKES LAND

Casey
AUSTRALIA

L
Ross Ice Shelf
*Roosevelt
Island*

M
Scott Base
NEW ZEALAND
McMurdo
UNITED STATES

N
ROSS SEA
Mount Erebus
12,448 FEET
3,794 METERS

VICTORIA LAND

MOUNTAINS

O
*ATLANTIC
OCEAN*
EQUATOR 0°
AFRICA

P
SOUTH
AMERICA
30°S

Dumont d'Urville
FRANCE
1992 South
Magnetic
Pole

INDIAN
OCEAN
30°E

Q
60°W
60°S
60°E

90°E
90°W

ANTARCTIC CIRCLE

R
ANTARCTICA
120°W
AUSTRALIA

S
SOUTH POLE
ANTARCTIC CIRCLE

■ Year-round
research station

0   KILOMETERS   700
0   STATUTE MILES   400

For map legend see page 21.

T

1   2   3   4   5   6   7   8   9   10   11   12   13   14   15   16   17   18

The Poles

Antarctica

In the 1770s British explorer James Cook sailed completely around this great white continent without ever sighting land. But he got close enough to conclude that if any land did lie beyond the ice-choked seas, "the world would not be benefited by it." The seal hunters, whalers, and explorers who came later found that land did, in fact, lie farther south, nearer to the South Pole. But Cook's assessment seemed correct.

Earth's southernmost continent, one-tenth of the world's land, is covered by a sheet of ice averaging two miles (3.2 km) thick. Winds howl across it at speeds up to 200 miles (320 km) per hour, and temperatures can plunge to minus 121°F (-85°C). So harsh is the climate that only a few mosses, lichens, and insects live on land.

Antarctica's interior remained largely unexplored until the early 1900s, when rival teams led by Norway's Roald Amundsen and Great Britain's Robert F. Scott raced each other to the South Pole. With the aid of dogsleds and good weather, Amundsen planted his flag at the Pole on December 14, 1911. Hauling their own sledges, Scott's party arrived 35 days later. On the way back, a blizzard trapped the British explorers in their tent, and they died of starvation.

The United Kingdom, Norway, and several other countries—Chile, Argentina, Australia, New Zealand, and France—have made sometimes overlapping claims to portions of Antarctica. But in the Antarctic Treaty, which went into effect in 1961, they agreed not to press those claims. This treaty, signed by some 40 countries, also decreed that Antarctica be used only for peaceful, scientific purposes.

Today more than 40 major research stations dot the Antarctic ice. Among other things, researchers are studying Antarctica's ice sheet to examine the possibility of global warming. Scientists have warned that increases in the earth's temperature due to an accentuated greenhouse effect could, in an extreme case, cause polar ice sheets to melt, raising ocean levels worldwide.

Scientists are also monitoring the "hole" that has been discovered in the ozone layer over Antarctica. Ozone shields the earth from the lethal effects of ultraviolet rays. Researchers are trying to discover whether excess radiation over Antarctica is slowing the growth of tiny marine organisms known as phytoplankton. Declines in phytoplankton could cause drops in other species, such as shrimplike krill, whales, penguins, and fish that abound in these coastal waters.

However, an encouraging report in 1993 indicated that, as a result of the 1987 Montreal Protocol—an international agreement to control ozone-destroying chemicals—ozone destruction should peak by the year 2000, and then the ozone layer is expected to begin replenishing itself.

Antarctica isn't only of scientific interest. Petroleum may lie under the continental shelf in large quantities, and other minerals, including coal, are known to be present. So far, the Antarctic Treaty and the huge costs of extraction have kept all mineral resources unexploited. But environmentalists object to any development in Antarctica. They say that oil spills or other mishaps could harm this fragile and still relatively unspoiled continent. Proposals have been made to set it aside as a nature reserve.

A compromise solution was hammered out in 1991, when Antarctic Treaty members banned all mining and oil exploration for 50 years. A two-thirds majority must agree to any lifting of the ban at the end of that period. It remains to be seen whether the agreement will succeed in protecting this unique region and the contributions it can make to global scientific understanding.

Arctic Regions

Earth's two polar zones are opposite in more ways than location on the globe. While Antarctica is an ice-covered continent surrounded by sea, the Arctic is an ice-covered ocean ringed by continents: North America, Europe, and Asia.

Because the Arctic ice pack is sea ice full of meltwater and open channels, it reflects less of the sun's heat back into space, and so the Arctic regions are warmer than Antarctica. Temperatures over the Arctic Ocean average 32°F (0°C) in summer and minus 30°F (-34°C) in winter.

In summer the ice pack shrinks, and the ocean abounds with fish, whales, and seabirds. Seals raise pups on floating ice-top nurseries, occasionally falling prey to polar bears or human hunters. Summer also melts the snow cover on the lands ringing the ocean. They spring alive with blossoming plants, shrubs, and grasses and support hares, foxes, caribou, and reindeer. Arctic lands are also home to several native peoples who have adapted to this frigid climate.

Adventurers from warmer lands have long been attracted to Arctic challenges. Sea captains nudged their boats along the Arctic's icy coasts, looking for northern trade routes. Later, explorers came seeking the North Pole.

More recently, developers have come north to tap the region's mineral wealth, which includes impressive stores of oil and natural gas, as well as coal and iron ore. Scientific studies have examined such problems as the effect of airborne pollutants from northern industrial areas and the extent of ozone loss.

In 1991, concerned with threats to the Arctic environment, the Arctic rim nations—Canada, the United States, the former Soviet Union, Iceland, Sweden, Norway, Finland, and Denmark (on behalf of Greenland)—adopted the Arctic Environmental Protection Strategy; it includes provisions to monitor the impact of development activities. Russia has since signed a trade and environmental agreement with the Nordic countries. These efforts may help reduce the pollution of the fragile Arctic ecosystems.

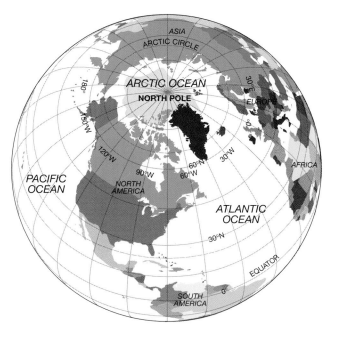

1 *Ellesmere Island, Canada*

2 *Baffin Island, Canada*

3 *Alaska, U. S.*

4 *Antarctica*

5 *Antarctica*

Arctic Regions

1 *An Inuit paddles his kayak past the village of Grise Fiord 950 miles (1,530 km) from the North Pole.*

2 *An Inuit grandmother at Pond Inlet baby-sits while stretching hides for use in clothing. The temperature around her is 40°F below zero (-40°C).*

3 *One of a migrating herd, an antlered caribou bull grazes the tundra. As summer draws to an end, caribou eat constantly to store up body fat for the long Arctic winter.*

Antarctica

4 *Emperor penguins stand with a two-week-old chick at their winter breeding ground on an ice shelf. Some penguin breeding colonies here number in the millions.*

5 *A scientist at the U. S. Amundsen-Scott Station at the South Pole checks solar radiation sensors to measure ozone-damaging air pollutants.*

Illustrations Credits

Abbreviations for terms appearing below: (t)-top; (b)-bottom; (l)-left; (r)-right; (c)-center; NGP-National Geographic Photographer; NGS-National Geographic Staff.

Cover, Michel Tcherevkoff. 2-3, Shusei Nagaoka.

Mapping Our World
9, Michel Tcherevkoff. 10-20, paintings by Shusei Nagaoka.

North America
22, (t) Annie Griffiths Belt; (c) Paul Chesley; (b) Philip Schermeister. 23, Tibor G. Toth. 25, Stephanie Maze. 28, Sandy Felsenthal. 29, (tl) NASA; (tr) Bruce Davidson; (bl) Wilbur E. Garrett; (br) C.C. Lockwood. 30, (t) Phil Schofield; (b) Bruce Dale, NGP. 30-31, Art Wolfe, All-stock. 31, (t) Robert W. Madden, NGS; (b) Bill Hess. 34, George F. Mobley, NGP. 34-35, Ann E. Yow. 35, (t) Paul von Baich, First Light; (c) Yva Momatiuk and John Eastcott; (bl) George F. Mobley, NGP; (br) Ivars Silis. 38, (t) Sisse Brimberg; 38, (b), 38-39 David Hiser, Photographers Aspen; 39, (t) and (cl) Danny Lehman; (cr) Chuck Place; (b) Sisse Brimberg. 43, Nicholas DeVore III, Photographers Aspen. 44, (t) Danny Lehman; (bl) Alain Keler, Sygma; (br) Matthew Naythons, Gamma Liaison. 45, (t) Joseph J. Scherschel; (bl) David Alan Harvey; (br) Loren McIntyre. 51, (t) Jodi Cobb, NGP; (bl) Tor Eigeland; (br) Cotton Coulson. 52, (t) Carole E. Devillers; (bl) and (br) Steve Raymer, NGS. 52-53, Bruce Dale, NGP. 53, (t) James L. Stanfield, NGP; (b) Tony Arruza.

South America
54, Loren McIntyre. 55, Tibor G. Toth. 57, William Albert Allard. 60, (t) O. Louis Mazzatenta, NGS; (bl) Fred Ward, Black Star; (bc) José Azel, Contact Press Images; (br) Georg Gerster. 61, (t) Uwe George, GEO Magazin; (b) Loren McIntyre. 64, (t) Cary Wolinsky; (b) Martin Rogers. 64-65, Ric Ergenbright. 65, (t) William E. Townsend Jr., Photo Researchers, Inc.; (b) Dieter and Mary Plage, Survival Anglia. 68, (t) Stephanie Maze; (b) Andrew L. Young. 68-69, Stephanie Maze. 69, Carole E. Devillers. 72, (t), 72-73, O. Louis Mazzatenta, NGS; 72 (b), 73 Loren McIntyre. 76, (t) O. Louis Mazzatenta, NGS; (bl) James P. Blair, NGP; (br) Frans Lanting, Minden Pictures. 76-77, David Alan Harvey. 77, Loren McIntyre.

Europe
78, (t) Farrell Grehan; (b) Bryan and Cherry Alexander. 79, Tibor G. Toth. 81, (l) Adam Woolfitt; (r) Horst Munzig. 84-85, Bob Krist. 86, (l) Sisse Brimberg; (r) Tor Eigeland. 87, (tl) Jodi Cobb, NGP; (tr) Bernhard Wagner; (b) Sven Hörnell. 90, 90-91, 91, (tr) and (bl) Larry C. Price; 91 (br) Jay Dickman. 94, (t) John Bulmer; (bl) Linda Bartlett; (br) Nathan Benn. 94-95, O. Louis Mazzatenta, NGS. 95, (l) and (r) Cotton Coulson. 98, (t) Nathan Benn; (b) James L. Stanfield, NGP. 99, (l) Jean-Paul Nacivet, After Image; (r) Gerd Ludwig, Visum. 102, Yva Momatiuk and John Eastcott. 102-103, James L. Stanfield, NGP. 103, (t) G. V. Faint, The Image Bank; (b) Yva Momatiuk and John Eastcott, The Image Works. 106, Bruno Barbey, Magnum. 106-107, Bruce Dale, NGP. 107, Steve Raymer, NGS. 110, James P. Blair, NGP. 111, (tl)

Stephanie Maze; (tr) David Burnett, Contact Press Images; (b) Bernard Wolf. 114, French National Railroad. 114-115, James L. Stanfield, NGP. 115, (tl) Charles O'Rear; (tr) Jodi Cobb, NGP; (b) Cotton Coulson. 118, O. Louis Mazzatenta, NGS. 119, (tl) Thomas Nebbia; (tr) and (br) James L. Stanfield, NGP; (bl) Cotton Coulson. 123, (tl) G. V. Faint, The Image Bank; (tr) P. Weisbecker, Explorer; (bl) Cary Wolinsky; (br) Alon Reininger, Contact Press Images. 124, (t) and (bl) Alon Reininger, Contact Press Images; (br) Klaus Reisinger, Black Star. 125, Steve McCurry. 128, (t) Hans Madej, Bilderberg; (b) James L. Stanfield, NGP. 129, (l) Comstock, H. Higuchi; (tr) James P. Blair, NGP; (br) Nicole Bengiveno.

Asia
130, (t) William Thompson; (b) Dean Conger. 131, Tibor G. Toth. 133, David Alan Harvey. 136, (tl) Eric Lars Bakke, Black Star; (bl) Sarah Leen; (br) Cotton Coulson. 136-137, Thomas Ernsting, Bilderberg. 137, (t) Vladimir Vyatkin; (b) Bruce Dale, NGP. 140, (t) and (b), 141, (tl) George F. Mobley, NGP; 141 (tr) H. Bakhshandagi, Black Star; (b) Tomasz Tomaszewski. 144, David Breashears. 145, (t) and (b) Nicole Bengiveno. 146, Hermine Dreyfuss. 146-147, Gerd Ludwig, Woodfin Camp & Associates. 147, (t) Alexandra Avakian, Contact Press Images; (b) Nicole Bengiveno. 151, (t) and (b) James L. Stanfield, NGP. 152, (tl) Georg Gerster, Comstock; (tr) James L. Stanfield, NGP; (b) Jodi Cobb, NGP. 153, (tl) Thomas Kern, Contact Press Images; (tr) Gerd Ludwig, Visum; (b) Steve McCurry. 156, Steve Raymer, NGS. 157, Mohamed Amin, Camerapix. 158, (tl) Thomas J. Abercrombie, NGS; (b) Jodi Cobb, NGP. 158-159, Robert Azzi, Woodfin Camp, Inc. 159, (t) Thomas Muscionico, Contact Press Images; (b) Lynn Abercrombie. 162, (t) Michel Plassart, Explorer; (r) Michael Coyne, The Image Bank. 163, (t) Klaus Reisinger, Black Star; (bl) James L. Stanfield, NGP; (br) Steve McCurry. 167, Henry Wilson. 168, Steve McCurry. 168-169, Raghubir Singh. 169, (t) David Hiser, Photographers Aspen; (bl) Steve McCurry, (br) Raghubir Singh. 172, (t) James L. Stanfield, NGP; (b) Cary Wolinsky. 173, (l) Bruce Dale, NGP; (tr) Thomas Nebbia; (br) H. Edward Kim. 174, Reinhold Messner. 174-175, Steve McCurry. 175, (t) and (b) Dean Conger. 178, (l) Charles O'Rear; (r) Michael S. Yamashita. 178-179, George F. Mobley, NGP. 179, (t) David Alan Harvey; (bl) Nathan Benn; (br) Yann Layma, Explorer. 182, James L. Stanfield, NGP. 183, (tl) Seny Norasingh; (tr) and (br) David Alan Harvey; (bl) Steve Raymer, NGS. 186-187, 187, (t) and (b) Steve McCurry. 188, (tl) James P. Blair, NGP; (bl) and (r) Dean Conger. 189, (tl) and (tr) Charles O'Rear; (b) David Robert Austen.

Africa
190, (t) Richard Packwood, Oxford Scientific Films, Ltd; (b) George F. Mobley, NGP. 191, Tibor G. Toth. 193, Steve Jackson, Black Star. 196, David Alan Harvey. 197, (t) Carol Beckwith; (b) Steve McCurry. 198, (l) Georg Gerster, Comstock; 198, (b), 198-199, Bruno Barbey, Magnum. 199, (t) Steve McCurry; (b) Pierre Boulat, Woodfin Camp Cosmos. 202, Ann B. Keiser. 202-203, (t) Dick Durrance II, Woodfin Camp, Inc.; (b) Robert Caputo. 203, (t) James L. Stanfield, NGP; (bl) Steve

McCurry; (br) Robert Caputo. 207, Olivier Martel, Gamma Presse Images. 208, (tl) Susan Pierres, Peter Arnold Inc.; (tr) and (b) Michael and Aubine Kirtley. 209, (l) Arthur Tress, Magnum; (r) Eugene Gordon. 212, (t) Douglas Waugh, Peter Arnold Inc.; (b) William Campbell, Sygma. 213, (tl) Georg Gerster; (tr) John Sleezer; (b) Anthony Suau. 216, 217, Anthony Suau. 218, (t) Robert C. Bailey; (b) James A. Sugar; 218-219, 219, (t) Georg Gerster. 223, (t) Mitsuaki Iwago; (b) George F. Mobley, NGP. 224, (t) Kevin Fleming; 224, (b), 224-225, 225, (b) Robert Caputo; 225, (tl) Gerry Ellis, Ellis Wildlife Collection; (tr) Chris Johns. 228, Frans Lanting. 229, (tl) Michael Friedel; (tr) and (b) Steve Raymer, NGS. 232, (t) Fred Ward, Black Star; (b) James L. Stanfield, NGP. 232-233, Eli Reed, Magnum. 233, (t) and (b) Bill Curtsinger. 237, (l) Carol and David Hughes; (r) Jim Brandenburg. 238, (l) Nicholas DeVore III, Photographers Aspen; (r) Frans Lanting. 239, (tl) and (b) James L. Stanfield, NGP; (tr) Thomas Nebbia.

Oceania
240, (t) Gordon W. Gahan; (c) Georg Gerster; (b) David Doubilet. 241, Tibor G. Toth. 244, (t) Penny Tweedie; (b) David Robert Austen. 244-245, George Hall, Weldon Trannies. 245, (t) Jim Brandenburg; (bl) Anne B. Keiser; (br) Yva Momatiuk and John Eastcott. 252, (l) Dilip Mehta, Woodfin Camp & Associates; (c) Nicholas DeVore III, Photographers Aspen; (r) Fred Ward, Black Star. 252-253, 253, (c) David Hiser, Photographers Aspen; 253, (l) Melinda Berge, Photographers Aspen; (r) James Balog. 254, 255, (tr) David Hiser, Photographers Aspen; 255, (tl) David Gillison; (b) David Doubilet.

The Poles
258, (t) Jim Brandenburg; (bl) Kevin Fleming; (br) Michio Hoshino. 259, (t) Doug Allan; (b) George F. Mobley, NGP.

Acknowledgments

We are grateful to the following for their assistance: National Geographic Society Library, including its Map and News Collections; Illustrations Library; Records Library; Messenger Center; Photographic Services Division; Production Services, Pre-Press Division.

We also thank the following individuals: Monica P. Bradsher, Ted Dachtera, Marguerite B. Hunsiker, Alice T.M. Rechlin, NGS; Harm de Blij; Charles Drake, Dartmouth College; Charles Dunne, U. S. Department of State; Terry Fenge, Canadian Arctic Resources Committee; Carl Haub, Population Reference Bureau; Zachary T. Irwin, Pennsylvania State University; Charles M. Love, Western Wyoming College; Jack M. Seymour, Jr., The Atlantic Council of the U. S.; Whitney Smith, Flag Research Center; John P. Snyder, U. S. Geological Survey; John D. Treadway, University of Richmond.

Facts at Your Fingertips

Earth's Extremes

Rainiest Spot
Mount Waialeale, Hawaii, U. S.; as many as 350 rainy days a year. Greatest rainfall in 1 year: Cherrapunji, India, August 1, 1860, to August 1, 1861; 1,041.78 inches (2,646.12 cm)

Driest Spot
Atacama Desert, Chile; rainfall barely measurable

Coldest Recorded Temperature
Vostok, Antarctica; -128.6°F (-89.2°C), on July 21, 1983

Hottest Recorded Temperature
Al Aziziyah, Libya, south of Tripoli; 136.4°F (58°C), in 1922

Highest Point
Mount Everest, China-Nepal; 29,028 feet (8,848 m)

Lowest Surface Point
In West Antarctica; 8,327 feet (2,538 m) below sea level

Longest River
Nile, Africa; 4,145 miles (6,671 km)

Tallest Waterfall
Angel Falls, Venezuela; 3,212 feet (979 m)

Largest Gorge
Grand Canyon, Colorado River, Arizona, U. S.; 290 miles (466 km) long, 600 feet to 18 miles (183 m to 29 km) wide, 1 mile (1.6 km) deep

Deepest Canyon
Colca River Canyon, Peru; 2 miles (3.22 km)

Longest Cave
Mammoth-Flint Ridge cave system, Kentucky, U. S.; more than 340 miles (547 km) of passageways

Largest Desert
Sahara, North Africa; 3,500,000 square miles (9,064,958 sq km)

Longest Reef
Great Barrier Reef, Australia; 1,250 miles (2,012 km)

Deepest Ocean Trench
Mariana Trench, Pacific Ocean; 35,827 feet (10,920 m)

Greatest Tides
Bay of Fundy, Nova Scotia, Canada; 52.5 feet (16 m)

Largest Ocean
Pacific; 64,185,999 square miles (166,241,000 sq km), average depth 12,925 feet (3,940 m)

Largest Sea
South China; 1,148,499 square miles (2,974,600 sq km), average depth 4,803 feet (1,464 m)

Largest Lake
Caspian Sea, Europe-Asia; 143,244 square miles (371,000 sq km), 3,363 feet (1,025 m) deep

Deepest Lake
Lake Baikal, Russia; greatest depth 5,371 feet (1,637 m)

Highest Lake
Unnamed glacial lake near Mount Everest, China-Nepal; 19,300 feet (5,883 m) high

Lowest Lake
Dead Sea, Israel-Jordan; surface of water 1,312 feet (400 m) below sea level

Largest Island
Greenland; 840,004 square miles (2,175,600 sq km)

Highest Town
Wenquan, China; 16,732 feet (5,100 m) above sea level

Lowest Town
Ein Bokek, Israel, on the shore of the Dead Sea; almost 1,300 feet (396 m) below sea level

Northernmost Capital
Reykjavik, Iceland; latitude 64°09′N, longitude 21°57′W

Southernmost Capital
Wellington, New Zealand; latitude 41°18′S, longitude 174°47′E

Largest Continent by Area
Asia; 17,176,102 square miles (44,485,900 sq km)

Smallest Continent by Area
Australia; 2,966,153 square miles (7,682,300 sq km)

Largest Continent by Population
Asia; 3,317,800,000

Smallest Continent by Population
Australia; 17,782,000

Largest Country by Area
Russia; 6,592,692 square miles (17,075,000 sq km)

Smallest Country by Area
Vatican City; 0.2 square miles (0.4 sq km)

Largest Country by Population
People's Republic of China; 1,165,771,000

Smallest Country by Population
Vatican City; 1,000

Most Crowded Country
Monaco; 50,000 people per square mile

Least Crowded Country
Mongolia; 3.7 people per square mile

Largest Metropolitan Area Population
Tokyo-Yokohama, Japan; 30,421,100

Engineering Wonders

Highest Bridge
Royal Gorge, Arkansas River, Colorado, U. S.; 1,053 feet (321 m) above water

Longest Bridge Span
Humber Estuary, Kingston upon Hull, England; 4,626 feet (1,410 m)

Longest Big Ship Canal
Suez Canal, Egypt, links the Red Sea and the Mediterranean; 100.6 miles (162 km)

Biggest Concrete Dam
Grand Coulee, Columbia River, Washington, U. S.; 10,585,000 cubic yards (8,093,000 cu m)

Biggest Earth-fill Dam
Syncrude Tailings, Alberta, Canada; 706,000,000 cubic yards (540,000,000 cu m)

Tallest Dam
Nurek, Russia; 984 feet (300 m)

Great Pyramid of Khufu
Giza, Egypt; 450 feet (137 m) tall; base covers 13.1 acres (5.3 ha)

Great Wall of China
3,930 miles (6,325 km) long; averages 25 feet (7.6 m) high; 15 feet (4.6 m) wide at top; 25 feet (7.6 m) wide at base

Largest Artificial Lake (Surface Area)
Lake Volta, formed by the Akosombo Dam on the Volta River, Ghana; 3,500 square miles (9,065 sq km)

Tallest Office Building
Sears Tower, Chicago, Illinois, U. S.; 1,454 feet (443 m); 110 stories

Longest Railroad
Trans-Siberian Railroad, Moscow to Nakhodka, near Vladivostok, Russia; 5,864 miles (9,437 km)

Tallest Freestanding Tower
CN Tower, Toronto, Canada; 1,815.5 feet (553.3 m)

Longest Rail Tunnel
Seikan Tunnel, from Honshu to Hokkaido, Japan; 33.46 miles (53.85 km)

Longest Road Tunnel
St. Gotthard, from Göschenen to Airolo, Switzerland; 10.1 miles (16.3 km)

Longest Artificial Seaway
St. Lawrence Seaway, on the St. Lawrence River from Montreal, Canada, to Lake Ontario; 189 miles (304 km)

Deepest Water Well
Stensvad Well 11-W1, Rosebud County, Montana, U. S.; 7,320 feet (2,231 m)

Glossary

Fact box explanation
At the end of each country account, you will find a fact box that lists basic information such as area, population, and so on. Most of the headings are self-explanatory. When the population of a capital city is preceded by the abbreviation *pop.* (meaning *population*), the figure includes only the people within the city limits. If the figure includes the whole metropolitan area, it is cited as *met. pop.*

Under the heading **Ethnic groups,** you will find descriptions of the people who live in each country. Where the populations are long established, as in Europe, country names may be used. Where they originate from a mixture of nationalities, as in the United States, terms such as *white* and *black* are more suitable. In some cases, continental ethnic origin is listed; such references may be explained in the country story. Only major ethnic groups, religious groups, and languages are listed, and we put the country's official language first.

The **Economy** of each country is split into agriculture *(Agr)* and industry *(Ind)*. Each is listed in roughly descending order of importance. *Agriculture* includes both food and export crops. In the countries where subsistence farming is of prime importance, food crops are listed first. *Industry* focuses on commercial activities that support a country's economy, including exports.

Abbreviations used in this book
Many of the figures and metric conversions have been rounded off.

°C—degrees Celsius or Centigrade	kg—kilograms
	km—kilometers
cm—centimeters	m—meters
cu m—cubic meters	mi—miles
°F—degrees Fahrenheit	sq km—square kilometers
ft—feet	sq m—square meters
ha—hectares	sq mi—square miles

adobe—brick made of sun-dried mud or clay.

alpaca—a domesticated mammal with long, woolly hair; related to the llama.

altiplano—a high plateau that lies between higher mountains.

apartheid—a former government policy of racial segregation and discrimination in South Africa.

aquifer—an underground reservoir of water contained within a porous rock layer.

Arabic—referring to the language and culture of the Arabs.

archipelago—a group or chain of islands.

atoll—a coral island or islets encircling a lagoon.

autonomy—the right of self-government or freedom from external control.

balkanize—to break up a large political region into smaller units or regions.

basin—a depression in the earth's surface, often filled with water at its lowest point; also the entire area drained by a river system.

bauxite—aluminum ore; an earthy, reddish-colored material used in the manufacture of aluminum.

bay—a body of water partially surrounded by land; bays are usually smaller and less deeply indented than gulfs.

Bedouin—a nomadic Arab of the desert.

Benelux—an economic and social alliance between the countries of Belgium, the Netherlands, and Luxembourg.

Berlin Wall—the wall built after World War II between East Berlin and West Berlin to prevent free movement from one part of the city to another.

Buddhism—a religion of Asia that grew from the teachings of Gautama Buddha in the 6th century B.C. He taught salvation through self-purification.

cacao—a tropical tree bearing seeds called cacao or cocoa beans, used to make cocoa and chocolate.

campesino—a resident of a Latin American rural area.

canyon—a deep, narrow valley with steep sides; it is usually wider and longer than a gorge.

cape—a piece of land that extends into a river, a lake, or an ocean.

capitalism—an economic system based on private ownership of businesses and a competitive market.

cash crop—a crop grown for sale, as opposed to food crops grown for family use.

cassava—a plant grown in the tropics for its edible, starchy root; sometimes called **manioc.**

caste—a hereditary social class in Hinduism.

CFA franc—currency of the Communauté Financière Africaine (African Financial Community); worth half a French franc.

chaco—lowland plain; specifically, the Gran Chaco of Argentina, Paraguay, and Bolivia.

channel—a waterway between two landmasses; also the part of a river that is deepest and carries the most water.

Christianity—a religion based on the teachings of Jesus Christ, who is believed to be the son of God.

city-state—an independent country made up of a city and sometimes the surrounding area.

civil war—armed conflict between opposing groups of citizens of the same country.

coca—a shrub whose leaves are made into a drug called cocaine.

collective farm—a collection of land holdings operated as a single unit, especially one owned and operated by a communist government; the workers receive a share of the returns.

colony—a foreign territory that enjoys some autonomy, but retains ties with its parent country.

the Commonwealth—a voluntary association of independent countries that maintains ties of friendship, cooperation, and assistance. The British monarch is the symbolic head.

communism—an economic system based on the idea that property is owned in common rather than privately and goods are distributed as needed.

conquistador—a soldier in the Spanish conquest of the Americas.

contiguous U. S.—the 48 states that adjoin each other in the United States; noncontiguous states are Alaska and Hawaii.

continent—one of the seven main land areas on the earth's surface: North America, South America, Europe, Asia, Africa, Australia, and Antarctica.

continental shelf—the shallow, gently sloping seafloor that surrounds each continent.

contras—an organized group of rebels who fought the Sandinista government in Nicaragua.

copra—dried coconut meat that yields oil.

coral—hard outer skeletons of tiny marine animals, called coral polyps, which form reefs and islands.

cottage industry—an industry whose labor force consists of family members working at home with their own equipment.

coup, coup d'état—the forcible overthrow of a government by a small group, usually from within.

Creole—a mixture of several languages, which serves as an indigenous form of speech.

crown colony—a colony of the United Kingdom over which the crown retains some control.

delta—a lowland composed of silt, sand, and gravel deposited by a river at its mouth.

democracy—a form of government in which power is held by the people and is exercised by them directly or through their elected representatives.

dependency—a geographically separate territory under the jurisdiction of a parent country.

desertification—deterioration of land within deserts and along their moister margins, caused by a combination of human use and drought conditions.

dhow—a West Asian boat with a triangular sail.

dialect—a regional variety of a language.

divide—the high boundary between areas drained by different river systems; water flows in a different direction on either side.

dormant volcano—a temporarily inactive volcano; a totally inactive one is called extinct.

drought—a long period without rain.

duchy—the territory ruled by a duke or duchess.

dynasty—a succession of rulers coming from the same line of descent.

economy—the system of a country's production, distribution, and use of goods and services.

emigration—the act of leaving one's native country or region to settle in another one; usually means moving to a foreign country.

enclave—a small land area entirely surrounded by foreign territory.

escarpment—a cliff separating two nearly flat land surfaces that lie at different levels.

estuary—the widening mouth of a river where it meets the sea; tides ebb and flow within this area.

ethnic group—a group of people who share a common racial, linguistic, cultural, or regional background.

European Community (EC)—an organization that promotes a common market in Europe.

fallow—farmland left unplanted during the growing season.

federation—a group of independent countries united by a treaty or alliance for joint action.

fjord—a narrow, steep-sided ocean inlet that reaches far into a coastline.

geothermal power—energy provided by heat from inside the earth.

glacier—a large, slowly moving mass of ice.

gorge—a narrow passage or valley with steep sides; it is narrower and shorter than a canyon.

guanaco—a mammal with a soft, thick coat; probably the original ancestor of both the alpaca and the llama.

guerrilla—a person who carries on warfare behind enemy lines through ambushes, raids, and sabotage of transport and communications.

gulf—a portion of the ocean partly enclosed by land.

hacienda—a large estate or plantation in Latin America, or its main house.

harbor—a body of water sheltered by natural or artificial barriers and deep enough to moor ships.

heavy industry—manufacturing that processes large amounts of raw materials, such as coal and iron ore, and uses heavy machinery.

Hinduism—the major religion of India; it teaches righteous living to achieve a final union with Brahman, the supreme power of the universe.

homeland—an area set aside for a people of a particular national, racial, or cultural origin.

hydroelectric power—electricity produced by capturing the energy of moving water.

ice sheet—a broad, thick layer of glacial ice that covers a large area.

iceberg—a large, floating chunk of ice broken away from a glacier or an ice shelf.

immigration—the legal or illegal movement of people into a country where they are not native residents.

Inca—an empire in the Andes that ruled an area from Colombia to Chile before the Spanish conquest.

irrigation—artificial watering of farmland.

Islam—a religious belief that there is one God and that Muhammad is the last of the prophets.

isthmus—a strip of land connecting two larger land areas and separating two bodies of water.

Judaism—a religion developed by the ancient Hebrews that teaches belief in one God.

kingdom—a form of government headed by a king or a queen.

ladino—a term used chiefly in Guatemala to describe a person who has adopted European ways of living.

lagoon—a shallow body of water that opens on the sea but is protected by a sandbar or coral reef.

landlocked country—a country surrounded by land, without access to the sea.

legumes—edible seeds such as peas, beans, lentils.

light industry—manufacturing that uses small amounts of raw materials and employs light or small machines; one example is food processing.

llama—a mammal used as a pack animal and a source of wool; related to the camel.

llano—an open, grassy plain.

loess—deposit of fine silt or dust that settles on the ground after being carried by the wind.

maharaja—a royal Hindu ruler.

maritime—bordering the sea; concerning navigation or commerce on the sea.

Maya—an Indian civilization of Mexico and Central America that built cities and temple-pyramids and devised a calendar and a writing system.

medieval—referring to a period of European history known as the Middle Ages, roughly from A.D. 500 to 1500.

mesa—a broad, flat-topped landform with steep sides found in arid or semiarid regions.

mestizo—a Latin American of mixed European and American Indian ancestry.

metric—a system of measurement based on units of ten; the meter is its principal unit.

millet—a grass cultivated for its grain, used for food.

monarchy—a government having undivided rule by a single person, such as a king or a queen.

monsoons—winds that produce either a dry or a wet season in southern and eastern Asia.

Moors—North Africans of mixed Arab-Berber descent; Moors ruled parts of the Iberian Peninsula between A.D. 711 and 1492.

moraine—an accumulation of debris carried and deposited by a glacier.

mosque—an Islamic house of worship.

mouth (of a river)—where a river ends by flowing into a large body of water, such as a sea or ocean.

mulatto—a person of mixed white and black ancestry.

Muslim—a follower of Islam.

nomads—livestock herders who migrate seasonally with their herds according to pasture and water.

oasis—a green area in a desert, with a spring or water hole often fed by an underground aquifer.

oil palm—a palm growing chiefly in western and central Africa, whose fruit and kernel yield oil.

outback—the remote backcountry of Australia.

outcrop—the part of a rock formation that appears at the surface of the ground.

pagoda—a tower with several successive roofs, used as a temple or memorial in the Far East.

pampa—an extensive grassland.

parliament—a group of representatives who meet to discuss national affairs and make laws.

patois—a regional dialect.

peer—a member of the British nobility, such as a duke, marquess, earl, viscount, or baron.

peninsula—a long piece of land almost surrounded by water but connected to a larger landmass.

per capita—a way of averaging "by heads," meaning by individuals; income, production, or other data are often given per capita.

permafrost—permanently frozen subsoil and bedrock, up to 1,500 feet (450 m) deep, that can produce the effect of completely frozen ground.

phosphate—organic compound used in fertilizers.

pidgin—simplified speech consisting of words adapted from other languages; used between people who speak different languages.

pilgrimage—a journey to a place of great religious significance.

plantain—a starchy fruit, similar to a banana, that is a staple in the diet of people living in the tropics.

plantation—a large estate that grows a cash crop; usually worked by unskilled or semiskilled labor.

plateau—a large, flat area that rises higher than the land around it; it is larger than a mesa.

poach—to capture or kill wild animals illegally.

polder—a tract of land reclaimed from the sea and protected by dikes. About 40 percent of the Netherlands consists of polders.

polyglot—a mixture of languages.

populous—having a large population; densely populated refers to the number of people per area.

principality—a territory or jurisdiction of a prince.

privatization—transferal of a business or property from public to private control or ownership.

Pygmies—groups of central African peoples who usually stand less than five feet tall.

pyrethrum—a chrysanthemum that is a source of insecticides.

rain forest—dense forest composed mainly of broad-leaved evergreens found in wet tropical regions.

reef—an offshore ridge of rocks, coral, or sand, that lies at or near the water's surface.

republic—a form of government whose chief of state is usually a president, not a monarch; also a country having such a government.

rift valley—a trough-shaped valley formed when the earth's crust sinks between parallel faults.

root crop—a crop grown for its large, edible roots, such as potatoes, turnips, cassava, taro.

Russia—until 1917 tsarist Russia was an empire in Eastern Europe and northern and western Asia; today the Russian Federation, known as Russia, is the largest of the former Soviet Union republics.

Sahel—the semiarid grassland directly south of the Sahara in western and central Africa.

savanna—a tropical grassland with scattered trees.

scale—the ratio of map distance to distance on the earth's surface, shown as a bar graph.

secession—formal withdrawal, such as from a country or federation.

socialism—an economic system based on the idea that a government should distribute the society's wealth equally.

sorghum—a tropical grass whose grain is used for food or whose stem may yield syrup.

sound—a long, broad ocean inlet usually parallel to the coast, or a long stretch of water separating an island from the mainland.

steppe—a grassland in the temperate zone where limited rainfall prevents tree growth and keeps most grasses from growing any taller than 20 inches (50 cm).

strait—a narrow passage of water that connects two larger bodies of water.

Sudan—the largest country in Africa, in the northeast; also the name given by Arabs to the region in north-central Africa between the Sahara and the equatorial forests. It includes the Sahel.

tableland—an extensive region of elevated land, usually with a level surface.

taiga—subarctic coniferous forest largely consisting of firs and spruces.

taro—a plant raised throughout the tropics for its edible, starchy root.

tartan—a plaid textile design usually associated with a distinctive Scottish clan.

territory—a geographical area belonging to or under the jurisdiction of an external government; also an administrative subdivision of a country.

traditional—refers to beliefs, customs, dress, and behavior handed down from one generation to another, often with no written record.

tributary—a stream that flows into a larger river.

tundra—a treeless plain found mostly in Arctic regions; it has permanently frozen subsoil and low-growing plants.

urban (metropolitan) area—the city and its surrounding built-up area and population, as far as the outer suburbs.

World War II—the name given to the global conflict of 1939-1945; battles were fought in Europe, Asia, Africa, and the Pacific islands.

yurt—a circular tent of felt or animal skins used by nomads in Central Asia; also called a **ger** in Mongolia.

Index

Map references are in **boldface
(74)** type. Letters and
numbers following in lightface
(P5) locate the place-names.
Refer to page 21 for more
detail. Illustrations appear in
italic (220) type, and text
references in lightface (106).
Diacriticals in the index
reflect what is in the book:
They appear in the text, but
not on the maps.

Type composition by the Typographic section of National Geographic Production Services, Pre-Press Division. Color separations by Chanticleer Co., Inc., New York, N.Y.; Graphic Art Service, Inc., Nashville, Tenn.; The Lanman Companies, Washington, D.C.; Phototype Color Graphics, Pennsauken, N.J. Printed and bound by R. R. Donnelley & Sons, Willard, Ohio. Paper by Consolidated Paper/ Alling & Cory, Philadelphia, Pa.

Library of Congress CIP Data

National Geographic Society (U. S.)
    National Geographic picture atlas of our world. — Rev. ed.
        p. cm.
    Includes glossary and index.
    Summary: Maps and text provide information on the geography, industries, and other vital facts of the countries of the world.
    ISBN 0-87044-960-5 (reg. ed.). — ISBN 0-87044-964-8 (library)
    1. Atlases. [1. Atlases.] I. Title. II. Title: Picture atlas of our world. III. Title: Our world.
G1021.N4 1993 <G&M>
912—dc20   93-4514
                                                        CIP
                                                     MAP AC